IMMIGRATION AT THE GOLDEN GATE

Passenger Ships, Exclusion, and Angel Island

Robert Eric Barde

D0103110

PRAEGER

Westport, Connecticut
London

Library of Congress Cataloging-in-Publication Data

Barde, Robert Eric, 1947—
   Immigration at the Golden Gate : passenger ships, exclusion, and Angel Island /
   Robert Eric Barde.
     p. cm.
   Includes bibliographical references and index.
   ISBN: 978-0-313-34782-5 (alk. paper)
1. San Francisco Bay Area (Calif.)—Emigration and immigration—History—20th century.
2. United States—Emigration and immigration—Government policy—History—20th century.
3. Asians—Legal status, laws, etc.—United States—History—20th century. 4. Angel Island
Immigration Station (Calif.)—History. 5. Asia—Emigration and immigration—History—
20th century. I. Title.
JV6923.B37   2008
304.8'7305—dc22   2007043639

British Library Cataloguing in Publication Data is available.

Library of Congress Catalog Card Number: 2007043639
ISBN: 978-0-313-34782-5

First published in 2008

Praeger Publishers, 88 Post Road West, Westport, CT 06881
An imprint of Greenwood Publishing Group, Inc.
www.praeger.com

Printed in the United States of America

∞

The paper used in this book complies with the
Permanent Paper Standard issued by the National
Information Standards Organization (Z39.48-1984).

10 9 8 7 6 5 4 3 2 1

Copyright Acknowledgments

The author and the publisher gratefully acknowledge permission to excerpt material from the
following sources:

A shorter version of Chapter 3, "An Alleged Wife," was originally published in *Prologue*, a
quarterly of the National Archives and Records Administration.

Portions of Michio Yamada's book on Japanese emigration ships, *Fune ni Miru Nihonjin Iminshi:
Kasato Maru kara Kuruzu Kyakusen e*, and his articles in *Sekai no Kansen* are used with his
permission.

Portions of Chapter 10, "The Great Immigrant Smuggling Scandal," were originally published as
"The Scandalous *Mongolia*" in *Steamboat Bill*, the journal of the Steamship Historical Society of
America, and are used with permission.

The diaries and personal papers of John Birge Sawyer are used with the permission of the Bancroft
Library, University of California, Berkeley.

To Beth and Russell,
whose immigrant roots touch Angel Island.

Contents

Illustrations

Preface

his book is categorized as a "monograph," indicating a single subject and
hinting that I am its sole author. Social science, however, is rarely such
a heroic, solitary endeavor, and that is certainly true of *Immigration at
the Golden Gate*. I have been the beneficiary of immense amounts of help
and advice—from friends, from colleagues, from service providers, and from people
"out there" on the Internet, people who will probably never meet me but
have generously contributed to this book, saving me from mistakes foolish and
otherwise.

I owe more to the Institute of Business and Economic Research than I can
ever express. Kathy Romain, my partner in running the Institute, has been
endlessly supportive of this distraction from my day job as an administrator of
other people's research. My other colleagues at IBER—especially Patt
Bagdon and Elizabeth Flora—have listened to me as this book has grown from
a single, quirky article to the present dozen chapters. They have proofread my
drafts and allowed me to try out material on them in the guise of staff research
presentations.

Susan Carter and Richard Sutch must bear some responsibility for this book.
In 1994 they generously took me on as a coauthor of the "International Migration" chapter of the *Millennial Edition of Historical Statistics of the United States*.
This was my introduction to immigration history and whetted my appetite for
writing it.

Neil Thomsen, former head archivist at the National Archives and Records
Administration, San Bruno, actually launched this book by introducing me to
the case file of Quok Shee, the "Alleged Wife." Bill Greene, Dan Nealand,
and the staff at NARA/San Bruno have been patient and supportive in helping
me wade through NARA's enormous collection and retrieve from it glimpses of
our past. Vincent Chin shared many of his findings from NARA's records of

Chinese businesses. Suzanne Harris at NARA/Washington, who knows me only from a distance, has been similarly helpful.

No one writes about American immigration history without help from Marian Smith, the Historian of the INS (as it once was known). Marian's knowledge of the INS published and unpublished records is exceeded only by her ability to suffer myriad requests with answers that are more informative than one has any right to expect.

Dan Lewis and Mario Einaudi at the Huntington Library helped me access the Pacific Mail archives and the Kemble maritime collection materials. Milt Ternberg and Marianne McDonald at the Long Business Library at UC Berkeley were always supportive of my requests for materials and tolerant of my rants about the microfilm readers. The Bancroft Library at UC Berkeley and its staff treated me like faculty member—a good thing, on the whole.

In a very roundabout, Internetworking way I had the great good fortune to locate and meet Jo Sawyer, the daughter of John Birge Sawyer, and her son, Craig Steele. Jo and Craig not only shared John Sawyer's precious documents and photos with me, but donated that collection to the Bancroft Library for other scholars to use. The chapter on "Mr. Section 6" would have been impossible without their help and friendship.

Noriko Shimada at Japan's National Women's University introduced me to Michio Yamada's work on Japanese emigration through ships. My Internet colleague Georg Fendt, who sailed on the modern *Nippon Maru* tall ship, helped me track down references to these ships.

Wesley Ueunten at UC Berkeley took time out from writing his dissertation to work on many of the Japanese-English translations of Michio Yamada's history of Japanese emigration ships. My neighbors Richard Nishioka and Mitsuko Okimoto relished translating the menus, but it was work all the same and I thank them for taking it on. Jeff Bradt, Tomoko Negishi, Yuko Okubo, Zeli Rivas, Anne Sokolosky, and Doug Welch translated other articles. Danian Lu, Peng Lou, Leo Yan, and Sophia Kam provided the Chinese-English translations.

Bill Kooiman at the Maritime National Historic Park's Library in San Francisco went overboard in helping me with this project. He encouraged me, shared his article on James J. Hill's maritime misadventures with the monstrous *Minnesota* and *Dakota*, dug out precious deck plans and photos from the Library's collections, and read the drafts of many chapters.

Drew Keeling offered comments on an early version of Asiatic Steerage. I am also most appreciative of the help given by Mr. Iwao Yamaguchi, Curator at the NYK Maritime Museum in Yokohama, and by Yuri Momose, staff editor at NYK's *Seascope* magazine.

Encouragement and advice came from many people, including Bob Chandler, Phil Choy, Barry Eichengreen, Alan Kraut, Ira Lapidus, Him Mark Lai, Howard Markel, Mae Ngai, Guenter Risse, Maria Sakovich, and Judy Yung.

Dan Krummes and Steve Potash are both "ship people" and collectors of images of historic steamships. They loaned me precious images of ships that were important to the immigration business. Robert Turner provided visual material and extensive comments on "Asiatic Steerage." Michio Yamada, a distinguished historian of Japan's maritime history, allowed me (thanks to the timely assistance of Yasue Yanai and Hannah Yoshii) to quote extensively from his history of Japanese emigration by ship, and kindly corrected my translations.

Gustavo Bobonis was most patient with me as we put together our article "Detention at Angel Island: First Empirical Evidence." The data in that article are the basis for my assertions about how long people were detained at the Immigration Station. What Gustavo learned about immigration history was far surpassed by what he taught me about econometrics.

My mother always encourages me when I venture into waters over my head— or where the sign says "No Swimming." My father, a historian in his own right, read many of the various chapters and added his comments and encouragement. Thanks, Dad.

My wife, May Ling, read the first part of this project, the chapter on Quok Shee, the "Alleged Wife." Her comment was my greatest incentive to finish *Immigration at the Golden Gate:* "Needs more research!" And so it did.

Abbreviations

CMSS	China Mail Steamship Company
CPR	Canadian Pacific Railway (steamship line)
CSYP	*Chung Sai Yat Po* (newspaper)
INS	Immigration and Naturalization Service. The name of the Federal agency charged with enforcing immigration laws, and the Department responsible for it, was changed several times during the period under consideration. For simplicity, INS and "Immigration Service" are used interchangeably.
NARA	National Archives and Records Administration
NYK	Nippon Yusen Kaisha (steamship line)
OSK	Osaka Shosen Kaisha (steamship line)
PMSS	Pacific Mail Steamship Company
TKK	Toyo Kisen Kaisha (steamship line)

— 1 —

Introduction

The story that launched this book might have begun on the first day of September 1916. Ponderous mountains of fog blanketed the Golden Gate. A gantlet of tricky tides, currents, and bars guarded the entrance to San Francisco Bay. There was no bridge across the Golden Gate, no span from which to see or hear the vessel laboring through the waters below.

At first light, a ship was making its way through the dense, enveloping fog and into San Francisco Bay: the historic, yacht-like passenger liner *Nippon Maru*, twenty-nine days and ten hours from Hong Kong. She carried 1,723 tons of silk and Asian merchandise, destined for Eastern cities. In her cabins were 106 first-class passengers, 10 in second class; below, in the steerage quarters, another 147. Two hundred and sixty-three Chinese, Japanese, and assorted Western passengers in a British-built ship, with a Japanese captain, all hoping to enter the United States of America. Two hundred and sixty-three American histories.

Among the passengers were Chew Hoy Quong and Quok Shee.[1] Chew Hoy Quong was a resident Chinese merchant, legally entitled to return to the United States, and after a few nights' detention on Angel Island, he was duly allowed in. Quok Shee, the woman he claimed to be his new wife, was not admitted. The Immigration Service believed that Quok Shee was being brought into the country for "immoral purposes"; her entry was denied and she was detained—imprisoned, really—on Angel Island for what would become an unimaginably long time, longer than any other person we know of.

At first, the project that became *Immigration at the Golden Gate* focused only on these two Chinese immigrants.[2] It was their story that fascinated me—how, despite Quok Shee's seeming unremarkableness, the Immigration Service went to great lengths to keep her out. How tenacious she was, refusing to be deported or badgered into returning on her own. How voluminous was the documentation that told the story, yet how many questions about her and her "alleged husband" remained unanswered. Little of Quok Shee and Chew Hoy Quong remains, just the public record, a folder of documents where brief portions of their lives were diligently written down, neatly assembled, preserved with bureaucratic thoroughness in the National Archives: Immigration Case file number 15530/6-29.

For twenty months, Quok Shee was held in detention on Angel Island. Eighty-five years later, such a case might have become a *cause célèbre*; in its day, it passed unnoticed, unremarkable, just another instance of the anti-Chinese abuse so common for the times and place. Her drama played out amidst the moral squalor of the Chinese Exclusion Act (and its equally ugly successors, referred to collectively here as the exclusion laws), on a set primed for corruption and scandal, with a cast of immigrants, smugglers, businessmen, officials honest and not, ambitious investigators-knights errant, lawyers of every stripe, racists and do-gooders, and the motherly presence of the "Angel of Angel Island."

What made Quok Shee's experience so fascinating, and what turned this singular, narrow tale into the present collection of essays, was that it led to so many other, unexpected stories that overlapped her own:

- The ship that she arrived on was one of the hundreds of ships that brought Asians to the New World, and one that had played a major role in a sinister event at the dawn of the twentieth century.

- Her detention on Angel Island coincided with one of the most sensational immigration smuggling scandals and investigations of the early twentieth century.

- The lawyers involved in her case (or rather, cases, as there were both administrative and judicial appeals) were characters in their own right and exemplified the various, frequently contradictory, ways in which the legal system could work against, or for, immigrants.

- Only one immigration officer on Angel Island left a diary: John Birge Sawyer, whose eighteen months there were smack in the middle of the years that Quok Shee was imprisoned.

- In detention, Quok Shee would have been ministered to by Deaconess Katharine Maurer, the "Angel of Angel Island," one of many churchwomen concerned with immigrants and their welfare. A fellow Chinese passenger on the *Nippon Maru* was "rescued"—unwillingly, it seems—from prostitution by what we would now call a social worker, the famous Donaldina Cameron, "Chinatown's Angry Angel."

- While in detention Quok Shee was exposed to smallpox and was consigned for six weeks to the Quarantine Station on Angel Island, a separate facility but one long associated with the control of immigrants.

- Among the other immigrants detained at this time were Japanese picture brides, as well as East Indians arrested in the so-called "Hindu conspiracy"—whose trial culminated in a sensational courtroom shoot-out.

The trail to each of these overlapping stories starts in Quok Shee's case file. When I first went to the National Archives, I had no intention of following these stories, nor did I have even the faintest notion of Quok Shee's existence. I shall be forever grateful to Neil Thomsen, the archivist at the Pacific Region branch of the NARA (National Archives and Records Administration) in San Bruno, California, who introduced me to Quok Shee's investigation case file in 1997.

I had been following a different trail, looking for a different sort of historical evidence. As part of the team producing the new edition of *Historical Statistics of the United States*, I was researching the "International Migration" chapter, of which I was coauthor with Susan Carter and Richard Sutch.[3] We were trying to find out what data the National Archives might have that would complement the official statistics of the INS (Immigration and Naturalization Service). Neil had enumerated the Archives' holdings of passenger manifests, lists of ships, court cases, and Chinese partnership records, and started to describe the San Bruno facility's treasure trove of "investigation case files."[4] He explained how anyone who was questioned by the Immigration Service between 1882 and roughly 1953 would most likely have had a case file. San Bruno's storage shelves held nearly 250,000 of them, but I had never seen one. Neil looked about and spied one that was lying on a nearby desk, it having conveniently not been returned to storage by the last user. Perhaps it was not sheer randomness that this turned out to be Quok Shee's case file, the documentation establishing hers as the longest known period of detention on Angel Island. I have often wondered about the identity of the researcher who left that file for me to find, and why he or she had been using it. Might it have been a descendant or relative? Someone who might answer the first questions that occur to everyone who has heard me tell Quok Shee's story?

What was in Quok Shee's case file was of no use at all for *Historical Statistics*, but it was absolutely riveting. One hundred and fifty pages, filled with more drama than I could have invented had I tried to write her life as a novel. The separate file containing her court cases was just as moving. One does not think of having emotional experiences in the National Archives, but when I unfolded the heavy, embossed paper that was the order to free her, I felt as though I was holding justice in my hands—justice delayed, but not denied. I was sure this was a story that would interest others.

It did not, of course. Knowing very little about immigration through San Francisco during this period, I presented Quok Shee's story unadorned, with little context or background. My telling of Quok Shee's incarceration was received as just another story of discrimination against immigrant Chinese, a tale too common to be of interest to those who write for a living about Chinese immigration. A narrow topic that did not go beyond the pathos of this singular, but single, experience.

But I was hooked, convinced that Quok Shee's story was worth telling because it spoke to the very ideals to which the Chinese exclusion laws did such violence, and to the tenacity of those who became Americans despite great obstacles. Researching Quok Shee and the stories related to hers brought out the immigrant in me: born in Japan, twice an immigrant (from the United States to Canada as a young adult, back to the United States as an older one), the grandchild of an immigrant from Germany whose true history was not the one he told his children, and the descendant of immigrants from Scotland, Wales, and England. I came to see *Immigration at the Golden Gate* less as a story of Chinese or Asian immigration and more as stories about *American* immigration and the complex, disjointed way that the San Francisco part of America dealt with another set of immigrants, albeit ones whose origins were different from, and less favored than, my own.

If the warp of the narrative fabric is the story of Quok Shee and her travails on Angel Island, the weft of this historical tapestry is formed by the many people and events that overlapped her imprisonment there. Beginning with the experience of Quok Shee, "An Alleged Wife," I followed as many of the threads of that experience as I could. My research went in so many directions that eventually it wove in the various economic and social institutions that would have touched her. As the scope of this tale widened to become the present book, it became less a story about two—or even all—Chinese immigrants and more about immigrants and natives bound together in a complex set of economic and social enterprises that constitute the "immigration industry." Angel Island was its focal point, but many of the activities that comprised the "immigration industry" were located elsewhere—ships and shipping companies, the Immigration Service itself, health inspectors, immigration lawyers, the churches and groups that assisted immigrants, and the newspapers that covered it all. Many of the immigrants were Chinese; most of those running the rest of the immigration business were not.

My purpose is not to provide an analysis of the "industrial organization" of the immigration business. Other historians have already tried to provide the "metadata" and overview that such an analysis would entail.[5] The goal of this book is more modest: to provide detail, the "thick" material that puts the flesh of description on the skeleton of analysis. The chapters in this book can be conveniently, if somewhat arbitrarily, grouped around a few major themes that advance this purpose:

DETENTION AND ANGEL ISLAND

"Exclusion, Detention, and Angel Island"—Angel Island, the largest island in San Francisco Bay, lies just inside the Golden Gate in a setting of extraordinary natural beauty. Today the entire island is a State Park, its tranquility seemingly incompatible with the throb of activity of a hundred years ago or with the neglect it suffered in the mid-twentieth century. A century ago the island hummed with the comings and goings of soldiers at its several Army installations. The Quarantine Station sent its officers and launches to inspect all ships entering the Bay, maintaining an extensive set of quarters and disinfecting facilities where the Park office is today. In a secluded corner of the Island, the Immigration Station, the smallest of these government operations, sat in judgment on all who would enter America through the "City by the Bay."

Perhaps 300,000 immigrants passed through the Angel Island Immigration Station during its lifetime, a tiny number compared to the 17 million who entered through New York's Ellis Island. Nonetheless, Angel Island's place in the consciousness of Americans on the West Coast is large, out of all proportion to the numerical record. This place is not conceded fondly or with gratitude. Angel Island's Immigration Station was not, as some have called it, the "Ellis Island of the West," built to facilitate the "processing" and entry of those welcomed as new Americans. Its role was less benign: to facilitate the exclusion of Asians—first the Chinese, then Japanese, Koreans, Indians, and all other Asians. This chapter offers a brief overview of the Island as it would have been experienced in 1916, the year Quok Shee arrived.

That same chapter uses new data that I discovered, providing partial answers to questions about how long people were detained at the Angel Island Immigration Station. As the primary the place of enforcement of the Chinese Exclusion Act and other anti-Asian immigration policies, it has been frequently asserted—even in the absence of substantiating data—that almost all entering Chinese were detained at Angel Island and that they were detained for weeks, months, even years. This chapter summarizes the first numerical evidence on how long people arriving at San Francisco were detained at the Angel Island Immigration Station and lets us know how "true" are the stories of Quok Shee and other detainees.

"An Alleged Wife" is where this book begins, spiritually if not logistically. This chapter recounts Quok Shee's experience, her six hundred-plus nights in detention at the Angel Island Immigration Station—her interrogations, her lawyers and attempts to free her, the secret testimony of an informer that kept her there, and the tribulations she went through as her fate was being decided. A somewhat shorter version of this chapter was previously printed in *Prologue*, the quarterly publication of the NARA.

"Before Angel Island" provides a new history of the location of enforcement of the Chinese exclusion laws before the opening of the Immigration Station on Angel Island in 1910. For the first twenty-eight years of the exclusion era, facilities for "processing" arrivals were located on the mainland in San Francisco, yet until now virtually nothing has been written about where or how that was done. For the first fifteen years of the exclusion era, a variety of make-do arrangements were used by the steamship companies and the immigration authorities. Only in 1898 did the Detention Shed on the Pacific Mail's docks become available to complement this system, but all sides found it unsatisfactory and the lobbying for new facilities soon began.

TRANSPORTATION ACROSS THE PACIFIC

"Asiatic Steerage" is an overview of maritime transportation in the first century of Asian mass migration to the New World, when several million Chinese, Japanese, Indians, and others made their way across the Pacific, Indian, and Atlantic Oceans. How did they make those journeys? What ships carried them? What was it like to be on them? How did the emigrants' experience in steerage differ from that of the wealthy travelers in cabin class? While there are many comments scattered throughout maritime and immigration history, and a number of treatises on the conditions of European migration, there are no accounts that address these questions in the context of Asian migration. "Asiatic Steerage" describes how so many emigrants were transported so far, from the facilities at the port of embarkation, to the ships they boarded and the life and conditions on those ships, to the facilities that awaited them upon arrival.

When Quok Shee began her long detention on Angel Island, the CMSS (China Mail Steamship Company) was nearing its first anniversary in the business of transporting people between San Francisco and East Asia. The China Mail is a stellar example of an immigrant community organizing a major, relatively long-lived enterprise to transport other immigrants to the United States. It was created in 1915, when most Asians would have traveled to the United States in ships that were white- or Japanese-owned. In the same year a unique convergence of events enabled Chinese and Chinese Americans to create the China Mail, which for over seven years would transport their countrymen (and others) across the Pacific and land them legally on America's front doorstep.

"The Life and Death of the China Mail" examines the events and institutions that led to the creation of the CMSS, the operation of the steamship line, the degree to which it was a "Chinese" enterprise, and the factors contributing to its demise. An examination of some of the claims that have been made on behalf of the China Mail—e.g., that it was an heroic effort to protest Japanese imperialism or U.S. racism—leads to more modest claims. Most important were the more immediate *opportunities* presented by the economic environment, the vision of its founders, and the local Chinese American institutions that made it possible for them to exercise leadership and seize the day. Its ultimate failure was similarly due only in small measure to actions that were clearly anti-Chinese, with internal conflict and changes in the broader society and in international trade playing larger roles.

"The *Nippon Maru*: A Career in the Immigration Trade" traces the "career" of the SS *Nippon Maru*. The ship that brought Quok Shee and Chew Hoy Quong to America had a history of its own—and a past. Recounting a portion of that past conveys something of the times that shaped the business of immigration in the United States, and of that historical space where the regulation of public health and of the immigration industry intersected and were fiercely contested.

The history of this extraordinarily beautiful ship is captured through three emblematic voyages. In 1899 the *Nippon Maru* became the first Japanese passenger ship to enter San Francisco Bay, causing quite a stir. Later that year, she was the central player in an incident that was a prelude to the first outbreak of bubonic plague on American soil. Seventeen years (and not a few adventures) later, the *Nippon Maru* brought Quok Shee to the United States. Between her first voyage and her last, she probably brought over 25,000 people across the Pacific and into San Francisco.

ENFORCEMENT

"The Great Immigrant Smuggling Scandal" is the first exploration of a smuggling scandal that rocked San Francisco in late 1915. Just as the China Mail was starting up, a huge group of stowaways was found on the last Pacific Mail ship to arrive as that line was winding down. San Francisco's newspapers made this front-page news, often displacing reports from the great conflict raging in Europe. The ensuing investigation into immigrant smuggling at Angel Island was led by John Densmore, the Labor Department's star investigator and a family friend of the Secretary. There were actually two Densmore Investigations—one in which he promised much but brought no one to trial and a second where illegal surveillance methods resulted in firings and convictions. The investigations revealed much about the workings of the immigration service and the lawyers who dealt with it.

Any discussion of immigrant smuggling must examine the community of lawyers who ingeniously challenged the exclusion laws, motivated by varying combinations of greed and altruism. This chapter relies on new primary material on Stidger and Kennah, the law firm fingered by Densmore as the principal source of corruption, and on the transcripts of Densmore's unauthorized wiretaps.

"Mr. Section 6" introduces John Birge Sawyer, whose diaries and professional papers are the only records left by an Immigration Service officer who served on Angel Island. Sawyer's life and active career with the Immigration Service and the Consular Service of the U.S. Department of State neatly coincided with the life of the Chinese Exclusion Act and its successors (1882–1943). He was a specialist in Chinese immigration whose career included postings at the Portland (Oregon) Immigration Station (1904–11), the American consulate in Hong Kong (1911–16), the Angel Island Immigration Station (1917–18), the American consulate in Shanghai (1918–42), and the American consulates in Ciudad Juarez and Nogales (1942–43).

The Sawyer papers include six volumes of diaries that I have transcribed and am making available as electronic files, plus a set of professional papers, letters, and photographs. The present chapter draws on these sources to provide an overview of Sawyer's career as one of the middle-level bureaucrats staffing the exclusion apparatus. A review of his various postings, the issues he dealt with, and his attitude toward the Chinese point out the moral ambiguity that surrounds enforcement of the exclusion laws: how could someone so honest and upright be part of something so patently unfair?

LISTENING FOR ANGEL ISLAND

Each of these chapters uses different types of sources. In some cases, the stories are told in the participants' own words, even though those words have been altered or muffled by the translators, Immigration Service stenographers, and lawyers as they found their way into the official printed record. For example, we hear Quok Shee's voice in her immigration and court files, from which also emerge the workings of the administrative machinery charged with interpreting and enforcing the immigration laws. From the transcripts of Densmore's investigation and interrogations, we see the workings of the enforcement apparatus from a different angle, from John Birge Sawyer's diaries yet another. "Asiatic Steerage" relies heavily on my translation of a Japanese-language source that until now has been inaccessible to American readers. "Before Angel Island" is based largely on newspaper accounts—both the English-language dailies of San Francisco and the Chinese-language daily *Chung Sai Yat Po*.

Throughout many of the chapters there is an undercurrent that is the era when the burgeoning power of a new bureaucracy, harnessed to a rampant public hostility to newcomers, posed grave threats to the liberties of all immigrants, and especially to those from Asia. The phrase "Angel Island" connotes more than a rocky outpost rearing up inside the mouth of San Francisco Bay, more, even, than shorthand for the various government outposts—military, health, and immigration—that guarded the Western Gate. If *Immigration at the Golden Gate* accomplishes anything, it should remind us of an important chapter in the history of immigration to the United States, one that was truly a "multicultural" enterprise long before that expression was even imagined.

With the restoration of the Immigration Station and the creation of a suitable museum/learning center, "Angel Island" may well become as much part of the American collective imagination as "Ellis Island"—but with its own, quite different, twist. The chapters that follow should give some sense of this larger "Angel Island," some indication of how natives and newcomers experienced the immigration process at one period in time. "Angel Island" should mean more than an alternately wind-swept, fog-shrouded, sun-baked, geological outcropping strategically ensconced in San Francisco Bay. It is an historical space with geographical, economic, and social-political dimensions, and it is that space that this book is meant to illuminate.

As John Gillis reminds us, "Islands...can represent both separation and continuity, isolation and connection. Over time, they have been the West's favorite location for visions of both the past and future."[6] Although Angel Island's role in American immigration was greatest at the dawn of the previous century, the process of immigration continues. The voices of a century ago—of exclusion, of bureaucratic and judicial nightmares, of the interwoven interests of migrants and businessmen, of the fear of foreigners and their diseases, of moral ambiguity and uncertainty—all echo to the present day.

NOTES

1. During her interrogation, she gave her names as "Quok Shee" and "Quok Sun Moy." "Shee" is an honorific, meaning simply "married woman," but "Quok Shee" was the only name used in all official documents. "Quok Shee," or "Married Woman Shee," she has become.Unless otherwise noted, all information on Quok Shee comes from Case

15530/6-29 Quok Shee; Immigration Arrival Investigation Case Files, 1884–1944; San Francisco District Office; Immigration and Naturalization Service; Record Group 85, Records of the Immigration and Naturalization Service; NARA—Pacific Region, 1000 Commodore Drive, San Bruno, CA 94066.

2. Chew Hoy Quong and Quok Shee are referred to as "immigrants," but one should use the term with caution. "Immigrant" implies that the move to a new country is voluntary and that there is some sense of permanence to the move. I think that both Quok Shee and Chew Hoy Quong intended to remain in the United States, but prevailing legislation prevented them from becoming citizens and cast doubt on whether they would ever be accepted as permanent residents. See the discussion of this in John Torpey, *The Invention of the Passport: Surveillance, Citizenship and the State* (New York: Cambridge University Press, 2000).

3. Robert Barde, Susan B. Carter, and Richard Sutch, "International Migration," in *Historical Statistics of the United States, from the Earliest Times to the Present: Millennial Edition*, ed. Susan B. Carter, Scott Sigmund Gartner, Michael R. Haines, Alan L. Olmstead, Richard Sutch, and Gavin Wright (New York: Cambridge University Press, 2006).

4. For details of the Archives' collection of case files, see Robert Barde, William Greene, and Daniel Nealand, "The EARS Have It: A Web Search Tool for Investigation Case Files from the Chinese Exclusion Era," *Prologue* 35, no. 3 (2003).

5. See Erika Lee, *At America's Gates: Chinese Immigration during the Exclusion Era, 1882–1943* (Chapel Hill: University of North Carolina Press, 2003); Andrew Gyory, *Closing the Gate: Race, Politics, and the Chinese Exclusion Act* (Chapel Hill: University of North Carolina Press, 1998); Roger Daniels, "No Lamps Were Lit for Them: Angel Island and the Historiography of Asian American Immigration," *Journal of American Ethnic History* 17, no. 1 (1997); and M. Mark Stolarik, ed., *Forgotten Doors: The Other Ports of Entry to the United States* (Philadelphia: Balch Institute Press, 1988).

6. John Gillis, *Islands of the Mind: How the Human Imagination Created the Atlantic World* (New York: Palgrave MacMillan, 2004), 3.

— 2 —

Exclusion, Detention, and Angel Island

Two somewhat contradictory facts underlie every chapter of this book. The first is the existence of the Chinese Exclusion Act and its successors. The second is that despite the Exclusion Act, Chinese were not completely "excluded" from the United States. Those already here were not deported, and not all those trying to enter were kept out. Resident Chinese went back to China and returned, and additional newcomers arrived. The tension between these two phenomena, between Exclusion and continued migration, creates the particular nature of the processes making immigration possible on the West Coast and at its principal port, San Francisco.

"Chinese Exclusion" refers to a series of Acts of Congress designed to put severe restrictions on the entry of Chinese into the United States. The first was the "Chinese Exclusion Act" of May 6, 1882, officially a law "To Execute Certain Treaty Stipulations Relating to Chinese" (22 Stat. 58); it was designed to keep out "coolies" by prohibiting Chinese in certain occupations from entering the United States, and by making it impossible for Chinese to become citizens. The "Geary Act" of May 5, 1892 (27 Stat. 25) tightened some procedures and extended the act for another ten years; and the Act of April 29, 1902 (32 Stat. 176) continued the Chinese Exclusion Act "until otherwise provided by law." Only in 1943 did President Franklin Roosevelt formally "provide otherwise" and rescind the Chinese Exclusion Act.

Following the Chinese Exclusion Act, severe restrictions were later imposed on the entry of other Asians, most significantly on Japanese through the 1907 Gentleman's Agreement and on people from South and Southeast Asia through the Immigration Act of 1917. The Chinese exclusion era partially overlapped another era of severe restriction, one based on the Immigration Act of May 26, 1924 (43 Stat. 153), also known as the National Origins Act.[1] After 1924, limitations on immigration were based on "a constellation of reconstructed racial categories, in which race and nationality—concepts that had been loosely conflated since the nineteenth century—disaggregated and realigned in new and uneven ways."[2] Visas were limited to 2 percent of a country's share of the 1890 population census. Aspects of this "quota" system lasted until 1965, when the current era of high-growth immigration began.

How effective were the Chinese exclusion laws at actually excluding the Chinese? For the last half of the 1870s, immigration from China had averaged less than nine thousand a year. In 1881, nearly twelve thousand Chinese were admitted into the United States; a year later, in anticipation of restrictive legislation, the number swelled to forty thousand. And then the gates swung shut. In 1884, only ten Chinese were officially allowed to enter this country as immigrants. The next year, twenty-six.

The effect of the exclusion laws on the Chinese population of the United States is captured in Figure 2.1. There was a precipitous falloff in official immigration following the 1882 legislation (measured on the left-hand scale). Between the 1880 census and that of 1890, there was a mild increase in the Chinese population of the United States—a product of the many arrivals in 1882—but after that it began to shrink. The number of Chinese dying or

Figure 2.1

Chinese Immigration and Population in the United States, 1860–1940. Statistics on Chinese officially admitted as immigrants only partially account for the persistence of a Chinese population in the face of the Chinese exclusion laws. After 1882, the flow of Chinese arrivals was chiefly composed of non-immigrant arrivals (the "exempt" classes) and returning American-born Chinese. Chinese immigration and arrivals are measured on the left-hand scale; Chinese residents in the United States, taken from the census, are measured on the right-hand scale.

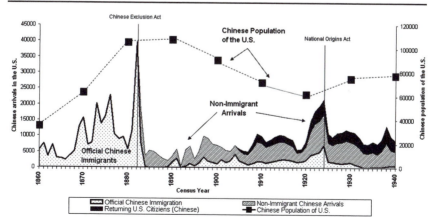

Source: Historical Statistics of the United States, From Earliest Times to the Present: Millennial Edition.

returning to China outnumbered the new arrivals and the few Chinese births that there were. While the total U.S. population continued to grow, the next three censuses saw a decrease in the number of Chinese on American soil (measured on the right-hand scale).

But the Chinese population did not shrink to zero. The new arrivals included both official immigrants and a larger number of long-term legal residents who could never become citizens and were counted as "non-immigrants" in the INS annual reports. Who were these "non-immigrants" who constituted the nucleus of future increases in the number of Chinese in the United States?

Among the salient features of the Chinese Exclusion Act were presumptions about class. Because the Chinese exclusion laws were justified as preventing "coolies" (laborers) from coming into the United States, there was a modest bias in favor of other classes, including Chinese merchants, students and teachers, ministers, bona fide tourists, and dependents of anyone in these categories. These were the "exempt classes"—those Chinese allowed to enter the United States despite the existence of the Chinese exclusion laws. The other important group of "Chinese" allowed to enter included persons of Chinese ancestry born in the United States and their children—*if* the former could furnish proof of such native birth and, for the latter, *if* they could prove that they were the children of such parents. As we shall see in the chapter on Quok Shee, "An Alleged Wife," this process of "sifting the arrivals" to verify their bona fides, plus appeals of unfavorable rulings, could take a very long time indeed.

The existence of such "exempt classes" is important to understanding why the Chinese population of the United States did not disappear altogether. They were central to its continuation and renewal and underpin arguments against the widespread notion that Exclusion produced a Chinese society of "aging bachelors."[3] Census figures show a Chinese population that was *not* aging, a fact accounted for by renewal (the phrase used by Chew and Liu is "substitution") through new arrivals not included in the statistics on official immigration. The new arrivals came in a variety of ways—as members (bona fide or not) of the "exempt classes," as illegals smuggled in, or as travelers "in transit" to some purported third country. To some extent, the "exempt classes" are represented in data produced by the Immigration Service on "non-immigrant arrivals." Including the "exempt classes" and Chinese who were returning residents or U.S. citizens gives a much different picture of the flow of Chinese into and out of the United States.

Recent scholarship has greatly expanded our knowledge of the Chinese Exclusion Act and its successors, shedding light on the changing mechanisms of enforcement and their legal underpinnings.[4] Erika Lee, in particular, reminds us that the Chinese exclusion laws brought about major changes in the way that *all* immigration into the United States was regulated. The Chinese Exclusion Act brought about the first federal immigration inspectors. It also engendered the first attempts to "identify and record the movements, occupations, and financial relationships of immigrants, returning residents, and native-born citizens."

Illegal immigration became a criminal offense. The mandatory registration of Chinese residents and the need to carry "Certificates of Identity" are direct ancestors of today's "green cards."[5] And the "visas" and documents establishing Chinese nationality were early versions of the passports later required of all persons entering the United States.[6] Each of these changes was part of the context in which the Angel Island Immigration Station and its predecessors evolved. Each echoes throughout this book and reverberates down to the present day.

The Chinese exclusion laws and the mechanisms for enforcing them are what make Angel Island different in purpose and procedures from Ellis Island. Although the Angel Island Immigration Station is often referred to as "The Ellis Island of the West," such a title does injustice to the histories of both stations. Ellis Island functioned to allow as many Europeans into the United States as possible, maintaining a façade of protecting the public by rejecting a small percentage as medically unfit or "likely to become a public charge."[7] The station at Angel Island clearly had a different purpose: not only was the clientele predominantly Asian rather than European, it was one that was not welcomed. While Ellis Island was built to let Europeans in, Angel Island was built to keep Asians out.

Today, the Immigration Station is synonymous with Angel Island, as though there was nothing else on the island. But when Quok Shee arrived in 1916, the Immigration Station was just six years old and shared the island with three older and larger Federal installations. On the northwest corner, at Hospital (today Ayala) Cove, was the Quarantine Station, built in 1891. On the southwest and southeast sides were U.S. Army bases. Camp Reynolds (aka "West Garrison") dated back to Civil War days (1863), while Fort McDowell (aka "East Garrison") was an 1899 child of the American conquest of the Philippines. The Immigration Station was very much the newest and smallest of the four Federal facilities. Even in regard to the arrival of travelers from overseas, it was distinctly junior to the Quarantine Station.

The National Quarantine Act of February 15, 1893 followed the New York epidemics of 1892 and was, in effect, a compromise between those who wanted to use "diseased immigrants" as a pretext for restricting *all* immigration, and those who favored separating public health issues from the debate over restricting immigration.[8] The Act called for a set of national quarantine regulations and a uniform way of inspecting incoming people and goods for diseases, but these were to be administered by the Marine Hospital Service in cooperation with local and state boards of health. By the time Quok Shee and Chew Hoy Quong arrived in 1916, the Federal health inspection apparatus had established its supremacy over its local counterparts and the Quarantine Station was a sizeable operation.

When a ship arrived in San Francisco, it was boarded well before it reached the dock by all sorts of uniformed employees of the federal government. Customs inspectors started looking for prohibited or dutiable goods. Members of the Public Health Service aboard the *Inspector* or the *Argonaut* began checking for contagious diseases. And officers of the Immigration Service began sifting the arrivals to see who was fit to enter the United States, and who was not. For "European" (i.e., white) passengers, chances were very good that they would be cleared for entry straight from the ship. But for others, especially if they were Asian, chances were high that they would be transferred by ferry or tug to the Immigration Station at Angel Island.

The Station's site at China Cove was—and still is—a truly lovely spot in many respects. On the leeward side of the island, hunkered down beneath the steep shoulders of Mt. Livermore, it offered some protection from winds blowing in through the Golden Gate. Facing northeast, it may have been spared the worst of the afternoon sun—although on a truly hot day, the wooden buildings could become very warm indeed. The island itself had been relatively denuded by many years of cattle grazing and woodcutting, but in 1908 the Army began a project to plant 200,000 pines and blue gum (aka eucalyptus) trees. What had been a barren corner of the island when the Immigration Station opened gradually became the wooded glade seen in most later photographs.

Mary Bamford visited Angel Island in 1916 on behalf of the Women's American Baptist Home Missionary Society. Her tour was something of an inspection, and in a booklet published by the Society she described the island, the Immigration Station, and its inmates in one of the earliest such narratives. In the passage below, she recounts how the island might have appeared to a first-time visitor, albeit one who was there for just the day.

> To visit Angel Island we must first obtain a pass from the Commissioner of Immigration. On visiting day, Tuesday or Friday, we go to Pier no. 7, San Francisco, to take the Angel Island Immigration Service boat, which makes several trips a day. We wait, toward the end of the long covered shed, for the coming boat. The cry of the sea-gulls is in the air, bells or whistles sound from different vessels, Chinese and Japanese wander about.
>
> The immaculate white boat for Angel Island comes alongside with its American, Japanese, and Chinese passengers. As they are discharged, the other Americans, Japanese and Chinese, who have been waiting, pass up the gangway and start on their Journey....
>
> Angel Island is seven miles in circumference, and has an altitude of nine hundred feet. On the south side of the island, the buildings and the khaki-colored tents that we see, do not mark the Immigration Station portion of the island, but comprise what is sometimes called the "Casual Camp," where soldiers from the Philippines are lodged. On the west of the island, out of sight of our boat, is Fort McDowell, the military station. On the north side of the island is the quarantine station.
>
> Our boat passes a little further and turns by a wooded bluff. We swing alongside a wharf. Connected with the wharf by a broad wooden walk, is the main building of the eighteen buildings on this section of the island devoted to the United States Immigration Service. Ten acres of the island are fenced in for this purpose.[9]

The Immigration Station was built as a successor to, and intended as an improvement upon, the Pacific Mail's detention shed on Pier 40 in San Francisco (see "Before Angel Island"). When the Immigration Station was completed in

1907 following an appropriation of $200,000, it was touted as a vast improvement, "The Finest Immigrant Station in the World." A full-page article in the *San Francisco Chronicle* lauded the achievements of the "Immigration Bureau" and supervising architect Walter J. Mathews for having created "the cleanest, best arranged and in all respects the finest and healthiest emigrant station ever established." These plaudits were, of course, handed out when the construction had been completed but several years before the Immigration Station was actually opened and occupied. A century later, it is ironic in the extreme to read of expectations that "the newcomers from foreign shores will probably think they have struck Paradise when they emerge from the steerage quarters of an ocean liner and land at the summer resort which the Immigration Bureau has provided for them."[10]

This, of course, proved wildly optimistic. Most detainees resented not only the lengthy detentions but also the conditions in which they were held. Many other early expectations went unmet as well. The *Chronicle's* reporter described "the big dock, where vessels of the greatest draft may tie up without difficulty," but such vessels never came to the Station, relying instead on ferries and tugboats to transport passengers from the mainland wharves to the Island. It was believed that there was water enough from wells, although later the station would rely on supplemental deliveries by water barge. The Immigration Station never lived up to its billing of having "a capacity of handling from 2000 to 2500 immigrants and sleeping and feeding accommodations for 1000."

From the larger roadway encircling the island, a side road ran sharply downhill to the level area fronting the beach where the wharf stood. On each side of the road, steep slopes led back uphill, creating a narrow, isolated little draw. Water tanks and nine small cottages for staff were perched atop the right slope, while mule stables and three other cottages were located high up the left-hand slope. At the bottom, near the gravel beach, were the Immigration Station's four principal buildings: the main administration building, the detention barracks, the hospital, and the power plant supplying electricity for the entire station. The cottages were torn down to the foundations long ago, and the administration building burned in 1940, but the hospital, detention barracks, and power plant remain. There is enough of the infrastructure left to make it easy to imagine the Immigration Station in its earliest days.

A detailed drawing that accompanied reporter Stellmann's article showed the layout of the three buildings actually housing immigrants. All three were two-story wood structures, designed to provide separate accommodations that the various "races" were deemed to require. While the uses of the various rooms undoubtedly changed during the Station's thirty-year lifetime, it is probable that his description held true for the years leading to Quok Shee's arrival:

> The principal building will be the administration building, close to the water front. This is designed for the receiving and discharging of immigrants. It contains separate dining rooms for Europeans, Chinese and Japanese, for employees, visitors and

officers, a baggage room, offices of the custom inspector, board of inquiry, Chinese Inspector, Commissioner of Immigration, etc., as well as Chinese and Japanese detention departments....

Immigrants are first received and taken to an examination room divided into compartments separated by iron railings. The Chinese and Japanese are separated from the Europeans and the women of the latter class are also received in a separate compartment....

The Europeans sleep in a dormitory on the second floor of the main [administration] building and will have excellent accommodations, including baths, lavatories and showers, a roof garden for daily exercises and most of the conveniences of a first-class hotel. [Offices] are in a wing entirely separated from the immigrant quarters. A feature of this building is that the Asiatic and European business is segregated in different wings. All immigrants are received and discharged without interfering with each other in any possible way and the handling of the two classes is thus greatly expedited. This is also the means of saving much confusion which could not but result from a mixing of the races in even the smallest degree.

The Oriental quarters are situated on a hill, not far away, and connected with the main building by a covered bridge which crosses the principal roadway, giving immigrants confined therein access to the Oriental dining room in the administration building without entering the grounds. The Oriental building is a two-story structure. One story is devoted to the Japanese, which are divided as to sex, and the other floor is given up to Chinese immigrants in the same way. Both floors have large dormitories for men and women, each with separate baths, sitting rooms, etc.[11]

The hospital building was similarly divided, with separate wards for Europeans, for Japanese, and for Chinese.

No sooner was this paradise opened than it became the target of very vocal, and well-placed, critics. Chief among them was Luther Steward, Acting Commissioner of Immigration for San Francisco. In a twenty-three-page letter to the Commissioner General in Washington, Steward blasted nearly every aspect of the design and construction of the new facility: "The plans show an ignorance of the necessities of an establishment of this character, from any phase, that is appalling."[12]

Steward was not alone in his dislike of the new station. In his Annual Report of 1915, Commissioner General Anthony Caminetti observed that "buildings in which detained persons are housed should undoubtedly be of fireproof construction, adequate size, and so arranged as to promote scrupulous cleanliness and sanitation as a safeguard to health. The quarters now in use at the Angel Island immigration station meet none of these conditions."[13]

Later that year, Secretary of Labor William B. Wilson requested, in his report to the President, that the buildings "be made more modern or be abandoned altogether." As an attempt to move the facility to Alcatraz had recently failed, Wilson recommended that any new station should be built on the mainland, preferably at Fort Mason.[14]

The station's remoteness was a frequent source of complaint. Anyone with business on the island was obliged to take the Angel Island ferry from the mainland which, though frequent, still presented an obstacle. Even the Immigration

Figure 2.2
Immigrants were transferred to Angel Island from arriving ships by tug or ferry, as shown in this lantern slide, ca. 1925.

Source: Photo Archives of the California State Parks.

Service's own Chinese Inspectors found the restricted number of ferry departures a burden. "The necessity of closing a hearing at a fixed time (4:15) and releasing the witnesses whether the case is in a state that will make it safe or not [is a real problem]. This condition is due to the fact that there is no boat leaving the Island after 4:35."[15]

The detainees, of course, had the most direct experience with the insufficiencies of the Immigration Station. The complaints of those held at the Immigration Station echoed many of Acting Commissioner Steward's: bad food, unsanitary conditions, rude treatment by the guards. But more than anything else, detainees experienced a deprivation of liberty that seemed both unjust and perhaps worse, of indeterminate length. Expressions of these wounds to the body and soul were carved into the wooden walls of the detention barracks by detainees from China, Japan, and other countries. Two of the many poems that have been preserved and translated convey what many detainees must have felt as the days without freedom multiplied.

> Imprisoned in the wooden building day after day,
> My freedom withheld, how can I bear to talk about it?
> I look to see who is happy but they only sit quietly.
> I am anxious and depressed and cannot fall asleep.

Figure 2.3
The *San Francisco Chronicle* called the new Angel Island Immigration Station "The Finest Immigrant Station in the World...the cleanest, best arranged and in all respects the finest and healthiest emigrant station ever established." Time would prove otherwise.

Source: Annual Report of the Commissioner General of Immigration, 1908.

> The days are long, and the bottle constantly empty; my sad mood, even so, is not
>   dispelled.
> Nights are long and the pillow cold; who can pity my loneliness?
> After experiencing such loneliness and sorry,
> Why not just return home and learn to plow the fields?[16]

Li Hai of Nancun, Taishan, wrote

> It's been a long time since I left my home village
> Who could know I'd end up imprisoned in a wooden building?
> I'm heartsick when I see my reflection, my handkerchief is soaked in tears
> I ask you, what crime did I commit to deserve this?[17]

How long were arrivals detained at Angel Island? Until recently, answers to that question were based solely on anecdotal evidence and surmise. The administration building burned in 1940, and many of the administrative records perished in the flames.[18] One can only guess at how many people were actually detained at Angel Island. My guess is that around 300,000 people were held there, based on an estimate that 340,000 aliens arrived through the Port of San Francisco between 1910 and 1940, that 70 percent of those arrivals were

Figure 2.4
The layout of main buildings of the Angel Island Immigration Station is shown at the time of its completion in 1907. It would remain unoccupied for over two years.

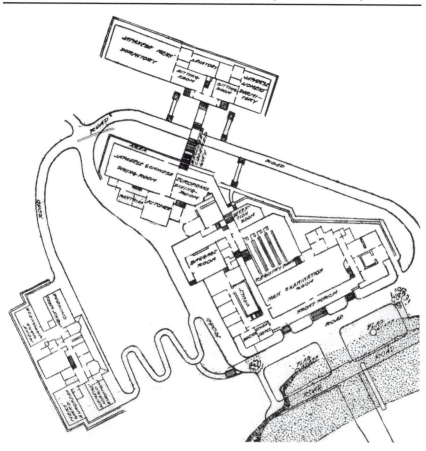

Source: San Francisco Chronicle, August 18, 1907. Thanks to John Soennichsen for directing me to this source.

detained, then adding in a guesstimate for deportees, passengers in transit, and undercounts in certain years.[19] Unfortunately, there is no comprehensive list of who was sent there nor of how long they were detained. There are numerous individual stories—including Quok Shee's—but there are no systematic data.

This is a rather glaring gap in American immigration history, one that we also find at the better-known immigration portal on Ellis Island. A standard history of Ellis Island states that the "actual time spent at the Island by the average immigrants was only a few hours."[20] A more popular account asserts that "80 out of 100 immigrants passing through Ellis Island went through quickly

Figure 2.5
Immigrants released from detention are shown boarding the government ferry *Angel Island* for the mainland.

Source: San Francisco History Center, San Francisco Public Library.

and easily; that 20 of each 100 were held, usually for a short while...."[21] However, there is no systematic evidence for such statements.

It is widely believed that just as the Chinese were singled out for special, negative treatment by the Chinese exclusion laws where eligibility for admission to the United States was concerned, so also were they given unequal treatment at the immigration stations. This is particularly true of Angel Island, where "Laws Harsh as Tigers" were enforced by the uniformed officers of the Immigration Service at the immigration station and, under other legislation, by those of the Public Health Service at the Quarantine Station.[22] It has been argued that "[a]ll Chinese seeking admission through San Francisco were subjected to detailed scrutiny and delay, and almost all of them were detained on Angel Island. Even elite Chinese arriving with student visas, whose right to enter was guaranteed by both statute law and Sino-American treaties, endured long delays."[23] A common comparison is that "most [immigrants] were ferried to the immigration station on Angel Island. In contrast, most European immigrants arriving at Ellis Island were processed in a matter of hours."[24] None of these assertions have data to back them up.

Figure 2.6
On August 12, 1940, the administration building at the Angel Island Immigration Station burned to the ground, destroying all of its records.

Source: San Francisco History Center, San Francisco Public Library.

Anecdotal evidence—the oral histories of Angel Island—is contradictory. My father-in-law, Koyee S.M. Ling, always insisted (correctly, we recently learned) that he had *never* been to Angel Island: as a graduate student sponsored by the Chinese Ministry of Education, he was landed directly from the SS *China* on October 1, 1917. Four years later, he endured a brief interrogation on Angel Island that did not involve actual detention.[25] In some Asian families, fear or shame led many to claim (incorrectly) that they had not been detained at Angel Island. At the other extreme, accounts of lengthy periods of confinement at Angel Island abound. Him Mark Lai, Genny Lim, and Judy Yung have compiled many such stories in *Island: Poetry and History of Chinese Immigrants on Angel Island, 1910–1940.*[26] Another chapter in this book, "An Alleged Wife," relates the ordeal of Quok Shee, a Chinese woman detained there for nearly six hundred nights from September 1916 to April 1918. Her experience was atypical, being the longest-known detention, but the story is extraordinarily well documented.[27] Thus, I have played a part in contributing to the notion that new arrivals, and especially the Chinese, were kept there "for, months, even years."[28]

A factual basis for answering the question, "How long were immigrants detained?" emerges from the records of the PMSS (Pacific Mail Steamship

Company).[29] The PMSS was charged for the upkeep of those of its passengers detained at the Angel Island Immigration Station, and it kept a record of these expenses. Two ponderous ledgers cover 29,344 passengers included in the records of 303 arriving ships between May 13, 1913 and August 16, 1919. The ledgers record how many nights the arrivals spent at the AIIS detention center, plus any time spent at the immigration station's hospital. Most passengers in the database were from ships crossing the Pacific, but 22 percent were from Pacific Mail ships that plied the west coast of Central and South America, representing 14 percent of all those detained.

The question "How long were arrivals detained at Angel Island?" contains an implied "on average," yet averages have a way of being misleading. We might ask, "average for whom?" Fully 8,873 of the "aliens" in the record (30%) never set foot on Angel Island; the number of nights for their stay was zero. Including them yields an average (mean) length of detention of 7.1 nights, with a median stay (where half the stays are shorter and half are longer) of 2. If we count only those who actually were sent to Angel Island, the average rises to 10.2 nights and the median to 4. Such large differences between "average" (mean) and "median" stays indicate that the "average" was pulled up by a relatively few people being detained for very long periods.

The Pacific Mail records clearly show that Chinese and Japanese were detained longer than all others, including Hispanics, Russians, Germans, English, the sample's 140 Indians, and a handful of passengers from the Philippines and Siam. Many Chinese (24%) did not go to Angel Island at all, but if they did, they were the ones most likely to be detained for lengthy periods (19.4% were detained for more than two weeks). Almost all Japanese (89.6%) were detained at Angel Island, but usually for only three days or less. Most non-Asians were likely to avoid Angel Island altogether or, if sent there, to have a very short stay.

Among the Chinese, there were marked differences in how long various categories of people were detained. "Sons of merchants" were detained longer than any other "exempt" category, as such men were suspected by the Immigration Service of trying to enter fraudulently as "paper sons." Even though Chinese women were generally thought to be actual or potential prostitutes, their frequency of being detained and the length of time of detention were comparable to Chinese men. Many of the Chinese detained at Angel Island were not even trying to enter the United States: they were "in transit," waiting to board a ship or (under bond) catch a train that would take them to, say, Mexico or Cuba.

Difficulties inherent in the sifting process explain why arrivals were held so long at Angel Island. Immigration officials had long professed difficulty in determining the identity of Chinese arrivals:

> The general resemblance of the race makes it very difficult to distinguish them apart: they all have the same black almond shaped eyes, copper complexion, coarse

black hair, while their heads are shorn alike with cue attachment....The height and size of the great majority are about the same, they are as near alike as cotton tailed rabbits.[30]

And, indeed, the forging of identity photographs was quite common. But a more apt explanation of the long delays is that Immigration Service inspectors believed that most Chinese trying to enter were untruthful about their occupation and, perhaps, about their name and family connections as well. In trying to ferret out the truth—or, more accurately, in trying to catch out suspicious cases in a lie—the officers of the Immigration Service developed a method of interrogation to which many would-be immigrants were subjected.

A well-known photograph shows a typical interrogation scenario confronting an Asian immigrant. A young Chinese man faces uniformed officers of the Immigration Service: a uniformed inspector in the Chinese Division conducting the interrogation, assisted by an Immigration Service interpreter and a stenographer. The immigrant was not entitled to legal representation at these sessions; he faced his interrogators alone. The number of questions asked often exceeded one hundred.

Before the opening of the Angel Island Immigration Station, the interrogations and detention of aliens were conducted at the detention shed on the wharf of the PMSS at Pier 40 in San Francisco (see "Before Angel Island"). The records of the interrogations from both the Immigration Station period and before are still available. They reside, waiting to speak to us, within the 250,000 investigation case files stored at the National Archives' Pacific Region branch at San Bruno, California.[31]

The subjects of the resulting investigation case files are overwhelmingly Chinese, although files for over eighty other national origins are also included—Japanese, Koreans, South Asians, Filipinos, Russians, Latin Americans, and the odd European. And not all the "Chinese" were Chinese nationals—a significant fraction were (or claimed to be) native-born Americans of Chinese ancestry attempting to reenter the United States.

Of all the so-called "Chinese case files" at the National Archives—Pacific Region, the oldest are for two people who arrived in San Francisco aboard the SS *Oceanic* on May 12, 1884. File 9228/1601 concerns Lui Fung, a merchant from Hong Kong. File 9228/1630 contains affidavits submitted on behalf of Leong Cum, a young woman who had been born in Lewiston, Idaho Territory, in 1868 and was returning to the United States after a visit to China. Both were briefly detained before being admitted, Lui Fung on May 13 and Leong Cum a day later. They represent some of the hundreds of thousands of new arrivals and returning residents who passed through the ports of San Francisco and Honolulu between 1882 and 1943, the years when the Chinese exclusion laws were in force.

A typical investigation case file contains the individual's name, place and date of birth, physical appearance, occupation, names and relationships of other family members, and family history. Specific INS proceedings are usually documented. Because of the nature of INS investigations, case files also provide links to file numbers for related cases, including those of other family members.

The files may contain certificates of identity and residency; correspondence; coaching materials used by "paper sons"; INS findings, recommendations, and decisions; maps of immigrant family residences and villages in China; original marriage certificates; individual and family photographs; verbatim transcripts of INS interrogations and special boards of inquiry; and witnesses' statements and affidavits. Some files are rather skimpy, while others are extraordinarily voluminous.

The time it took to verify the qualifications of an "exempt" Chinese was often measured in months, especially if the Immigration Service had to contact stations in other cities for information, witnesses, or records. No case took longer than that of Quok Shee, who arrived in 1916 with Chew Hoy Quong. "An Alleged Wife" is her story.

NOTES

1. For summaries of the various acts, see Michael LeMay and Elliott Robert Barkan, *U.S. Immigration and Naturalization Laws and Issues: A Documentary History* (Westport, CT: Greenwood Press, 1999). A superb treatment of enforcement of the Chinese Exclusion Act is Lee, *At America's Gates*.

2. Mae M. Ngai, "The Architecture of Race in American Immigration Law: A Reexamination of the Immigration Act of 1924," *Journal of American Ethnic History* 86, no. 1 (1999): 69.

3. Kenneth S.Y. and John M. Liu Chew, "Hidden in Plain Sight: Global Labor Force Exchange in the Chinese American Population, 1880–1940," *Population and Development Review* 30, no. 1 (2004).

4. Lee, *At America's Gates*; Mae M. Ngai, *Impossible Subjects: Illegal Aliens and the Making of Modern America* (Princeton: Princeton University Press, 2004); Lucy Salyer, *Laws Harsh as Tigers: Chinese Immigrants and the Shaping of Modern Immigration Law* (Chapel Hill: University of North Carolina Press, 1995); Sucheng Chan, *Entry Denied: Exclusion and the Chinese Community in America, 1882–1943* (Philadelphia: Temple University Press, 1991); and Jennifer Gee, "Sifting the Arrivals: Asian Immigrants and the Angel Island Immigration Station, San Francisco, 1910–1940" (PhD Dissertation, Stanford University, 1999).

5. Erika Lee, "The Chinese Exclusion Example: Race, Immigration, and American Gatekeeping, 1882–1924," *Journal of American Ethnic History* 21, no. 3 (2002).

6. See Torpey, *The Invention of the Passport*.

7. See Amy L. Fairchild, *Science at the Borders: Immigrant Medical Inspection and the Shaping of the Modern Industrial Labor Force* (Baltimore: The Johns Hopkins University Press, 2003).

8. See Howard Markel, *Quarantine! East European Jewish Immigrants and the New York City Epidemics of 1892* (Baltimore: Johns Hopkins University Press, 1997), 153–82, for the quarantine/immigration restriction nexus.

9. Mary Bamford, *Angel Island: The Ellis Island of the West* (Chicago: The Women's American Baptist Home Mission Society, 1917).

10. Louis J. Stellmann, "San Francisco to Have the Finest Immigrant Station in the World," *San Francisco Chronicle*, August 18, 1907.

11. All quotes attributed to Stellmann are in Ibid.

12. National Archives and Records Administration, "Luther C. Steward, Acting Commissioner, Immigration Service San Francisco, to Commissioner General, Immigration Service Washington, D.C., Dec. 19, 1910."

13. U.S. Department of Labor, "Annual Reports of the Commissioner-General of Immigration," 1903–32.

14. Secretary of Labor's annual report to the President, quoted in *San Francisco Examiner*, "Angel Island Station Shift Is Supported," December 17, 1915.

15. John Birge Sawyer, *Diaries of John Birge Sawyer: Holograph and Typescript, 1910–1962*, vol. 2 (Berkeley: Bancroft Library, University of California), 127.

16. Him Mark Lai, Genny Lim, and Judy Yung, *Island: Poetry and History of Chinese Immigrants on Angel Island, 1910–1940* (San Francisco: Hoc Doi [History of Chinese Detained on Island], San Francisco Study Center, 1980), 68.

17. Architectural Resources Group, "Poetry and Inscriptions: Translation and Analysis" (San Francisco: 2004).

18. Many, but not all. The NARA facility at San Bruno, California, holds an enormous collection of 250,000 "investigation case files" and administrative records. See Barde, Greene, and Nealand, "The EARS Have It," on the development of a Web-based search engine for the investigation case files index (http://iber.berkeley.edu/casefiles). Chen (1940) alludes to records kept at the Immigration Service office in the city of San Francisco, but these records, too, seem to have been lost.

19. Maria Sakovich, "Angel Island Immigration Station Reconsidered: Non-Asian Encounters with the Immigration Laws, 1910–1940" (master's thesis, Sonoma State University, 2002), 237–42.

20. Thomas M. Pitkin, *Keepers of the Gate: A History of Ellis Island* (New York: New York University Press, 1975), 67.

21. David Brownstone, Irene Franck, and Douglass Brownstone, *Island of Hope, Island of Tears* (New York: Wade Publishers, 1979), 203.

22. Salyer, *Laws Harsh as Tigers*.

23. Daniels, "No Lamps Were Lit," 8.

24. Lee, *At America's Gates*, 82.

25. Case file number 20498/1-2 for Ling Sze Moo, "Arrival investigation case files, 1884–1944," Records of the Immigration and Naturalization Service, 1891–1957, Record Group 85, National Archives and Records.

26. Lai, Lim, and Yung, *Island: Poetry and History*.

27. Case file number 15530/6-29 for Quok Shee, "Arrival investigation case files, 1884–1944," Records of the Immigration and Naturalization Service, 1891–1957, Record Group 85, NARA—Pacific Region facility, San Bruno, CA.

28. Iris Chang, *The Chinese in America: A Narrative History* (New York: Viking, 2003), 82.

29. The Pacific Mail data are explored and explained more fully in Robert Barde and Gustavo Bobonis, "Detention at Angel Island: First Empirical Evidence," *Social Science History* 30, no. 1 (2006): 103–36.

30. U.S. Bureau of Customs, "Press Copies of Letters from the Collector of Customs, San Francisco, to the Secretary of the Treasury, 1870–1912," Collector Sears to Secretary McCulloch, December 30, 1884.

31. Barde, Greene, and Nealand, "The EARS Have It."

— 3 —

An Alleged Wife

Chew Hoy Quong and his "alleged wife," Quok Shee, crossed my path quite by accident, two among thousands of Chinese would-be immigrants who had tried to enter the United States in 1916. Their experience was one of hardship, tenacity, and sadness. It was unusual, and it was puzzling, for through it runs a thread of mystery.

Their story begins in the thirty-fourth year of the Chinese Exclusion Act. It is a tale now over eighty years old. If today it seems dramatic, back then it surely passed unnoticed. No newspaper headlines, no memoirs. Only the public record remains, a folder more than an inch thick, begun in September 1916 and not closed until August 1918. It startled me when I first read that, for it meant that Quok Shee had been held in detention at the Angel Island Immigration Station for almost two years. As I leafed through her file, the dry and dated pages jumped to life as she was repeatedly interrogated, denied access to a lawyer, plagued by depression, subjected to smallpox, isolated from a husband she scarcely knew yet who was her only contact in America, pulled this way and that. One hundred and fifty pages of inquisitorial interrogations, legalistic maneuvering, medical evaluations, intrigue, and court orders, an extraordinary use of state power to prevent one little Chinese woman from entering the United States.

Her case was not ordinary, but then neither were the times, the place, and the other characters.

Here is the story of Quok Shee and her "alleged husband" (as the Immigration Service always referred to him), Chew Hoy Quong—or at least the part we can document. Their testimony is stored safely in the records of the National Archives, and if we listen carefully we can imagine their voices, sense the times, and feel the dramas that once swirled around Angel Island.

COMING TO AMERICA

Whereas, in the opinion of the Government of the United States the coming of Chinese laborers to this country endangers the good order of certain localities within the territory thereof. . . .it shall not be lawful for any Chinese laborer to come, or, having so come after [August 4, 1882], to remain within the United States.[1]

Chew Hoy Quong had first come to California as Congress was debating the Chinese Exclusion Act. He arrived in San Francisco from Hong Kong in 1881 and immediately went to work in his uncle's store on Washington Street. When his uncle died in 1896, Chew inherited the business. Like many other merchants, he saw his store destroyed in the earthquake and fire of 1906. He told immigration authorities that he had run a company in Holt Station, a railroad station eight miles west of Stockton, until 1915, when he joined the Dr. Wong Him Company, a prominent Chinatown firm dealing in herbs and medicines.

Having lived in the heart of the San Francisco Chinese community for nearly twenty-five years, Chew probably knew the procedures for coming to the United States. He would have known that if Chinese merchants wanted to leave the country and reenter, their firms were required to register with local authorities. The Dr. Wong Him Company had done so. On February 2, 1915, Chew joined the firm, investing $1,000 to buy out the share of one of the founding partners. As a principal in a legitimate business, he could now apply to the Immigration Service for a Form 431, which he did on March 25. When this was approved, he became entitled to leave the United States. More importantly, he became entitled to *return*—and to bring with him any wife or children he might have.

Carefully, Chew had laid the groundwork for the next, and perhaps last, big change in his life: to find a wife and get married. On May 15, 1915, at the age of 55, he boarded the SS *Manchuria* for Hong Kong. He later testified that, using a go-between, he met a Hong Kong woman named Lee See who had a daughter whom she hoped to marry off: Quok Shee, age 20.

Chew subsequently testified that on February 21, 1916, he and Quok Shee were married. We do not know when Chew told his bride that they would be going to *Gam San* ("Gold Mountain"—i.e., the United States). Perhaps her mother told her that the prospective husband resided in the United States. Or perhaps Quok Shee only found out after the wedding. But she had over five months to adjust and prepare for the future, five months during which she and Chew said they lived in rented space on the third floor of a Hong Kong building.

In June or July, Chew arranged for passage back to America on the Japanese ship *Nippon Maru*. Ship owners in the business of transporting immigrants clearly understood that should a passenger be turned back or delayed at the U.S. port of entry, the shipping line would incur additional costs—the immigrant's upkeep on

Figure 3.1
Quok Shee and Chew Hoy Quong were issued certificates of health in Hong Kong prior
to sailing on the *Nippon Maru*.

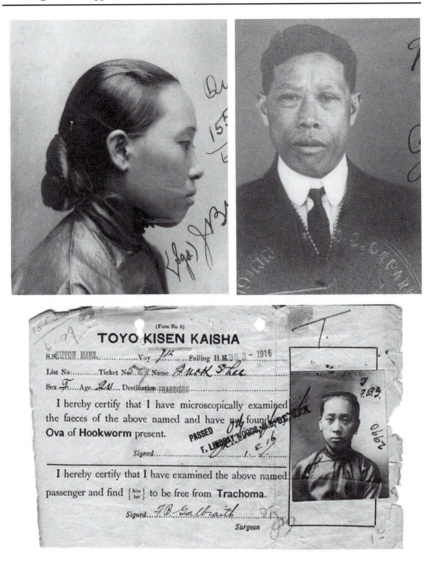

Source: National Archives and Records Administration.

Angel Island and, should the would-be immigrant be refused entry, the responsibility of transporting that person back to the country of origin.

Thus, the TKK (Toyo Kisen Kaisha) line, owner of the *Nippon Maru*, had an
incentive to see that their passengers' documents—especially their evidence of

good health—were in order. In Hong Kong, Quok Shee was taken to the TKK office, where she presented her photograph and obtained a certificate stating that she was free of hookworm and trachoma.

On August 3, 1916, the *Nippon Maru* sailed from Hong Kong, arriving in San Francisco on September 1. From the ship's passenger list, signed by Captain Nagano as required by American law, we know that she carried 188 passengers: 90 Japanese, 75 Chinese, and 23 others of various nationalities (mostly Europeans and Americans).[2] Among the Chinese were Chew and his wife of six months, Quok Shee. Quok Shee had crossed the Pacific, but in many ways her journey to America had just begun.

ARRIVAL

When a vessel bearing immigrants to California sails into San Francisco Bay, through the Golden Gate, anchorage is made at Meiggs' wharf, the vessel signals by whistling, and the immigration officials go aboard. The vessel proceeds to its dock in San Francisco, where the first-class passengers land, but all others are sent to Angel Island, which corresponds to Ellis Island on the Eastern Coast.[3]

For most non-Asian passengers, whether immigrants, returning citizens, or passengers in transit, passing through the port's health and immigration controls would have been done quickly. Visas were not necessary, and there were few formal requirements for entry. But for Chinese like Quok Shee and Chew, the process was quite different. Along with other Chinese passengers on the *Nippon Maru* they were taken to Angel Island, several miles away in San Francisco Bay. The island's Immigration Station was assigned the role of enforcing the grossly unfair Chinese exclusion laws, and that this was done in a callous manner only compounded the injury and resentment. First-hand testimony—some carved into the very walls—of former detainees speaks of injuries physical and emotional. Quok Shee and her husband were about to enter that labyrinth.

"TWENTY QUESTIONS," PLAYED FOR KEEPS

Fat Noon, you say that you first came to the United Sates in 1881 or 1882. Write in a book the testimony you once gave at the hearing in the Immigration Office; such as, the dates and the steamers on which you arrived in and departed from the United States. You two, be sure to learn the testimony thoroughly.[4]

The next day, September 2, J.P. Hickey, acting assistant surgeon of the U.S. Public Health Service, examined Quok Shee. He would have found her to be 4-foot-9, able to read and write, and with $10 and a ticket that her husband had paid for. Hickey signed her "Medical Certificate of Release." One hurdle had been cleared, but the couple was still held in the island's detention barracks.

On September 5, Quok Shee and her "alleged husband" were interrogated by the Chinese Division of the United States Immigration Service. The interrogation was an expected—and dreaded—part of the entry process for most Asians. The standard interrogation contained a minimum of fifteen questions; Quok Shee was asked eighty-four questions, Chew was asked over one hundred.

Chinese immigrants complained bitterly about such interrogations, whose unnerving, inquisitorial style were liable to trip up even the most honest immigrant. Immigration inspectors were convinced that most Chinese trying to enter as children or wives of resident Chinese were, in fact, fraudulent. These suspicions were not unfounded; many entering males were "paper sons" (i.e., fictitious sons), and there probably was a trade in women being brought in for "immoral purposes." Chew would certainly have been aware of the interrogation that loomed before them, and surely he and his wife used the long trip from Hong Kong to prepare for it.

There were two initial interrogations on September 5: one for Quok Shee and a separate one for Chew. Both were conducted by Inspector J.B. Warner (through interpreters) and stenographer H.F. Hewitt. Quok Shee's case file contains the verbatim transcripts of both interviews, and I present them here in their tedious fullness. Reading them today conjures up images of interrogations in a police state; imagine how nerve-wracking it must have been in 1916 to answer such questions—all these opportunities for even an innocent person to make a false step from nervousness, fatigue, or faulty memory.

Q: What is your name?

A: Quok Shee—Quok Sun Moy

Q: Where were you born?

A: Hong Kong.

Q: Whereabouts in Hong Kong?

A: 34 Tai Ping Street

Q: What is your father's name?

A: Quok Wah.

Q: What is your mother's name?

A: Lee Shee.

Q: Is she living?

A: Still living.

Q: How old is she?

A: 47.

Q: What kind of feet has she?

A: Natural. [i.e., not bound—Ed]

Q: Is your father living or dead?

A: Dead.

Q: How long has your father been dead?

A: Died when I was 13 years old.

Q: How many brothers and sisters have you?

A: One brother younger; no sisters.

Q: What is his name and age?

A: Quok Soo Tai, 18.

Q: Where is he?

A: He is a student, in Hong Kong.

Q: Had your father any brothers or sisters?

A: One brother younger.

Q: What is his name?

A: Quok Tim.

Q: What other name has he?

A: Quok Wing Chung.

Q: Are you married?

A: Yes.

Q: Who arranged your marriage?

A: Sam Por was the go-between.

Q: Did your uncle have anything to do with your marriage?

A: Yes.

Q: When were you married?

A: C.R. 5/1-19 (1916, Feb. 21).

Q: What are your husband's names and age?

A: Chew Hoy Quong; I don't know his other name.

Q: You don't know his marriage name?

A: He did not tell me.

Q: How old is he?

A: 56.

Q: What is his native village?

A: Nom Moon village, H.S. district.

Q: Did you ever visit his village?

A: No.

Q: Did your husband visit it after your marriage?

A: Yes.

Q: How long was he away from you?

A: 10 some odd days—A number of times.

Q: A number of times?

A: Yes. I don't remember how many times.

Q: Was your husband ever married before?

A: No.

Q: Are there any children who he claims he has?

A: None that I know of. He told me he had a nephew, Chew Nee Leung.

Q: Did you ever see this boy?

A: No.

Q: Are you positive you never saw Chew Nee Leung?

A: Yes. He accompanied me to the steamer.

Q: Who did he come with from his village?

A: With his father and my husband.

Q: What is his father's name?

A: Chew Kai Quong.

Q: Has this boy any brothers or sisters to your knowledge?

A: Three brothers.

Q: Did you ever see his three brothers?

A: No.

Q: Where did this boy and his father sleep while they were in Hong Kong?

A: I don't know. They never mentioned it.

Q: Did they eat at your house?

A: No.

Q: Did your husband eat at home with you while his brother and his nephew were in Hong Kong?

A: Sometimes he ate with me and sometimes he ate with his brother.

Q: Do you know where they ate when he ate with his brother?

A: I don't know.

Q: Where did you marry your husband?

A: Wah Hing Street, west.

Q: What number?

A: Number 20.

Q: On what floor were your rooms at this address?

A: Third floor.

Q: Did you occupy the entire third floor?

A: The whole floor.

Q: How many rooms were on that floor?

A: A private room (bedroom), reception room and a kitchen.

Q: How was the bedroom furnished?

A: One small round table, 4 American chairs, two cuspidors, one dressing bureau and one iron bed.

Q: How was the bedroom lighted?

A: Electric light in the reception room. A coal oil lamp in the bedroom and also in the kitchen.

Q: How was the reception room or parlor furnished?

A: Clock and round table, 4 chairs, American, one cuspidor and looking glass.

Q: Did you have a servant?

A: No.

Q: Did you do the cooking?

A: Yes.

Q: How was your bedroom lighted in the day time?

A: There is a hallway, parlor, bedroom and kitchen. The bedroom was lighted from a window in front of the building.

Q: How was the parlor lighted?

A: From a window in front of the building.

Q: What time did you arrive at your husband's home the day of your marriage?

A: About 6 p.m.

Q: What mode of conveyance did you use from Tai Ping street to Wah Hing street?

A: Sedan chair.

Q: Were you veiled when you came to your husband?

A: Yes.

Q: What color veil?

A: Red.

Q: Was there a feast held on the night of your arrival?

A: Yes.

Q: Where was it held?

A: Soo Fung Loy restaurant, third floor.

Q: Were you present?

A: No. But I served tea and wine.

Q: Was there a table set at the feast for women?

A: Yes, one table.

Q: What presents did your husband make you before or after marriage?

A: Pair of bracelets which I have on. (Exhibits pair of rattan bracelets mounted with gold.)

Q: Nothing else?

A: No.

Q: Did your husband ever take you to his home village?

A: No.

Q: Did you ever see your husband before you married him?

A: No.

Q: Did your husband ever visit your home, that is, where your mother lives?

A: No. My mother visited me a couple of times and my husband saw her then. He never visited my mother's home.

Q: Did you ever go home after you marriage?

A: Yes.

Q: Did you remain at home for any length of time?

A: No.

Q: Then you lived at 20 Wah Hing street all the time, from the time of your marriage up to the time of your departure for the United States?

A: Yes.

Q: Did your husband ever take you in Hong Kong after your marriage?

A: No.

Q: Did he ever take you out shopping?

A: No.

Q: Did he give you any money while you were in Hong Kong?

A: No.

Q: Did your husband pay the bills?

A: Yes.

Q: What rent did he have to pay for your apartments?

A: $15 per month.

Q: Did your husband take you to the Doctor?

A: Yes.

Q: Do you know what your husband's occupation is in the United States?

A: Merchant, druggist, I don't know the name of the store.

Q: Your husband's nephew accompanied you to the steamer landing the day you departed from Hong Kong?

A: Yes.

Q: Tell us exactly how many times your husband was away from home over night, after you married him the 19th day of the first month of this year?

A: I don't remember how many times—A number of times.

Q: Did he tell you he was going to his home village each time?

A: Yes.

Q: Did he go more than once?

A: Number of times—I don't remember how many times—more than two times.

Q: Is this your husband? (Showing photo of the all. Husband in this case.)

A: Yes.

Q: After the death of your father, how were you, your mother and brother supported?

A: Seamstresses.

Q: Are you an expectant mother?

A: No.

Q: Have you anything further to state?

A: No.

Q: Have you understood the interpreter?

A: Yes.

> Interpreter A.M. Alves asked the applicant if she had understood interpreter Chin
> Jack; she replied in the affirmative.
> Signed by Mark: X
> HFH/9/5/16

Inspector Warner must have entertained some doubts about their story. Later that same day, he and stenographer Hewitt recalled "the all. Husband" for further questioning. He was cautioned to be careful in his answers. Wrapping up that day's events, Inspector Warner made a favorable recommendation: he, at least, was convinced, and Quok Shee was on her way to being admitted to the United States. Or so it seemed.

MORE QUESTIONS

In fact, the Immigration Service did not release Quok Shee. Chew was already a legal resident and free to enter the country, which he did on September 5. But something was amiss, and Quok Shee remained in detention on Angel Island. More ominously, the Immigration Service wanted to talk to Chew again.

On September 13, Chew took the 8:45 a.m. steamer from Pier 7 back to Angel Island. He and his wife were again subjected to extensive questioning: 115 questions were put to him, 65 to his "alleged wife." As before, they were questioned separately and given no chance to talk to each other. This time, the interrogation was conducted by "Law Officer" W.H. Wilkinson. Again, only the stenographer and an interpreter were present. The same questions were asked again and again, each time in a slightly different way, brusquely jumping back and forth. The point was to catch them out and prove that they were not husband and wife.

This time, the interrogations explored how the "alleged husband's" story diverged from that of his "alleged wife." Wilkinson's questions focused on three areas: Quok Shee's knowledge of the furnishings and other occupants of the building they inhabited in Hong Kong, Chew's visit(s) to his native village, and the matter of getting onto the ship in Hong Kong. After the interrogations, he wrote a "Memorandum for the Commissioner." In it, he emphasized discrepancies in the number of visits made by the alleged husband to his home village, the nature and number of occupants on the second floor of their Hong Kong building, whether their apartment on the third floor was on the top floor or if people lived above them, whether the apartment had a metal clock or a wooden one, whether

Chew's adopted son lived on the ground floor or not, and the number of men accompanying them from the house to the steamer.

Wilkinson's conclusions were brief but brutal: "In view of the fact that the above contradictory statements appear incompatible with the relationship claimed, I recommend that the applicant be denied admission." That same afternoon, September 15, Commissioner Edward White ordered Quok Shee deported. The brisk "Notice to Rejected Chinese Applicant, Under Rule 5" was thoughtfully printed in both English and Chinese. Quok Shee was advised that she had two days to launch an appeal.

Two days for a poor immigrant to get a lawyer? Who would take such a case? Had she known what lay in store for her, she might have resisted engaging one. She surely had no idea how long and how tortuous her struggle would be.

ENTER THE LAWYERS

As in the 3 preceding years the cases coming under [petitions for writs of habeas corpus] *have been not only numerous but in the main hard fought, the petitioners being represented by experienced, able, and resourceful attorneys.[5]*

Chew was not unprepared. As soon as he sensed that something was amiss he engaged the services of the San Francisco legal firm of McGowan and Worley, well known as specialists in the problems of Chinese immigrants.

Housed in the Bank of Italy Building, McGowan and Worley was one of a number of law firms dealing largely in immigration law. It had been started in 1906 by Alfred Lincoln Worley and George A. McGowan. Worley was an immigrant himself, his father having moved the family from England to California in 1870, when young Worley was a year old. Worley's father went on to become a police Judge and City Attorney of San Francisco. This respectable social pedigree enabled young Worley to begin his professional life as an editor of the commercial department of the *San Francisco Chronicle*, but he soon switched to law and became a specialist in "Chinese immigration practice."

His partner was not a native San Franciscan, but came from Arcata, Humboldt County, in northern California. McGowan had been admitted to the bar in 1897 and subsequently became heavily involved in Republican politics: member of the legislature (1905–6), chairman of the San Francisco delegation, and coordinator of all emergency legislation following the 1906 disaster. McGowan was active in the Masons and in one other fraternity, the Native Sons of the Golden West.

By 1916 McGowan and Worley were established names in their trade, but with a whiff of the less-than-respectable about them, especially Worley. Where McGowan was a Republican insider aspiring to social acceptance, Worley (a Democrat) played the role of legal bomb-thrower. He had frequent run-ins with the Immigration Service and with the courts and was not shy about taking on unpopular cases. In 1915 he was debarred from practicing before immigration officials after he criticized their conduct toward one of his Chinese clients—the Immigration Service objected to a boy suffering from beri beri being visited by a private physician recommended by Worley, and the boy died. Worley was so incensed by such callous treatment, and by the subsequent denial of a death certificate and clinical report, that his vociferous and public criticism drew the ire of the Commissioner of Immigration in Washington. Worley was later exonerated, but within a year managed to attract further attention: he publicly charged that the detention of an immigrant from India has been inspired by a British plot to make life difficult for all Indian nationalists. This so-called "Hindu conspiracy" competed with World War I battlefront reports for space on the front page of the *San Francisco Examiner*.[6]

They were competent lawyers, and it was not at all unusual for them to be defending Chinese clients. The Chinese in California had a long history of using American lawyers and the American legal process to fight the Chinese Exclusion Act and its various successors, as well as discriminatory local ordinances. They also launched many legal actions against specific instances of unfair application of the exclusion laws. In the first ten years of the exclusion laws, more than 7,000 legal appeals were filed by the Chinese,[7] and between 1891 and 1905, an additional 2,600.[8] There was plenty of work, and no shortage of able and willing white lawyers to earn the fees.

McGowan took charge of Quok Shee's case and started working on it. On September 11, acting on behalf of Chew as the "alleged husband," he requested Quok Shee's records, including the report of the examining inspector and the review of the law officer. These, however, were withheld by the Immigration Service because "said report does not contain any evidence whatsoever." While this refusal would later be used against the government, its initial effect was to keep Quok Shee on Angel Island.

McGowan and Chew kept testing the government's resolve to exclude Quok Shee. On September 22 they filed a sworn affidavit in which Chew stated his background as a law-abiding citizen, provided details on his marriage to Quok Shee and their stay in Hong Kong, and showed how discrepancies in their interrogation testimony could be easily explained.

The affidavit was forwarded to Commissioner White on September 23, along with two other documents: a request to interview Quok Shee and a nine-page "Application to Re-open Case: Misunderstanding of purport of questions propounded and mistake of effect of Chinese customs bearing upon competency and relevancy of certain inconsistencies on the face of the record."

McGowan tried to use to his clients' advantage of existing notions of how alien and incomprehensible were the ways of the Chinese. He quoted at length from *Things Chinese*, a book first published nearly twenty-five years earlier, to demonstrate how Chinese customs are different from "civilized" ones, especially those that concern the status and treatment of women.[9] In trying to explain discrepancies in their testimony, Quok Shee's lawyer argued that Chinese women were sheltered, uneducated, unworldly, and basically, incompetent: "Matters of this kind only go to show that too much has been expected in this examination of the testimony of this Chinese wife."

Commissioner White was not in the least persuaded. On September 26 he notified McGowan and Worley that their request to reopen the case was denied. Further, the request that Quok Shee be able to confer with her "alleged husband" and with her lawyer was also denied.

The next day McGowan tried appealing to whatever sense of compassion the Immigration Service might have:

> This applicant having been held incommunicado at your station since the 1st day of September, 1916, she having been kept separate, apart, and away from her husband during all of that time, the husband now desires to request that he be permitted to see, talk to, comfort and console his wife, who journeyed with him to this country on the same boat and to whom you have denied admission.

The Immigration Service was not in the compassion business. Permission was denied.

For McGowan and Worley, the next stage was to appeal to the Secretary of Labor in Washington. On September 28, Commissioner White in San Francisco forwarded a copy of Quok Shee's file to Washington. In the dossier was all the Immigration Service's information on Quok Shee that had been shown to McGowan—and some that had not.

This administrative appeal, too, was rejected on November 21, 1916, when the Secretary of Labor ordered Quok Shee deported, "said deportation to take effect Saturday, the 25 day of November, 1916." It seemed that Quok Shee's attempt to enter the United States had failed, and that after three months in captivity on Angel Island she would be forced to return to China.

Rather than accept defeat, Chew turned to the courts to free his wife. To do so, he somehow brought in additional legal firepower: Dion Holm, a young, brilliant lawyer whose family had been in business in San Francisco since the Gold Rush. Holm worked in the office of Samuel Shortridge, a future Senator and a lawyer with a long history of representing Chinese merchants, even though he early opposed Chinese immigration. "The warfare of Californians against the Chinese is a patriotic and righteous warfare, justified by the principle of self-protection."[10]

Holm resorted to a widely recognized remedy in the Anglo-American legal system for violations of personal liberty: the writ of habeas corpus. The most important version of this writ directs someone who holds another in custody to produce the body of that person before the court in order that the court may rule on the legality of the detention. In other words: "produce the body of the person you hold, and charge that person with a crime or release him." Or her.

The Chinese in the United States had a long experience with writs of habeas corpus, with their American lawyers using it from the inception of the Exclusion Act to prevent the Immigration Service from denying entry to the Chinese women. According to Vincente Tang, the most successful were the Chinese criminal gangs (tong) who brought in prostitutes. With ample financial resources to hire lawyers, file writs, appeal deportations, and "grease the wheels" where needed, tong members were able to secure the entry of many prostitutes. So many, in fact, that gaining entry via a writ of habeas corpus practically labeled a woman a prostitute. In 1890, Mrs. S.L. Baldwin complained that

> Cargoes of such women are landed here without certificates while wives of respectable Chinese...cannot land. It is maddening to think of the writ of habeas corpus, that sacred birth right of Anglo Saxons, and the safeguard of our liberties, being turned into a slave chain to drag these women down to hell.[11]

Petitioning the court for a writ of habeas corpus was thus a necessary last resort. On November 24, the day before Quok Shee was to be deported, Dion Holm went to the Federal District Court for Northern California on behalf of Chew and filed a petition for a writ of habeas corpus.

Judge Dooling of the U.S. District Court was known for being more favorably disposed toward immigrants (and opposed to administrators denying immigrants "ordinary fairness") than most judges. He immediately issued a court order for the Commissioner of Immigration to appear on November 29. The delay was brief. On December 15, Judge Dooling ruled in favor of the government and denied the petition of a writ of habeas corpus. Four days later, Immigration Commissioner White issued yet another order regarding Quok Shee to the inspector in charge, Deportation and Detention Division, Angel Island Station: "You will see that she is deported on the next available steamer of the line that brought her unless this office is in the meantime served with an order of Court staying such deportation."

The last document for 1916 in Quok Shee's case file is lawyer Holm's letter of December 22 to the Immigration Service: "You were served with an Order staying all proceedings in this matter and also a Citation to show cause why the judgment in the case as rendered by the District Court should not be corrected. These two papers constitute sufficient notice to you to stay deportation." Quok Shee's case would now go to the court of appeals, and Quok Shee would remain on Angel Island.

THE LONG WAIT

Today is the last day of winter,
Tomorrow morning is the vernal equinox.
One year's prospects have changed to another.
Sadness kills the person in the wooden building.[12]

Compared with the speed with which administrative appeals had been acted upon, the progress of Quok Shee's court case was interminably slow. Not until August 1917 would the court of appeals rule on her case. In the meantime she remained in limbo—neither charged with any crime nor free to enter the United States—and in detention on Angel Island.

Many detainees have told of the lamentable conditions of incarceration on Angel Island, of their isolation and emotional exhaustion. Told to oral historians or written on the walls of the barracks, their words speak of a desolate period in their lives. For women, the effects of incarceration were even worse. Chinese women of that period were much more likely to be uneducated and less worldly than male detainees. Their social support networks, too, were weaker. Their numbers were perhaps but one-tenth that of the men, making it less likely that they would have the companionship of someone who spoke their own dialect. Quok Shee's fate was this, and more.

Early in 1917, smallpox broke out in the female quarters on Angel Island. Quok Shee was held for observation at the Public Health Service's Quarantine Station on the opposite side of the island, then released on March 20. One can only imagine how the threat of smallpox and subsequent removal to the Quarantine Station must have compounded her sense of isolation and despair.

Her desperation did not escape notice by the Immigration Service. Less than a week after being released from quarantine, Quok Shee was interviewed by Inspector Charles Mayer and badgered to drop her appeals:

Q: Is it true that you want your case in the courts abandoned and that you desire to be deported on the "Sib. Maru" on April 3?

A: Yes.

Q: Why do you want to go back and not wait for the court's decision in your case?

A: Well I don't know how long that is going to be and I have been here 7 months already.

Q: Do you want to be landed in the U.S.?

A: Within this few days, if I can be landed, if not I will go back on the "Siberia."

Q: Why do you want to go back on the "Siberia" rather than any other vessel?

A: Because I understand there are some others going on the same boat and I wanted to go.

Q: If none of those others go back on the "Siberia" do you want to go on the "Siberia" anyway?

A: Yes.

At around the same time, an anonymous handwritten note on the Department of Labor paper appears in her file:

Kwok Shee has had no money for seven months—is wearing shoes and stockings that have been given to her by American friends. She doesn't know what has been done about her case and desires earnestly to be sent back to China. She feels very much neglected because she is clinging to the idea that she is really married and gets no response either from her Chinese friends or her lawyer. She has sent word to her lawyer on an average of once in six weeks. She owes about $8 which has been borrowed from girls.

Drawing on emotional resources we can only imagine, Quok Shee resisted the pressures to have her returned to China.

She may also have been succored by one of the numerous groups who provided assistance to new arrivals at various stages in the process of establishing themselves in a new country. The Travelers Aid Society—claimed to be the forerunner of Legal Aid—helped travelers of all sorts, both domestic and international. Jewish arrivals at Angel Island, especially those coming across the Pacific from Russia, were assisted by the Hebrew Immigrant Aid Society. A priest from the Russian Orthodox Church in San Francisco frequently visited Russians (Orthodox or not) detained at Angel Island.[13] The Tung Wah Dispensary, established in 1900, and the Chinese YMCA, established in 1911, were examples of the Chinese community providing new organizations independent of the older clan-based mutual aid societies, such as the Chinese Consolidated Benevolent Association (aka "Chinese Six Companies"). Several Protestant denominations provided what today would be called social workers: in addition to their religious "ministry" work, they would conduct visitations to detainees and offer everything from counseling to the more dramatic forms of "rescue" (see the reference to Donaldina Cameron, below). Overwhelmingly women, they constituted an unsung, but important, part of the immigration industry.[14]

One in particular was an immigrant herself (from Canada) who helped other immigrants on Angel Island for nearly the entire life of the Immigration Station: Deaconess Katharine Maurer (1881–1962).[15] A striking figure— tall, handsome, dignified, always "in uniform" in a black dress and bonnet, white ties and cuffs, and a long black cape as protection against the wind—she became almost as much a part of the Immigration Station as the inspectors, guards, and matrons. In time she became known to the Chinese as "Kuan Yin" ("Goddess of Mercy") and to the newspapers as the "Angel of Angel Island."

In 1911, Maurer graduated from the San Francisco National Training School of the Methodist Episcopal Church. As a new Deaconess, she became part of a movement begun in the late nineteenth century, one that trained young women for Christian education, social work, and home visitation—all part of the ministry that the pastor of a large parish could not do alone, and one of the few Church careers open to women.[16] A year earlier, the Church's WHMS (Women's Home Missionary Society) had begun to work with Japanese and Korean picture brides detained on Angel Island. A year later, Deaconess Maurer succeeded Miss Carrie Isabelle Pierson as the WHMS provider of "welfare work" on Angel Island.[17] It is inconceivable that Quok Shee would not have met her, just as one must imagine Maurer taking an interest in such a pitiable case.

Maurer's salary was paid by the WHMS, with assistance from churches, Sunday schools, and the Daughters of the American Revolution.[18] The government allowed her to use two rooms at the Immigration Station as a library and office, and according to Maurer's predecessor, "The deaconess is the only person not in the government employ who is allowed to visit freely among these aliens."[19]

Figure 3.2
Deaconess Katharine Maurer of the Methodist Episcopal Church ministered to detainees
on Angel Island from 1912 to 1940.

Source: California Historical Society, FN-18240.

Both Pierson and Maurer had to maintain a delicate balance between keeping
the confidence of the detainees and having the Immigration authorities continue to allow them access, between being an advocate for detainees and playing
within bounds set by the Immigration Service. With the latter goal in mind,
Maurer would tell detainees, "You must have faith the American officials will
not hurt you. When you answer their questions, be truthful. Then you will have
nothing to fear. Good will come out of it all."[20] Her advocate-cum-social worker
activities were prodigious:

> The list of activities carried on by Miss Maurer is a long one. Daily visits to the
> various quarters on the island; letter writing; interpreting, shopping for supplies,
> teaching English, attending court, seeing girls safely married; follow-up work and
> subsequent visitation in the homes of people who have been landed; classifying
> and checking out library books; supplying clothing for those in need; securing
> employment for men and women; furnishing materials for occupational work—
> weaving, knitting, wood carving, sewing; sitting with the women and listening to
> their problems, giving helpful advice when requested.[21]

In her Annual Report for the year 1915–16, Maurer tallied some of her activities:

Calls made (not including Angel Island): 550

Meetings attended: 290

Letters written: 453

Bouquets of flowers: 653

Garments distributed: 300

Nationalities: 32[22]

She eventually learned to speak some Chinese and Japanese but in 1916 her Chinese was limited. But perhaps her language skills were sufficient for giving comfort.

She recalled one troubled little woman whose depression and loneliness were growing serious. One day she motioned Miss Maurer to kneel with her beside a chair. The deaconess knew only a little Chinese, but it included the Lord's Prayer and the hymn "Jesus Loves Me." To these she added her own petition for light and courage to come to this lonely woman.[23]

TROUBLE ON ANGEL ISLAND

Since the Geary Chinese Exclusion act (of 1892) went into effect there have been scandals innumerable....In the days when enforcement of the Geary act was being first attempted the ousting or disgracing of an immigration official of San Francisco was news of common occurrence.[24]

Any artificial scarcity—such as entry into the United States—inevitably leads to a black market. In immigration it takes the form of forged papers, sale of genuine papers, smuggling, and bribes. The various Chinese exclusion laws had made legal entry a scarce commodity. Chinese women were even scarcer: the first act had driven the ratio of the Chinese men to women to over 26 to 1. This ratio improved over time, but in 1916 there were still more than ten Chinese men for every Chinese woman in the United States. In the same year, only 300 Chinese women officially entered the United States, of whom 111 were of the category that Chew hoped to use: "merchants' wives."[25]

This black market was a multiracial enterprise, and those in it profited handsomely. With many willing to pay, many others were willing to be paid— kitchen help smuggled in coaching materials, watchmen looked the other way, inspectors changed their recommendations, file clerks helped files disappear temporarily while photographs were switched, lawyers took and paid bribes. Corruption flourished, a phenomenon explored further in a subsequent chapter on the Densmore investigation into the smuggling of immigrants. It was no wonder that the Immigration Service was skeptical of Chew and his "alleged wife."

APPEALS

On August 6, 1917—nearly a year after Quok Shee had arrived in San Francisco, after more than eleven months of detention on Angel Island—the Circuit

Court of Appeals for the Ninth Circuit ruled on Quok Shee's case. Or, more precisely, on *Chew v. White, Immigration Com'r*, Case No. 2926.

Surprisingly, while the courts upheld the exclusion laws in general, individual Chinese had fared rather well when seeking individual relief. Of the 2,288 Chinese petitions for habeas corpus filed between 1891 and 1905, well over half had been decided in favor of the petitioners. It seemed that many judges—even avowedly exclusionist ones—had an allegiance to the rule of law, to the notion that even the Chinese, as alien and unassimilable as they might be, deserved some elemental constitutional protections and due process.

Holm based his appeal of the district court's ruling on the only arguments possible under the law: that the Immigration Service had not correctly followed its own procedures and that Holm should have been allowed to present new evidence to explain the discrepancies in his clients' testimony. His arguments were completely rejected by the court of appeals. This decision again gave the Immigration Service authority to deport Quok Shee. Other developments in the courts, however, boded ill for the government.

On August 22, 1917, Commissioner White noted that "it seems probable that a petition for rehearing will be filed by the appellant, based on the recent decision in the case of Mah Shee, Bureau No. 54176/56." In this case, the court of appeals ruled against the government because immigration authorities had refused the request of Mah Shee's lawyers that they and Mah Shee's husband be allowed to interview her jointly—without advising the lawyers that they would have granted permission to him alone. And who were the attorneys for Mah Shee? None other than McGowan and Worley. Commissioner White was certain that Dion Holm would hear of this ruling and "present the point to the Court in an application for a rehearing." And he did.

Holm and Chew went back to the district court, launching another petition for a writ of habeas corpus, this time arguing that Quok Shee's lawyers (at the time, McGowan and Worley) had been prevented from interviewing her. The government still found a sympathetic ear in the person of Judge William C. Van Fleet, and the petition was denied.

On November 19, Holm went to the circuit court of appeals with another petition for a writ of habeas corpus. This one would have a very different outcome, however, for Holm had learned that the Immigration Service had a dirty little secret: it had been withholding information.

THE INFORMER

Unknown to Quok Shee, Chew, or their lawyers, "Law Officer" W.H. Wilkinson of the Immigration Service had made additional inquiries shortly after the couple arrived on Angel Island. It was he who conducted the second round of interviews on September 13, 1916. And it was Wilkinson who secretly talked with an informer. What he learned, and the source of his information, was to be the

Immigration Service's closely held secret. It is revealed in the following "confidential" memo found in Quok Shee's case file:

15530/6-29   September 15, 1916

CONFIDENTIAL

In accordance with your instructions, I called upon the Assistant Attorney-General and there interviewed his informant in the case of Quok Shee, an applicant for admission at this port as the alleged wife of a merchant, ex SS "Nippon Maru" September 1, 1916. I was advised that said informant had been a client for many years and that she was a woman of refinement and culture, and one in whom full confidence could be placed—facts which were obvious to me after seeing and conversing with the lady and her daughter, who accompanied her, and who speaks English fluently.

Said informant stated that a friend of hers had told her of a confession made to her by the alleged husband wherein he admitted that the applicant is not his wife but that he is bringing her to this country for immoral purposes for which action he will receive the sum of $3,000, and that said applicant had formerly been a prostitute in Hong Kong. The informant stated that the alleged husband had also admitted to her that the applicant was not his wife and that he was bringing her into this country for Lew Quong (who, the informant stated, is at present an interpreter employed by the T.K.K. SS Co. in Hong Kong, and formerly a resident of the United States), and that he intended to take her to the country immediately upon her landing (this latter statement is in strange contrast with his statement before this office that he intended to take his alleged wife to his store at 1268 O'Farrell Street, San Francisco, Cal).

The informant was very fearful of vengeance if her connection with the case became known, and it was only upon assurance that her name would not be mentioned that she consented to convey the above information; and it is in conformity with that assurance, and as a precaution against any possible disclosure of the information contained herein, that I have withheld all names. If the Bureau directs that such names be disclosed, the information can of course be furnished.

Signed: W.H. Wilkinson, Law Officer

Wilkinson and the Commissioner set great store by the information of the unnamed informer. Commissioner White wrote to Washington requesting that

> Every possible precaution has been taken to prevent this confidential information, and the name of the informant from becoming known to parties interested in the case; and it is for this reason that the above-mentioned report of inspector Wilkinson has not been made a part of the record...owing to the extreme danger to the informant which would undoubtedly result from an exposure of her identity.

Commissioner White was convinced that Chew was attempting to bring in Quok Shee as part of "a concerted move to import Chinese prostitutes" by men from Chew's village of Nom Moon. As Quok Shee was repeatedly questioned, and as the length of her confinement grew, it would become apparent that no amount of persuasion or explanation by her lawyers could convince the Immigration Service that Quok Shee was more than an *alleged* wife. Immigration officials were persuaded to the contrary by a few minor discrepancies in testimony, buttressed by the word of an informer. That testimony was unchallengeable in its anonymity, a fact that would one day, perversely, be used against the Immigration Service.

A TEST OF WILLS

If Chew was tenacious in pursuing appeals on behalf of Quok Shee, the Immigration Service was just as determined to assert its authority and to prevent her entry. One of Quok Shee's female fellow-passengers on the *Nippon Maru* was a prime example of what the Immigration Service thought it was up against: widespread fraud, especially where it involved Chinese women.

According to the ship's passenger manifest, Jung Oy was in some ways quite similar to Quok Shee: aged 24, height 4'11", black hair, dark eyes, yellow "complexion," coming from Kwangtung province and destined for San Francisco. But there were some major differences: she was single, listing "housework" as her occupation, traveled in second cabin (where Quok Shee traveled steerage), and claimed to be an American citizen by virtue of having been born in San Francisco. She was initially denied admission, but diligent work by lawyers McGowan and Worley produced a string of prominent Chinese witnesses attesting to Jung Oy's American birth. After several administrative appeals and seventy days in detention on Angel Island, she was admitted on November 15.

This was not the last entry in Jung Oy's case file. Immigrant Inspector John Robins reported that two months after her release he encountered her again—at the Panama Hotel, "a Chinese House of prostitution, 1134 Grant Street." He had gone along on a raid by the local police, who were accompanied by four women from the Presbyterian Mission. That foursome was led by Donaldina Cameron, "Chinatown's Angry Angel," who saw her mission to be the rescue of Chinese "slave girls" from prostitution.[26] Cameron had obtained an arrest warrant for Jung Oy from the Juvenile Court—but Jung Oy's age put her well past the reach of the Court and Ms. Cameron. While the other young women in the brothel's sitting room were taken away under the warrant, Jung Oy simply refused to be rescued.[27]

On November 9, 1917, and again on November 20, and yet again on December 13, Immigration Inspector Mayer interviewed Quok Shee. He did not need to threaten her, but he did attempt to manipulate her isolation and vulnerability to get her to return to China voluntarily.

Q: Quok Shee, the highest court in San Francisco has recently decided that we had a right to deport you and we would have deported you today if your alleged husband had not taken your case to the courts again. As it is you may have to wait some time until the court again decides your case. Are you willing to wait awhile for the court now to decide your case or do you still wish to be sent to China as soon as possible?

A: How much longer will it take to know about my case?

Q: It is impossible to state; it may be decided within a week or two and it may not be decided for months. Did your alleged husband or your attorney or anyone else consult you about having this new case brought before the court?

A: No I was not consulted.

Q: If you had been consulted about it would you have agreed to the bringing of the new case before the court?

A: No I would not. I would like to have my husband not bring this case in court. I would rather be sent back.

Q: How long is it since you last saw your husband?

A: I haven't seen him for about 8 months. He has not been to see me at the Island.

Q: Has he sent any word to you within the last 8 months?

A: No. My lawyer brought me over $10 one day.

Q: Did you ever get any money from your husband or from anyone else since you have been at the station here up until the time you received that $10 last?

A: No nothing. I would like to have you tell my husband to send me back to China.

Q: Do you still maintain that you are the lawful wife of your alleged husband?

A: I was married to him in China.

Q: Have you any reason to think it was not a legal marriage?

A: Yes I think it was a legal marriage, my mother had me married.

Q: How do you explain the indifference that your husband has shown towards you since you have been here?

A: He is in the city. I don't know why he didn't come.

On December 13, Inspector Mayer again tried to persuade Quok Shee to demand that her lawyer drop her petition for a writ of habeas corpus:

Q: It will probably take three or four months for your case to be decided in court.

A: I am not willing to wait that long, since I have waited so long already.

Q: Would you be willing to wait two months for the Court to decide your case?

A: My lawyer has already promised me in two weeks, so I am not willing to wait any longer than that.

Q: With due deference to your lawyer, I can state that your case cannot possibly be decided for two or three months at the very least.

A: I have already asked him to ask my friends not to appeal my case any longer....I am determined to go back.

Q [to the interpreter]: Mrs. Wisner, please explain to her that we have no right to urge upon the Court that she be deported day after tomorrow, irrespective of the wishes of her husband unless she herself absolutely demands it of us. (Interpreter complies)

A [by Applicant]: I have nothing else in my mind now, except to return on the Nippon Maru on Saturday the 15th. I have nothing else to say about it; I insist upon going.

A [statement by Mrs. Wisner, the interpreter]: During the last month, every time I have seen this woman, I have been asked to take a note to Mr. Hayes or the Commissioner or Mr. Mayer, *begging them to use their utmost endeavors to send her back on the first Japanese boat. I have explained this statement to the applicant, and she says it is correct.*

By this time, Quok Shee had been held on Angel Island for nearly fifteen months. The cycle of appeal and denial, hope and disappointment, had taken its toll. Her lawyer wrote to Commissioner White that he had applied for Quok Shee to be released on bail, and he implored the commissioner not to oppose that request. "Quok Shee is in a highly nervous state and I really believe that she will undergo great physical suffering, as well as mental if confined at Angel Island any longer. I have been told that she has on many occasions threatened to commit suicide if not released."

This was not an idle threat. Interviews with detainees contain references to a few cases of suicide by those who were to be deported, including a case reported by an interpreter of a woman who, fearing deportation, forced a sharpened chopstick through her ear to her brain and died. Even the Immigration Service was becoming concerned about Quok Shee: it would not do to have a suicide on their hands.[28] "This woman is in a wrought up condition over the matter and it would be a great relief to her and to this office if a dismissal of the [appeal] could be secured."

Bail was denied. The appeals were not dropped. And Quok Shee did not commit suicide. Instead, she continued to bear the tedium and anxiety of confinement. It would be another four months until the court rendered its verdict.

ISSUE THE WRIT

On March 6, 1918, Dion Holm went before the Circuit Court of Appeals in San Francisco to argue his side of *Chew v. White, Immigration Com'r*, Case No. 3088. His brief, printed and formally presented, is part of Quok Shee's court file. He accused the Immigration Service of refusing him an opportunity to confer with Quok Shee and of withholding information about the informer.

After nearly four weeks, the Circuit Court of Appeals, Ninth Circuit, issued its ruling on April 1, 1918. The case had been heard by Judges Gilbert, Ross, and Hunt, the same trio who had heard Chew's first appeal. In his opinion, Judge Gilbert this time expressed his clear opposition to the behavior of the Immigration Service.

> The denial of the right of the applicant's attorneys to interview her...was, we think, in itself sufficient ground for holding that the hearing was unfair....Aside from that, we hold that the fact that the immigration authorities received a confidential communication concerning the applicant's right to admission, upon which they acted, and which was forwarded to the Department of Labor for its consideration, was sufficient to constitute the hearing unfair. However far the hearing on the application of aliens for admission into the United States may depart from what in judicial proceedings is deemed necessary to constitute due process of law, there clearly is no warrant for basing a decision, in whole or in part, on confidential communications, the source, motive, or contents of which are not disclosed to the

applicant or her counsel and where no opportunity is afforded them to cross-examine, or to offer testimony in rebuttal thereof, or even to know that such communication has been received.

The judgment is reversed, and the cause is remanded, with instruction to issue the writ.

There is something majestic in witnessing the delivery of justice, even from a remove of more than eighty years. Quok Shee's case had been building for so long, and the documentation already so voluminous, that I was unprepared for the effect of unfolding yet another document. This one was dated May 2, 1918, printed on a stiff, heavy paper, embossed and weighty in its officialness: the actual order from the court of appeals, commanding that a writ of habeas corpus be issued for Quok Shee. Invoking the awesome power of the President of the United States, it left no doubt that the judicial system was now working *for* Quok Shee and her liberty.

References to "alleged husband" and "alleged wife" disappeared. The order recognized "Chew, as Petitioner for and on Behalf of His Wife, Quok Shee." In the name of "the Honorable Edward Douglas White, Chief Justice of the United States," the district court was told to issue the writ "as according to right and justice and the laws of the United States." That same day, the actual writ of habeas corpus issued by the district court commanded that Commissioner White bring Quok Shee, "the said person by you imprisoned and detained," before the court on May 11 to be released on $250 bond. The bond was arranged through C.T. Hughes of the National Surety Company. Quok Shee pledged to "personally appear at the...Court...at any and all times or time." She was free to enter the United States of America.[29]

REFLECTIONS

At first blush, this case is both a powerful example of the harsh treatment often afforded Asian immigrants during the period of the exclusion laws and an indictment of how the Immigration Service abused the broad powers given to it.

Yet there are reasons why one might *not* want to write about Quok Shee's case. Hers was not "typical," being the longest known detention at Angel Island and turning out reasonably well in the end. Did "the system" work? Is this proof that immigrants could and did receive fair treatment?

Many questions remain unanswered: Who was the unnamed informant? Why did the Immigration Service decide to contact her about Quok Shee? How did Chew decide on engaging first McGowan and Worley, then Dion Holm, as his lawyers? Why, really, did the Immigration Service come down so hard on Quok Shee and Chew even *before* talking to the informer?

Why were they pursued so doggedly—almost obsessively—when the discrepancies in their stories seemed so minor, so plausible? Were they being shaken down, the inspectors hoping for a bribe? We cannot know for certain, but these are not unreasonable suspicions, especially in light of the concurrent Densmore Investigation into immigration smuggling. Even Densmore thought it enough of a possibility that he specifically asked to examine her file.

Two questions, in particular, await answers:

Was Chew *really* the husband of Quok Shee? Or was he, as the Immigration Service claimed, bringing her to the United States for "immoral purposes"? It seems unlikely that a merchant whose entire resources amounted to less than $1,350—his stake in the Dr. Wong Him Co. plus an IOU—could pay the substantial legal bills incurred over nearly two years of administrative appeals and court cases. Perhaps his legal costs really were underwritten by a criminal element with sinister designs on Quok Shee. Might the Dr. Wong Him Co. have been a front for individual immigrant smugglers? Or, more benignly, perhaps the legal fees were paid by the Chinese Consolidated Benevolent Association, better known as the Chinese Six Companies. It is quite possible that *all the above are true*.

But something in the consistent, determined testimony of Quok Shee argues otherwise. Despite her isolation, her manipulation at the hands of Immigration Service inspectors, her fragile emotional and physical state, and the frequent examples of the women being deported and forced by the Immigration Service to leave the country, Quok Shee stuck to her story. She always insisted that she had been legally married, and that Chew was her husband. Even in moments of despair when she asked to be sent back to China, she never recanted or disavowed Chew as her husband. It would have been so easy to do. She did not, and one is inclined to believe her.

Most tantalizing of all: What happened to them? The court released her on $250 bond, the Immigration Service closed her case file, and this story ends. Or is it just a chapter that ends? Where the official documents leave off, perhaps a much longer story begins: Quok Shee's life in the United States.

NOTES

1. Chinese Exclusion Act, approved May 6, 1882; U.S. Statutes at Large, vol. 22, 58 ff. See LeMay and Barkan, *U.S. Immigration and Naturalization Laws and Issues*.

2. Data on the *Nippon Maru*'s passengers are from the passenger lists on microfilm held by the National Archives and Record Administration: Record Group 85, series M140, Roll 91.

3. Bamford, *Angel Island*.

4. Coaching material in Immigration Service administrative files, NARA, San Bruno, CA. Translated literally by Interpreter H.K. Tang, May 30, 1918.

5. Report by the Commissioner of Immigration for San Francisco, contained in the *Annual Report of the Commissioner General of Immigration to the Secretary of Labor*, 1917, 201.

6. Sources: For both Worley and McGowan, see J.C. Bates, ed., *History of the Bench and Bar of California* (San Francisco: Bench and Bar Publishing Co., 1912), and Worley's obituary in the *San Francisco Chronicle*, September 30, 1939.

7. Chinese Admiralty Cases, Private Admiralty Docket; from Christian Fritz, "Due Process, Treaty Rights, and Chinese Exclusion, 1882–1891," in *Entry Denied*, ed. Chan (Philadelphia: Temple University Press, 1991), 29.

8. Figures represent Chinese habeas corpus cases in the Northern District Court of California and in the U.S. Circuit Court for the Northern District, cited by Salyer, *Laws Harsh as Tigers*, 80–82.

9. J. Dyer Ball, *Things Chinese: Being Notes on Various Subjects Connected with China* (London: S. Low, Marston, 1892).

10. Oscar T. Shuck, ed., *History of the Bench and Bar of California* (San Francisco: The Commercial Printing House, 1901), 1808.

11. Esther Baldwin, *Must the Chinese Go? Examination of the Chinese Question* (New York: Elkin Press, 1890), quoted in Vincente Tang, ed., *Chinese Women Immigrants and the Two-Edged Sword of Habeas Corpus, The Chinese American Experience: Papers from the Second National Conference on Chinese American Studies* (San Francisco: Chinese Historical Society of America, 1980), 49.

12. One of the poems written by Chinese detainees on the walls of the dormitories of Angel Island, collected by Lai, Lim, and Yung, *Island: Poetry and History*, 52.

13. See Sakovich, "Angel Island Immigration Station Reconsidered."

14. See Peggy Pascoe, *Relations of Rescue: The Search for Female Moral Authority in the American West, 1874–1939* (New York: Oxford University Press, 1990).

15. Her first name is variously spelled Katherine or Katharine. I have used the latter, as it corresponds with the spelling used by the United Methodist Church Archives.

16. See Mary Agnes Dougherty, *My Calling to Fulfill: Deaconesses in the United Methodist Tradition* (New York: General Board of Global Ministries Women's Division, United Methodist Church, 1997). For background on "home mission" work among the Chinese in San Francisco, see Jeffrey L. Staley, "'Gum Moon': The First Fifty Years of Methodist Women's Work in San Francisco Chinatown, 1870–1920," *The Argonaut (Journal of the San Francisco Museum and Historical Society)* 16, no. 1 (2005).

17. Constance Willis Camp, *Kuan Yin, Goddess of Mercy of Angel Island* (Cincinnati: The Woman's Home Missionary Society, Methodist Episcopal Church, n.d.).

18. *San Francisco Examiner*, "Angel Island Station Shift Is Supported," December 17, 1915.

19. Carrie Isabelle Pierson, "The Immigrant on the Pacific Coast," *Woman's Home Mission*, 1912.

20. See items in the Katharine Maurer collection, California State Library, Sacramento, CA.

21. Camp, *Kuan Yin, Goddess of Mercy of Angel Island*, 4.

22. Katharine Maurer collection, California State Library.

23. Eunice Jones Stickland, "More Than an Angel," *World Outlook*, 1944, 15.

24. *San Francisco Examiner*, November 20, 1915.

25. Excellent sources of information about Chinese women in San Francisco during this period are two works by Judy Yung: *Unbound Feet: A Social History of Chinese Women in San Francisco* (Berkeley: University of California Press, 1995) and *Unbound Voices: A Documentary History of Chinese Women in San Francisco* (Berkeley: University of California Press, 1999).

26. Mildred Crowl Martin, *Chinatown's Angry Angel: The Story of Donaldina Cameron* (Palo Alto, CA: Pacific Books, 1977).

27. Memo from Robinson to Commissioner of Immigration, San Francisco, dated May 10, 1917, is in Jung Oy's case file, 15530/4-4, at the NARA, San Bruno, CA.

28. Lai, Lim, and Yung, *Island: Poetry and History*, 63.

29. Case 16119, In the Matter of the Application of Chew Hoy Quong for a Writ of Habeas Corpus for and on Behalf of his Wife Quok Shee; Admiralty Case Files, 1851–1966; United States District Court for the Northern District of California; Record Group 21, Records of District Courts of the United States; NARA—Pacific Region, 1000 Commodore Drive, San Bruno, CA 94066.

—4—

Before Angel Island

Immigration through San Francisco seems inextricably linked to Angel Island and its Immigration Station, with all things related to West Coast and Asian immigration projected onto the 787-acre rock in San Francisco Bay. This preoccupation, when it comes to the early locations for controlling immigration through San Francisco, might be diagnosed as a severe case of "islomania."

That Angel Island has exerted this power over our imagination is, in some ways, a natural occurrence. Our historical memory easily ignores physical objects that are no longer present in favor of ones that are. In other ways, our preoccupation with Angel Island's Immigration Station is a "socially constructed" phenomenon, the product of the political process of generating interest—and funds—to rehabilitate what remains of the Immigration Station. The many community groups and scholars involved in this process know the importance of having a reference point that can be seen, visited, touched, and easily invoked. To stand in the Detention Barracks dormitory and read the heart-reading poems incised in its walls is a powerful experience, one that captures the Chinese Exclusion Act and its successors, discriminatory laws in force from 1882 to 1943.

This fixation with the Angel Island Immigration Station, opened in 1910, has an unfortunate side. It ignores the locus of the first twenty-eight years of enforcement of the Chinese exclusion laws. Despite laws aimed at severely restricting the Asian presence in America, the process of moving persons into and out of San Francisco constituted an ongoing set of vibrant economic activities employing thousands of people—from shipowners to ships' crews, from customs watchmen and immigration inspectors to lawyers and labor brokers. Even before the Chinese Exclusion Act of 1882, this thriving industry was scrutinized and sporadically regulated. Only gradually did there come to be physical locations that symbolized the industry, a process that began long before Angel Island had an immigration station.

SYMBOLS OF THE IMMIGRATION INDUSTRY

No enterprise symbolized the immigration industry more than the PMSS. The Pacific Mail was founded in 1848 and began transporting passengers across the Pacific Ocean in 1867. A mail contract with the federal government provided a revenue base for establishing service between San Francisco and China and Japan, and over the years the PMSS became arguably the most famous American steamship line. The history of the Pacific Mail, and especially its role in bringing Asians to the Western Hemisphere, is discussed in greater detail in the chapter on "Asiatic Steerage."[1]

No shipping line brought more Asians to the United States than did the Pacific Mail. For many years, it had a near-monopoly on regular service between Hong Kong and San Francisco. Although in the late 1890s it began to have competition from the CPR (Canadian Pacific Railway) and the Japanese TKK line, it remained the dominant carrier until well into the twentieth century. By the early 1870s, the Pacific Mail had come to symbolize the numerous shipping lines that promoted and profited from the movement of people from East Asia to the United States. Nearly every representation of Chinese arriving in San Francisco depicts them using some facility of the PMSS: ensconced in "Asiatic steerage" aboard a PMSS steamer, coming down the ramp onto the Pacific Mail's covered pier, or being inspected in the PMSS warehouse and searched by Customs officers for contraband. An unflattering cartoon (Figure 4.1), probably from around 1890, shows streams of immigrants being disgorged from steamers and making their way to San Francisco's Chinatown. The ships are those of the CPR and the Pacific Mail.

As the prime mover—and beneficiary—of migrants across the Pacific, the Pacific Mail was also the prime target of those opposed to Asian, and especially Chinese, migration to the United States. Headlines in the *San Francisco Call* typified how the vilification of big business—a popular tactic in trust-busting times for selling newspapers—could be coupled with anti-Chinese prejudice. "The Dishonest Chinese Passenger Traffic of the Pacific Mail...a Gigantic Plot of the Steamship Company to Flood the Country With Coolies."[2]

CHAOTIC ENFORCEMENT OF EARLY "RESTRICTION" LAWS

Well before the Chinese Exclusion Act, arrivals at the port of San Francisco had been inspected. The Customs Service at San Francisco had a long history of dealing with arriving Chinese, usually in the guise of collecting customs duties on such items as silk and opium. Arriving ships were greeted by a Customs Service boat (often referred to as the "customs barge") while still out on the Bay, one that enabled uniformed Customs officers to make a cursory appraisal of the situation on board. At that time the ship's captain would present the ship's passenger manifest, as had been required by the Steerage Act since 1820, containing a listing of all the "persons taken on board...at any foreign port or place."[3]

Figure 4.1
In a contrived view of San Francisco, ca. 1890, Chinese from ships of the Pacific Mail and the CPR pour into Chinatown.

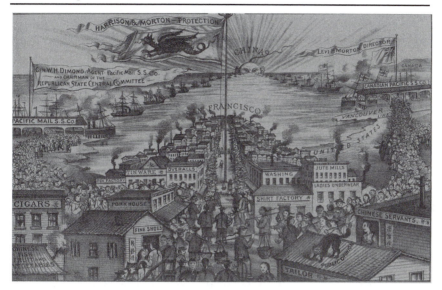

Source: Bancroft Library, University of California, Berkeley.

As a general rule, cabin-class passengers would have their baggage inspected in their cabin, while steerage passengers, always the more numerous, would be inspected ashore. Contemporary drawing in *Harper's Weekly* convey a chaotic, Dickensian scene where arriving passengers—if they were not white—had little expectation of privacy or confidentiality.

San Francisco's health officials constituted a second set of authorities monitoring the arrival of ships with passengers. According to California law, the Governor appointed San Francisco's Quarantine Officer (in fact, its entire Board of Health), and it was he who decided which passengers could land and which could not. Before the establishment of the Quarantine Station on Angel Island in 1892, passengers deemed to be carrying a contagious disease could be kept aboard ship during a prescribed quarantine period. San Francisco's Board of Health and its Quarantine Officer decided on how to care for those whom they would allow ashore, and whether to send them to the Pesthouse or to the city hospital on 26th Street.

The National Quarantine Act of 1893 was meant to establish a role for the federal government vis-à-vis local health officials in protecting the nation from diseases coming from abroad. However, even the presence of a Quarantine Station on the northwest corner of Angel Island did not unequivocally establish Federal primacy over State officials. The "turf wars" between the Federal

Quarantine Office and his local counterparts continued—sometimes openly, sometime sub rosa—until the bubonic plague epidemic that broke out in 1900. The response to that outbreak at last made clear that the federal government was in charge.[4]

Yet a third institution monitored the comings and goings at the port: San Francisco's daily newspapers. The *Examiner*, the *Chronicle*, the *Daily Alta*, and the *Call* all covered the waterfront with varying degrees of zeal, reporting on the arrival of ships of note and on the human cargo they carried. The papers were highly partisan and their reporting was well larded with editorial comment on the Chinese and on those charged with enforcing immigration, customs, and health regulations. The reportage was, with occasional exceptions, highly disparaging of the "wily" "heathens," "pigtails," "Mongolians," "Celestials," or other derogatory terms for the Chinese.[5] The *Call* seems to have been the most zealous in reporting on immigration and on attempts to evade the Restriction Act (as it was often termed).

ENFORCING THE "CHINESE RESTRICTION" LAWS

The Chinese Exclusion Act was approved on May 6, 1882, to take effect ninety days hence. The Act stipulated that it was to be enforced by the United States Customs Service, in the person of the Collector of Customs of each port. Little thought was given to the facilities and procedures that would be needed to enforce the Act, and no one seemed to have foreseen the possibility of there being detainees or where to hold them. Certainly not on dry land. The first Chinese to arrive after the Exclusion Act went into effect on August 9, 1882, came from Sydney aboard the Pacific Mail's *City of Sydney*. After first being inspected by the (state) quarantine officer, the ship was directed to proceed to the dock. But Customs officers found her to be carrying sixteen Chinese crewmen without passports, so the ship was directed to wait in the stream (i.e., not docked, but still out in the bay). After a brief dispute between the Captain and Customs, the cabin passengers and mails were landed by a tug, the Chinese were transferred to the hulk *China*, and ten hours later, the ship finally docked at the Pacific Mail pier.[6] The following day, seventy-two Chinese crewmen on the O&O's *Oceanic* were similarly consigned to the *China* while authorities determined their ability to enter the country.

The first place of detention, the hulk *China*, was a storied part of San Francisco's maritime history. The first of several Pacific Mail ships to bear that name (thus known generally as *China I*), the *China* was launched on July 1, 1867 and was among the largest wooden-hulled oceangoing side-wheelers ever built. Like her sister ships *Great Republic*, *America*, and *Japan* (see Figure 6.2), she was built specifically for the transpacific trade, capable of carrying 1,500 passengers, most of them in steerage. After about thirty round-trips, the *China* became victim of the move to iron-hulled, screw-driven ships and was consigned to the scrap heap. But before being broken up and burned, she had a stationary career as accommodations for detained immigrants and as a quarantine station for smallpox victims.

At around the same time, the city's health authorities were looking for places to accommodate passengers arriving with smallpox. In May 1882, the ship *Altonower* had arrived with "her horde of infected coolies." Infected white men from the crew were removed to the city pesthouse, but it was decided that neither it nor the city hospital would take the Chinese. However, "the old bark Columbia, lying on the mud flats...was found to be admirably suited, her spacious dimensions and general structure answering in every respect....She was evidently used as an emigrant vessel...and will hold fully 1,000 patients."[7] It seems that "the hulk of the old bay steamer Contra Costa" was also used, as the number of incoming smallpox cases was quite large.[8]

The early "interrogations" must have differed from the famous photograph on the cover of Lucy Salyer's *Laws Harsh as Tigers*, where a lone Chinese male is being questioned by a stern-faced, uniformed immigration officer and an equally stern-faced, suited, non-Chinese interpreter (and an unseen stenographer). Anecdotal evidence from the San Francisco newspapers implies that the questioning of new arrivals was not conducted in private, but aboard ship in full view (and hearing) of one's fellow passengers. An article from early in the exclusion era related that Customhouse officials had "decided that when the next steamer arrives to examine each trader separately, as it was noticeable during the examination of the last arrivals that Chinamen in the crowd would occasionally prompt one of the passengers under investigation."[9]

FROM SHIP TO SHED

For many years, San Francisco was without a dedicated, government-managed space for holding arriving passengers detained for questioning or for deportation. It would not be until 1910 that such a place was opened. In the intervening years, all manner of other solutions were tried, including release on bond, jails, ships, mission homes, and the infamous "Detention Shed" on the docks of the Pacific Mail.

The simplest means of housing those who were not immediately landed was to release them on bond. Even in the absence of reliable statistics for the pre-1900 period, we can infer that this was done quite frequently. The San Francisco daily newspapers regularly printed stories like the *Examiner*'s of June 1, 1883, which noted that "the United States Customs authorities have allowed eleven of the Chinese passengers on the steamer Glenelg to come ashore on $1,000 bonds each." In addition to articles about such "outrages," there were complaints by the Collector himself that the courts' rulings "leave a Chinese to enter the United States temporarily *in transit* or otherwise when not allowed to enter permanently under the statutes and if permitted to enter temporarily cannot he remain permanently?"[10]

For those who could not post bond, or who had already been ordered deported, the County Jail seems to have been used rather frequently. There are numerous newspaper accounts of arrivals being "remanded to the Sheriff." The Collector of Customs wrote regularly to the Secretary of the Treasury, requesting reimbursement for funds that he had expended on the upkeep of Chinese being deported by immigration authorities at some other city. A typical case was from 1893, where he had paid Joe Tape (a noted Chinese labor broker and bonding agent) $10 for "transporting Chinese and Inspectors from County Jail to steamship dock" and board for the Chinese at the County Jail at 40¢ per day. Another read: "I respectfully forward herewith for payment voucher in duplicate, duly receipted and certified in favor of J.J. McDade, in the sum of $10.40, for board and maintenance of seven Chinese in the County Jail, pending sailing of steamer."[11]

As can be imagined, jail conditions were miserable for criminal and immigrant alike. In 1903, the San Francisco Chinese newspaper Chung Sai Yat Po reprinted a report on the San Francisco County Jail. The following is the reporter's description of the jail—translated from English to Chinese by Chung Sai Yat Po, and here translated back to English.

> The jail was built on Broadway near Dupont Street with bricks and cement about 50 years ago. It is used to detain Chinese who don't have papers to establish their right to be here.... The Chinese are detained here to wait for hearings when US officials get around to it....
>
> The other night I paid a personal visit to the jail. The darkness and filthiness of this Chinese detention area is beyond description.... The smell was hard to describe and the place was like hell on earth....
>
> The Chinese people coming to the United States are not criminals; why are they treated like this? It's only because the American government is trying to delay their hearings so as to have more time to find fault with the Chinese.[12]

A rarer method probably applied only to young women traveling alone. In such cases, the Collector of Customs would arrange to have them housed at one of the homes run by a religious or missionary organization in the city. Donaldina Cameron's Chinese Presbyterian Mission Home at 920 Sacramento Street was probably the most famous, but the Methodist Episcopal Church (with which Deaconess Katharine Maurer was associated) also ran one, as did other churches. In 1893, the Collector paid the Rev. F.J. Masters, "Superintendent of the Chinese Mission," for ninety-seven days board and lodging of a Chinese girl who was eventually deported on the O&O's Gaelic (which also billed the Collector for nine days maintenance of three Chinese, including the girl).[13] Another way of "storing" arrivals while their cases were sorted out was to let the steamship companies do it on their ships. This was noted quite early on. In 1883, "Judge Hoffman ordered the Pacific Mail company to retain the (Chinese habeas corpus) petitioners on board the steamer [City of] Tokio until their cases are decided."[14] Surely the PMSS would have kept them in a detention facility ashore were it possessed of one, but the use of steamers as floating detention facilities, maintained at the companies' expense, persisted.

In 1895, the Department admonished the Collector that "when Chinese merchants are refused landing and appeals are taken, they should remain in the custody of the steamship company." Collector Wise responded that such was normally the procedure at San Francisco,

> but of late I have found the number of transfers from the importing vessel to another of the same line, where notices of appeal have been served on me, increasing to such an extent that great confusion has ensued, to say nothing of the danger of escape from the steamers or substitution....If I am compelled to allow [this to continue], it will be but a short time before there will be a large floating Chinese alien population in the Bay of San Francisco.

A few weeks later he wrote that "I have had Chinamen transferred from steamer to steamer ever since last May, and it is a very tiresome job."[15]

As late as 1909 the *Call* reported that of the three thousand Chinese coming through San Francisco that year,

> the bulk have been handled through the Pacific Mail steamship company's offices and divided between its detention shed and the ships of the company. There are now 236 Chinese in the detention shed and 142 quartered on ships....With the shed already crowded, the [350 additional Chinese arriving on the *Mongolia*] must be shifted from ship to ship and quartered there until either granted admission or deported.[16]

The steamship companies, of course, resented having to bear the Federally-mandated cost of accommodations for detained passengers. When they complained to Collector Wise in 1898, it mattered not at all whether they were keeping detainees aboard ship or in some PMSS facility ashore.

> The steamship companies complain urgently and bitterly against the delay in passing upon these cases of "native born" applicants. They claim it to be an injustice that they are compelled to board such applicants during so long a delay in the hearing of their cases. They dogmatically say, "Either land or reject these applicants at once, and let us take them back, if rejected, without a large expense bill for board."[17]

In 1898, the outbreak of the Spanish-American War disrupted this system—briefly, but long enough to encourage other solutions. The American invasion of the Philippines required a small armada of ships to transport its troops across the Pacific, but neither the Navy nor the Army had troop transport ships of their own. They resorted to chartering (or commandeering, as the shipping companies had little choice in the matter) most of the passenger ships based in San Francisco. In May 1898, the invasion fleet consisted of two ships that had been purchased and seventeen that had been chartered, among them the lion's share of the ships providing transoceanic service out of San Francisco: the *Australia* and the *Zeelandia* (of the Oceanic Steamship Company), the *City of Puebla*

Figure 4.2
The Pacific Mail's Pier 40 was the site of the Detention Shed, indicated on the 1899
Sanborn Fire Insurance Maps as "Chinese Quarters."

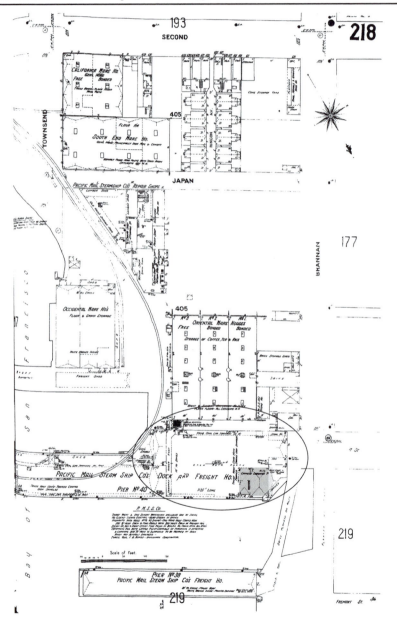

Source: 1899 Sanborn Map of San Francisco, Vol. 2, Sheet 218. Courtesy of the Sanborn Library,
LLC.

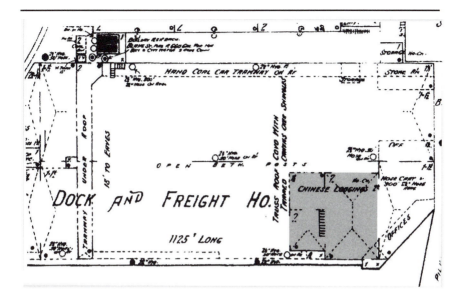

(of the Pacific Coast Steamship Company), and the *China, City of Para, City of Peking, City of Sydney, Colon, Newport, Peru,* and the *City of Rio de Janeiro* (all of the Pacific Mail). The ships that had collectively formed a floating holding tank for would-be immigrants suddenly became unavailable to their owners and to the Chinese Bureau's inspectors. To make up for the decrease in its ability to hold passengers waiting inspection, sometime in mid-1898, the Pacific Mail converted a portion of its "general offices" into a detention facility. By November, what would become known as the "Detention Shed," or simply "the Shed," was in full use.

The "Detention Shed" was part of the "Pacific Mail Dock," located on Pier 40. The largest such structure on the San Francisco waterfront, Pier 40 jutted out perhaps 250 ft., then made a ninety degree turn to the right and continued another 1,125 ft.—long enough to accommodate the largest ocean liners of the day. The Sanborn Fire Insurance Maps for 1886–87 clearly show the Pacific Mail's facilities at the foot of Brannan Street. Well south of the Ferry Building, the PMSS pier was served by a spur of the Southern Pacific Railroad that went directly onto the long projection into the Bay that was Pier 40. Handcar tramways for loading coal on the big liners also extended to the very end of the pier. The PMSS complex was quite extensive, including coal storage, all manner of repair shops, a large "Oriental Ware House" for "storage of coffee, tea & rice," and of course the covered pier itself. A wooden structure nearly 1,000 ft. long, the "Mail Dock" had a "truss roof covered [with] tarred canvas over shingles." At the corner of First Street and Brannan, the covered pier gave way to a two-story structure of about 150 ft. by 100 ft., 18 ft. to the second story eaves.

A two-story wooden structure for offices overlooked the slip between Pier 40 and neighboring Pier 38. The Sanborn maps of 1886 showed this as only "general offices," but by 1899 the PMSS had converted the second story to "Chinese Lodgings," a space approximately 100 ft. by 50 ft.[18] This was not the first time that steamship companies had provided accommodations for those of their passengers being detained by government gatekeepers. In 1892, the Oriental and Occidental Steamship Company erected two wooden barracks that were capable of holding over 500 passengers detained at the Quarantine Station on Angel Island, run by the predecessor of the Public Health Service.[19] How the Pacific Mail would have financed the Pier 40 "lodgings" and shifted the risk from their treasury to the pockets of individual travelers is, however, somewhat cloudy. Perhaps the PMSS demanded a bond or deposit from certain types of passengers—those most likely to be detained. What is likely is that, in the end, the Chinese would have financed their own confinement and the operation of the new detention quarters on the Pacific Mail's dock.

The first description of the new facility is contained in a remarkable article by J.F. Rose-Soley in the *San Francisco Call* on November 6, 1898, "Chinese in Bond on the Mail Dock." Despite its racially biased reportorial style, this article is one of the few first-hand descriptions of the "Detention Shed" that we have, and certainly the earliest.

> "The Pacific Mail dock looks deserted these days, but housed up aloft in the main building are hundreds of Chinese. The extraordinary employment of the big China mail steamers for transport duty has sidetracked these 'native sons,' 'merchants,' 'travelers' and 'professional coolies,' all struggling to find a hole in the Chinese restriction law and gain admission to this country. Not only does the Pacific Mail Company guard these 'bonded Chinese' with vigilant care, for it means a payment of $500 if one of them escapes, but a lynx-eyed Federal customs house officer watches them night and day."
>
> It must not be supposed, however, though there are such a large number of Chinese at the Mail dock hotel, that there has been any great increase in immigration of late. It simply happens that there are no steamers in port, and consequently the Chinese have to be detained ashore. When a steamer is in port the company prefers to keep them on board a vessel.

The author—most likely a freelance writer, rather than a staff reporter—explored the detention facilities located on the second floor.

> At last...we were free to walk through this human warren, threading our way, as best we could, amid confused throngs of Chinamen. The place, which forms a kind of mezzanine story to the dock, was originally used as an office by the Pacific Mail Company. It has only one floor, and is not much bigger than an ordinary four-roomed cottage. Yet, on the day of my visit, no less than 357 Chinamen, including two women, were confined in this narrow compass. There they were, squatting on the floor around boxes and bundles of all kinds, each one shoveling in rice with a pair of chopsticks. The rooms are of all sizes and shapes. It is a perfect honeycomb of small apartments and the mat-covered bunks rise in tiers five or six high. Right

up on top, close to the ceiling, Chinamen in every stage of deshabille were perched; everywhere there was surfeit of humanity.

Yet, to do the Mongolian justice, it must be admitted that, in spite of the overcrowding and insanitary conditions, the atmosphere was by no means as bad as might have been expected.

"We treat a Chinaman just as if he was a chest of tea, or a box of opium," said the inspector. "We hold him until we get authority to set him free, and the company, meanwhile, is responsible for his safe-keeping. If a Chinaman escapes, the Mail Company has to pay a fine of $500, so you can understand that it is careful."

Note the crowding—357 people given the space and, presumably, the sanitary facilities equal to a "four-roomed cottage"—that would become a source of constant complaint.

In 1903 the space was modified after the Commissioner General of Immigration insisted that conditions be improved. Even so, ample motivation to escape remained. Successful escapes and not-unrelated complaints about conditions contributed to the push for a more secure and better-equipped site.

Late in 1908, twenty-one Chinese escaped from the Shed after they had "sawed through the stout wire meshes and two iron bars at one of the windows, and crawled out." As part of its coverage of the story, the *Call* provided a drawing of the interior of the Shed, and the *Chronicle* a description of its layout.

The detention rooms are reached by a narrow flight of stairs, and this is the only means of entrance or exit except through the windows that overlook the roof of the shed. Upstairs are the big detention room, where tiers of bunks are arranged for the accommodation of detained immigrants; a small office for the Federal authorities; and a small room which is used as a hospital ward.

In addition to any Chinese women who might have been paroled to the Christian "missions" in town, the "Mail Dock" had at least one separate room for two Chinese women. The *Call's* drawing also showed a separate "Women's Quarters" and a small "Cook Room."[20] Thus, there were separate facilities for women, if only at the outset, when the number of women arriving was small.

In one corner of the building, after passing through a maze of narrow rooms, we come upon a jealously locked door. "The women's quarter," says the attendant, as he feels for his key.

There are but two Chinese maidens here now, and, squatted on their bunks, they greet us with feminine coquetry. Obviously they know their importance and the difficulty which attends their admission to Uncle Sam's land of gold. Eve, a vivacious little thing, gnaws smilingly at her apple, and poses for the artist with the utmost composure. "Look, see," she cries, as he exhibits the rough draft of her picture.

The basis of some complaints may have been that there was but a single room for *all* women, regardless of class.

Toward the very end of the Shed's existence, the Acting Commissioner of Immigration at San Francisco requested that the facilities be inspected by the Admeasurer of Vessels of the Customs Service. In April 1909, Admeasurer

Figure 4.3
Drawings in the *San Francisco Call*, accompanying a lengthy article, are the first depictions of the Detention Shed of the PMSS.

Source: San Francisco Call, November 6, 1898.

J.C. Eagan filed his report, "proceeding as if admeasuring steerage passenger spaces of a vessel in accordance with...the Passenger Act of 1882."

1. Front Room, West Side: 2,368 cu. ft., 263 sq. ft., 20 passengers
   Front Room, with three rooms partitioned therein:
2. East side (Japanese): 1,333 cu. ft, 111 sq. ft., 11 passengers
3. West Room: 1,589 cu. ft., 132 sq. ft., 11 passengers
4. North Room: 3,593 cu. ft., 299 sq. ft., 26 passengers
5. Main Room (Male, Chinese): 28,273 cu ft., 2,356 sq. ft., 195 passengers
6. Female (including dining room): 3,093 cu. ft., 258 sq. ft., 32 passengers

The Admeasurer added several interesting findings:

- the berths are generally in tiers of four high;
- that the berths are not constructed in accordance with Sec. 2 of the Act, not being of sufficient length, 6 feet, nor with sufficient interval, 2 feet, 6 inches, between berths;
- that two separate hospitals are not maintained;
- that no space is set apart for the use and exercise of those detained, corresponding to the required deck space; and
- that in the case of the male occupants, no tables and seats are provided for their use at meals.

That said, he found the space (3,420 sq. ft. for 295 people), construction, lighting, and ventilation satisfactory. Had the Shed been a ship, it would have passed the Admeasurer's inspection.[21]

In situations where time hangs heavy—in prisons, aboard ship—food assumes an importance beyond mere sustenance. At the Shed, it appears that there were minimal cooking facilities and, as implied in this report, no separate dining facility. A "restaurant keeper" had the concession for feeding the detainees, as the author of the *Call* story witnessed when

> a couple of huge trucks...appeared at the entrance to the dock. More Chinese, emboldened by the retirement of the officer, emerged from above, pigtailed heads peered surreptitiously over the barrier: there was a subdued chorus of "heap good."
>
> From a Mongolian point of view, it was undoubtedly "heap good." The trucks were laden with huge baskets of snow white rice, great tins of vegetable soup, hot and greasy, evil smelling fish of the kind which the Chinaman delights in, and, to wind up with, many cans of steaming black tea. It was a feast to win the heart of an Oriental, though a Caucasian would have turned from it in disgust.
>
> "The great thing," said Mr. Busse, the restaurant keeper who feeds all these men by contract, "is to give them good rice. If the rice is of poor quality or is burned or not properly cooked, there is sure to be a kick coming. I have learned from experience what they want."

The concluding paragraphs of the *Call* article seek to put the story into perspective and, perhaps unintentionally, hint at the future of the facility on the "Mail Dock." One might infer that despite the large number of Chinese held there, and the machinations of the (white) lawyers that seemed to drag out their stay in the "Shed," in the long run the problem of where to house arriving Chinese would simply go away. A diminishing Chinese population and airtight administration of the exclusion laws would see to it—although both projections proved wildly inaccurate.

> B.E. Meredith, the chief of the Chinese bureau, is of opinion that the number of Chinese in the State is rapidly decreasing. "The annual departures," he said, "exceed the arrivals by at least 2000. That is to say, if 6000 Chinamen leave in a year, only 4000 return. A little over twenty years ago there were more than 60,000 Chinamen in San Francisco alone. To-day there are less than that number in the whole State."
>
> The application of the exclusion law is now so stringent that it is exceedingly difficult for a Chinamen to get in fraudulently. . . . In these disputed cases the examination may be a long and tedious one. . . . The attorney and the customs officers fight it out, and meanwhile the unfortunate subjects of the dispute are imprisoned at the Mail dock, paying *their own board* [emphasis added] and uncertain whether they will not have also to pay for a return ticket to China.

Although the space on the Pacific Mail dock had only recently come into use as a detention facility, the reporter notes that some Chinese have been detained— first aboard ship, now ashore—for very long periods of time.

> There are men in this place who have been detained for weeks and months owing to some defects in their papers. In one instance the term of imprisonment was lengthened to over half a year, yet this was an exceptional case. On the whole the Chinamen seem cheerful and happy. Their meal over, they settle themselves down to gamble, though heaven knows most of the poor wretches have little enough to lose. Dominoes, exactly like those used by the Europeans, seem to be the favorite sport, but there are many who prefer the funny looking Chinese playing cards, long and thin, and covered with all sorts of curious spots.

We have no way of knowing if the reporter's hint of long periods of incarceration at the Shed was exaggerated. There are no systematic data for the Detention Shed, and those that exist are even skimpier than those for Angel Island.

The one glimmer of evidence on lengths of detention at the Shed comes from the Bureau of Immigration and Naturalization (as the Immigration Service was known), then a branch of the Department of Commerce and Labor. Shortly before the Angel Island facility opened, the Commissioner General in Washington wrote to the Commissioner in San Francisco, asking for a report on the status of returning "domiciled merchants" being held in the "Detention Shed." There was some concern, perhaps in response to protests from the Chinese community or the Chinese Consul General, that "domiciled merchants"—arriving Chinese merchants who had been living in the United States—were being kept there too long.

On February 9, 1909, Commissioner General Daniel Keefe wanted to know how many of these "domiciled merchants" then detained in "the Shed" had been "pre-investigated, how long each was detained, and what were the reasons which led to the detention?" In response he received a "Statement showing the number of Chinese in the Detention Shed week by week, from August 30th, 1908, to January 10th, 1909," together with the number of days each had been held. Thus, it included *all* Chinese in detention, not just domiciled merchants.[22]

"Chinese in the Detention Shed" lists the name of the steamer, its arrival date, the number of passengers from that ship still in detention, and how long each person had been kept in the Shed. Included are not only PMSS ships but several ships from the TKK line: thirty-four ship arrivals (some of which had made port well before August 30), representing 1,261 Chinese passengers detained.

By following the fate of a ship's passengers week by week, it is possible to construct a rough gauge of how long each was kept. This gauge is imperfect, and might slightly overstate the typical length of stay. The average (over twenty-three days) and the median (eighteen days) are both substantially higher than what we find for stays on Angel Island. One can see why there might have been protests over merchants being held there for so long.

The Detention Shed was not reserved for the humble alone. It held its share of illustrious names—people famous in their own right, or whose names became landmarks in immigration history. One of the more notable cases in immigration law involved an unwilling guest at the Detention Shed. In 1903, the U.S. District Attorney in San Francisco appealed a ruling by the district court that allowed Ju Toy, a cook from Oakland, to reenter the country after a trip to China. Ju Toy had claimed he had been born in the United States, and while the Immigration Service did not believe him, the district court upheld his appeal. In *United States v. Ju Toy*, Chief Justice Oliver Wendell Holmes ruled that the lower courts could not overturn the decisions of immigration officials (in this case, the Secretary of Commerce and Labor). The latter's greatly increased powers would subsequently lead to more stringent enforcement of the exclusion laws. Ju Toy's attorney, Oliver Stidger, referred to his client as a "United States prisoner."[23]

Perhaps the most famous person to reside at the Shed, decidedly against his wishes, was Sun Yat-sen, leader of the 1911 revolution that overthrew the Manchu dynasty and founding father of the Republic of China. In 1904, however, he was treated simply as another Chinese would-be immigrant attempting to evade the exclusion laws. The Commissioner of Immigration at San Francisco denied his claim to American citizenship (as having been born in Hawaii) and ordered him "deported to the port whence he came upon the departure of the next vessel of the line bringing him here." Sun "was held incommunicado in the wooden immigration shed," but was able to smuggle out a note and launch an appeal that eventually led to his release.[24]

COMPLAINTS ABOUT THE SHED

The Shed was the subject of complaints almost from the time it was first used in 1898. Not only the Chinese, but the Federal enforcement agencies, the San Francisco press, and outside observers all found it objectionable in some way. There were frequent allegations that the Shed was cramped and dirty, that it did not sufficiently isolate detainees, that escapes were too easy and too frequent, and that it cost the steamship companies money to operate (particularly the locally powerful Pacific Mail). Within a very few years, the chorus of complaints rose to a crescendo that the Immigration Service could not ignore, and the search began for another site. That search would eventually lead to the construction of the Immigration Station on Angel Island.

Stanford Professor Mary Roberts Coolidge, in her classic work *Chinese Immigration*, judged the facility as harshly from her first-hand visits as did her Chinese informants.

> No one of the inconveniences incident to the enforcement of the law, has created more criticism and ill-feeling, than the place and manner of detention of all classes of applicants for admission. There is no immigration building at San Francisco. The detention station used by the department of immigration was provided by the Pacific Mail Steamship Company in order to avoid keeping the immigrants on board ship till they were admitted. The Shed—rightly so-called—is a cheap, two-story wooden building, at the end of a wharf, built out over the water where the odors of sewage and bilge are most offensive; unclean, at times overrun with vermin, and often inadequate to the numbers to be detained....It was in this place that the [Chinese] merchant exhibitors who came to the Louisiana Purchase Exhibition were detained and it is not surprising that they reported: "The Americans are a race of pigs."[25]

Roberts was not alone in deploring conditions at the Shed. Even the Commissioner General of Immigration expressed similar sentiments, perhaps out of sympathy with those imprisoned there, but also as a way of pressuring Washington for funds for a new station.

> At San Francisco there is no immigrant building. Chinese aliens have been temporarily landed from vessels, by permission, and placed in detention quarters furnished by the transportation lines. These quarters were so disgraceful—cramped in dimensions, lacking in every facility for cleanliness and decency—that it was necessary to insist upon an immediate remodeling thereof. As a temporary expedient, the result of my protest to the steamship lines has been the reconstruction of a better, cleanlier, and more commodious building, but it does not obviate the pressing demand for a structure to accommodate all alien arrivals.[26]

Immigration authorities also found it unsatisfactory because it was not sufficiently isolated. Its proximity to downtown San Francisco made it easily accessible to those who could help Chinese evade the net of exclusion. Easy access to the Shed and its occupants would facilitate the coaching of arrivals, enabling them to coordinate their (presumably false) stories with those of their sponsors. A story in the *San Francisco Chronicle* from 1899 typified this concern:

> Customs Inspector Stephens made an important find on the Pacific Mail dock yesterday afternoon. He noticed one of the Chinese confined in the detention shed throw two letters through a window to the wharf. The letters were picked up by a Chinese who gave the name of Tang Ho and who claimed to be a member of the firm of Wong, Hop & Co. on Stockton Street. Stephens arrested Ho, placed him in the custody of another inspector and took the letters to [Chinese Bureau interpreter] Dr. Gardiner, who on translating them, found them to contain full details as to the expense of importing Chinese coolies and female slaves.[27]

What could be done to isolate those in the Shed from persons who might influence their testimony? In 1901, Collector of Customs Stratton decided to keep agents and lawyers out of the Shed and "to exclude attorneys from the Chinese Bureau during the hearings of applications for admission of Chinese to this country." As Stratton's predecessor had allowed attorneys to participate in these hearings, his decision elicited a howl of protests. Nonetheless, the decision stood: arrivals would henceforth confront the Immigration inspectors alone.[28]

The Chinese Bureau at San Francisco was also seen as insufficiently isolated from local pressures and politics. In 1898 the *Call* launched a series of attacks on corrupt practices within the Chinese Bureau, focusing its special ire on the Bureau's chief, Inspector R.E. Meredith. A series of stories alleged that Meredith was in cahoots with "slave dealers"—Chinese brothel owners and their white lawyers and agents—attempting to bring in Chinese women as prostitutes. The *Call* took credit for the launching of an investigation by Special Agents Linck and Smith, whose report led to the Chinese Bureau being separated from the Customs Service in 1899. Henceforth, the Bureau would have a proper, well-paid Chief (not just a regular customs inspector). No longer would the Chinese Bureau report to the Collector of Customs (a position historically seen as a lucrative patronage appointment) but, rather, directly to the Secretary of the Treasury in Washington, who appointed him. Similarly, rather than relying on Inspectors seconded from the Collector of Customs' force, the new Chief would control his own set of Chinese Bureau Inspectors.[29]

The Shed was also viewed as being unsafe because, as Commissioner General of Immigration Frank Sargent noted during a visit to San Francisco in 1903, "Oriental peoples...are the principal mediums for the introduction of dangerous communicable diseases." A greater distance from the mainland would also "prevent communication with [aliens] by persons who find their interest in landing aliens unlawfully."[30]

The Chinese, of course, bore the brunt of detention and its bitter inconveniences. Despite the assertion by the *Call*'s reporter that Chinese detainees bore their imprisonment with good humor, those who were actually detained in the Shed found it barbaric.

The detention shed is another name for a "Chinese jail." I have visited quite a few jails and State prisons in this country, but have never seen any place half so bad. It is situated at one end of the wharf, reached by a long, narrow stairway. The interior is about one hundred feet square. Oftentimes they put in as many as two hundred human beings. The whitewashed windows and the wire netting attached to them added to the misery. The air is impure, the place is crowded. No friends are allowed to come in and see the unfortunate suffering without special permission from the American authority. No letters are allowed either to be sent out or to come in. There are no tables, no chairs. We were treated like a group of animals, and we were fed on the floor. Kicking and swearing by the white man in charge was not a rare thing. I was not surprised when, one morning, a friend pointed out to me the place where a heartbroken Chinaman had hanged himself after fourth months' imprisonment in this dreadful dungeon, thus to end his agony and the shameful outrage.[31]

Chinese bitterly resented the attitude of their jailors. In 1906, Wong Hock Won wrote from his jail cell in Portland (where he was being detained) about his experience trying to enter San Francisco.

Entering (the detention shed) one may look to the right and to the left and see only bunks and a few benches. "You stay here, you stay here" is all they say. Here you are cramped and doomed never to stretch. You complain that the shed leaks and they say "Why should you care? You will be here but a day." No words can express such misery.[32]

Their plight was occasionally taken up by Chinese on the outside—through newspapers such as *Chung Sai Yat Po*, through letters to immigration authorities, by the resident Chinese Consul General, and less directly, through the anti-American boycott of 1905. Some of these complaints were occasionally reported in the white press.

The one hundred and seventy-five Chinese immigrants confined by the steamship companies in the detention shed on the Mail dock have entered into a conspiracy to make a break for liberty next Tuesday, when the Hongkong Maru sails for China. A few weeks ago they made an attack upon several Customs Inspectors and were clubbed into submission. An English-speaking Chinese immigrant informed Larry Brannigan and Night Watchman Wasley that the Chinese were desperate, most of them having been confined in the detention shed for nine months awaiting the decision of the Supreme Court on their appeals from the action of the Customs Collector refusing them a landing. The Chinaman said further that they had petitioned their agents in China and the officials of the steamship company to send them home again, as they were sick and tired of their imprisonment in the detention shed, and that if they were not placed on board the Hongkong Maru next Tuesday they would batter down the doors and make a break for liberty. Captain Anderson of the Mail dock has been notified of the plot.[33]

A few days later, at a mass meeting, inmates of the Shed threatened to "tear the shed apart" unless they were immediately returned to China—a threat that never materialized.[34]

Even though the Collector of Customs had men "assigned to duty guarding the Chinese at the so-called 'Barracks' on the Pacific Mail Steamship Company's dock,"[35] escapes were not unknown. The press eagerly reported all attempted escapes, successful or not. In 1900 it was reported that six Japanese stowaways from the *Nippon Maru,* "ordered deported because they were paupers, escaped from the detention shed of the Pacific Mail during the night" and were probably in the interior, looking for work. The New Associated Press noted that the PMSS was liable for a $500 fine for each escapee.[36] In 1901, "only an accidental discovery prevented the escape of about 150 Chinese from the detention shed over the Pacific Mail wharf early this morning. Five Chinese escaped, and a sixth was caught by Watchman Stein as he was getting away. The men crawled through a hold cut through the roof with a cleaver, and slid down a sewer pipe to the wharf."[37]

Such escapes continued to occur at infrequent intervals throughout the life of the Shed. In 1908, twenty-nine Chinese escaped from the Detention Shed, and the subsequent investigation was followed avidly by the press.[38]

The press diligently reported all ruses, proven or otherwise, of which the Chinese were suspected in their attempts to evade or resist the exclusion laws. In 1896 the *Call* reported that "one of the practices at this port...is to allow local Chinese to go aboard ship any day from 12 to 1 and talk with their brethren from across the sea. It is said that the incoming Chinese are then coached in such a way as to almost defy the most careful cross-examination."[39]

FROM THE SHED TO ANGEL ISLAND

The campaign to build an immigration station began quite soon after the Shed went into use as a detention facility. In 1905, Congress approved construction of a station on Angel Island. Land was obtained from the War Department, and funds were allocated to build the new facility. The 1906 San Francisco earthquake and fire delayed construction, but it was essentially complete by 1908. When the Immigration Station would actually open was a matter of some debate. Arguments for delay came from the Chinese, concerned about the hardships that such a remote location would create for passengers, and from the Immigration Service, which wanted to wait for the influx of European passengers that the new Panama Canal would bring.

This interlude—when the Angel Immigration Station was complete but unoccupied—was awkward for all concerned. In June 1909 Special Inspector Fred Watts recommended that the "government...not permit other Chinese be placed [in the Shed]: place death-trap unsanitary."[40]

Several temporary schemes were explored, including building new "detention sheds" on the new Pacific Mail Pier 42 or 44, or on adjacent land owned by the Harbor Commission. Vice President R.P. Schwerin of the PMSS successfully argued that the new detention quarters "would have to be heavily stockaded and guarded...built and erected as a prison, as they must necessarily be, would be a continual source of irritation to the public and in daily view through the press."[41] Another promising suggestion was to use the old Pacific Mail steamer *City of Peking* as a floating detention center anchored in the Bay. This PMSS proposition was approved by Washington in the fall of 1909, then dropped as the date for opening Angel Island was moved forward.

By 1909 the extension of San Francisco's seawall south from the Ferry Building had extended San Francisco's waterfront "so far out into the bay that the site of the old Pacific Mail dock seems to be marooned inland. Beginning with the Pacific Mail dock...docks and slips that were long known to commerce have disappeared and the spaces that they occupied have become solid land."[42] "The earth has been filled in around the dock, [and] Chinese are able to congregate under these windows and communicate with their countrymen."[43]

The Harbor Commission built a new Pier 40. Concrete pilings and steel replaced wood in a new structure several hundred yards from the old Pier 40.[44] Where "the detention shed was formerly located at the end of the long pier... now it is on land and the inmates are able to communicate with people on the outside."[45] The increased possibility of immigrants being coached contributed to greater local pressure to open the Immigration Station.

That pressure must have come to a head during President Taft's visit to San Francisco in October 1909. The extensive newspaper coverage this triumphal tour received reminds us how rare such visits were; every word of every speech—by the President or his hosts—and the gist of seemingly every conversation were printed in the local newspapers. Returning by boat to San Francisco after giving a speech at Berkeley,

> Collector of the Port Stratton had a short talk with the president on official business. The president told the collector that he favored the immediate opening of the immigrant station on Angel Island to be used as a detention station for oriental immigrants pending their deportation. It had been the intention of the government not to use the station until the Panama canal was opened and European immigrants had begun to come directly to California.[46]

What had prompted the President to press this issue? Had friends in missionary circles (and he had many) urged him to do so? Did the many businessmen he met during innumerable ceremonies argue the need to present a more dignified face to their Chinese counterparts? Was the Collector of Customs eager to reduce the scrutiny attracted by the immigration business, moving it offshore? The *San Francisco Call* gave the following plausible interpretation:

> While he was in San Francisco, word came to the president that the Chinese and Japanese travelers and immigrants alike entering at that port were all landed in an old shed, where the facilities were the crudest possible and where the higher class of oriental visitors might easily feel that they were suffering an indignity. Knowing the oriental character well, President Taft felt that while the Chinese, for instance, might submit to the conditions in silence, they nevertheless would feel the matter keenly and might in time retaliate with a boycott.[47]

Three days later, President Taft ordered the opening of the new Immigration Station on Angel Island. Presidential authority being what it was,

> Secretary [General of Immigration] Nagel reported to the president here tonight that he had found a way to open the new station, had authorized the immediate purchase of necessary furniture and other essentials and had instructed the officials not even to wait for the installation of electric lights, but to use lanterns for a temporary lighting system.[48]

Politics were not the only factor behind the Shed's days being numbered. There had been a sharp increase in the number of Chinese arrivals in the United States, with San Francisco, as always, receiving the largest number. Arrivals over the past several years had more than doubled and appeared to be headed steeply upward—a trend commented upon frequently by the newspapers. Although the increase may have been tiny in relation to total immigration, the impact on San Francisco's limited facilities was substantial.

The end of the Shed as a detention facility came on January 22, 1910 when, as the *San Francisco Examiner* so delicately put it, the "Detention Shed Is Emptied of Chinese; Mongolians Are Taken to New Immigration Quarters at Angel Island." The *Call* was a bit more circumspect, leading with "Doubtful Aliens on Angel Island; Great Excitement Attends Embarkation from Old Sheds on the Mail Dock," and following with a lengthy description of the event.

> There were 101 Chinese and one lone and gloomy Hindu in the party transferred to the new home for doubtful aliens.
>
> The time set for the transfer of the inmates was 9 a.m. but long before that scores of Chinese coaches gathered around waiting for a last word to their fellow countrymen before a heartless government sent them across the water.
>
> The moment the first of the Chinese appeared at the head of the long stairway and gazed in blinking wonder around him a storm of language broke loose. The immigration inspectors shooed away the wise ones on the sidelines as best they could, but they would return again and again, yelling their last words of advice.
>
> The transfer was made in installments. A large dray was backed up to the foot of the stairs and into this would be loaded a gang of Chinese, as many as it would hold. Then, surrounded by a group of inspectors and government officials the dray started for the pier, where a tug lay waiting for the cargo. . . .
>
> W. T. Boyce, in charge of the operations, gave strict orders to keep the local Chinese as far away as possible from those being transferred. There was a fear that some oriental at the last moment would make the desperate break for American citizenship but none attempted it.
>
> In the crowd were four Chinese women. They seemed to regard this affair as a picnic. They laughed, chatted, giggled, and chatted pidgin to the grinning inspectors. The lone Hindu was last. He moved down in majestic stride and strode on board the tug as if it belonged to him.
>
> Among the Chinese of the detention quarters there is one man who has been there since last August. . . . When he stepped on board the tug he wrapped himself in a shawl and gazed curiously at the spot which he had left and which he had entered on landing six months ago.[49]

Leaders of the Chinese community were not as sanguine about exchanging the Shed for the Island. An editorial in the *Chinese World* on the day of the move expressed Chinese resentment at conditions in the Shed (pictured in a rare waterside view) and forebodings about the new facility at Angel Island.

> The detention station at San Francisco's port, commonly called the Wooden House, where immigrants were kept before being questioned, was moved to Angel Island at 9 a.m. today. Currently there are 101 Chinese in custody. Also moved there to wait for investigation were the detained passengers from the *Siberia*, including 85 Chinese (1 female), 3 Japanese, and 4 Indians. The Chinese arrested by patrol boats today were also shipped to Angel Island this afternoon. It has been many years since the Wooden House was first built. . . . Chinese detainees in the Wooden House have been treated worse than prisoners. Its walls are covered with the inmates' poems complaining of their treatment, and traces of their tears can been seen on the floors. There has even been a case of suicide due to the unbearable misery. The rope that the man used to hang himself is still there in the building, a hateful symbol to anyone who sees it. Now that the detention station is relocated and our countrymen will be kept on a deserted island, we hope that the photo published today will help us to remember the Wooden House. For our posterity, the image of the Wooden House will be a token by which to remember the exclusion of Chinese, as well as a source of empathy for what the early generations of immigrants have gone through.[50]

During the 1906 earthquake and fire, the Shed had been saved in what marked a turning point for the firefighters, preventing the destruction of all the

Figure 4.4
A rare photograph shows the Detention Shed of the PMSS, San Francisco, ca. 1904.

Source: Healy and Chew, *A Statement for Non-Exclusion*, 1.

other piers,[51] but it could not withstand the redevelopment of the waterfront. Completion of the seawall meant that "within the next three months the present detention shed...must make way for modern improvements."[52] The Shed became a fish quite out of water, deprived of its direct connection with ships at the pier. A new era in Exclusion enforcement had begun, although there would be little improvement in the lot of detainees at the Golden Gate.[53]

CONCLUSION

It is puzzling that prior to 1910 San Francisco had no dedicated facility for holding Asian detainees. Many smaller entry points, such as Suma, Washington, and Portal, North Dakota, had Chinese inspection and detention stations by 1901. At San Francisco, neither the steamship companies nor the Customs Service thought it worthwhile to invest in building a more permanent facility, perhaps because they expected that the diminishing Chinese population would eventually make such a facility unnecessary. And so the use of make-do facilities persisted.

The Angel Island Immigration Station represented a change in who bore responsibility for housing arrivals while their admissibility was being determined. Heretofore, the steamship companies were charged with providing accommodations for their passengers while in detention. Not only did the companies provide for the passengers' upkeep, but they were also liable for a large fine for every passenger escaping their care. Having the federal government assume the responsibility, if not all of the costs, of detention was a subtle but important change in the enforcement of Exclusion.

An assumption underpinning the use of the Pacific Mail's Detention Shed that it was, in effect, an extension of its ships: the Shed was not on American *terra firma*, and Chinese (and other inadmissible aliens) had not entered the United States. As one report put it, "the Chinese, while physically off the ship, are held constructively to be aboard."[54] Moving the locus of detention to an island maintained part of the fiction that aliens had not truly "landed," but the fiction was an easy target for anti-Chinese critics. Angel Island was clearly American soil, and the presence of the detainees was due not to some capitalist plot, but rather to the workings of federal government policies.

One thing that did not change was that the federal government did not assume the full burden associated with daily upkeep of those detained by its orders. At the Detention Shed and on Pacific Mail ships, the PMSS directly provided meals for detainees. Even at Angel Island, where the Immigration Service provided the meals (through a concessionaire), the Pacific Mail (and presumably other steamship companies) were charged for each and every meal consumed by their passengers. It is highly unlikely that the Pacific Mail would bear all the risk—and cost—of the hugely variable periods of detention its passengers endured. It must have had a way of passing some of the cost along to its passengers. In more ways than one, the Chinese probably paid for their own incarceration.

NOTES

1. René De la Pedraja, *The Rise and Decline of U.S. Merchant Shipping in the Twentieth Century* (New York: Twayne Publishers, 1992), 13–22; John Haskell Kemble, *One Hundred Years of the Pacific Mail* (Newport, VA: Mariners Museum, 1950); and E. Mowbray Tate, *Transpacific Steam: The Story of Steam Navigation from the Pacific Coast of North America to the Far East and the Antipodes, 1867–1941* (New York: Cornwall Books, 1986).

2. *San Francisco Call*, April 29, 1899.

3. The Act of March 2, 1819 (also known as the Manifest of Immigrants Act, 3 Stat. 489) took effect on January 1, 1820.

4. For an account of this interplay between local politics and public health, see Robert Barde, "Prelude to the Plague: Public Health and Politics at America's Pacific Gateway, 1899," *Journal of the History of Medicine and Allied Sciences* 58, no. 2 (2003).

5. See Jules Becker, *The Course of Exclusion, 1882–1924: San Francisco Newspaper Coverage of the Chinese and Japanese in the United States* (San Francisco: Mellen Research University Press, 1991).

6. *San Francisco Examiner*, August 10, 1882.

7. *San Francisco Examiner*, May 19, 1882.

8. *San Francisco Examiner*, May 23, 1882.

9. *San Francisco Examiner*, October 31, 1883.

10. *San Francisco Examiner*, December 30, 1884, Collector Sears to Treasury Secretary McCulloch. Fifteen years later, on May 12, 1900, the *Call* reported "another outrage" when "Coolies Marched from the Vessel to the Dock Before the Arrival of the Federal Officers."

11. U.S. Bureau of Customs, "Press Copies of Letters from the Collector of Customs, San Francisco, to the Secretary of the Treasury, 1870–1912." February 11, 1893, and September 20, 1893.

12. *Chung Sai Yat Po*, "American Newspaper Describes Prison as Inferno," December 18, 1903.

13. U.S. Bureau of Customs, "Letters from the Collector of Customs," January 24, 1893 (Volume of correspondence July 7, 1892 to February 9, 1893, 470).

14. *San Francisco Examiner*, October 25, 1883.

15. *San Francisco Examiner*, November 15, 1895.

16. *San Francisco Call*, October 8, 1909, "Immigrant Station Pleases Senator."

17. *San Francisco Call*, August 16, 1898. Collector Wise to Secretary.

18. Sanborn Fire Insurance Maps for San Francisco, 1886/1887 (Volume 1, sheets 18 and 19) and 1899/1900 (Volume 2, sheets 218 and 219).

19. John Soennichsen, *Miwoks to Missiles: A History of Angel Island* (Tiburon, CA: Angel Island Association, 2001), 85.

20. *San Francisco Call*, November 30, 1908.

21. Admeasurer of Vessels to Surveyor of Customs, San Francisco, April 2, 1909. RG 85, Entry 9, File 52270/21. 17W3, 14/16/02, Box 468, NARA.

22. Alan Kraut and Randolph Boehm, eds., *Records of the Immigration and Naturalization Service*, vol. Reel 9 (Bethesda, MD: University Publications of America, 1992). Reel 13, item 52363/14, dated February 9, 1909.

23. The letter from Stidger to the Inspector In Charge, Chinese Bureau, is found at http://gallery.unl.edu/picinfo/21649.html.

24. Immigration ruling quoted in Neil L. Thomsen, "No Such Sun Yat-Sen: An Archival Success Story," *Chinese America: History and Perspective*, 1997, 21.

25. Mary Roberts Coolidge, *Chinese Immigration* (New York: Henry Holt and Company, 1909), 299–300.

26. U.S. Department of Labor, "Annual Reports of the Commissioner-General of Immigration, (1903–32)," 1903, 63.

27. *San Francisco Chronicle,* May 7, 1899.

28. *San Francisco Call,* January 3, 1901.

29. *San Francisco Call,* April 1, 1899.

30. "Favors a Site on Angel Island," *San Francisco Call,* November 4, 1903.

31. Fu Chi Hao, "My Reception in America," *Chinese America: History and Perspective,* 1991, 153.

32. Wong Hock Won, "Composition on the Advantages and Disadvantages of America, from a Chinese Standpoint." Translated at Portland immigration station, ca. October 30, 1906. Enclosure in letter from J.H. Barbour to Commissioner General of Immigration F.P. Sargent. Record Group 85, Entry 133, File 13928, 17W3, 4/22/05, Box 207, NARA.

33. "Penned Chinese Grow Desperate," *San Francisco Call,* April 11, 1902.

34. Lee, *At America's Gates,* 125.

35. Collector Wise to Treasury Secretary, May 12, 1899.

36. *Los Angeles Times,* February 14, 1900.

37. *Los Angeles Times,* October 26, 1901.

38. See, for example, "Investigating Escape of Detained Chinese," *San Francisco Call,* January 12, 1909.

39. *San Francisco Call,* July 12, 1896.

40. Fred Watts's telegram to Immigration Bureau, June 3, 1909. RG 85, Entry 9, File 52270/21, 17W3, 14/14/02, Box 468, NARA.

41. Schwerin to Hart North, Commissioner of Immigration, San Francisco, July 13, 1909. RG 85, Entry 9, File 52270/21, 17W3, 14/16/02, Box 468, NARA.

42. "Harbor Being Prepared for the Vast Commerce," *San Francisco Call,* December 11, 1909.

43. Immigrant Inspector Richard Taylor to Commissioner General of Immigration, March 25, 1909. RG 85, Entry 9, File 52270/21, 17W3, 14/14/02, Box 468, NARA.

44. "Approves Plans for a New Pier; Harbor Commission to Build Structure to Replace Old Mail Wharf," *San Francisco Call,* June 23, 1908.

45. "Immigrants to be Closely Guarded," *San Francisco Examiner,* June 1, 1909.

46. "Favors New Station," *San Francisco Call,* October 7, 1909.

47. "Taft Opens Island for Immigrants," *San Francisco Call,* October 10, 1909.

48. Ibid.

49. The quotations from the *Examiner* and the *Call* are from their editions of January 23, 1910.

50. "The Wooden House," *Chinese World,* January 22, 1910, trans. Danian Lu.

51. Gordon Thomas and Max Norgan Witts, *The San Francisco Earthquake* (New York: Stein and Day, 1971).

52. "Immigrant Station Pleases Senator," *San Francisco Call,* October 8, 1909.

53. For details on the opening of Angel Island, see Lee, *At America's Gates.*

54. Asst. Secretary of Commerce and Labor Wm. R. Wheeler, "Memorandum for the Secretary," January 28, 1909. RG 85, Entry 9, File 52270/21, 17W3, 14/14/02, Box 468, NARA.

—5—

Moving Migrants across the Pacific

Wen Quok Shee and Chew Hoy Quong landed in San Francisco, they joined the several million Chinese, Japanese, Indians, Filipinos, and other Asians who made the long journey across the Pacific—and sometimes the Indian *and* Atlantic Oceans as well, if Brazil or the Caribbean was their destination—in the first century of Asian mass migration to the New World.[1] While such figures may seem modest when compared with the tens of millions involved in the great transatlantic migrations from Europe in the pre-1924 period or with Chinese migration within Asia, the Asian migrations to the Western Hemisphere were nonetheless important for adding a significant element to the peopling of the New World. The Asian migrations to the New World can be put into perspective by comparing them with other mass migrations taking place during this period. Whether the destination was the Americas, Southeast Asia, or the Asian mainland, "migrations across the globe were broadly comparable in size and timing."[2] Curiously, little has been written about how so many people were moved so far.

Quok Shee and Chew Hoy Quong, like nearly all Asians, migrated by ship. Like most Asians, they traveled in the near anonymity of steerage class—"Asiatic steerage," as it was commonly known on the Pacific. They were also among the tens of thousands of Asians who made the voyage to the New World aboard a ship that was Japanese. The ship that brought them, the Japanese *Nippon Maru*, was part of this larger universe of ships and other facilities that made it possible for Asians to cross the Pacific Ocean.

At the turn of the twentieth century, ships carried symbolic and emotional freight—as well as the real stuff—that today they do not. In an age when ships were the only means of crossing oceans, the fates of countries, as well as mere travelers, depended on them. The commerce of nations, and in some cases their

Figure 5.1
Chinese and Japanese migration to the Western Hemisphere in the period 1801–1925 was important, but considerably smaller than their respective international migrations within Asia.

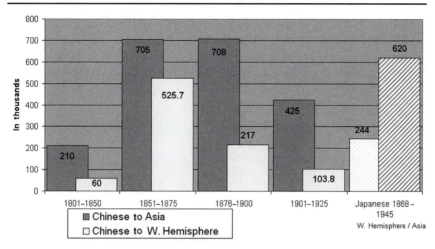

Sources: For Chinese, see Pan, *Encyclopedia of the Chinese Overseas;* Carter et al., *Historical Statistics of the United States, Millennial Edition;* Lee, *At America's Gates.* For Japanese, see Kikumura-Yano, *Encyclopedia of Japanese Descendants in the Americas,* table 1.3, 67.

very survival, was affected by the merchant ships that entered and left their harbors. Immigration was just one of the many businesses tightly dependent on ships.

There was an inherent tension between the immigration–shipping complex and the Chinese exclusion laws. Keeping the Chinese out—or, more realistically, severely limiting the entry of Chinese and other Asians—may have been good politics, but it was bad for the shipping business and for those in the import-export business. Passengers provided an important contribution to any company's bottom line. Whether white- or Asian-owned, businesses required regular and frequent ship service to move their goods in and out of North America. Thus, there was ample incentive for shipping companies like the Pacific Mail, and for trade groups like the San Francisco Chamber of Commerce, to work to soften the enforcement of the exclusion laws, and to maintain the supply and flow of ships.

It is sometimes argued that on the Atlantic, advances in ship technology—from sail to steam, from paddle wheels to screw propulsion—made possible the great migrations of the nineteenth and early twentieth centuries. But did the succession of newer, faster, larger ships make migration possible, or just more comfortable?[3] Did causation perhaps run the other way, with a greater demand for space on long-distance passenger ships making it feasible for steamship companies to commission more advanced vessels? Improvements in shipboard conditions were rarely the result of government intervention. On the Pacific as on the Atlantic, legislation was largely ineffective in improving conditions, due to "careless drafting of legislation, inadequate enforcement, unwillingness to yield jurisdiction in the interests of international regulation and, above all, the effectiveness of the highly organized shipping lobby."[4]

There is good reason to think that the Pacific market was quite different from the one that prevailed on the North Atlantic. The volume of business on the Pacific was much lower, perhaps a tenth that of the North Atlantic. Demand was regulated not by the business cycles on both sides of the ocean—as Brinley Thomas long ago demonstrated that it was on the Atlantic[5]—but by governmental actions. These policies included American laws prohibiting or restricting the entry first of Chinese, then of Japanese, and finally of all other Asians, as well as such actions as the Japanese government's policy of encouraging emigration. The government of China was virtually incapable of any effective involvement in the emigration of Chinese, unlike many European countries that could control predeparture conditions, if not conditions on the ships themselves.

Despite occasional fare wars, fares were remarkably stable in nominal dollars; for over half a century, it cost $50 to travel from Hong Kong to San Francisco. Asian steerage customers were, it seems, more price sensitive than their European counterparts, eschewing the improved conditions offered by second-class or enclosed/partitioned third-class in favor of low fares. Certain technological advances, such as the screw propeller, were adopted much later on the Pacific, where there was less competition. Contract labor, rare on the North Atlantic, was important for certain periods for several New World destinations—for Japanese going to Hawaii, Peru, and Brazil, and for South Asians going to the West Indies.

None of these differences should obscure the basic similarity: that a multinational enterprise involving privately owned shipping lines, railroads linking ports with interiors, networks of agents and publicists, government regulators and gatekeepers, and industrialists and land developers, all collaborated in the intercontinental movement of tens of millions of people.

A complete portrait of all the elements that went into transporting immigrants is beyond the scope of this book. One might want to examine in depth the involvement of governments (especially of Japan, Canada, and the United States) in developing maritime policies that promoted (or hindered) the sea-born transportation of immigrants.[6] There were networks of ticket agents both in Asia and in North America—how were they structured, who ran them, and what tactics did they use to entice their clients into purchasing tickets for transoceanic journeys?[7] How successful were the shipping companies in lobbying for less onerous enforcement of laws restricting Asian immigration? What was the social life among cabin-class passengers, where Asians and whites were from (presumably) similar social milieux?[8]

What I offer here is the beginning of that portrait, sketches—in increasing detail—of three of its principal features. "Asiatic Steerage" surveys a broad range of ships and destinations, looking specifically at the conditions of those who did not travel in cabin class, the great masses in the age of mass migration. "The Life and Death of the China Mail" narrows the view, examining one steamship company run by and for immigrants. "The *Nippon Maru*" is a close inspection of a single ship, one whose entire "career" was predicated on being in the business of transporting Asians across the Pacific. Together, these three chapters may begin to close the gap between what we know about the Pacific crossings and our knowledge of the European crossings to North America.

NOTES

1. The three largest Asian groups making the journey eastbound were Chinese, Japanese, and East Indians. Figures for Chinese migration for the century after 1840 are scattered, but would include roughly 400,000 to North America, around 140,000 to the Caribbean (especially Cuba), 100,000 to Peru, and a few thousands to Brazil and Mexico. See Pan (1999), Emmer (1990), and Castro de Mendoza (1980). A conservative estimate of Japanese immigration to the Americas for the period 1868–1941 (620,000) can be found in Akemi Kikumura-Yano, ed., *Encyclopedia of Japanese Descendants in the Americas* (Walnut Creek, CA: Altamira Press, 2002). Of those traveling westbound, East Indians were by far the most numerous. Over 500,000 migrated from British India to British, French, and Dutch possessions in the West Indies between 1839 and 1917. See Piet C. Emmer, "Immigration into the Caribbean: The Introduction of Chinese and East Indian Indentured Labourers between 1839 and 1917," *Itinerario* 14, no. 1 (1990): 66.

2. Adam McKeown, "Global Migration, 1846–1940," *Journal of World History* 15, no. 2 (2004): 155.

3. Drew Keeling, "The Transportation Revolution and Transatlantic Migration, 1850–1914," *Research in Economic History* 19 (1999).

4. Maldwyn A. Jones, "Aspects of North Atlantic Migration: Steerage Conditions and American Law, 1819–1909," in *Maritime Aspects of Migration,* ed. Klaus Friedland (Koln: Bohlau Verlag, 1989), 331.

5. Brinley Thomas, *Migration and Economic Growth: A Study of Great Britain and the Atlantic Economy* (Cambridge: Cambridge University Press, 1954). See also Keeling, "Transportation Revolution."

6. For Japanese government policies on emigration, see William Wray, *Mitsubishi and the N.Y.K, 1870–1914: Business Strategy in the Japanese Shipping Industry* (Cambridge, MA: Harvard University Press, 1984); and Alan Takeo Moriyama, *Imingaisha: Japanese Emigration Companies and Hawaii, 1894–1908* (Honolulu: University of Hawaii Press, 1985).

7. For a study of merchant/brokers and lawyers in the Seattle and Portland areas, see Todd Stevens, "Brokers between Worlds: Chinese Merchants and Legal Culture in the Pacific Northwest, 1852–1925" (PhD Dissertation, Princeton University, 2004).

8. John Malcolm Brinnin, *The Sway of the Grand Saloon* (New York: Delacorte, 1971).

— 6 —

Asiatic Steerage: Ship Travel and Asian Mass Migration

At daybreak on September 1, 1916, the "yachtlike liner Nippon Maru steamed into port through a dense fog." By 6:35 a.m. she was safely tied up at San Francisco's Pier 34. As was customary, the *San Francisco Chronicle* announced her arrival in its Maritime News.

> The greater part of her cabin list (is) composed of missionaries returning to their homes in the United States after many years of absence in foreign territory.... Among the passengers on the Nippon were John de L. Caldwell, Minister from the United States to Persia, his wife and two sons; Ralph H. Rader, United States vice-consul at Teheran, Persia; K. Honda, Director of Agriculture in Korea;...and Charles A. Bonte, dramatic critic of the Philadelphia Ledger, who was in Japan to study the native drama. The complete list of passengers arriving aboard the Nippon follows.[1]

Far from being complete, the list included only the 116 cabin-class passengers. Nowhere did it give the names of the 147 passengers in "Asiatic steerage," nor indicate that 68 of them were Chinese, 75 were Japanese, 2 were Russians, and 2 Indians.[2] It did not say that among the steerage passengers was a Chinese man in late middle age, hoping to bring his young wife into the United States. Not a word indicated that Chew Hoy Quong and Quok Shee had arrived in America.

They were simply two more Chinese traveling in steerage, too insignificant to merit even the briefest mention. A century later, we hunger for details of their travels, of how they and the great masses of Asians crossed the Pacific. What was the steerage passenger's experience? How were these ships laid out? In what ways did the steerage experience differ from the cabin-class experi-ence or from steerage on the North Atlantic?[3] Did the steerage experience change over time? This chapter explores these questions, focusing largely on Japanese, American, and Canadian ships. An introduction to the concept of steerage is followed by two lengthier sections: the ships that made steerage travel possible, and the nature and conditions of steerage travel aboard those ships.

AN INTRODUCTION TO "STEERAGE"

Emigrants were carried in ships of every sort, from converted cargo ships to the most luxurious of passenger liners. The latter are well known to us, largely through documentation produced by the shipping companies themselves that focused on the cabin-class cruise experience. Their glossy magazines showed well-heeled passengers in palatial settings, on their way to exotic destinations. The TKK line's San Francisco office published both *T.K.K. Topics* and *Japan: Overseas Travel Magazine*. The latter was a rather lavish magazine that frequently used the artwork of San Francisco-based Japanese artist Chiura Obata to impart a sense of the japonesque to potential clients, all the while employing photographs that emphasized the plush, Western-style accommoda-tions of TKK's ships on the run from San Francisco to the Orient. Rare is the hint of the many passengers in steerage, those who would never partake of this experience; deck plans for prospective passengers showed only vacant spaces where steerage quarters actually were.

Most early definitions of "steerage" referred to some aspect of guiding (or steering) a ship—the mechanisms used in doing so, or the very act itself. The *Oxford English Dictionary* refers back to Hakluyt's *Voyage* (1599), where "The English shippes using their prerogative of nimble stirrage...came often times very neere upon the Spaniards."

Another meaning from the days of sailing vessels refers to the space below decks in the stern of the vessel. In the sixteenth and seventeenth centuries, "steerage" was the place from which the ship was actually steered. Early in the eighteenth century, the wheel was placed on the open deck, so that the vessel was no longer steered from the "steerage" which, however, retained the name.[4] In that "steerage" room, various parts of the steering mechanisms might still have intruded into the compartment. Such space made for straitened and uncomfortable accommodations—just the place where junior officers might have been assigned.

In the nineteenth century, the term came to mean that part of a passenger ship assigned to people traveling at the cheapest rate. On a TKK liner like the *Nippon Maru*, the cost difference for the trip between San Francisco and Hong Kong could be substantial—$225 in first class, $100 in "European steerage" (sec-ond cabin), and $50 in "Asiatic steerage." The latter denoted both the lowest class of accommodation and the fact that "white" people were expected to travel in some other class.

A TKK fare sheet illustrates the relative costs of travel in the various categories of accommodation. As the leisured class, those traveling in first class were expected to travel with servants, either "European" or "Asiatic." Missionaries were given special rates, as were their servants. In both cases, Asian servants were expected to dine with the steerage passengers, while European servants ate with second-class passengers. "European steerage" was likewise a combination of either steerage sleeping quarters and second-class dining or somewhat more private steerage quarters and European, rather than Asian, steerage cuisine. The brochure further advised that "[t]he Asiatic Steerage is for the sole use of Asiatics, and cannot be occupied by, nor rates applied to, any other class."[5] Professor Jean Gontard, a Frenchman, was one of those whites who insisted on traveling in "Asiatic steerage," but when he arrived in San Francisco he and his wife were subjected to a lengthy detention on Angel Island as a result.[6]

The CPR's 1902 promotional brochure noted that on the *Tartar* and the *Athenian*—older ships formerly on the Alaska route—the following restrictions applied: "The classes of accommodation are First cabin, Intermediate, and Asiatic Steerage....Chinese, Japanese and other Asiatics only will be booked in the Asiatic Steerage. Females will not be carried in Asiatic Steerage."[7]

The location of the cheapest (and least desirable) quarters may have shifted over the course of the century. In the era of side-wheelers, this may even have been amidships or, as the *Harper's* article (see below) indicates, forward. "Steerage" has always carried the principal distinction of being far from the comfort and respectability of cabin class, regardless of its physical location. Generally, "steerage" meant below decks (or on the "between deck"—between the main deck and the cargo hold), with conditions ranging from uncomfortable to unsanitary to scandalously dangerous. By the later part of the century, "steerage" would have referred to accommodations near the ship's stern, where the noise of the ship's screws and engines was unrelenting, or nearer the bow, which could shake and vibrate in heavy seas. These locations are typified by the cutaway drawing of the CPR's *Empress of India*, with the highlighted steerage areas located fore and aft.

"Steerage" crept gradually into the American legislative lexicon beginning, somewhat curiously, with what has come to be known as the Steerage Act (or, more formally, the "Act of March 2, 1819, An Act Regulating Passenger Ships and Vessels")—curiously, for nowhere in the text of the law does the word "steerage" appear. This Act is best known for marking the beginning of the collection of data on immigration, the master of each vessel being obliged to furnish the local collector of customs with a list of the name, age, sex, and occupation of each of his passengers—except those Americans in cabin class. As Senator Newton of Virginia noted when presenting this bill to the Senate, it also contained provisions regulating the number of passengers (per ton of ship) and

Figure 6.1
A cutaway plan of the CPR's steamer *Empress of India,* ca. 1891, shaded areas show
"cargo or steerage" areas on the main and lower decks. Only the steerage smoking room
on the upper deck was not amenable to conversion for cargo.

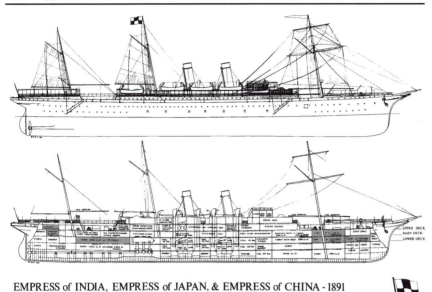

EMPRESS of INDIA, EMPRESS of JAPAN, & EMPRESS of CHINA - 1891

Source: *The Pacific Empresses,* 24. Courtesy of Robert Turner.

the amount of provisions per passenger required of all ships *arriving* in the United
States, provisions whose purpose was "to give to those who go and come in
passenger vessels a security of comfort and convenience."[8] This, of course, was
when the United States was concerned only with European immigrants coming
to Atlantic ports.

The word "steerage" did not make its first official appearance until Congress
passed the Act of March 3, 1855, "An Act to Regulate the Carriage of Passengers in Steamships and Other Vessels." Throughout the long nineteenth
century, Congress made a number of attempts (1847, 1848, 1855, 1860, 1882,
and 1908) to improve conditions for passengers "other than cabin passengers,"
as the Act of May 17, 1848 put it. The requirements of the 1819 Act were gradually made more rigorous and extended to ships arriving at and departing from the
United States, including Pacific as well as Atlantic ports. Investigators even
traveled the Atlantic *incognito* to ascertain actual conditions; what they found
horrified the legislators, indicating that enforcement was, and would remain, a
problem.

"Cheap," "malodorous," and "lacking privacy" seem the three phrases that
best sum up the concept of "steerage." On today's commercial airplanes, "coach"

(as opposed to "first class" or "business class") contains some of the same class of service and social class distinctions, but without many of the corollary implications that made "steerage" of a hundred or so years ago a decidedly different, utterly *déclassé* experience. We might also think of "steerage" in terms of what it was NOT: nowhere near as luxurious as "first class cabin" private accommodations on a ship, not even as comfortable as the "second cabin" accommodations shared with a few other passengers. It was neither glamorous nor expensive, nor even private, having a faint connotation of "undesirable."

SHIPS AND STEERAGE, CHANGING OVER TIME

On the Pacific, the steerage experience changed over time and over place, encompassing five broad, somewhat overlapping, geographical-historical phases to the transpacific steerage experience.[9] The first phase was the era of sailing ships, with movements of people (almost exclusively Chinese) eastward. For the purposes of this chapter, this period began with the first Chinese arriving in California in February 1848, aboard the brig *Beagle* from Hong Kong. A second phase began with the introduction of steam-powered ships around 1867, was centered on the Hong Kong–San Francisco route, and lasted until about 1885. The third phase, commencing about 1880, added sizeable Japanese and Chinese migration to Hawaii. In the 1890s, Japanese ships began competing on the run from Hong Kong and Japan to Seattle (1896) and San Francisco (1899) with the established American lines headed by the PMSS and its partner line, the Occidental and Oriental Steamship Company, and those of Canada and Britain, primarily the CPR's steamship line service to and from Vancouver. A fifth phase saw South America begin receiving Chinese and Japanese at the end of the nineteenth century, especially with the establishment of Japanese shipping routes to Peru (1899) and Mexico (1901), with the massive migration of Japanese to Brazil, beginning in 1908, adding the long journey via South Africa to the catalogue of steerage experiences.

Certain ships can be thought of as exemplars of these periods, either in their design, ownership, or choice of routes.[10] The following sections touch briefly on the kinds of ships that plied these routes and epitomized the steerage experience on them.

Steerage Under Sail

The first Asian emigrants to the New World came on ships powered by sail—American, British, Dutch, Spanish, Peruvian, and even the occasional Chinese junk. While there are familiar stories of Chinese coming to "Gold Mountain" after the 1848 discovery of gold, those migrations were largely voluntary. A larger, more harrowing set of migrations is less well known.

As the African slave trade was being suppressed, plantation and mine owners in South America and the Caribbean searched for alternative sources of cheap, servile labor and found it in the "coolies"[11] supplied by Western merchants and their Chinese agents. Hundreds of thousands of Chinese "coolies" were taken in mid-century to work the plantations and hellish guano deposits of Peru's Chincha Islands (100,000–150,000 from the late 1840s to 1863), Cuba (a similar number, between 1850 and 1875), and other plantation-type economies in the Caribbean.[12] Between 1849 and 1874, some 656 trips were made by ships bringing Chinese laborers to the British Caribbean, Peru, Cuba, and Surinam.[13] Notwithstanding occasional elaborate charades attempting to create the illusion that the "coolies" had willingly entered into a labor contract, these were *involuntary* migrations: most of the Chinese laborers in those three countries claimed to have been deceived, coerced, or simply captured and put on a ship. Many of the most beautiful American clipper ships—including the *Sea Witch* and the *Swordfish*—engaged in this lucrative trade.[14]

The "coolie" trade with Peru was very much an international affair. In the period from 1849 to 1874, for instance, over 90,000 Chinese "coolies" were brought to Peru, carried on 207 different ships from eighteen different countries. Peruvian ships—or at least, ships flying a Peruvian flag of convenience—topped the list, followed by ships of Italian or French registry, with American, British, Spanish, and Dutch ships far down the list. It appears that ships of all nations experienced episodes of mutiny, shipwreck, or disease.[15]

It would be misleading to describe the "coolies" of this period as "steerage passengers" in the conventional sense. "Human cargoes" would be more appropriate, as ships in the "coolie trade" were frequently described as "floating hells" or "devil ships." To gain some idea of the conditions on such ships, it is worth quoting Basil Lubbock in *The Coolie Ships and Oil Sealers*:

> Accommodations on these sailing ships were little different from those on African slavers.
>
> "Down the whole length of both lower decks were tier on tier of berths, or rather shelves," and the space allotted each man and boy was "something less than two feet in width and five [feet] in length." The decks and hatchway openings of most "coolie" vessels were "barred and barricaded like the old convict ships." An iron grating was bolted to the hatchway entrance, leaving an opening for those below of no more than nine inches in diameter. An armed sentry was often posted on top. One vessel employed cannons that face each hatchway opening "with the muzzles pointed forward."[16]

Food and hygiene often matched the wretched accommodations, which in addition to being prison-like were invariably packed far beyond any legal limit that might have existed. When captives were chained to their berths, a ship's sinking meant the loss of all human cargo. To be subjected to such conditions for long periods of time was bound to produce a high death rate from sheer brutality, disease, suicide, and the not infrequent rebellion. In the 1850s the voyage from Hong Kong to Callao, Peru, generally took 120 days, and the death rate was around 30 percent; on the trip to Cuba by way of Cape Horn, which generally took around 170 days, anywhere from 15 to 20 percent died. Indians suffered similarly on the long voyages to South Africa and the even longer sailings via the South Atlantic to the West Indies.[17]

Conditions on "coolie ships" did vary. In general, British ships and colonies were under the scrutiny of the antislavery forces. This led to somewhat better enforcement of regulations on indenture contracts and on food, medical assistance, and the amount of space allotted per passenger. Spain, too, established extensive regulations for all ships taking laborers—white, Chinese, and indigenous people from Yucatan—to Cuba, but enforcement was weak.[18]

It appears that the advent of service by steamship did little to lower death rates. Rather, steam seems to have made it more profitable to service a more widely distributed set of planter-clients. Toward the end of the Chinese "coolie" trade with Cuba, "the Spanish steamer 'Rosa Nena,' which left Macao with 850 coolies destined for a voyage of ten months and seven days, with stops at Batavia, Reunion and the Cape of Good Hope. . . arrived in Cuba to report a loss of 125 persons."[19]

The forced-labor "coolie trade" began to decline in the 1860s. The abuses inherent in such a trade became widely known—as much as anything by virtue of the frequent revolts by the Chinese passengers themselves. In 1875, a speaker in the House of Lords stated that there had been thirty-four mutinies on Chinese "coolie ships," including occasions when the Chinese set on fire the ship that was carrying them to their particular hell.[20] Similar testimony was given to a Joint Committee of Congress in 1876. The British stepped up enforcement of antislavery laws, and in 1874 legislated an end to the trade in Chinese laborers from Macao and Canton. The American Congress passed a law in 1862 prohibiting Americans from engaging in the trade. China's government also established diplomatic agreements with Peru, Brazil, and Spain (for Cuba), effectively putting an end to the worst aspects of the Chinese coolie trade by 1881.

Although the migration of laborers from the Indian subcontinent to the Caribbean is outside the scope of this essay, it makes for an interesting comparison. The enormous Indian "coolie trade" involved perhaps 500,000 East Indians migrating to the British, French, and Dutch possessions in the West Indies. It was highly regulated by the British government through the London Colonial Office, the British Viceroy in India, and officials in various British colonies. By the 1850s, "coolies had to be given seventy-two cubic feet for every adult, (while at) this time, British soldiers on troop-transports were allowed sixty-six cubic feet."[21] Surgeons—of varying levels of experience and ability—were required to be aboard each coolie ship. Yet such regulation did not prevent all abuses and merely allowed planters and mine owners in the colonies to take advantage of the immiseration of Indian peasants in a way that soothed the British conscience. By 1917, complaints from the Indians themselves finally put an end to such large-scale contract labor emigration.

Early Steam

The earliest nineteenth-century descriptions of Chinese coming to North America are also from the era of sailing ships, but the context was rather different. The lure of gold (and, later, work on the railroads) induced many Chinese to voluntarily borrow from clansmen or fellow countrymen the money needed for passage to California. This was the origin of the "credit-ticket" system. The lender—often also a labor broker—had a financial interest in seeing that his client arrived safely in the United States and commenced working to pay off his ticket-credit. This made for conditions in steerage more like those on the North Atlantic, and less like the gruesome "floating hells" described above. Such conditions ranged from uncomfortable to unhealthy, with overcrowding, lack of sanitation and proper ventilation, poor food badly prepared, and inadequate medical treatment among the chief culprits. This was also true of the first attempt to bring Japanese laborers to Hawaii in 1868 (when Hawaii was still an independent kingdom) aboard the three-masted American square-rigger *Scioto*.[22]

Conditions of the great European migrations over the North Atlantic improved following the introduction of steam around 1850. Similarly, conditions improved on the North Pacific as the voyage from San Francisco to Hong Kong was shortened significantly. Where even the fastest clipper ships required forty-five days to make the crossing, steam lowered that considerably—thirty-four days on average via Yokohama (twenty-two days just to Yokohama, later down to twelve days by the end of the century)—with a commensurate decrease in mortality and general perceptions of the risky nature of the journey. Legislation in the United States and, especially, Great Britain dating from the 1850s also played a role in ameliorating overcrowding and lack of hygiene.[23]

The transition from sail to steam began in 1852, but it was a slow one. On the Atlantic, even with its higher passenger volume, it took nearly twenty years for the various passenger lines to build up capacity to where steamships could completely replace sailing ships in transporting passengers arriving in New York from Europe.[24] The first regularly scheduled steamship service between San Francisco and China via Yokohama was not inaugurated until 1867, when the wooden-hulled paddle-steamer *Colorado* was shifted from the Pacific Mail's San Francisco–Panama service to the run to the Far East. Even on Pacific Mail ships built specially for service on the turbulent North Pacific—*America, Japan, China*, and *Great Republic*—sail continued to augment steam.[25]

As the dominant carrier, the Pacific Mail was slow to introduce the technological innovations that were rapidly incorporated into ships on the Atlantic. Only in 1874 did the Pacific Mail put into service its first iron-hulled screw steamers, years after the last wooden side-wheelers had been built for the Atlantic by Cunard (1862) and the Royal Mail Steam Packet Co. (1865). The lack of competition meant that the Pacific Mail could charge the high fares needed to support its inefficient, coal-burning monstrosities—albeit ships that long retained their popularity with the public.

Figure 6.2
The large side-wheel passenger liner *Great Republic* was the sister ship of the *Japan,*
the *China,* and the *America,* all of the PMSS. This particular image is an 1867 lithograph by Endicott Lith of New York.

Source: Photograph by Cathy Forbes. From the collection of Stephen J. and Jeremy W. Potash.

In 1866 the company's agents in Hong Kong and in California concluded that
there was a substantial demand for the proposed steamer service.[26] Such "market
research" surely contributed to the Pacific Mail's decision to build its huge side-
wheelers. The *Great Republic* was 380 ft. long, 3,881 tons, and capable of carrying
1,500 tons of coal, 250 cabin passengers, and 1,200 steerage passengers. Such a
ship was clearly predicated on there being a substantial movement of steerage
passengers—presumably Chinese—in both directions, and average loads of
1,000 eastbound and 800 westbound eventually bore this out. Passenger traffic
proved to be a mainstay of the Pacific Mail's revenues, generally exceeding revenues from hauling freight, merchandise, and "treasure." In light of subsequent
anti-Chinese agitation and legislation, official San Francisco's effusive expression
of delight at the prospect of hundreds of thousands of Asian laborers being transported there by the Pacific Mail's new ships is not a little ironic. "If China and
India will send us that (needed labor) and cultivate a trade with us, in a few years
we shall be able to do for them what England, nor Russia, nor France can ever
do—send their starving people cheap bread and make famine impossible."[27]

Where commerce was concerned, the attitude of Californians toward the
Chinese was as ambiguous aboard ship as it was on land. Not only were the ships'
crews predominantly (i.e., excluding the officers) Chinese[28] and held in high
esteem by the company, but the Pacific Mail was publicly quite solicitous of its
Chinese customers. "[The ship's surgeon] is to note particularly the conduct of
subordinates and servants towards Chinese passengers and report . . . any neglect

of duty or unkind treatment. On the confidence and friendship of these people, the prosperity of the company chiefly depends."[29]

But business is business, and the Pacific Mail was not averse to boosting profits at the expense of its steerage passengers. In the first year of its transpacific service, "as many as fourteen hundred were in the steerage on a single voyage. At such times, air and space were at a premium and the potential for illness was exceedingly high."[30] In 1873 the Secretary of the Treasury launched an investigation following a stream of complaints that

> steerage passengers were being crowded to excess, not only on decks corresponding to those on which sailing vessels were restricted, but also on the orlop deck [the deck farthest down in the hold, usually reserved for cargo—Ed.]). "Thus the darkness, the foul-smelling bilge water, the tainted atmosphere, and kindred evils of the early sailing days were repeated."

The U.S. District Attorney sued the Pacific Mail, but on appeal the fine was reduced to a mere $16,000. In his ruling, Judge Ogden Hoffman implied that the Chinese needed less than the minimum space and fresh air required under Federal law, as steamships on the Pacific could transport "a number of passengers

Figure 6.3
An illustration from *Harper's Weekly* is a not unsympathetic depiction of Chinese in steerage on the Pacific Mail's *Alaska*. May 20, 1876.

Source: Bancroft Library, University of California, Berkeley.

Figure 6.4

The deck plan of the Pacific Mail side-wheeler *Japan* reveals steerage accommodations (shaded areas) *forward* of the great paddle wheels amidships.

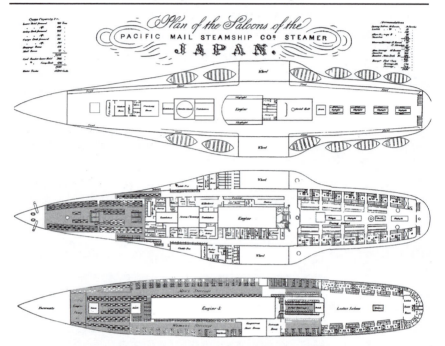

Source: Mariners' Museum, Newport, VA.

considerably greater than was actually carried with less comfort or danger... than usually attends an Atlantic voyage of an immigrant ship."[31]

The layout of early Pacific Mail steamers made concessions to the presence of large number of passengers in steerage. Many ships carried cannon, and there would have been an arms room filled with rifles, revolvers, cutlasses, and boarding pikes—mostly for protection against Chinese pirates, but also handy in the event of "a rising among steerage passengers"—undoubtedly a legacy of the more unpleasant aspects of the coolie trade.[32] There was also "a system for spraying steam and hot water on all the decks," useful not only for cleaning but as an efficient form of crowd control.[33] Curtained-off areas in steerage were designated for opium smoking. Most steerage accommodations were on the berth deck, with additional steerage *forward* on the main deck. In the deck plan for the Pacific Mail's *Japan*, note how steerage quarters were placed close to the gigantic paddle wheels, forward and amidships, while the cabin and "saloon" accommodations were toward the rear. Note the separate, and relatively large, areas designated as Women's steerage. Light was brought to the ladies saloon aft on the lower deck through skylights, but there were none for the steerage passengers.

The *Japan* was a glamorous member of the Pacific Mail's transpacific fleet, as renowned as her sisters *Great Republic, America,* and *China,* but steerage was an extremely important part of her carrying capacity: In addition to listed capacity of 190 cabin berths are 908 steerage berths. Kemble notes that "In the steerage there were three berths one above another in both the open standees and the doorless state-rooms. The arrangements on the berth deck to steerage men and women are interesting, but whether these were used in actual practice may be doubted in the light of accounts of travelers in the ship and her sister vessels."[34]

Enter the Japanese

Important changes came to the Pacific shipping scene in the 1880s and 1890s. In 1891 the CPR launched the three *Empresses* (*India, Japan,* and *China*), providing competition for the Pacific Mail's through service to San Francisco, Portland, and Seattle with its shorter and faster route by way of Vancouver and Victoria. But the biggest change came when the Japanese government set out to develop a substantial maritime presence and individual Japanese began to leave the home islands in significant numbers. As the stream of Japanese emigration swelled and flowed east toward North America, then toward the west coast of South America, and finally toward Brazil, the mix of ships and shipping lines changed to accommodate it. Japanese ships and shipping companies were instrumental in transporting that flow of immigrants, and for a time dominated that trade.

Two early experiences with migration to the New World clearly influenced many of the subsequent developments surrounding Japanese emigration and the ships that facilitated it. Both were negative experiences, highlighting the pitfalls of mass migration to foreign lands. Combined with an emerging Japanese nationalism that verged on chauvinism, these events contributed to a government presence in the migration industry that was infinitely more forceful and intrusive than any efforts of the Chinese government.

The first set of formative experiences involved three groups that, in 1868–69, were the beginnings of organized emigration from Japan: the 148 *Gannenmono* (or "people of the first year of Meiji") who went to Hawaii aboard the *Scioto* in 1868; the 40 contract laborers who went to Guam in the same year; and the party of 40 that went to North America in 1869. All three groups went under arrangements that had not been vetted by the new Meiji government. The *Gannenmono,* in particular, had been virtually spirited out of the country by a labor recruiter (albeit one with diplomatic trappings).[35] Many of the *Gannenmono* who worked on the Hawaiian sugar plantations returned at the end of their labor contracts, while the "gold hill" settlers from Aizu were unsuccessful in establishing themselves in California.

Also in the early years of Meiji (1872), the *Maria Luz,* bound for Peru from China, entered Yokohama seeking refuge from a violent storm. One of the Chinese "coolies" on board escaped and reported to local authorities that the

Maria Luz was a slave ship. An investigation confirmed this, and all the Chinese were set free. This incident not only exposed slave transport by Peruvian ships and led Peru to adopt the principle of free immigration, but heightened awareness on the part of Japanese officials of the need to monitor the conditions of all nationals traveling under labor contracts.[36]

The first steps toward large-scale, organized migration came in 1884 when a special representative of the Kingdom of Hawaii, Robert Irwin, set about recruiting 600 people for the first group of *kanyaku imin*, or government-sponsored emigrants to work on Hawaii's sugar plantations. In requesting the cooperation of the Governor of Tokyo, Irwin specified the ships to be used to transport the emigrants: "Transport from Nagaura (near Yokosuka) to Honolulu will be on the Pacific Mail's *Tokyo Maru* (aka *City of Tokio*), the Kyodo Unyu Company's *Yamashiro Maru*, or on a similar first-class passenger steamer. My government will furnish all transport costs on these steamers."[37]

This ushered in the period of Japanese labor emigration to Hawaii under government contract. Irwin's letter conveys how persistent the Hawaiian Kingdom was in trying to recruit Japanese emigrants. The two ships specified by Irwin were much superior to the old, cheap, chartered ships that were used in the *shiyaku imin* (private contract) period that followed. A formal treaty between Japan and the Kingdom of Hawaii, the Convention on Japanese Immigration, was signed in 1886 and specified that emigrants were to be treated as steerage passengers on first-class ships vetted by the Japanese government, and that their passage to and from Hawaii was to be free. The *City of Tokio* (and her sister, the *City of Peking*, which carried the third group of contract laborers to Hawaii) was one of the Pacific Mail's newer ships, an iron-hulled screw steamer normally on the run from San Francisco to Japan and on to Hong Kong—definitely a "first-class passenger steamer."

The voyage of the *City of Tokio*, bringing the first group of contract workers[38] from Japan to Honolulu, presaged many aspects of future Japanese migration by ship. On the *City of Tokio*, "the emigrants were orderly."

> Although they were in steerage class, because there were no Chinese emigrants aboard they were fed Japanese food. *Kumi*, or groups, organized the assignment of accommodations. Each *kumi*'s leader was responsible for its behavior. This self-management system was also used on later emigration ships to South America. Since the majority of the emigrants were from rural, agricultural villages, the common attire included *hitoe* (single layer *kimono*), *tsutsusode* (tight-sleeved *kimono*), *momohiki* (close-fitting trousers), *shirushi banten* (livery coats), and *geta* (wooden clogs). The only people wearing Western clothing were passengers from Tokyo and Yokohama.[39]

The period of government-sponsored emigration lasted for ten years, the last group traveling on the steamer *Miike Maru* when it arrived at Honolulu on June 15, 1894: twenty-six emigration voyages to Hawaii, with a total of 29,069 emigrants landing there. Nearly half of those early emigrants traveled in the

Kyodo Unyu's *Yamashiro Maru*, which made twelve voyages. The *Yamashiro Maru* was the first Japanese ship to carry emigrants. It was considerably less palatial than the *City of Tokio* (even in steerage), and its history, too, presaged the way in which the construction and subsidization of "emigration ships" was designed to support Japan's growing military might.

The Kyodo Unyu Kaisha was one of the forerunners of the mighty NYK (Nippon Yusen Kaisha)[40] line, and when it was formed in 1882 the Kyodo Unyu had as patrons such high officials as the Foreign Minister and the Minister of Agriculture and Commerce. It was established to contribute to the nation's status as a sea power, bringing in senior Navy officers as part of its management, such as Rear Admiral Ito Shunkichi and Captain Totake Hideyuki, who later became presidents of the company. Such a strong military involvement naturally produced ships more like a volunteer fleet, ready for service in time of war, than a commercial fleet. The *Yamashiro Maru* and its sister ship, the *Omi Maru*, were ordered from the Armstrong shipyards in Newcastle—not coincidentally, a big supplier of warships for the Japanese Navy. Subsequently, an internal company report concluded that the *Yamashiro* and the *Omi* were built to warship specifications as demanded by the Naval Ministry, "built to be used in emergencies and are thus not suitable for use as commercial vessels."[41] Nonetheless, they carried over 13,000 *kanyaku imin* to Hawaii.

The second most used ship was the aforementioned *Miike Maru*, which made five voyages on the Hawaii run. The *Miike Maru* was the largest of the eight newly built ships that NYK purchased from Britain upon its establishment in 1885. At the time it was Japan's largest ship, one of only two Japanese ships (along with the *Hiroshima Maru*) over 3,000 tons.[42]

Michio Yamada is of the opinion that the ships used to transport Japanese laborers in steerage during the government contract period (1884–94) were much better ships than those used during the period when the private sector managed emigration, largely through private emigration companies. Still, the ten- to fourteen-day voyage from Yokohama to Honolulu held many possibilities for things going awry, and the Japanese government took its responsibilities as sponsor quite seriously. The first group of laborers traveling under the Convention was accompanied by six Kanagawa prefectural policemen acting as guards, and a Japanese Section was set up within the Hawaiian Bureau of Immigration, entrusted with supervising and protecting emigrants.[43]

Some idea of the interior of these ships comes from the writings of Masaoka Shiki in "Jugun Kiji (War Correspondence)." Shiki, who had volunteered to be a war correspondent during the Sino-Japanese War, was a passenger on the *Kaijo Maru* (originally the P&O passenger ship *Assam*, 3,231 tons, built in 1873) from Japan to Dairen (Dalian). From his writings we know that the ship's steerage quarters were large rooms with double-decker (i.e., bunk) beds and that the cabin was similar to the large cabins on present-day outer island ships in Japan—except that there was a shelf to separate the top and bottom of the cabin's space. Lacking in comfort, these cabins could carry twice as much as cabins on outlying island ships. Such cabins were extremely efficient in carrying large number of people. The *Kaijo Maru* had been owned by NYK and since it was the same type of ship as those conveying contract emigrants to Hawaii, its interior was probably similar.

On the way back to Japan from Dalian, Shiki rode the *Sadokuni Maru* (originally the German *Ashington*, 1,246 tons, built in 1872) and was put in the same type of large sleeping spaces with shelves. In his collection of essays "Byō-shō Rokushaku" ("A Six Japanese-foot Sickbed"), in uniquely graphic language, Shiki described the dark and unbearably cramped quarters. Due to the hardships on his voyage, he fell ill and began to cough up blood. He struggled with his illness for seven years, but succumbed to tuberculosis at the age of 36.[44]

A second, somewhat darker period of Japanese emigration to Hawaii began in 1896 following the conclusion of the Sino-Japanese War and ended in 1907 with the so-called Gentlemen's Agreement. Conditions for traveling in steerage to Hawaii probably worsened during this period, and for a number of reasons. Less government supervision certainly gave the for-profit Japanese emigration companies that recruited emigrant laborers more opportunity to exploit them. Having just three lines (Pacific Mail, O&O, and TKK) providing the transport services to Honolulu created many possibilities for collusion and price gouging. Sometimes this took place on the ship (overcrowding, selling supplies on board at inflated prices), sometimes before the emigrant even boarded: doctors performing unnecessary operations (especially for trachoma), emigrants being told that there was no space on their intended ship and they would have to spend additional nights at the port's hostel. The Japanese government eventually recognized the severity of these problems and began regulating port-city providers of services to emigrants.[45]

To North America

Until the very end of the nineteenth century, passenger traffic between the west coast of North America and Asia was dominated by American, British, and Dutch shipping lines.[46] Foremost among them was the PMSS, based in San Francisco, a line whose story has been well told.[47] The Pacific Mail was eventually absorbed by the Dollar Line, the direct predecessor of today's American President Lines. Along the way, a small but interesting interloper was the CMSS, a Chinese American–owned line that operated out of San Francisco from 1915 to 1923.[48]

In the late 1880s and in the 1890s, newcomers appeared who would provide additional competition in the market for steerage passengers and eventually drive out the Pacific Mail. First was the CPR's entry into the shipping business, followed by the arrival of two Japanese lines, the NYK and the TKK. This section emphasizes these three lines; a separate chapter focuses on the TKK's pioneering ship, the *Nippon Maru*.

There were, of course, alternatives on the northern Pacific run. Numerous tramps, charters, and one-time sailings brought thousands of Asians to North America. At the low end, perhaps the most infamous of these was the 1914 sailing of the *Komagata Maru*, a decrepit Japanese collier hired by an Indian Sikh to carry 150 of his compatriots from Hong Kong to Vancouver. Accommodations were described as "533 wooden benches, something like third-class railway seats without backs...there were no tables or chairs, simply benches, spaced every one and a half metres, on which the passengers were to throw their bedding."[49] At the high end, were the lines owned by the CPR and other American lines.

In 1905, for instance, railroad tycoon James J. Hill deployed two new ships whose design he had personally commissioned. The largest commercial ships in the world, the *Minnesota* and the *Dakota* were simply monstrous. Each displaced 37,500 tons—over six times the size of the *Nippon Maru*. They were capable of carrying "1500 Asiatic passengers in open steerage, in addition to 290 in cabin-class. Following the custom of the times and for the pleasure of Chinese addicts, a small space labeled 'The Opium Den' was reserved for this use."[50] However, they were not successes as passenger ships. Underpowered and slow, they were scarcely faster than the *Colorado* in 1867. Passengers preferred the faster ships of other lines even if meant taking a slightly longer route to reach their destination.

The CPR offered its own service between North America and China and Japan. Beginning in 1887, in chartered three aging steamers to connect the CPR's rail service to Vancouver with the Far East. The *Abyssinia* steamed into Vancouver on June 14, 1887. It was indicative of future trends that of her eighty Chinese steerage passengers, only thirty were headed for British Columbia; the others were all bound for the United States.[51] The carriage of Chinese passengers south—and flour north—to Portland and other U.S. ports was an important mechanism for making the CPR routes to the Orient profitable.

As on the Pacific Mail's first generation of steamships, conditions aboard the CPR's *Abyssinia, Parthia,* and *Batavia* were not luxurious. One traveler noted that on the *Abyssinia*:

> She was low in the water and in bad weather seas would break over the upper deck, making it impossible for passengers to stay dry.
>
> There was no running water, no refrigeration, no steam heat. Somewhere towards the bow was an ice room which carried a certain amount of fresh meat, but the main reliance was placed on the live stock which was carried on deck. Along the upper deck, amidships, were pens for sheep and fowl of all kinds, chickens, ducks, turkeys, geese, etc. Once in a while these would be swept away in bad weather.[52]

Forward and on the deck below was accommodation for an undetermined number of Chinese passengers. Occasionally there would be as many as five or six hundred, and if there were less, the space was given over to cargo, and the berths temporarily removed. In 1889, a mail subsidy from the British and Dominion governments made it possible for CPR to consider purchasing a trio of new ships for the North Pacific route. Two years later, the *Empress of India*, the *Empress of China*, and the *Empress of Japan* all made their debuts. These beautiful ships, with their bowsprits, Clipper bows, and traditional figureheads, were transition ships: equipped with the most modern triple-expansion engines and twin screws, they still carried sail as insurance against failure of the steam-powered engines. They were elegant to the point of opulence in their cabin accommodations, as "throughout the saloon, and to a less extent, the second-class quarters, the finest of materials were used." This did not apply to the steerage quarters, of course, which "were allocated to the less desirable areas in the ship.... The lower deck had large areas reserved for steerage passengers, and the remainder was required for coal bunkers and the ship's machinery. Even more steerage space, available for cargo should the need arise, was allotted in the lower reaches of the ship."[53]

Deck plans for the first *Empresses* (1891) clearly showed the interchangeability of cargo and steerage passengers. While the lower deck carried no passengers, the main deck and the upper deck had areas set aside for them. The upper deck had spaces allocated for "baggage room or cargo" and for "cargo or steerage," while on the main deck, "cargo or steerage" spaces were located forward, aft, and amidships. Thus, all space allotted for steerage passengers was also capable of being turned into cargo space. Twenty years later, deck plans for the *Empresses of Russia* and *Asia* showed a mild change: most steerage compartments were labeled "Asiatic steerage" only, with but two large compartments on the main deck indicated as being for "portable steerage or cargo."[54] Clearly, by 1913 there were enough Asians returning to China or Japan to warrant quasi-permanent steerage quarters.

In 1896 the NYK's *Miike Maru*, the ship that had delivered so many Japanese to Hawaii, became the first regularly scheduled Japanese passenger ship to sail to the U.S. mainland. Her arrival in Seattle on August 31 prompted a spectacular celebration.

> Boats of all descriptions—hundreds of them—anchored in Elliott Bay to enjoy the spectacle. Fireworks soared overhead while a brass band entertained the crowds onshore. The din intensified, according to one local reporter, as "the yells of thousands of people on the docks and the blowing of every steam whistle for five miles along the waterfront...celebrated the glad event and welcomed the Oriental visitor of the East to the Occident."[55]
>
> Carrying thirty-seven first- and second-class passengers and a cargo of teas, silk goods, raw silk, camphor, curios, matting, soy oil and paper, the *Miike* was escorted to Schwabacher's wharf, serenaded by "Dad" Wagner's First Regimental Band on board the fireboat *Snoqualmie*, playing the *Miike Maru March*."[56]

The *Miike Maru* and the two ships that later joined her—the *Yamaguchi Maru* and the *Kinshu Maru*—were old and relatively small at 3,225 tons and 320 ft. long. A year later they were replaced by a trio of larger (5,000 tons) ships, and in 1901 by a quartet of ships in the 6,000 ton class. Even a cursory inspection reveals their true calling—the hauling of goods, rather than people. These ships all followed what Yamada calls the "cargo first, passengers second" model, part of an arrangement whereby NYK agreed not to compete head-on with James J. Hill's Great Northern Steamship Company, a maritime extension of his Great Northern Railway.

Ships on the Seattle run followed the "cargo first, passengers second" rule. This made them different from those on the San Francisco run, where the order of importance was reversed. Japanese ships included those of the TKK line and later the NYK and OSK (Osaka Shosen Kaisha) lines, while the American ships were those of the Pacific Mail and its successors—the China Mail, the Dollar Line, and the American President Line. Most were glamorous passenger liners of the sort featured in *Japan, Overseas Travel Magazine*. Their archetype was the *Nippon Maru* (430 passengers, built in 1898 by Sir James Laing in Sunderland, England) and its successors, the *Tenyo Maru* class (1,100 passengers, built by Mitsubishi in Nagasaki in 1908). Because of the *Nippon Maru*'s pioneering role in the expansion of Japanese shipping into the migration business, and because of its long involvement in it, a subsequent chapter is devoted to a brief biography of this ship.

The *Nippon Maru*, a Japanese ship, was in the emigrant trade for twenty years. Many other ships, of course, were involved in moving emigrants to and fro across the North Pacific. In addition to the TKK line, NYK, CPR, and the successors to the Pacific Mail (Dollar and American President Lines) maintained fleets of large ships that carried Asian migrants, as well as European and Asian businessmen, tourists, missionaries, and diplomats. The CPR's *Empress* ships on the run to Asia from Victoria and Vancouver catered particularly to first-class passenger travel, although steerage class and high-value cargoes were extremely important. These "tri-purpose" ships—steerage passengers, cabin passengers, and cargo—continued until well after World War II.

South and Central America: Mexico, Peru, and Brazil

After the end of the Chinese contract labor trade with Peru in 1874, Asian migration to South America went into the doldrums for nearly thirty years. Although "some (Peruvian) planters...even made an unsuccessful attempt to establish a steamship route between Hong Kong and the Peruvian port of Callao via Hawaii in 1874," in general the "slow and expensive passage, made either by sailing ship or by steamer via San Francisco, as well as the bad reputation of Peru, discouraged further migration."[57] That migration began to revive around the turn of the century as political and economic conditions improved. Passenger ship service, heretofore largely in the hands of the Pacific Mail, improved with the arrival of Japanese competitors, making it more practical for Asians to migrate to South America.

The first Japanese emigrated to Latin America in 1893 (Meiji 26) when 132 Japanese sugarcane plantation workers in Hawaii moved to plantations in

Guatemala, traveling to their destination via San Francisco. Over the course of time the principal destinations for Japanese traveling to Latin America shifted, first to Mexico, then to Peru and Brazil. The ships involved in these migrations were a diverse lot, reflecting variations in the direction and intensity of the flow of migrants.

In 1897, small groups of Japanese contract laborers came via ships such as the *Gaelic*, a White Star Line ship that had long been chartered by O&O for the San Francisco–Yokohama–Hong Kong run. Other ships involved in taking Japanese contract workers to Mexico were of Japanese registry but constructed elsewhere. The *Kotohira Maru* and the *Kotohira Maru No. 2* had both been purchased during the Russo-Japanese War by the Kawasaki Senpakubu (Kawasaki Shipping Department, which later became Kawasaki Kisen Kaisha) and later chartered by the Continental Colonization [Tairiku Shokumin] emigration company to transport migrants to Mexico. The *Kotohira Maru*, of 3,657 gross tons, had one triple expansion reciprocating engine and a top speed of fourteen knots. Built in 1887 in England as the Glenline's *Glenshiel*, her passenger capacity was forty-three in first class, eight in second class, and an unspecified number in third class, most likely on standee beds placed in the cargo hold. The *Kotohira Maru No. 2* had been the P&O's *Nankin*: 4,367 gross tons, one triple expansion reciprocating engine, top speed fourteen knots, with a passenger capacity of seventy in first class and forty-six in second class.[58]

Another ship that carried Japanese emigrants had an unusual experience in that all the Mexico-bound emigrants returned on the ship that brought them. On June 19, 1904, 500 mine workers sailed from Kobe aboard the TKK's *Akebono Maru* (formerly the English *Crown of Arragon*, an iron-hulled steamship of 2,450 gross tons capable of making eleven knots). On arriving at the Boreo Copper Mine in Baja California, the emigrants found that in addition to a sweltering climate and high costs of living, the mining equipment was so inferior as to be life-threatening. After fruitless negotiations with the mine owners, the entire contingent sailed back to Japan.[59]

The Japanese experiment with group migration to Mexico was short-lived, as many found the conditions so unpleasant that perhaps 5,000 of the 8,000 contract laborers fled to the United States before finishing their contracts.[60] Coupled with the restrictions placed on direct Japanese migration to the United States by the so-called "Gentleman's Agreement," the flow of emigrants to Mexico virtually dried up by 1908. Soon, however, it was replaced by Peru and, shortly thereafter, by Brazil. These two very different destinations involved quite different ships and styles of transportation.

The Ships to Peru[61]

Japanese emigration to Peru began much later than Chinese migration to the same country, but under less oppressive conditions. Working closely with the Japanese Foreign Office and the Peruvian government, the Morioka Emigration

Company (*Morioka Imin Kaisha*) negotiated an agreement to send 798 contract laborers to work on agricultural plantations.[62] The first shipload of 790 who actually boarded, along with twelve supervisors—all men—departed on February 27, 1899, in a festive atmosphere of a band and cannon salutes. Their ship was the *Sakura Maru* (ex-*Mogul*, built 1887), chartered from NYK.

The *Sakura* had already made a brief, sad appearance in the immigration trade. In 1897 she had carried 316 Japanese laborers to Hawaii, only to have them all refused admission on the grounds that the money they were carrying was insufficient. This time her destination was farther away, a thirty-six-day journey of 8,600 nautical miles. Even outfitted with auxiliary sails and undoubtedly modified to increase the range of its single coal-burning triple-expansion engine, the little (2,953 tons) *Sakura* would have been unlikely to have made the trip without stopping for water and fuel. Captain Brett Knowlton had indicated that he would stop in Seattle on the return; perhaps he did so outbound as well.

Yamada speculates that the passenger quarters were large open rooms with bunk beds. The onboard conditions were probably similar to those in Tatsuzō Ishikawa's *Sōbō* (see below), worse than later South American emigrant ships. But they were surely not as difficult as what awaited emigrants on the various plantations, where an unfamiliar climate and an "oil and fat" local cuisine made them prone to malaria and dysentery.[63]

Many other aspects of this initial arrangement were unsatisfactory. The Japanese government took note and had its Consul in Mexico launch an inquiry. We can assume that future improvements were partly a result of this continued governmental interest in the conditions under which emigrants left Japan, and partly the emigration companies' self-interest in delivering healthy bodies to their foreign clients. When subsequent groups left on the *Duke of Fife* (initially a charter, later purchased and operated by Morioka as the *Itsukushima Maru*), they were accompanied by four doctors. The gender mix changed as well. Where the first group had been entirely male, the 981 contract laborers in the second group included 98 women.

A variety of ships were employed in carrying Japanese emigrants to Peru. At first, older ships from the North American run were shifted to the run to Peru, usually traveling via Manzanillo or Salina Cruz on their way to Callao (Lima's port) and Iquique, Chile.

In 1905 TKK established a schedule of three trips per year between Japan and the west coast of South America. The limited number of Japanese migrating to that region could not have long supported such a schedule. What made possible the continued regularly scheduled service was a second client base: Chinese emigrants to Peru. "The years from 1905 until May 1909 were the golden years of free emigration to Peru, with as many as three thousand Chinese a year arriving in Callao." Even after political reaction set in against Chinese immigration, "from 1911 to 1930, Chinese migration to Peru was...swinging between periods of complete suspension and ever larger numbers of new arrivals."[64]

The resumption of Chinese migration thus coincided with the new Japanese migration to Peru, creating a demand for ships to service it.

Various efforts were made to establish service between Peru and Hong Kong. Beginning in October 1904, the British-owned Compañía Marítima Occidental used the *Kensington* (8,669 gross tons) for two trips. Although 356 Chinese passengers were carried on the first trip, there was virtually no cargo on the return, and the CMO quickly folded. Chinese businesses in Lima and Hong Kong then set up their own line for transporting emigrants between Hong Kong and Callao, the Lee Chay company. They advertised for potential migrants in the Hong Kong newspapers, and in April 1906 the *Lennox* made its first voyage, carrying 630 Chinese passengers as well as rice, medicines, foodstuffs, silks, and other staples of the migrant economy.[65]

Later efforts included a vessel owned by the government of China, perhaps part of an effort to assert responsibility for its nationals living in Peru. A contemporary American observer reported that the *Hwah Ping*, "a vessel of 4,254 tons registered gross, owned by the Chinese Government, has made two round-trips within the past year between China and west South and Central American ports. This vessel also carries both freight and passengers and the itinerary is much the same as that of the Toyo Kisen Kaisha. Whether this will develop into a regular service or not is problematical."[66] This may refer to the Chungwha Navigation Company, founded in 1921, by Lima-based Chinese merchants with support from Chinese investors in other parts of Latin America, Honolulu, Hong Kong, and Shanghai.[67]

As many as 600 Chinese were on each sailing to Peru. With TKK extending its route back as far as Hong Kong at around the same time, clearly quite a number of Chinese could be carried in its ships. At first the TKK used non-Japanese ships so as not to offend the Chinese (especially during the anti-Japanese boycott of 1907), but as Chinese migration to Peru soared, TKK became the preferred means for Chinese to reach their destination.[68]

There is such a thing as business being "too good," and this is especially true in the migration business. Wherever Asian immigration was limited (as it was in Peru), a certain amount of corruption ensued, with the usual suspects being consular and port officials, representatives of the migrating community, and those supplying the transportation. There would often be a reaction to what host country nationals saw as the shipping company owners being overly eager to bring in "coolies" merely for profits (both legal and not). Many of the same arguments used against the Pacific Mail's facilitation of Asian immigration in the United States during the Chinese exclusion period were used in Peru. There, they had an even more negative effect on the fortunes of shipping lines which, other than the Japanese, were poorly financed.

Between 1905 and 1911, TKK used three ships on its state-subsidized service to Peru: a refurbished oil tanker, the *Kiyo Maru* (9,287 tons, built 1910); the *Buyo Maru* (5,238 tons, built 1908); and the *Hong Kong Maru* (6,064 tons, built 1898, sister to the *Nippon Maru* and the *America Maru*), which was transferred from the North American run. However, none of these ships were specifically designed for carrying large number of migrants in one direction and freight in the other. Yamada adds that the *Kiyo* and the *Buyo* "having been converted from oil tankers, were barely strong enough to handle the sea conditions on that route. With that in mind, TKK decided to study the actual conditions along the South American West Coast shipping route and create a ship that, matched to those conditions, would be efficient."

That ship was the TKK's *Anyō Maru*, the first Japanese ship specifically designed to transport emigrants. Begun in 1911 in Mitsubishi's shipyard and completed two years later, it was designed to handle TKK's service to the west coast of South America. In 1911 TKK also purchased a 6,500 ton freight and passenger ship built in England and christened it the *Seiyo Maru*, to replace the *Buyo Maru*. Together with the *Seiyo Maru* and the *Kiyo Maru*, the *Anyō Maru* offered scheduled service to South America every other month until the mid-1920s. The trip from Hong Kong to Valparaiso took twelve weeks (eleven to Callao in Peru), two weeks less from Yokohama.[69] She was a frequent visitor to San Francisco on her way to Peru, the U.S. Customs Bureau recording fifty-one instances of her arrival. As the *Anyō Maru* was seen as a prototypical emigration ship, it is worth exploring Yamada's account of this vessel in greater detail.[70]

> At 9,500 tons and with twin screws capable of doing up to 15.3 knots, the *Anyō Maru* was among the faster ships of its day. It could carry 4,877 tons of coal (converted to oil in 1918), enabling it to travel 92 days—covering 30,000 nautical miles—without replenishing fuel. Much of this efficiency was due to the use of geared turbine engines, a technology licensed to Mitsubishi by the British company Parsons. The *Anyō Maru* was one of the very first ships on the Pacific to use this design, for which it received more contemporary attention than it did for its role in the emigration industry.
>
> The *Anyō Maru* was an improvement on the previous generation of emigrant-carrying ships, among which were converted oil tankers or freighters more fit for carrying cargo (say, Chilean nitrates) in-bound than people out-bound. The steerage rooms were consigned to four large blocks of space along the upper deck and in the aft section of the second deck.
>
> In the forward section of the upper deck is the steerage for Chinese passengers. There were two main rooms, one with a capacity of 126 persons and a second block area accommodating 148 persons. Add to that one block of cabins with toilet and bathing facilities, for use by women and children (thirty people). The cooking room and a room for use by the Chinese were separate and situated inside the foremast derrick platform.

In 1918, the U.S. Customs Service inspected the *Anyō Maru* when she arrived in San Francisco on her way back from Valparaiso. Records of that inspection reveal some intriguing, additional detail of her layout. The steerage area took two forms: "permanent" bunks (or berths) that could accommodate 127 passengers, plus an "area [of] open desk space" that could be converted into sleeping accommodations for an additional 750 passengers. The bunks were reported as much the same as on other ships with steerage quarters: 2 ft. by 6 ft., arranged in two tiers, each bunk six inches off the deck, with the top bunk 2½ ft. from the ceiling, and 2½ ft. between tiers of bunks.

Note that the Chinese accounted for 304 places in steerage, an important complement to the 334 Japanese steerage passengers. In addition to the multiethnic steerage nature of the passengers in steerage, there was a leavening of cabin-class accommodations. Ten cabins catered to first-class passengers (with their own dining saloon, smoking room, and pub), and another ten were for second-class passengers (with their own dining room and separate smoking room). Thus, the *Anyō Maru* reproduced in miniature some of the class distinctions found on the more glamorous, larger ships.

In 1924 the TKK added three new ships to its run to Peru and Chile. Designed especially for the route to South America via the San Francisco, they were clearly designed to appeal to emigrants traveling steerage, as "even the third class [cabins] are above the waterline."[71] Adding new ships in the depressed business climate of that year was a gamble, one that did not pay off. Two years later, TKK sold to NYK, which absorbed its South American routes.

Ships on the Route to Brazil

The movement of Asian emigrants to Brazil, at least where it concerned the Japanese, was fundamentally different from emigration to Peru: labor contracts brought entire families to Brazil, whereas Peru largely attracted single men.

While the *Anyō Maru* was the "first [Japanese] ship especially designed for emigration," other types of ships provided the carrying capacity to Brazil. Migration to Brazil began in 1908 and was principally on a family basis through the Kōkoku Shokumin Gōshi Kaisha ("Imperial" colonization company).

The first shipload of 781 Japanese emigrants who traveled on the *Kasato Maru* (ex-*Kazan*, built 1900) achieved an iconic place in Japanese (and Brazilian) history, and their voyage was recognized at the time by Japanese as a trailblazer of a new kind of emigration. The newspaper *Osaka Asahi Shimbun* reported this event the next day with the headline "Great Hopes for Brazilian Emigration."

> The first 781 contract immigrants went aboard on April 28, at 2:00 in the afternoon, and were sent to Brazil, 18,000 miles away. The significance of this emigration is that they are families. They are well prepared and most of them are dressed in western clothing. They are quite different from labor emigrants of the past. Therefore, [this reporter] assumes that these well prepared immigrants will give Brazilians a good impression of our country and people.[72]

The emigrants' quarters on the *Kasato Maru* were set up steerage style, both fore and aft on the main deck and on the deck below. Each steerage block was like a big warehouse filled with a honeycomb of bunk beds. As there is no official layout of the *Kasato Maru*, the precise details of how the rooms were arranged are unknown. We do know that the emigrants from Okinawa, Hiroshima, Kumamoto, Yamaguchi, and Ehime were placed in the forward steerage, and those from Kagoshima in the stern. There were separate rooms in the very rear of the stern that were especially designed for the few "free (i.e., noncontract) emigrants" that were on the ship, a room shared by fifteen other passengers, bunk beds having been provided for them. A doctor's office was right next door. Although this was an "emigrant ship," there were six "first-class" rooms on the bridge deck, along with a first-class dining room. Officials from the Immigration Company and their translators occupied these quarters.

From the diary of Rokurō Kōyama, a free (noncontract) emigrant, we have a description of that first, memorable journey.

> After sailing through the Formosa Strait, they set up an awning for shade on both fore and aft decks. Many emigrants spent time in the shade, escaping from the hot, stuffy passenger rooms. The fore deck especially became a communal space for the emigrants where they did *Sumo* (wrestling) and Kenjutsu (Japanese fencing). In the South China Sea, a swimming pool made from canvas was also used on the deck.

May 15, the eighteenth day after leaving Kobe, found the *Kasato Maru* in the Indian Ocean at latitude 1° 25' north, longitude 89° 24' east. They celebrated Neptune's crossing, and cultural numbers from each prefecture were performed on deck. The Okinawa party was reported to be extremely talented entertainers, with their traditional songs and dances accompanied on the *Jabisen* (a stringed musical instrument made from snakeskin). Young emigrants helped prepare a celebratory feast. Later on, OSK's steamships adopted the tradition of "crossing the line." In this as in many other things, the *Kasato Maru* was a model for ships taking emigrants to South America.

In his diary, Ryō Mizuno, president of Kōkoku Shokumin Gōshi Kaisha, recorded the basic progression of the trip.

- May 5th (8th day of the trip), in latitude 15° 33' N., longitude 113° 5' E., 274 *ri* (approximately 1068.6 km or 667.9 miles, 1-ri = 3.9 km = 2.4 miles). The heat makes sleeping difficult.
- May 7th, Lat. 8° 15' N., Long. 108° 48' E., 254 *ri* (619.1 miles). A sailor bothered the emigrants while he was on night guard duty. The lower ranking crew, such as cooks/cleaners, sneak into the emigrants' rooms and attack and rape women and children.
- May 9th at 2:00 p.m., arrived Singapore. There is a rumor that a crewman will attack Haruyoshi Kataoka (a free emigrant from Kochi Prefecture). We must keep an eye on him.
- May 10th at 3:00 p.m., leaving for Cape Town. The hot weather is not as bad as we expected and sick passengers are many fewer than we had expected.
- May 16th, Lat. 0° 44' S., Long. 86° 40' E., 204 *ri* (497.3 miles). A strong wind from the south shakes entire ship for four days. Many passengers are seasick.
- May 27th, Lat. 28° 52' S., Long. 46° 31' E., 271 *ri* (660.6 miles). We saw Madagascar Island at first light.

- June 2nd at 10:00 p.m., arrived Cape Town, cast anchor outside the bay (went ashore the next morning at 7:00 a.m.)
- June 4th at 9:00 a.m., stayed outside the bay and weighed anchor at 1:00 p.m. Waves are extremely high.
- June 8th, Lat. 28° 10' S., Long. 0° 36' E., 222 *ri* (541.1 miles). Waves caused the ship to shudder and some objects fell from shelves.
- June 15th, Lat. 24° 57' S., Long. 33° 8' W., 260 *ri* (633.8 miles). Things get worse. A sailor tried to attack me. Luckily I was saved by one of the officers, but he got stabbed.
- June 18th at 9:00 a.m., finally arrived Santos after 12,000 *ri* of journey (29,250 miles).

The following citation is from the diary of Mineo Nomura of Hiroshima Prefecture, an emigrant who embarked at Kobe for Brazil in August 1913 (five years after the emigrants of the *Kasato Maru*) via the Takemura Colonial Trading Company's charter ship, the *Teikoku Maru* (5,163 tons, completed 1894). Mineo Nomura, bringing his wife, Sayo, and his younger brother, Shigeyuki, became a steerage passenger on the *Teikoku Maru* and sailed for fifty-one days to Santos.

As for the cabins allotted to the emigrants, *silkworm shelf* style beds had been set up. The "beds" were only mats spread out on bare planks and in order to increase the number of beds, the space between beds was extremely tight, so that an adult could finally get between, if he turned his body sideways. For the next two months, the emigrants would have to pass their time here.[73]

In the 1920s, a second generation of emigration ships was built at Mitsubishi's Nagasaki Shipyard. The *Santos Maru* class of ships were the first large-scale diesel-powered passenger ships built in Japan, and the first with automatic steering guided by gyrocompasses. In its route guide, the OSK line touted the new engine, one "that does not spit out soot and smoke, and as a result everywhere on board is always comfortable and clean. In addition, (everything is electrified, so) there is absolutely no unpleasantness from annoying noises that come from loading and unloading cargo, raising and lowering the anchor, etc."[74] In addition to greater comfort, the *Santos Maru* ships promised shorter travel times: more powerful engines and fewer, shorter port calls along the way reduced the travel time from sixty-two-plus days (*Tacoma Maru-* and *Kanagawa Maru-*class ships) to forty-seven days. The reduction in port calls was a result of lines like OSK expanding their fleets so that goods to, say, East Africa could be transported on ships dedicated to that route, rather than using emigrant ships bound for Brazil. Emigrants were also aided by there being three competing lines— NYK, OSK, and Kaigai Kogyo—who eventually agreed to keep fares low, forcing the lines to make economies elsewhere.

While Chinese passengers were an important component on the transpacific route to Peru, they were much less so for the Japanese ships traveling to Brazil. Where the *Anyō Maru-*class ships had entire sections reserved for Chinese steerage passengers, ships of the *Santos Maru* class had none. Where ships did pick up Chinese passengers in, for instance, Hong Kong, "a large room or compartment was prepared if there was a substantial number of Chinese emigrants, with the intent of segregating them from the Japanese as much as possible."[75]

THE STEERAGE LIFE
Dry-Land "Steerage"

The dry-land steerage experience was as different from that of the cabin-class passengers as was the onboard experience. Such establishments as the Oriental Hotel in Kobe or the Palace in San Francisco catered to the wealthy cabin-class travelers who, perhaps, purchased their ship passage and hotel accommodations as a package. A similar first-class experience awaited travelers who connected to the port by rail. TKK, for instance, offered such "land-sea" packages to passengers crossing the North Pacific in either direction. But steerage passengers did not travel in such luxury, neither by sea nor by land.

The steerage experience frequently began long before travelers set foot on their ships, and often it did not end when their ships reached port. Sometimes weeks in advance, emigrants would prepare for departure by gathering at ports and staying in hotels or hostels.

It was not unusual for them to stay in similar lodgings upon arrival in their country of destination. We might think of these predeparture/post-arrival periods as an extension of the steerage experience.

Emigrants often needed to spend some days in port prior to departure. In China, there were arrangements for passage to be made, often with countrymen who worked a ticket-credit system for financing passage to the destination of choice. In Japan, for those going to the United States, after 1893 it was required that they pass a medical inspection for trachoma and hookworm. These inspections were conducted by physicians in the employ of the steamship companies—the company being responsible for the return passage of those rejected at the U.S. port of entry. All of this took time, and while waiting the emigrant needed a place to stay.

Steamship companies were active in the hotel business, but usually at the upper end. They usually left the provision of lodgings for steerage class passengers to small-scale "steamship inns." The largest numbers of Chinese going overseas went to Malaya, Singapore, Thailand, and Indonesia.

While awaiting departure in a Chinese port, prospective emigrants would stay at a local inn. Most inn operators were from the same place of origin as the lodgers. The coast sprouted inns which proclaimed their native-place affiliations by carrying door signs that read "Fuqing Inn," "Quanzhou Inn" and so on. They also specialized by their guests' designation.... The inns made it their business to buy blocks of boat tickets from shipping brokers. These they sold to the (labor) recruiter-couriers with whom they worked closely or, in some cases, had entered into partnerships....

The recruiter-couriers themselves would lodge in the same inn as their charges while awaiting the ship to their overseas destination.[76]

The flow to southeast Asia dwarfed those going to the New World—but the apparatus for handling emigrations to North America was probably quite similar for all who left from such southern Chinese ports as Amoy, Shantou, Canton, and Hong Kong. There were hotels in Hong Kong, such as the Taishan and the American, that catered to travelers between Taishan County and the United States.[77]

This sort of cozy relationship between shipping companies, labor recruiters, and innkeepers was not unique to southern China. A similar development took place in Europe in the late nineteenth century, where municipalities prodded the shipping companies into seeing to it that facilities were available to the enormous number of emigrants flowing through the principal ports, waiting for ships. In Liverpool, the steamship companies controlled a multitude of boarding houses. In Germany, the Hamburg-America Line "in 1901 and 1902 built a little town on the outskirts of the city and near the harbor [which eventually] could house 5000 persons at one time."[78] In Japan, "emigrants complained about illegal practices and collusion between shipping companies and emigration companies.... They are very closely connected through the brokers and hotel-keepers, and it is hard to draw a line of separation of interests."[79]

The abuses are easily imagined, to the point where staying at such an inn in Kobe or Yokohama could be quite an adventure in itself. Emigrants were often victimized by the emigration agents and others in cahoots with unscrupulous steamship inns.

> Often, even though a ship was scheduled to sail on time, they found a pretext to detain emigrants and have them stay in the inn for a week to 10 days. Or emigration agents pretended that a ship was completely filled. Announcing that travelers would be delayed one sailing, they extorted 10 or 20 yen from prospective emigrants as bribes to hasten their departure.[80]

Henry Kawabe describes his experience in 1906:

> I went to Yokohama and...lodged at an emigrant house. A worker at this emigrant house took me frequently for trachoma and hookworm examinations, but as for the most important thing—he wouldn't let me board. Presumably they were calculating to prolong my stay at the lodging house day by day. I was kept there for three weeks. I spent all my money there, and so I went back home, managed to get the necessary money once more, came back to Yokohama and again stayed at an emigrant house.[81]

Emigrants were also prey to unscrupulous doctors, perhaps in league with the inn owners. Tamie Tsuboi was victimized in 1920 when she attempted to join her new husband in the United States:

> I was to follow him, but when I took my physical examination at the emigrant house in Kobe, the doctor said I had trachoma. Therefore I had twelve eye operations.

Looking back on it now, I suspect that the operations, instead of curing me, made it worse. I was afraid that the doctor, shaking hands with the operators of the lodging houses, was deliberately delaying me, whereupon I went to Nagasaki, took the examination, and passed it at once.[82]

In Hong Kong, the major port of embarkation for Chinese coming to the New World, a similar situation existed. Chinese complaints concerned many aspects of the immigration process and administration of the American exclusion laws. One law which disproportionately affected Chinese and Japanese involved the debarment of aliens with "loathsome and dangerous contagious diseases."[83] If emigrants were found to have trachoma or hookworm, they were rejected at the port of entry and returned to their port of origin at the steamship company's expense. Thus, it was in the interests of the steamship companies to make sure that their passengers would pass medical inspection at the U.S. port. The resulting predeparture screening could save an emigrant potential hardship and heartache and the steamship company from fine and an unpaid return passage. Or it could hold up the emigrant to what was virtually medically-based extortion. American Vice-Consul John Birge Sawyer saw how this operated in Hong Kong and explained it in a 1915 letter to a colleague at the Seattle immigration station:

For several years, and until quite recently, all the steamship lines carrying Chinese to the States were in agreement with one firm of doctors to examine their applicants for passage. The firm was Jordan, Forsyth, Grone, Aubrey and Woods. The steamship lines of course entered into this agreement with the idea that it better protected themselves. The Jordan firm secured commodious quarters, known as the Wanchai Hospital, put in a good equipment for hookworm work, and delegated Woods and Grone to examine the applicants. No other doctor or firm of doctors has devoted equal attention to the subject nor made any very strong bid for the business.

Whether Jordan's firm has succeeded reasonable well in barring diseased aliens . . .my opinion would necessarily be formed on a few meager facts such as the case of a Section 6 student who was treated and "cured" by Jordan's firm three times. After the first time he went to Vancouver and was rejected; after the second time was refused at Seattle; and after the third time he finally gained admission at San Francisco; or at least I assume that he did as several months have elapsed since he left here and he has not yet re-appeared before me. . . .

Complaints circulated about continually from both Chinese and other doctors who were cut out of the business. . . .As a result. . .the Pacific Mail tried a new departure and located on of their doctors on shore here to make examinations instead of Jordan's firm. This man, Dr. Richter evolved the idea of passing all who stood a good chance of being cured on the voyage through treatment by the ship's doctors. As a result of this program the Pacific Mail got the business away from other lines, particularly the T.K.K., and some people were greatly wrought up about it. The program did not prove satisfactory to the Pacific Mail, however, because the treatment by the ship's doctors did not come up to what Richter expected and the company lost in fines what it was making in increased business. . . .Finally matters came around to the present situation in which the lines generally have thrown over the Jordan monopoly and accept the certificates of all doctors.[84]

Of course, many of the innkeepers and other entrepreneurs provided real services for emigrants. In Hong Kong in the 1920s, "the Eastern Ocean Shipping Company, run by Liu Canchen...offered to assist people traveling from their village to the United States by handling 'paperwork' and conducting eye tests."[85] Hong Kong was also a major staging point for those traveling from India to Canada or the United States. "The Sikh temple in Hong Kong was especially important, for emigrants sometimes had to remain there as long as a month before they could book passage. As a principle, Sikh temples maintained free lodging for wayfarers and usually provided one free meal a day. Non-Sikhs were also welcome to use the temple as a hostel."[86]

While emigration companies were an important factor in promoting Japanese emigration, they did not control all of the pre-embarkation experience. There were also "free immigrants," traveling without labor contracts and hoping to find jobs or education abroad through social connections or simple industriousness. Several organizations, formed explicitly to promote such travel and to educate the travelers, operated as counterweights to the exploitative behavior of the emigration companies by providing information to those going abroad.

Such organizations included the Christian Nihon Rikkōkai (Japan Endeavor Society) and Katayama Sen's Associations for the America-Bound. Nihon Rikkōkai's founding chairman, Nagata Shigeshi, opened the Yokohama Institute for Travelers and "went to great lengths to bring travelers from emigrant inns.... Since the operators of emigrant inns conspired with doctors and officials to take unfair profits, they were annoyed by intrusions of righteous people and tried in any way possible to keep travelers from attending the institute."[87]

With conditions in the United States and other countries becoming so inhospitable to the emigration of Japanese bachelors, Nagata felt that would-be emigrants needed to be prepared intellectually and physically to enter foreign societies. In 1924, he went so far as to open a "stowaway training school," where "students swam the four kilometers from Misaki to Jōgashima and back, carrying on their head packages of clothes wrapped in oiled paper."[88] While this was taking pre-embarkation preparation to the extreme, there was, more generally, a movement to target the pre-embarkation period for providing information to would-be travelers about the emigration process, and about the ships that would be carrying them.

With the Japanese government so involved in either sponsoring or facilitating emigration, it eventually began to regulate port-city boarding houses. "[O]fficials set standards for the rooms. To hold down costs for boarders the government put a limit on their stay in these houses, required that rates be approved by local authorities and clearly posted.... [T]he government divided boardinghouses into two classes with rates appropriate for each class."[89]

Until 1928, Kobe alone had eight *Imin-Yado* or "emigrant inns," two-story wooden building in the port area, each capable of housing one hundred emigrants. Yamada describes how emigrants filled their days, and how these inns may have provided essential services for those getting ready to depart.

Emigrants were very busy during their stay in Kobe. They had to obtain their own passports (which they had to apply for in their hometowns or prefectures), purchase their tickets, undergo physical inspections, get inoculated for diseases and checked for trachoma and hookworm, and have their baggage sterilized....Shipping companies designated the emigrant hotels as agents, and many of the health and medical procedures were taken care of by the hotels or the emigration companies.... Emigrants also had to procure articles for the duration of their ocean voyage. For emigrants, most of whom were farmers, it was the first time that they experienced such arduous days. The complexity of the experience taxed their bodies and minds.[90]

In 1928, a facility managed by the national government was opened in Kobe. Run by the Ministry of Foreign Affairs, the Kobe facility was a response to the private hotels' inability to handle properly the large number of emigrants destined for Brazil that were part of the national policy of encouraging emigration. This five-story concrete building became known as the "Imin-shūyōsho" or "National Emigration Center."

With fifty rooms housing twelve emigrants each, the Kobe facility could handle approximately the steerage capacity of an NYK or OSK ship on the South American run. Accommodations were purposefully designed to closely resemble steerage quarters; along with lectures about life aboard ship and in their new country, the intention was clearly to acclimate emigrants—largely rural folk— to their new circumstances. Emigrants were instructed, for instance, in what to bring with them on the ship:

1. A few sets of cotton work clothes with turned-down collar (dress shirts and neckties are unnecessary), shirts, pants, socks, Japanese-style clothes (sleeping clothes only), etc. It will be convenient for women to bring simple cotton Western-style clothes, boys to bring short pants, and girls to bring short skirts (*hakama*).

2. Women must bring *sarumata* (drawers) for themselves and underwear for their young children. (As women at that time did not use such underwear, this makeshift expression indicates that *sarumata* were encouraged for reasons of public morality rather than personal appearance.)

3. Hats. Men should bring caps, straw hats, or fedora. Women do not need hats.

4. Shoes. Men should have sturdy shoes that are similar to military shoes. Women should have low shoes (their socks should be long so as to not expose their legs).

5. Mosquito net, blankets, and *futon*. (These items are to be used after landing. They will be unnecessary on board because similar items are provided.)

6. Sleeping clothes should be *yukata*. Anything that has buttons or anything else that prevents the front from opening is acceptable.

7. Toiletries, kettle, tin eating utensils, knife, spoon, pots and pans, saw, hammer, hand towel, pocket knife, soap, paper, envelopes, toothpaste, tooth brush, scissors, razor, mirror, notebook, needles, thread, pen shaft and tip, pencil, etc.

8. A familiar farming implement that is easy to carry.[91]

Yamada notes that "Japanese clothing other than sleeping clothes was determined not to be necessary. In the Meiji and Taisho Periods, photos of men and women emigrants who went overseas show most of them wearing Japanese clothing, but from the end of the Taisho Period and into the Showa Period (i.e., circa 1920), the emigrants gradually switched over to Western style clothing."[92]

Harry S. Kawabe of Seattle tells of his getting outfitted for his 1906 crossing on the English ship *Salisbury*. "Western clothes were important after all, so I traveled in clothes given to me by my father's thirty-five-year-old cousin—a suit, a hat and a watch. Only about sixteen, here I was, dressed in the style of a middle aged-man. I must have cut a strange figure in the eyes of people who knew anything about fashion."[93]

Steerage Accommodations

Once they were on board, where did steerage passengers sleep? As one might expect, their actual accommodations changed over time. A white passenger aboard one of the early Pacific Mail transpacific steamers described the steerage accommodations:

> Except for a comparatively few door-less staterooms, these passengers slept in standee berths consisting of wooden frames over which canvas was stretched which were set up in open spaces within the ship. Their quarters were well-ventilated and the ship's officers saw that they were kept clean. Chinese steerage passengers usually stayed below decks, playing games of chance or lying in their berths....Deck space was provided for them, and in warm weather or at the time of meeting ships at sea they swarmed out into the open.[94]

Kemble's description of steerage conditions differs only in tone from a widely read popular account. An 1876 image in *Harper's Weekly*, "Chinese emigration to America, sketch on board the steamship *Alaska* bound for San Francisco," may have captured the flavor of steerage life aboard one of the Pacific Mail's 4,000-ton side-wheelers and, presumably, most steamships plying the Pacific. The *Harper's* reporter went on to describe the steerage accommodations at some length:

> Our double-page engraving represents a company of the Celestials [i.e., Chinese] on board the vessel *Alaska*, bound for San Francisco. The price of steerage passage from Hong-Kong to San Francisco is $50. This includes subsistence from port to port. The middle deck forward and amidships is fitted up with a framework, upon which comfortable stretchers are placed, each one provided with a canvas bottom. These are all single bunks. The emigrant, as a general thing, furnishes his own bedding or blankets, although when such things are wanting they are furnished by the ship. The food supplied consists of bountiful rations of soup, meat, and vegetables. Tea is regularly given out, and the water supply is, of course, abundant. The food is served in large earthen bowls, and, as every Chinaman carries his "chop-sticks," neither forks, knives, nor spoons are necessary. The emigrants are in charge of an agent of one of the companies, whose business it is to look after them during the voyage and deliver them safely at their destination. Whatever may be the truth in regard to these corporations, there is either good in them, or else they are so terribly

enslaving that remonstrance and protest are of no avail, for the parties most interested do not rebel or murmur against their arrangements.[95]

Although the references are to Chinese steerage passengers, comparable conditions were undoubtedly experienced by the first Japanese colonists coming to the U.S. mainland, who arrived in California on May 29, 1869 aboard the Pacific Mail's side-wheeler *China* from Yokohama. Note the reference to the social control mechanism, the "agent of one of the (Chinese) companies," referring to the labor brokers who recruited and transported Chinese laborers. This was not dissimilar to the social control that was later adopted by Japanese emigration companies aboard their ships. Both were rather different from conditions on the North Atlantic. There, ship brokers contracted for various amounts of square footage in steerage and endeavored to cram in as many of their "clients" as possible, leaving "discipline" to the captain and his crew. Schwendinger feels that this happened more frequently on the Pacific than is allowed for in the more optimistic view. Those who had made the journey knew the costs and benefits of "buying up." An anonymous Chinese traveler described the divisions this way:

> The richer ones spend more money on a better seat, which would cost about, I would say, three hundred dollars American money. This is first class. First class is about $350, $400. Then the second class runs about $250. Then there's semi... between second and third. The third one is way down in the bottom. You sleeping like dogs more or less. In big rooms you know, not much privacy. I was fortunate to get into what they called between second and third. That means you stay with about four or six people in one compartment, in double bunks.[96]

The appearance of the first Japanese ships, carrying contract laborers to Hawaii and to Peru and Brazil, brought about changes in steerage. Reactions to the accommodations in ships like the *Yamaguchi Maru*, which carried around two hundred passengers in steerage, are conveyed by Tokuji Hoshino in *Ikyō no Kyaku* ("Guest in a Strange Land," 1903):

> In this place, a cabin in name only that must also be seen as a mere cellar within the ship, pillows were lined up on shelves positioned around the room; it slept over a hundred. The rays of light that leaked in from some small round windows were, in terms of dimness, weaker than the light of twilight. Inside [the room], the color of the faces of the squirming people were pale and, surrounded by gloom, they halfheartedly endured the difficulties and the inevitable stench. Even I felt as though I had committed a crime and had been thrown into prison for life.[97]

Yamada further notes that "at the time of embarkation, Hoshino brought his own futon mattress, blanket, pillow and some type of sleepwear, and so we understand that in this period emigrants brought their own bedding materials."

Tatsuzō Ishikawa, in *Sōbō*, gives a description of steerage quarters in a Brazil-bound ship of the interwar period:

> The emigrants boarding the ship finally found the entrance to go downstairs to their assigned rooms after having wandered around on the deck with their carry on bags

for a while. When they went down, they saw five or six carbon lamps in the gigantic room. Along the perimeter of the room were double-decked rows of closely packed gratings shaped like birdcages. These were our beds. The room was divided into four sections and held 180 to 220 people.[98]

On the routes to North America, Japanese ships had steerage accommodations similar to what would later be adopted for their ships going to South America. An NYK guidebook for would-be passengers, printed in 1901, gives a rare glimpse below decks at sleeping arrangements in steerage. The beds pictured in the "third class steerage cabin" are much deeper than bunk beds, appearing to be about 6 ft. deep. One would think these suitable for families traveling together, but not for individuals traveling alone.

In general, NYK's ships to Seattle were smaller and less glamorous, and the conditions on board could be far from elegant, and they set the tone for many of the other lines. Heitaro Hikida told how he traveled from Hikone City (Shiga Prefecture) via Kobe to Seattle via Vancouver in 1907:

Figure 6.5
An idealized depiction of third-class (steerage) accommodations aboard a Japanese passenger ship, ca. 1904, shows an unlikely multinational group of Japanese, Chinese, and Caucasian passengers sharing an open room in steerage.

Source: Jokyaku Annai Yusen Zue by Shokoku Yamamoto; published in a 1906 special edition of the annual periodical, *Fuzoku Gaho*.

The English boat *Willwich* [actually the *Woolwich*], which I boarded appeared to be a former cargo boat pressed into service for passengers because of the transportation shortage.

As the boat was a freighter turned passenger boat, the miserable state of the third class cabins was beyond words. In the hold they had built wooden bunks in two rows like silkworm racks. As my little space was right below the airvent pipe, it was awfully cold when the ocean wind blew through. Not knowing anything else to do, I put my straw hat over the hole.[99]

The *Anyō Maru*, designed specifically for carrying Japanese and Chinese emigrants to Peru, set the tone for the next stage in the evolution of steerage accommodations. Following the *Anyō Maru*, many of the Japanese ships on the long routes to South America switched over from two-tiered, dormitory-style bunk beds to the "silkworm shelf" bed model pictured in Figure 6.5. This innovation seems not to have been adopted by non-Japanese lines on the routes to North America.

Food on Board

Along with entertainment and sightseeing at ports of call, food is one of the three major attractions in modern cruise ships. Such things were important in the age of mass migration, too, even though passenger ships like the *Nippon Maru* (built for speed and comfort) and emigrant ships like the *Anyō Maru* (which carried people more as cargo than as passengers) were as different as night and day. For all passengers, the three daily meals (or more, in the case of leisure cruises or first- and second-class travels) did more than sustain the body; they spiced up onboard life and helped pass the time.

A first-cabin meal was—and still is—something of an event, a spectacle not necessarily reproducible in daily life. Steerage fare was something else entirely. It was meant to be adequate, but reduced to the bare essentials. What constituted "the bare essentials" changed over time. The 1876 description of steerage fare on the Pacific Mail's *Alaska* (quoted above) notwithstanding, it is widely thought that steerage meals (at least before 1945) were anywhere from poor to terrible. There is certainly much anecdotal evidence to support this view. Yamada describes the meals given to the first contingents of Japanese contract laborers migrating to Brazil as "poor and basic." They had barley, fish, pickles, and sometimes *miso* soup. The emigrants usually ate in bed or on the floor, even though a small dining room was provided for them. A gong sounded at mealtime.[100]

Even on the North American route, there is a presumption that the food in steerage was generally unpalatable. Heitaro Hikida described his 1907 journey from the Kobe to Vancouver on the *Woolwich*:

The stewards, cooks and boys who served the Japanese passengers were all Japanese. The cooks and boys for the higher class crewmen such as the officers were Chinese,

Figure 6.6

A game of fan-tan takes place aboard the Pacific Mail's *China*. According to the accompanying article, such games were one of the few places where people of all classes and races could mix socially aboard ship.

Source: San Francisco Call, November 6, 1898.

as were the lower-class crewmen such as boatswains, stokers, carpenter, and pilot.... As for the menu, all three meals were Japanese. I remember that the soup served every morning contained only two or three small pieces of dried tofu (bean curd) and was watery and tasteless. Anyway, the meals were of the poorest quality. Not only were the meals bad, but we didn't eat in the dining room. Bowls, cups and dishes were issued to us at the beginning and we kept them throughout the trip, eating in the bunkrooms.[101]

Fare surely varied from ship to ship, but Harry Kawabe had a similar experience in 1906 on the *Salisbury*, traveling from Yokohama to Seattle: "The cooks and the ship's boys were Chinese, and every day we had curry rice only. The Chinese came around selling sweet bean cakes and a sweet, pasty soup."[102]

Fare on the Canadian ships was not much better. Hong Len Jung traveled in steerage on the *Empress of India* in 1912. As a fifteen-year-old, he found the long journey tedious.

> There was rice—not very tasty—just all stirred up together in a wok. You were never full because they, the Chinese crew, wanted you to buy from them. Those sailors sold rice to us with Chinese sausage, salted duck eggs. They never made good food for us for the regular meals. Your regular meal was 5–6:00 p.m. They, the sailors, would sell you their food around 10:00 at night. That was the good food. The Chinese cooks and sailors saved the food and took it from the ship's stores to sell to us. They charged us 20 cents a bowl.[103]

A description of the first dinner after leaving Kobe, which appears in the historical novel *Sōbō*, sums up the general view of meals in the pre–World War II era:

> At 5:00 p.m., the first meal began in all the rooms. In the center of each room there was a large hatch hole. A board was used to cover the hole. Tables were arranged on this cover and wooden benches placed along them for people sit on. This was the cafeteria. The passengers in each room were divided into three groups to eat in shifts. The meal consisted of a slice of salted fish, a clump of spinach, and boiled barley and rice.[104]

Maritime historian Michio Yamada, who originally shared this low opinion of steerage cuisine, has revised his view, concluding that—at least on Japanese ships in the years after World War I—it was, at a minimum, tolerable. The cooking staff on the principal Japanese ships created food supply manuals to prevent the volume and quality of the meals from being different from voyage to voyage. Below are examples from such a manual, indicating a concern with providing meals along the lines that Yamada describes.

To anyone accustomed to Japanese food, there is nothing repugnant in these menus, especially if the hinted-at variety actually materializes over the course of a thirty- to sixty-day voyage. Remembering his family's experience of emigrating from Japan to Brazil in the 1930s, painter Manabu Manabe felt that eating this sort of earthy, familiar "comfort food" also served to ease the pain of leaving one's homeland.

> Meals were also something we looked forward to. We were summoned with a gong that was similar to those used at educational institutions. When it was time, it went "*jaan.*" Probably for sanitation reasons, no fish was bought at ports-of-call and there were a

SAMPLE STEERAGE MENU[105]

KANAGAWA MARU (NYK line), eastbound voyages

Breakfast

(1) Dried sardines, lotus root cooked Korean style, *miso* soup (radish, fried tofu), pickled radish, *ume*, steamed wheat/rice
(2) Small salmonid (ayu) cooked in sweet sauce, wakame (brown algae)/ fried tofu in vinegar sauce, *miso* soup (ground soy beans, green onion), pickled radish, *ume*, steamed wheat/rice
(3) Quail bean cooked in sweet sauce, salted salmon, dried squid in sweet sauce, *miso* soup (radish, fried tofu), pickled radish, *ume*, steamed wheat/rice

****

Lunch

(1) Tuna teriyaki, grated radish, bamboo shoots cooked in sweet sauce, pickled radish, *ume*, steamed wheat/rice
(2) Broiled salted baby sea bream, preserved turnip, pickled radish, *ume*, steamed wheat/rice
(3) *Tamago tōfu-pudding, kinpira gobō* (burdock roots and carrots stir-fried with sugar and soy sauce), pickled radish, pickled ginger root, steamed wheat/rice

****

Dinner

(1) Beef cooked with Chinese cabbage in sweetened soy sauce, soup broth made with fish bones, pickled radish, *ume*, rice cooked with azuki beans
(2) Fried buckwheat noodles with beef, clear broth (Sea bream, kelp), pickled radish, *ume*, steamed wheat/rice
(3) Beef curry, clear broth (sliced fish, Chinese cabbage), preserved radish, vegetable preserved in *miso* sauce, steamed rice with chopped vegetables

lot of dishes using pickled mackerel. The *zenzai* (sugared bean soup with rice cakes) we had for snacks was sweet and tasty.[106]

Yamada also traveled on postwar emigration ships and experienced this sort of cuisine first hand, describing it as "unexpectedly good."

My opinion from looking at the menus is that they were typical of the era's middle class households. Moreover, the emigrants were likely to be farmers who barely made a living in their home villages and whose meals had been frugal. The onboard meals consisted of Japanese food and featured simple dishes and pickled vegetables. Nutritionally speaking, they were balanced meals. The staple was a boiled mix of one-fifth barley and four-fifths rice. This combination was served to prevent beriberi. In any case, people in the olden days ate a lot of rice.[107]

Food served by the ship could be supplemented with purchases from the ship's store. Japanese emigrants to South America had been instructed to bring "carry-on items," which included personal items and food:

> Since the ship gets wet, it is desirable to have at least one pair of rubber-soled slippers, leather-soled slippers, or rubber shoes. A water jug, bucket, wash basin, and an aluminum or enameled container for boiling water will be needed on the ship. Further, it is also advantageous to prepare enough *umeboshi* (salted and pickled plums) *shiokonbu* (salted seaweed), sugar, and long-lasting snacks for children (e.g. dried candy, biscuits, drops, etc.). There is also a store on board.[108]

Stores aboard ship, and more generally the practice of selling goods to steerage passengers, were targets of complaints in the early days. Emigrants frequently felt that the stores were selling inferior, unsanitary, or overpriced goods. After initially allowing the crews to run the stores as concessions, both OSK and NYK eventually operated the stores directly and forbade their crews to sell goods.

Safety

An incident that befell the *Empress of China* in 1911 typified one of the risks associated with traveling in steerage. As she neared the coast of Japan she struck a reef. Water began to flood the forward holds and the ship developed a two degree list to starboard. Closing the watertight doors controlled the flooding and the crew began to evacuate the passengers.

The process, however, affected the 35 passengers in cabin class differently from the 150 in steerage. The former were served breakfast, then taken off by Japanese fishermen. But deep in the bowels of the ship, the situation provoked panic among some of those in steerage. Order was restored only when the ship's officers displayed their revolvers, and only then were the steerage passengers finally transferred to shore—four hours after the cabin passengers.[109]

Health and Hygiene

The health of Asians traveling in steerage was a major preoccupation of those involved in the migration business—passengers and shipowners, of course, but the receiving countries as well. In the United States, there was a long history of "medical scapegoating" on both coasts, a phenomenon that did not lessen even when steam replaced sail and reduced travel times. On the East Coast, public health failures were blamed successively on the Irish, then the Italians, then East European Jews.[110] On the West Coast, the Chinese had long been blamed for outbreaks of everything from cholera to typhoid fever to syphilis. Writing in

1876, one San Francisco physician noted: "The Chinese were the focus of Caucasian animosities, and they were made responsible for mishaps in general. A destructive earthquake would probably be charged to their account."[111]

Conditions aboard incoming ships, especially tramps, could be wretched, and newspaper reporting often reflected white San Franciscans' fear of contagion from foreigners. In 1882, just as the Chinese Exclusion Act was being signed, a series of ships brought hundreds of Chinese to San Francisco who had been exposed to smallpox. As the *San Francisco Examiner* reported, the

> steamer *Strathairly*, which arrived Sunday, thirty-four days from Hongkong, with a cargo of 813 Chinese, had shown that it was the dirtiest vessel that has come from China for years. The filth and excrement had accumulated during the entire passage, and at present it is impossible to board the ship without becoming covered with it. The wooden houses on the decks had been destroyed while at sea and thrown overboard. In consequence, all of the Chinese are forced to go below, and the hold is greatly overcrowded. The ship will have to be cleaned, fumigated, and whitewashed....The water closets were made of common sail cloth, and such had been the accumulation of filth and dirt that it was necessary to wear gum boots while making the inspection.[112]

Much of the American legislation regulating the transporting of immigrants was aimed at improving health conditions on board so as to prevent the arrival of disease on American shores. Another line of defense against microbial invaders was inspection at the port of arrival. At New York's Ellis Island, inspectors were hard-pressed to inspect the thousands of arriving immigrants—frequently 5,000 a day, with 16,209 passengers arriving one record day in 1907. A busy day left doctors but two minutes for each patient or, as one doctor put it, about "six seconds per eyelid."[113] Although handling nowhere near the traffic that came through New York, the Quarantine Station on Angel Island played a similar role for San Francisco.

But even this defense was not thought stout enough to protect the United States from invading contagious diseases brought by immigrants. Typhus and cholera epidemics on the East Coast, attributed to East European Jewish immigrants, frightened the American public into supporting the National Quarantine Act of February 15, 1893. The President was granted power to (among other things) post officers of the Marine Hospital Service to the U.S. consulates in foreign ports. Every vessel leaving for the United States was to have its cargo and passengers inspected, and the "consular bill of health" presented to the Collector of Customs on arrival in the United States.[114]

This "Disease Early Warning" system in the Pacific saw Sanitary Inspectors attached to the U.S. consulates in Yokohama, Manila, Honolulu, and various ports in China. Their reports on local health conditions included developments that might affect ships and people traveling to the U.S. mainland: outbreaks of disease, the thoroughness of predeparture inspections by the local health establishment, and the effectiveness of the disinfection of ships bound for the United States.

Health authorities on the American mainland would pay special attention to any vessel arriving from a port where, say, plague, meningitis, or cholera had broken out and where the isolation and disinfection processes were known to be inadequate.

Dr. Stuart Eldridge, the American Sanitary Inspector in Yokohama, stated the case crisply in his report of October 1899:

> The position of Yokohama renders it, in some sense, the sanitary gateway of the Far East. Through this port passes all the travel from China, that center of infection, where epidemics rage with little or no effort made for their control, where plague and cholera seem to have become endemic and small pox, ever present. . . . Through it or from it go, too, all the Japanese passengers for United States ports in numbers already large and steadily increasing. . . . Precautions of the most stringent character on the part of the United States seem fully warranted. It was, undoubtedly, a knowledge of these facts that induced you in 1894 to appoint a representative of the Bureau at this point.[115]

As American Sanitary Inspectors had little in the way of resources, they had limited leverage in getting local authorities to act according to American standards when it came to inspecting and disinfecting ships bound for the United States. At best, they could exert two forms of economic leverage on the steamship companies. Passengers denied entry at the U.S. ports would be returned to their country of origin at the steamship line's expense. Holding a ship in quarantine at a U.S. port would inconvenience not only its passengers but its cargo as well: delay and the possibility of spoilage from fumigation were incentives to merchants at both ends to strengthen predeparture health precautions. Passengers from the Japanese interior, for instance, were inoculated and quarantined if coming from a known area of infection, then inspected and their passport or ticket stamped before being allowed to board a ship headed directly to an American port. Ships originating in Yokohama were inspected by the resident *American* Sanitary Inspector and, if passed, given a consular bill of health. The same was true for ships originating in China or the Philippines. "Should any sickness of suspicious nature exist on board at arrival at Yokohama, (the Sanitary Inspector will) immediately visit the vessel, *irrespective of the fact that she has successfully passed the Japanese inspector of quarantine*, afterwards acting according to the circumstances."[116]

The American government's obsession with transpacific hygiene was shared by other nations. The government of independent Hawaii stationed sanitary inspectors in Hong Kong, Amoy, Nagasaki, Kobe, and Yokohama. They feared that Chinese and Japanese laborers coming to work on the plantations would bring infections with them, and upon arrival all Asian laborers were subjected to "from fourteen to twenty-one days' detention at the quarantine station on Mauliola Island, where their clothing and baggage is disinfected."[117] A quarantine station was maintained near Victoria for incoming ships from Asia bound for Canadian ports on the Pacific.

While it is unlikely that other Western Hemisphere countries stationed sanitary inspectors abroad, there were collective efforts to alert receiving countries about unfavorable health conditions along international migration routes. For instance, in 1928 the League of Nations office in Singapore sent out a worldwide alert about a cholera outbreak in Saigon, a city visited by Japanese ships on their way to Brazil, and this warning was transmitted by the Japanese government to its ships at sea.

Even if a receiving country's health laws were less stringent than those of Canada or the United States, the Japanese government insisted that, at least on Japanese ships, its emigrants be protected by having a doctor present. The Chinese government had virtually no control over ships leaving its ports, and whatever health protections afforded to the Chinese steerage passengers were those provided by non-Chinese carriers out of self-interest. As with the "coolie ships" surgeons, whose presence was required by the British colonial authorities in India, ship doctors varied in their competence and in their ability to protect the passengers' health in the face of the imperatives of a ship's progress and profit.

It is not clear when it became common practice for passenger ships to have a sick bay. I suspect that this happened at the very end of the nineteenth century, perhaps coinciding with the advent of Federal health controls described above, and certainly well before 1930, when American law finally made it obligatory to provide one. Although in the U.S. Public Health Service's *Annual Reports* "there seems to be little evidence...that there was a ship doctor on board by custom or law,"[118] there is good reason to believe that having a physician on board became common at around the same time. Customs Service examinations of scheduled passenger ships arriving at San Francisco in 1918 indicated that every ship had at least one physician on board.[119] Some combination of competition between shipping lines and government regulation on both sides of the Pacific led to facilities designed and equipped to provide passengers and crew with medical attention. Deck plans for the CPR's ships reveal something of the timing of the evolution to providing more professional medical care on board. In 1891, the *Empress* ships (*India, China, and Japan*), built expressly for the Asian market, had no facilities dedicated to handling health or medical issues. Twenty years later, the new *Empress of Russia* and *Empress of Asia* both had such facilities. Aft on the shelter deck were several rooms next to the laundry: an embalming room, mortuary, an infections hospital, and the men's hospital.[120] The *Arabia Maru*, a less glamorous ship used by OSK on the Seattle run from 1918 to 1931, had a sick bay. The *Anyō Maru*, designed to carry immigrants on the long haul to South America, similarly had separate sick bays for men (capacity of five) and for women (capacity of three) in the stern. There was a drawback to putting the sick rooms in the stern, as the pronounced pitching and vibrations from the propeller shaft made for a poor location for medical treatment. Having them there would, however, help isolate people with infectious diseases. Later emigrant ships were similarly laid out, and in the *Santos Maru* class, the sick bays were situated aft on the less-remote boat deck.[121]

Steerage accommodations had long been associated with disease. And not only in the popular imagination, American health authorities routinely exempted cabin-class passengers from any but the most cursory health examinations, while subjecting steerage passengers to more detailed inspections.[122] In 1903, an American physician stationed at Yokohama explained that only "steerage aliens" were manually inspected for trachoma as "the aversion of eyelids essential for the diagnosis of trachoma, would, if practiced upon cabin passengers, be likely to embarrass the work of the Service here."[123] There was a long-held bias in favor of the "better classes" that traveled in cabin accommodations, but occasionally a bit of quasi-scientific evidence emerged to reinforce such notions. The Anyō Maru incident described below is a good example: on returning to Balboa its passengers were tested to see if they were meningococcus carriers; 22 percent of steerage passengers tested positive, yet none of the first-class passengers—well isolated from the others—were infected.

In the days of sail, steerage accommodations may well have been the cause of much disease. This would have been especially true in the coerced migrations of the "coolie ships" taking Chinese laborers to Cuba or the Chincha Islands off Peru. Overcrowded and virtually imprisoned in the hold, the "coolies" were subjected to conditions clearly hazardous to their health, including attacks of panic, violence against each other or the crew, and fires set to get them allowed on deck. A diet of rice, salt fish, and tea produced nutritional deficiencies on the long voyages under sail.

Under steam, which markedly shortened travel times, it is more likely that diseases simply walked aboard with the passengers. Steerage accommodations were not infrequent conveyors of diseases of the respiratory tract, including pneumonia and influenza. In 1890, cerebrospinal fever joined the list, breaking out on a ship transporting "coolies" from Calcutta to British Guiana. There was another outbreak of cerebrospinal fever in 1918, this time on the Anyō Maru: it had carried 500 Japanese and 100 Chinese steerage passengers, stopping in Hong Kong (where a major outbreak of cerebrospinal fever was in progress), Japan, San Francisco, San Diego, and Salina Cruz (Mexico) before arriving in Balboa. The passengers, who had been aboard ship for over a month, were also variously afflicted with beriberi, influenza, pneumonia, and acute rheumatism. By the time the Anyō Maru reached Callao, Peru, two weeks later, the cerebrospinal fever had reached the point where Peruvian health authorities refused clearance, sending the Anyō Maru back to quarantine at Balboa. There were three deaths among the steerage passengers.[124]

Recall that one of the National Emigration Center's primary functions was to assure, both to the emigrants and to their host countries, the good health of those going overseas. Thus, it was ironic that among the very first group of emigrants processed at the Kobe facility, traveling on the Hawaii Maru, seventeen should die from of an outbreak of cholera—brought aboard, it was suspected, when the ship called at Saigon.

While the Japanese government and its licensed emigration companies seem to have made significant efforts to promote personal hygiene and to have adequate medical facilities on emigration ships, health catastrophes did occur. In "Epidemic Outbreaks," Yamada touches on three such incidents, including the one involving the *Hawaii Maru*. The worst occurred in 1918 aboard the *Wakasa Maru*, sailing from Kobe via Singapore to Santos, Brazil, with 1,800 passengers. By the time the ship reached Singapore, one passenger was already dead from cerebral meningitis, and the ship was denied entry. Although the captain was for returning to Kobe, he was persuaded to continue to Brazil. By the time the ship reached Santos, fifty-three people were dead. What made this doubly scandalous were the NYK's efforts to stifle accurate reports of the event.[125] On the whole, however, Yamada implies such catastrophes were kept to a minimum by the Japanese government's requirements that ships have adequate medical personnel, sick bays, and even birthing facilities.

Despite these precautions, there were many instances of diseases making their way eastward across the Pacific. Anecdotal evidence abounds, especially in the reportage of San Francisco's daily newspapers, which avidly covered the immigration scene. The first ship sent to the Quarantine Station on Angel Island after it opened was the *China*, in April 1891, which arrived from Hong Kong carrying two cases of smallpox. Nearly a decade later, bubonic plague arrived on a ship (Marilyn Chase accuses the *Australia* as the guilty vessel, a supposition unsupported by evidence[126]), as described above and in the chapter on the *Nippon Maru*.

Life Below Decks

Life above decks in first class was undoubtedly grand. Or at least full of diversions and opportunities for socializing. Surveying the passenger lists and photographs in steamship publications, one is struck by the multinational, multiracial nature of the body of cabin passengers. Though Americans predominated, there was always a leavening of Chinese, Japanese, and other Asians and Europeans. Assuming that the class composition of those with cabin accommodations was similar to that on the North Atlantic, then the ambience described in Brinnin's *The Sway of the Grand Saloon* may well have been replicated on the Pacific. The activities for cabin-class passengers would be familiar to those on modern cruise ships—"seven meals a day," opportunities for bridge in the clubroom, bathing in the salt water tank, deck golf, deck baseball, deck tennis, exhibitions of *kendo* and *sumo* (at least on the TKK's ships), a movie in the ballroom.[127] Illustrations in NYK's 1906 guide for passengers, *Jokyaku Annai Yusen Zue*, certainly give the impression of "the Grand Saloon."

In general the cabin-class passengers were kept apart from those in steerage, especially on the glamour runs from San Francisco, Seattle, or Vancouver to Japan and China. Robert Louis Stevenson noted a similar convention on the North Atlantic, where it was considered "a gross breach of the etiquette of sea life, and a shocking exhibition of bad manners and low inquisitiveness, for passengers to visit unasked the quarters of an inferior class."[128] This generally applied to the on-deck airing and promenade areas as well as to the dining and sleeping accommodations. The *Empress of Russia* and the *Empresses of Asia* of the CPR, for example, allowed steerage passengers a small "airing space" aft on the shelter deck, but located next to the hospital, mortuary, and embalming room—and separated from the second class promenade by a steel bulkhead.[129]

Segregation by class occasionally broke down, of course. Jack London's 1904 photos of passengers and crew of the Pacific Mail's *Siberia* show "Chinese, Japanese and Caucasian passengers at the railing...[in] traditional and modern wearing apparel."[130] Clearly these are steerage passengers mixing with cabin-class passengers, gazing out over the ocean as they while away the long hours. And occasionally, cabin passengers dropped down to watch the "entertainment of the Oriental passengers," as shown in a photograph of a wrestling match included in a TKK passenger's notebook of a 1915 trip on the *Shinyo Maru*, "From San Francisco to the Orient."[131]

From the passenger's point of view, a successful trip depended on having enough of everything—food, drink, space, and activities. From the ship operator's point of view, establishing order among a large number of steerage passengers was essential. This was especially true on the seemingly endless journeys from Japan to Brazil or to Peru. On Japanese ships, social control was maintained through "self-governing" committees (*sennai jichi han*) formed jointly by the ship's crew and by the emigration companies that had recruited the passengers. Asserting such control began in the emigrant hostels and was reinforced by instructions given to passengers when they boarded:

> During the long period of time living on board, which can range from 44 to 56 or 57 days, because you are unaccustomed to sea travel and also because we will pass through tropical regions, much care must be taken with hygiene. We serve boiled barley and rice to prevent beriberi and for your health, so you should not complain. You need to be especially careful regarding gastrointestinal disorders that arise from lack of exercise, beriberi, contagious diseases from ports-of-call, and children's measles. Make an effort to keep regular habits, get enough exercise, keep good hygiene, and refrain from excessive eating and drinking. At ports-of-call, avoid buying food or drink. Be also careful about your dress and behavior so as to not invite the ridicule of foreigners. A transport supervisor and his assistant will be onboard (and) we need everyone's cooperation in following the instructions of the supervisor and the ship's crew. During the voyage, there will be primary school classes, language lessons, sports competitions, variety shows, an equator crossing ceremony, and other activities. Further, since you will be able to go sightseeing at ports-of-call, the long voyage will seem to end in a matter of days.[132]

The supervisor from the emigration company controlled the initial setup of the self-governing committees. He convened a meeting of all the heads of households as soon as the ship left port, during which they met the ship's officers and crew, were briefed by the ship's doctor, and were instructed in the use of toilets, the schedule for bathing and laundry, and rules for conserving water. The supervisor designated room leaders (*kumicho*) and assistant room leaders for each steerage compartment.

Additionally, a youth group (*seinendan*) and a women's auxiliary (*fujinkai*) were established as work details. Officers of these organizations below the level of president were elected: the contact officer, sports officer, variety show officer, education officer, onboard newspaper officer, hygiene officer, public morals officer, surveillance officer, and meal service officer.[133]

These groups would meet daily, either in the steerage dining area on OSK ships or, on NYK ships, in the *tatami*-covered resting room or around the hatch covers. During those meetings, they would organize the many activities described below.

Managing Water

These modern mariners were all confronted with the ancient problem of "water everywhere, but not a drop to drink." This was, of course, true on the extraordinarily long distances covered by ships going from Japan and China by way of South Africa, but it was also a problem on the crossings from Japan to North America. Heitaro Hikida's recollection was that in 1907,

> On board the [*Woolwich*] they prepared a bath every evening. However, it was not fresh water but water pumped out of the ocean and heated. We could not wash our bodies as we do when we use fresh water because the skin would sting. They gave us one dipper of fresh water when we got out of the tub. This could be used for rinsing off our skin, or we could rub the salt-water off with our small dampened towels. Not only that: Only 50 or 60 of the people could take a bath in one evening, and that means that we could bathe only twice a week.[134]

One of the principal responsibilities of the self-governing group was to enforce discipline around the use of freshwater. The routes to South America, and especially those to Brazil, involved long stretches between port calls, and as evaporators and desalinators were not in general use, it was imperative that the ship's supply of freshwater be conserved. Ships' rules included such admonitions as

"Treat each drop as you would one *sen*" [Treat water like money]

"A drop of lingering water is a drop of a *sen*"

"A ship has neither a well nor a spring"[135]

Until World War II , Japan's "Ship Inspection Bylaws" required two *sho* (3.6 liters) of fresh drinking water per person per day. By way of comparison, English law required one British gallon (4.5 liters) per person per day on ships departing England. But that was just for drinking. Fresh water was also needed for washrooms, laundry rooms, showers, and kitchens. NYK's experience on the

Brazil route was that each person actually required about 36 liters of fresh water per day. With over 900 people on board, for ships like the *Santos Maru*, normal daily consumption would be over thirty tons of water—for a ship whose fresh-water tank held but 406 tons.

Where Japanese standards of cleanliness confronted the ships' limited water supply it created problems, solutions to which were largely enforced by the self-governing committees. One solution was for steerage passengers to use seawater for most bathing and for toilets. Another was to restrict the hours for bathing, or the amount of fresh water one could use. Some ships issued tickets good for a fixed volume of water, while others simply limited the number of times one could bathe to two or three times per week. On Japanese ships traveling to Brazil through the intense heat of the low latitudes, this presented a hardship for many passengers, although rules were relaxed on special days such as sports festivals or cultural events.[136]

Leisure Activities

Life in steerage had its own rhythms and its own sets of activities distinct from those of travelers in cabin class. These activities differed, too, by the nature of the destination and the length of the voyage. Even in 1916, the voyage from Hong Kong to San Francisco took four weeks (two and a half weeks from Yokohama)—a long time to be cooped up. Activities were primarily a way of passing time. A traveler going from Yokohama to Seattle in 1908 found the *Aki Maru*

> crowded with passengers. About thirty of them were first and second class, and about 300 non-immigrants and 30 immigrants made up the third class, where I was.... During the 16 days from Yokohama to Seattle, talent shows were held on board. People applauded the *noh* singing, popular songs, *shigin* (the chanting of Chinese poems) and *biwa* (Japanese guitar) solos, as well as Japanese dramas. The boat boiled with youthful activity.[137]

On the North Pacific runs, one of the most popular below-decks diversions was " [g]ambling, such as Fan Tan, which began as soon as the meals were finished, was a major activity for many on board. For those uninterested in gambling there was sleep, conversation and walking in the limited deck space reserved for the steerage passengers."[138] Harry Kawabe recalls that when he crossed in 1906 on the *Salisbury*, from Yokohama to Seattle, "On deck they played a Chinese gambling game called *shiko* (*fan-tan*). Japanese people at that time, especially the victorious veterans, looked down on the Chinese, calling them '*chankoro*.' When *shiko* began, the Japanese went around recruiting players, but every time it was the Japanese who lost."[139]

Fan-tan was one of the few activities where steerage passengers might rub shoulders with swells from cabin class. An 1899 article in the *San Francisco Call* described a voyage from San Francisco to Hong Kong on the *China* in which "there were three games of fan-tan going night and day." Games were not part of the ship's formal program of entertainment, but rather were run as private enterprises by various members of the ship's crew. The captain's "boy" (steward) and saloon staff ran one; coal passers another; and Chinese members of the boatswain's crew a third. Although the latter was "Chinese only" (meaning crew and steerage passengers), the first two were open to all.

A drawing accompanying the story captures some of the multicultural, class division-crossing nature of the games, as do the sub-headlines "Passengers and Crew Rub Elbows in Their Zeal to Play the Games" and "Chinese Sailors, Stripped to the Waist, Crowd Around, and the Soldiers, Missionaries, Globe-trotters and Other Travelers are Tempted to Take a Hand."[140]

Several sources indicate that most ships carrying Chinese immigrants had some space set aside for opium smoking. Kooiman says of the mammoth *Minnesota* and *Dakota* that, "following the custom of the times and for the pleasure of Chinese addicts, a small space labeled "The Opium Den" was reserved for this use."[141] Yamada, too, is quite explicit about opium smoking on ships carrying emigrants. In discussing ships on the North Pacific run to San Francisco, he says that in the Chinese section there were also smoking room facilities called the "opium den." Such facilities were also established in public rooms for use by the Chinese on passenger ships between China and Nagasaki.[142] He adds that on "TKK's passenger ships the atmosphere was traditionally one of warm hospitality toward the Chinese passengers. An opium den-style opium smoking room was furnished in the *Tenyo Maru* class steerage for Chinese passengers, but naturally the *Anyo Maru*, like the other, lesser ships on the South America run, had none."[143]

The early *Empresses* of the CPR also had opium smoking rooms, designated "steerage smoking room" aft on the main deck. Such rooms appear on the deck plan of the *Empresses of India, Japan,* and *China.* The deck plan of the *Empress of Russia,* built in 1913, clearly shows an "Opium Smoking Room" in the steerage section forward on the main deck.[144]

For many Chinese headed to the United States, the long journey was a last opportunity to study their "coaching books." Such books were prepared by professional writers, largely for the benefit of "paper sons" and others who needed to memorize a new life story, including the names of their ("paper" or bogus) relatives, the details of the village they were supposedly from, and the answers to the myriad questions of the sort that Immigration Inspectors put to Quok Shee and Chew Hoy Quong. Many migrants—even those legally entitled to enter—relied on such books to get them through the dreaded interrogation by Immigration Service officers responsible for enforcing the Chinese exclusion laws.

Occasionally the study time was devoted to practicing the language needed in the immigrants' new home—occasionally with curious results. Traveling in 1908 from Yokohama to Seattle, Saburo Hirata of Kobe observed

> A certain gentleman from Hiroshima Prefecture who had apparently studied in advance, explained the American situation in detail to us all, saying that he had no difficulty with English conversation. One day we saw him talking with a white

lady who was taking a walk on the top deck. He was frantically using gestures, while the lady grimaced and finally reproved him by saying, in perfect Japanese, "You aren't making any sense. Study English more!"[145]

An even greater inventiveness would be needed to fill the time on the long runs to South America. For those headed to Peru or Brazil, where trips could last up to two months, a significant amount of time was devoted to getting ready for life in their country of destination. Most Japanese emigrants traveled under the aegis of an emigration company, one that had incentives to get its "clients" safely to their destination and to prepare them for their new country. Classes devoted to acquiring language skills or learning about the new country's culture were occasionally held on deck or, in the case of OSK ships, in the third class dining saloon.

> Among education activities, the most serious consideration was the...establishment of the ship's elementary school. Classes were held in the morning. Among the emigrants there were often people with teaching experience who were able to guide children. For adults, there were short lectures on Portuguese and on the conditions of their destination. The women's group held courses on cooking and western dressmaking.[146]

Emigrants also organized themselves to provide classes for adults and for children. Another regular activity was *Kokumin* exercises, roughly comparable

Figure 6.7
Language lesson aboard a Japanese ship bound for Brazil, early in the Taisho period (1912–26), was one of many activities fostering group cohesion and preparing emigrants for life in a new land.

Source: Photo from the collection of Michio Yamada.

to today's exercise videos, the daily exercises which children did in the morning and adults after dinner, both taking place on the rear deck. On postwar emigrant ships, the daily exercises took place after everyone got up.

On the long journeys to South America, social control was exercised over the steerage passengers at all times. The "Onboard Regulations" in Kaigai Kogyo's *Toko Annai* (Voyage Guide) warned passengers to follow the orders of the emigration company's supervisor when they disembarked at ports of call. The Japanese Ministry of Foreign Affairs allowed emigrants to go ashore unless the local port of call authorities refused them permission to land or if it was known that the port had suffered an outbreak of an infectious disease. Since it was believed that emigrants (especially those going to South America) were not used to traveling and would be prone to getting lost or into trouble, the Ministry gave detailed instructions for the emigrants to follow when they disembarked and encouraged them to move about in groups.

Logs of emigrant ships traveling from Japan to Brazil via Singapore and Cape Town show that it was not unusual for passengers to be confined to the ship in the face of local outbreaks of disease. This was a blow to passenger morale: while the primary purpose of port calls was to take on cargo, fuel, and supplies, they also relieved the tension and tedium of the two-month journey to Brazil.[147]

Aboard any ship, one nearly universal activity is celebrating the crossing of the equator, and Japanese emigrant ships both before and after World War I were no exception. On such vessels the celebration included a short play called "The Dragon King" that had Neptune give the ship's captain the key to the gates of the equator. After the dragon king performance, a masquerade line of emigrants and crew formed and paraded.[148] On postwar emigrant ships, dinner on the day of the "Crossing the Line" festival was held on deck. On the menu was Argentinean *asado*, a South American–style barbecue. The rustic charm of meals on deck is carried on even now by the cooking staffs of OSK (today's Shosen Mitsui) passenger ships—a meal that Yamada reports eating with great gusto when he went on a long cruise with them. Though it was customary to hold an *Engeikai* (entertainment by emigrants and crew members), after the on-deck dinner, there was no special event on the night of the Equator Crossing Festival on prewar emigrant ships.

A variety show was held on a different day. Organized by the entertainment chairperson of the *Seinendan* (Youth Group), it had none of the exotic, Western flavor of the Equator Crossing Festival that the emigrants were not completely comfortable with. Rather, the variety show, like the sports festival, was something intimately familiar. In *Sōbō*, the variety show was held when the ship passed the island of Madagascar. A passenger described the event:

> The sound of drumming and singing from the morning of the day that the variety show was held made it feel as if we were on a pleasure cruise of entertainers. From the afternoon, under the direction of the culture committee, the *Seinendan* officers built a stage and a *hanamichi* (a passageway to and from the stage to the backstage)

on D deck (author's note: this was above the fourth hatch). By 6:00 p.m. when the show began, a large audience of emigrants formed in front of the stage. Even the first class guests came down to see the show. The purser and the chief engineer also were present. The doctor, forsaking his malnutrition and pleurisy patients, also came with two nurses.[149]

The show included various performances ranging from children's skits and songs, sword dances, *Yasugi-bushi* and *Yagi-bushi* (local and comical dances with song), and *Nagauta* (lyrical *Kabuki* song). Among the emigrants, who had come from all over Japan, were those who sang the folk songs of their home regions. As there are photographs of emigrants clearly dressed in Okinawan style, we can assume that Okinawan cultural activities were presented along with those of the main Japanese islands.

On most emigration ships going to Brazil, there seemed to be no lack of entertainers. Some were quite talented, perhaps prompting those watching to think it was a waste for them to immigrate to South America. In *Sōbō*, there is the following exchange between the Director and the emigrant supervisor:

"It's a shame to send them into the boondocks of Brazil, isn't it? They could make a living if we put them in the Tokyo vaudeville."

"I guess. But if we did that, we'd have our hands full on the next ship with Tokyo entertainers."[150]

Among the more popular special events were the sports festivals and plays. The sports festivals on the postwar route to Peru were held when the ships passed the region off Acapulco, which on the Brazil route were held after the ships left Singapore, often around Colombo. The sports festivals included footraces, bread eating contests, paper lantern races, *daruma* races, two- and three-legged races, and obstacle courses. Other events on postwar South American emigrant ships included cigarette lighting contests, bread eating contests, candy eating contests, *binzuri* (bottle hanging) races, balloon popping races, and ball passing contests. On the *Santos Maru*-class ships, the sport festivals were held on the deck aft.

Given the immense popularity of the sports festivals, anticipation started to build several days before the event, in the course of which the emigrants might put aside their homesickness, boredom, depression, or anxiety about their new home. Sports events included *Kokumin Taisō* (group calisthenics knows as "radio exercises"), judo and kendo, and sumo wrestling. Temporary canvas pools filled with seawater were set up by the crew for the children. This temporary pool could not be used in even moderate seas, since it was feared that children might be washed over the side and into the ocean.[151]

End of the Line

The cabin class–steerage divide also existed at the American and Canadian ends of the Pacific run. Where luxurious establishments such as the Palace Hotel awaited well-to-do cabin class travelers arriving in San Francisco, those in steerage were more likely to land in the Tamura Inn or the Nagamoto Inn (in San Francisco) or a small Japanese-run hotel in Seattle. These class-based differences in accommodations also surfaced if passengers were detained at the port of arrival for health or immigration reasons.

An earlier chapter ("Before Angel Island") described the various sorts of "accommodations" that awaited Asians arriving in San Francisco prior to the opening of the Angel Island Immigration Station in 1910. But if they arrived on a ship flying the yellow flag that signaled disease on board, then their first nights might well have been spent at the federal Quarantine Station on Angel Island. Opened in 1891, it reproduced many of the class distinctions between "cabin class" and "steerage." There were quarters for first-class passengers, and a small "Second Class Passengers Building" was also available, perhaps for non-Asians not traveling in first class. Quarantined steerage passengers were directed to either the Japanese Barracks or the larger Chinese Barracks. It was the O&O steamship line that had originally provided the various barracks for its passengers, precisely so that they could be detained in the relative comfort and social separation to which they had been accustomed aboard ship. The cabin-class detention barracks were one of the first attempts to furnish the quarantined cabin passengers with accommodations similar to those aboard ship, insuring a greater level of privacy and comfort. The suggestion and design for this building was made by D. A. Carmichael, Senior Surgeon in the Marine Medical Service.[152] The MMS (forerunner of the Public Health Service) maintained and expanded these two quite different sets of accommodations for passengers detained while they waited out the ten- to fourteen-day quarantine period for cholera, plague, smallpox, or yellow fever.

Even the medical treatment of quarantined passengers differed by class. In the early 1890s,

> the steerage passengers and crew always were required to undergo quarantine, whereas the cabin passengers who had not actually been exposed to the disease were allowed to leave the station. Each morning and evening the steerage passengers lined up, and received an inspection by one of the medical officers to make sure there were no new outbreaks of the disease and to check for escapes. Every morning the barracks were fumigated by the pot methods with sulphur dioxide, and then flushed out with salt water.[153]

During the 1899 bubonic plague scare, all the passengers and crew of the *Nippon Maru* were detained at the Angel Island Quarantine Station. Even though the cabin-class passengers found their new quarters frightfully unacceptable, those quarters were a distinct step up from the accommodations provided for the steerage passengers. Later, at the Angel Island Immigration Station, the distinctions in accommodations were less pronounced, based more on race than on class, but real nonetheless.

Conditions at the Quarantine Station seem not to have improved over time. In 1912 the *San Francisco Call* described the twenty-four first-class "staterooms with two bunks in each room" as insufficient to handle big transpacific liners bringing up to three hundred cabin-class passengers. "For the steerage passengers and crew the accommodations are even more inadequate...the Chinese barracks...is now unfit for human habitation."[154]

THE RETURN VOYAGE

Migration was not necessarily a permanent move. There were those whose sojourn was for a limited time, eventually returning to their country of origin. Many others simply went home for a visit—to get married or to reunite with a wife, perhaps, or to see parents. Or to retire. For some groups, such as the Japanese in North America, the volume of traffic returning to Japan in many years was equal to the number of Japanese leaving the country.[155] From North America, overall passenger traffic back to Asia was only about 70 percent of traffic *from* Asia, with probably an even greater drop-off in steerage. These return trips were undoubtedly different in many respects. There would be fewer passengers, and those passengers certainly experienced less excitement or anticipation than those emigrants who were leaving home for the first time.

Maedakō Hiroichirō conveys something of that difference in his 1920 story *Santō senkyaku* (*Third Class Passengers*), based on notes from his own return from the United States. In it, he portrays Japanese who have begun the homeward journey from San Francisco to Japan after having emigrated to America. Coming on board, their baggage included "a sense of longing, retaining preconceptions about Japan, the trip, and returning to life in Japan." Throughout the story, the narrator describes the characters' day-to-day activities in third class. Aboard the ship, the immigrants are consumed with their anxieties and the mundane experience of life as a third class passenger.

> In each of the beds, the men and women with healthy bodies were tormented with loneliness, the weight of "time" that occupied their future prospects almost suffocated them, without a thought as to how they would pass it, while they were granted a short release from their second instinct of manual labor, they just didn't know what to do and simply stared absent-mindedly at the stained ceiling or at the top sailcloth bed that was plump with the body of a human being.[156]

Many of the larger ships also catered to a return passenger of sorts. Several scholars have noted the desire of Chinese to have their bones or ashes returned to China for burial. In many cases this involved disinterring remains from their grave in North America and shipping them home. As early as 1863, the Panyu charity house in San Francisco raised a substantial sum to ship the remains of 258 people back to China. By 1903, San Francisco alone had nine such charity organizations.[157] This was good business for the steamship companies, whose ships also had mortuaries and a supply of coffins to avoid burials at sea.

One story, offered by the notably anti-Chinese *San Francisco Call*, alleged that elderly Chinese were not above taking advantage of the restrictive immigration laws to economize on the final journey home. They would simply turn themselves in to the immigration authorities as illegal immigrants, expecting that after a few nights in the detention shed they would be deported.

> The [600] Chinese who sailed on the Lothian were nearly all old men, who are going back to China to die. Under ordinary circumstances many of them would have availed themselves of the various Oriental schemes for making Uncle Sam send them home.... This rate war is pleasing to the officials of the Chinese Bureau, much of whose time is taken up with these old men, who, for the sake of a free ride home, acknowledge themselves illegally in the land of the free.[158]

CONCLUSION

Not all Asians traveled steerage. A small fraction traveled in first or second cabin. How many? Absent a thorough review of, say, American Customs and Immigration records, our best guess comes from the detailed records kept by the PMSS for the period 1913–19. Of Chinese passengers crossing the Pacific, 88 percent came in steerage. For Japanese, the percentage was identical. The rest came cabin class, either because they cherished (and could afford) the comfort, or because they hoped of more lenient treatment from medical and immigration inspectors.[159] These figures may cover only one steamship line over a limited period, but the PMSS was then the dominant carrier on the Pacific. Despite the Chinese Exclusion Act, this was a period when many Asians were on the move to North America as migrants, if not permanent immigrants. It is quite possible, of course, that this percentage changed over time, due to changing economic conditions or to perceived vagaries in enforcement of the immigration laws. But there would always have been some Asians who did not travel steerage.

Why did the "steerage" concept persist so long on passenger ships crossing the Pacific? One is struck by the differences in accommodations between these emigration ships and the passenger ships plying the North Atlantic, a difference that becomes even more pronounced when one looks at the Japanese ships going to South America. A sort of "maritime enclosure movement" began on the North Atlantic in the last quarter of the nineteenth century, with lines such as Cunard converting to cabins the large, open, steerage quarters pictured in many articles about transatlantic migration. Drew Keeling has speculated that beginning in the late nineteenth century, "better travel conditions, not lower fares, [were] the primary means by which steamship companies facilitated population flows between the labor markets of Europe and the United States."[160] The implication is that the European (and, to some extent, American) market demanded it, while Asian customers did not.

A 1931 deck plan from the Dollar Lines' *President Hoover* and *President Coolidge*, with room for 800 in steerage aft (in addition to 320 in first class and 120 in "special" second class), shows that this open steerage concept was still used extensively on the Pacific after it had fallen from common use on the

Atlantic. Yamada's evidence, including photos from the 1950s, shows that Japanese ships continued to employ the more open "steerage" concept (including the "silkworm shelves"—family-size sleeping platforms) long after ships on the routes from Europe to North America had discarded such arrangements. Clearly, Asians were more price-sensitive when it came to transoceanic travel. How else to explain that American and Japanese lines retained the concept of semi-open steerage so long after it went out of vogue on the Atlantic?

A different argument as to why conditions improved on the Pacific is that advances in ship design and onboard conditions seem to have flowed from improvements in the terms and conditions of the future work that led Asians to come aboard ship. As Asians came to exert greater individual control over their labor, so they more resembled "customers" who, unlike "cargo," could exert market power to achieve better food, accommodations, sanitation, and safety.

Some of the shipping lines that carried steerage passengers to the New World are still operating. The NYK bought out the TKK line in 1926. Today, it is a global corporation which, among many other things, operates the elegant Crystal Line of cruise ships. The miscellaneous ships that transported the odd lot of migrants, usually in grossly inferior conditions, are still with us, too. Although the carrying of large number of Asian emigrants is now largely in the hands of the airlines, less frequently they are consigned to the not-so-tender mercies of operators of such ships of ill-repute as the *Golden Venture*, whose "four-month nightmare voyage...ended [June 6, 1993] when the tramp freighter dumped its starving and frightened cargo of nearly 300 Chinese immigrants into frigid waters off one of New York City's most popular public beaches. Six passengers died from drowning or exposure, several had to be hospitalized and the remainder were sent to detention centers to await Federal hearings."[161]

NOTES

This chapter owes a great debt to the work of Japanese maritime historian Michio Yamada, author of a series of twenty articles that appeared in *Sekai no Kansen* (1993–95) on Japanese emigration through ships and a subsequent book on that subject, *Fune ni Miru Nihonjin Iminshi: Kasato Maru kara Kuruzu Kyakusen e* [The History of Japanese Emigrant Ships: From the *Kasato Maru* to Cruise Ships] (Tokyo: Chūō Kōronsha, 1998). I am very grateful to Mr. Yamada for his permission to quote extensively from his work and for improving my team's translations from the Japanese.

1. *San Francisco Chronicle,* September 2, 1916.

2. Passenger list of the *Nippon Maru,* U.S. Bureau of Customs, "Customs Passenger Lists of Vessels Arriving in San Francisco, California, 1903–1918" (NARA, San Bruno, CA).

3. For the cabin class experience on the North Atlantic, see Brinnin, *Sway of the Grand Saloon.* For the steerage experience, see Edith Abbott, ed., *Immigration: Select Documents and Case Records* (Chicago: University of Chicago Press, 1924; repr., New York: Arno Press and the *New York Times,* 1969), 6–97; and Brownstone, Franck, and Brownstone, *Island of Hope, Island of Tears.*

4. *Oxford English Dictionary*, online edition.

5. Toyo Kisen Kaisha brochure, ca. 1910, a rarity in that it clearly showed there *was* a steerage class, with published steerage fares.

6. Jean Gontard, "Second Class on Angel Island: Immigrant Hell," *The Californians: The Magazine of California History* 12, no. 4 (1995).

7. Robert D. Turner, *The Pacific Empresses: An Illustrated History of Canadian Pacific Railway's Empress Liners on the Pacific Ocean* (Victoria: Sono Nis Press, 1981), 59.

8. Immigration Commission, *Steerage Regulation, 1819–1908*, vol. 39, *Reports of the Immigration Commission* (Washington, DC, 1911) (aka, the Dillingham Commission), can be found *in toto* on the Web at http://www.ebrary.com/stanford/Dillingham1.html. Volume 39 also contains Senator Newton's remarks on page 341.

9. For the north-south migrations of Japanese and Chinese into Southeast Asia and Australia, consult Lynn Pan, ed., *The Encyclopedia of the Chinese Overseas* (Cambridge, MA: Harvard University Press, 1999). For the migrations of Indians going as contract laborers to Mauritius, South Africa, Ceylon, Fiji, and the West Indies (via the Cape of Good Hope), see Hugh Tinker, *A New System of Slavery: The Export of Indian Labour Overseas, 1830–1920* (London: Oxford University Press, 1974).

10. An excellent introduction to the many ships that crossed the Pacific is Tate, *Transpacific Steam.*

11. For explanations of the origin of "coolie," see Patricia Buckley Ebrey, ed., *The Cambridge Illustrated History of China* (New York: Cambridge University Press, 1996), 251; the *Oxford English Dictionary*; and Tinker, *New System of Slavery*, 41–43.

12. For Cuba, see Duvon Clough Corbitt, *A Study of the Chinese in Cuba, 1847–1947* (Wilmore, KY: Ssbury College, 1971). For Chinese in the Caribbean more generally, see Andrew Wilson, ed., *The Chinese in the Caribbean* (Princeton: Markus Wiener Publishers, 2004). For Peru, Mario Castro de Mendoza, *El transporte marâitimo en la inmigraciâon China, 1849–1874* (Lima: Consejo Nacional de Ciencia y Tecnologâia, 1989).

13. Wilson, *Chinese in the Caribbean.*

14. This story is powerfully told by Robert J. Schwendinger, *Ocean of Bitter Dreams: Maritime Relations Between China and the United States, 1850–1915* (Tucson, AZ: Westernlore Press, 1988), especially 19–60. Another source is Lisa Yun, "Under the Hatches: American Coolie Ships and Nineteenth-Century Narratives of the Pacific Passage," *Amerasia Journal* 28, no. 2 (2002): 38–61.

15. See Mario Castro de Mendoza, *La Marina Mercante en la Republica, 1821–1968*, 2 vols., vol. 1 (Miraflores [Peru]: Talleres de Artes Gráficas Martínez, 1980), 310 ff.

16. Basil Lubbock, *The Coolie Ships and Oil Sealers* (Glasgow: Brown, Son and Ferguson, 1981), 33.

17. A powerful account of the Indian "coolie" system is found in Tinker, *New System of Slavery.* Trip-by-trip death rates are in Piet C. Emmer and A.J. Kuipers, "The Coolie Ships: The Transportation of Indentured Labourers between Calcutta and Paramaribo, 1873–1921," in *Maritime Aspects of Migration*, ed. Klaus Friedland (Koln: Bohlau Verlag, 1989), 403–26.

18. See Corbitt, *Study of the Chinese in Cuba*, 47–62 for Spanish attempts to regulate conditions under which laborers of all sorts were brought to Cuba.

19. Corbitt, *Study of the Chinese in Cuba*, 59.

20. Tinker, *New System of Slavery*, 168.

21. Ibid., 145.

22. For the so-called *Gannenmono*, see John E. Van Sant, *Pacific Pioneers: Japanese Journeys to American and Hawaii, 1850–80* (Urbana and Chicago: University of Illinois Press, 2000), 97–116.

23. See the *Reports of the Immigration Commission* (aka, the Dillingham Commission). Volume 39 contains an excellent section on "Steerage Regulation, 1819–1908," including particularly lurid descriptions of disease outbreaks aboard sailing ships packed with immigrants from Ireland in 1847–48.

24. See Raymond L. Cohn, "The Transition from Sail to Steam in Immigration to the United States," in *Maritime Aspects of Migration,* ed. Klaus Friedland (Koln: Bohlau Verlag, 1989). See also Drew Keeling, "The Transportation Revolution and Transatlantic Migration, 1850–1914," *Research in Economic History* 19 (1999), who notes that by 1870, "over ninety per cent of the immigrants to America were traveling on the iron-hulled screwships of a dozen steamship lines."

25. John Haskell Kemble, "Side-Wheelers Across the Pacific," *American Neptune* 2, no. 1 (1942): 4–38; and Tate, *Transpacific Steam,* 27–31.

26. See Kemble, "Side-Wheelers Across the Pacific," 31.

27. Editorial in the *Alta California,* December 31, 1866, quoted in Tate, *Transpacific Steam,* 23.

28. For the role of Chinese crews in American maritime history, see Schwendinger, *Ocean of Bitter Dreams.*

29. San Francisco headquarters to Captain Freeman of the *Japan,* letter dated December 1, 1869, California Collection of the San Francisco Public Library. Quoted in Dorothy Perkins, ed., *Coming to San Francisco by Steamship, 1906–1908, The Chinese American Experience: Papers from the Second National Conference on Chinese American Studies* (San Francisco: Chinese Historical Society of America, 1980), 27.

30. Schwendinger, *Ocean of Bitter Dreams,* 79.

31. Robert J. Schwendinger, "Investigating Chinese Immigrant Ships and Sailors," in *The Chinese American Experience: Papers from the Second National Conference on Chinese American Studies,* ed. Genny Lim (San Francisco: Chinese Historical Society of America, 1980), 19–20. See also his *Ocean of Bitter Dreams,* 78 ff.

32. Kemble, "Side-Wheelers Across the Pacific," 14.

33. Tate, *Transpacific Steam,* 43.

34. John Haskell Kemble, "Notes: Cabin Plan of the Pacific Mail Steamer *Japan,*" *American Neptune* (1942), 243.

35. While little is known about the Guam group, the other two groups are described in Van Sant, *Pacific Pioneers,* 97–130.

36. Toraji Irie and William Himmel, "History of Japanese Migration to Peru," *Hispanic American Historical Review* 31, no. 3 (1951): 442. This document is a translation of selected chapters of Irie's *Hajin Kaigai Hattenshi,* 2 vols. (Tokyo: Iida Shoten, 1942).

37. From Kuga-mura Monjo (official document of Kuga Village, on Oshima Island, Yamaguchi Prefecture), quoted in Michio Yamada, "Emigrants to Hawaii in the Meiji Era, Part 1," *Sekai no Kansen,* November 1993.

38. For both the *kanyaku imin* (emigrants under government contract) and the *shiyaku imin,* see Alan Takeo Moriyama, *Imingaisha: Japanese Emigration Companies and Hawaii, 1894–1908* (Honolulu: University of Hawaii Press, 1985).

39. Yamada, "Emigrants to Hawaii, Part 1."

40. Mitsubishi Mail Steamship Company and Kyodo Unyu Kaisha merged on September 29, 1885 to form NYK, and the new company commenced operations on October 1 with fleet of 58 steamships.

41. *Kindai Nihon Kaiun Seisei Shiryō* (NYK Line: 1988), quoted in Yamada, "Emigrants to Hawai'i, Part 1."

42. Michio Yamada, "Emigrants to Hawaii in the Meiji Era, Part 2," *Sekai no Kansen* (December 1993).

43. Ibid.

44. Quoted in Ibid.

45. See Moriyama, *Imingaisha*, 79–81.

46. An excellent overall survey of the shipping lines on the Pacific is Tate, *Transpacific Steam*.

47. See works by Kemble and Schwendinger.

48. See the following chapter.

49. See Hugh Johnson, *The Voyage of the Komagata Maru: The Sikh Challenge to Canada's Colour Bar* (Delhi: Oxford University Press, 1979), 27. The passengers of the *Komagata Maru* were denied entry at Vancouver, and after a two-month standoff the ship and passengers returned to Hong Kong.

50. William Kooiman, "James Hill's Great 'White Elephants,'" *Sea Classics*, 1991, 12.

51. Turner, *Pacific Empresses*, 22.

52. Ibid., 21.

53. Ibid., 21–26.

54. Ibid., 24 and 78–79.

55. Sharon Boswell and Lorraine McConaghy, "Arrival of the Miike Maru," *Seattle Times*, 1996.

56. Quoted in NYK Lines, "First Arrival of Miike Maru to the Port of Seattle," *Ripples in Time*, 2001, http://www.nykline.co.jp/english/seascope/200011/.

57. Adam McKeown, *Chinese Migrant Networks and Cultural Change: Peru, Chicago, Hawaii, 1900–1936* (Chicago: University of Chicago Press, 2001), 44–45.

58. Michio Yamada, "Emigration to Mexico and Peru in the Meiji Era," *Sekai no Kansen*, March 1994.

59. Ibid.

60. Ibid.

61. This section relies heavily on Michio Yamada, "Emigration to Mexico and Peru in the Meiji Era," and "The First Ship Specially Built for Emigrants, the *Anyō Maru*," *Sekai no Kansen*, June 1994.

62. For the negotiations, see Irie and Himmel, "History of Japanese Migration to Peru," 438–44.

63. Ibid.

64. McKeown, *Chinese Migrant Networks*, 44–46.

65. Ibid., 146–47.

66. John H. Smith, *Letter from Jno [John] H. Smith to Henry Rose Carter, May 10, 1923*; available from http://etext.lib.virginia.edu/etcbin/fever-browse?id=01102019.

67. See McKeown, *Chinese Migrant Networks*, 166–67.

68. See Yamada, "The *Anyō Maru*."

69. See Toyo Kisen Kaisha Line, "Sailing Schedule of South American Line," *Japan: Overseas Travel Magazine*, November 1916.

70. This section relies heavily on Yamada, "The *Anyō Maru*."

71. Quoted in John Sharrock, "Three Seas and Two Oceans," *Japan: Magazine of Overseas Travel*, 1924.

72. Quoted in Michio Yamada, "First Emigrants to Brazil by the *Kasato Maru*," *Sekai no Kansen*, April 1994, trans. Tomoko Negishi, with Robert Barde. The section on the *Kasato Maru* relies heavily on Yamada's article.

73. From *Sōbō no Daichi* [The Earth of the People], Yukiharu Takahashi (Kōdansha 1990). Quoted in Yamada, "The *Anyō Maru*."

74. Michio Yamada, "The First *Santos Maru*, Part 1," *Sekai no Kansen*, September 1994, trans. Wesley Ueunten.

75. Ibid.

76. Lynn Pan, *The Encyclopedia of the Chinese Overseas*, 57.

77. Madeline Y. Hsu, *Dreaming of Gold, Dreaming of Home: Transnationalism and Migration Between the United States and South China, 1882–1943* (Stanford: Stanford University Press, 2000), 139.

78. See Gunter Moltman, "Steamship Transport of Emigrants from Europe to the United States, 1850–1914: Social, Commercial, and Legislative Aspects," in *Maritime Aspects of Migration*, ed. Klaus Friedland (Koln: Bohlau Verlag, 1989), 316.

79. W.M. Rice to the Commissioner General of Immigration, April 24, 1899, U.S. Congress, House, p. 7. Quoted in Moriyama, *Imingaisha*, 80.

80. Hisashi Tsurutani, *America-Bound: The Japanese and the Opening of the American West*, trans. Betsey Scheiner with Yamamura Mariko (Tokyo: The Japan Times, 1989), 65.

81. Kazuo Ito, *Issei: A History of Japanese Immigrants in North America*, trans. Shinichiro Nakamura and Jean S. Gerard (Seattle: Japanese Community Service, 1973), 12.

82. Ibid., 15.

83. See Fairchild, *Science at the Borders: Immigrant Medical Inspection and the Shaping of the Modern Industrial Labor Force* (Baltimore: The Johns Hopkins University Press, 2003).

84. Letter from J.B. Sawyer to (Henry) Monroe, October 18, 1915, in John Birge Sawyer, "Professional Papers of John Birge Sawyer" (Bancroft Library, University of California, Berkeley, n.d.).

85. Hsu, *Dreaming of Gold*, 139.

86. Joan M. Jensen, *Passage from India: Asian Indian Immigrants in North America* (New Haven: Yale University Press, 1988).

87. Tsurutani, *America-Bound*, 74.

88. Ibid., 75.

89. Moriyama, *Imingaisha*, 81.

90. Yamada, *Fune ni Miru Nihonjin Iminshi*, 149. Translations by Wesley Ueunten.

91. Ibid., 161. See also Michio Yamada, "Voyage of Sōbō: Part 1: National Emigration Center," *Sekai no Kansen*, November 1994.

92. Ibid., 162.

93. Ito, *Issei*, 13.

94. Kemble, "Side-Wheelers Across the Pacific," 32. His sources are contemporary travelogues and memoirs.

95. "Chinese Passengers Being Searched, San Francisco," *Harper's Weekly*, 1876.

96. A Chinese traveler from the 1930s, quoted in Hsu, *Dreaming of Gold*, 33.

97. Cited by Yamada, "The *Anyō Maru*." The voyage referred to took place in 1898 aboard the *Yamaguchi Maru*.

98. *Sōbō* by Tatsuzō Ishikawa. Quoted in Yamada, *Fune ni Miru Nihonjin Iminshi*, 93, trans. Zelideth Rivas.

99. Ito, *Issei*, 42.

100. Yamada, "First Emigrants to Brazil."

101. Ito, *Issei*, 42.

102. Ibid., 13.

103. Quoted in Turner, *Pacific Empresses*, 40.

104. *Sōbō* by Tatsuzō Ishikawa. Quoted in Yamada, *Fune ni Miru Nihonjin Iminshi*, 197.

105. From Michio Yamada, "Voyage of Sōbō: Part 2: Meals on Japanese Emigrant Ships," *Sekai no Kansen*, December 1994, trans. Richard Nishioka and Mitsuko Okimoto.

106. This quotation appeared in a column by Manabu Manabe in the *Nihon Keizai Sinbun* newspaper in December 1993. Cited by Yamada, *Fune ni Miru Nihonjin Iminshi*, 200.

107. Yamada, "Meals on Japanese Emigrant Ships," trans. Wesley Ueunten.

108. "Tokō Annai" [Guidance for the Voyage] by Kaigai Kōgyō, 1936, 61. Quoted in Yamada, *Fune ni Miru Nihonjin Iminshi*, 206, trans. Wesley Ueunten.

109. Turner, *Pacific Empresses*, 69.

110. Alan Kraut, *Silent Travelers: Germs, Genes, and the "Immigrant Menace"* (New York: Basic Books, 1994).

111. From *Pacific Medical and Surgical Journal* 19 (June 1876): 36–37, quoted in Joan B. Trauner, "The Chinese as Medical Scapegoats in San Francisco, 1870–1905," *California History* 57, no. 1 (1978): 7.

112. *San Francisco Examiner*, May 23, 1882.

113. E.K. Sprague, "Medical Inspection of Immigrants," *Survey* 30 (1913), quoted in Anne-Emanuelle Birn, "Six Seconds Per Eyelid: The Medical Inspection of Immigrants at Ellis Island, 1892–1914," *Dynamis* 17 (1997): 309.

114. Markel, *Quarantine!*

115. U.S. Public Health Service, "Annual Report of the Supervising Surgeon-General, Fiscal Year 1899," 557–58.

116. Ibid., 560; emphasis added.

117. Ibid., 550, report of Surgeon D.A. Carmichael, stationed at Honolulu.

118. Associate Historian of the United States Public Health Service, personal communication to author, November 2005.

119. U.S. Customs Service, "Report of Examination of Passenger Vessels," Records of the U.S. Customs Service (RG 36), NARA—Pacific Region (San Bruno, CA).

120. Cutaway drawings for both sets of ships are in Turner, *Pacific Empresses*, 24 and 78–79.

121. Yamada, "The *Anyō Maru*."

122. For examples of how these class prejudices operated on the North Atlantic, see Markel, *Quarantine!* and Kraut, *Silent Travelers*.

123. Quoted in Howard Markel, "Which Face? Whose Nation? Immigration, Public Health, and the Construction of Disease at America's Borders, 1891 to 1928," in *Immigration Research for a New Century: Multidisciplinary Perspectives*, ed. Ruben G. Rumbaut, Nancy Foner, and Steven J. Gold (New York: Russell Sage Foundation, 2000), 102.

124. Iwao M. Moriyama, "Epidemic Cerebrospinal Fever Among Transpacific Steerage Passengers," *University of California Publications in Public Health* 2, no. 2 (1936): 183–234.

125. Michio Yamada, "Voyage of Sōbō: Part 4: Epidemics Aboard Emigrant Ships," *Sekai no Kansen*, February 1995, trans. Wesley Ueunten.

126. Marilyn Chase, *The Barbary Plague: The Black Death in Victorian San Francisco* (New York: Random House, 2003).

127. Observations in "From San Francisco to the Orient." Author unknown, published by Toyo Kisen Kaisha line, ca. 1915.

128. Robert Louis Stevenson, "The Amateur Immigrant," 1895, quoted in Brinnin, *Sway of the Grand Saloon*, 262.

129. See Turner, *Pacific Empresses*, 79, for cutaway drawings of these two Empresses.

130. Schwendinger, *Ocean of Bitter Dreams*, 201.

131. Unknown author. Notebook from the collection of the Huntington Museum.

132. "Tokō Annai" [Guidance for the Voyage, 64] by Kaigai Kōgyō, 1936. Quoted in Yamada, *Fune ni Miru Nihonjin Iminshi*, 167–68, trans. Wesley Ueunten.

133. Ibid.

134. Ito, *Issei*, 43.

135. Slogans developed by passengers in Tatsuzō Ishikawa's novel *Sōbō*. Quoted in Yamada, *Fune ni Miru Nihonjin Iminshi*, 113–14, trans. Ann Sokolsky and Wesley Ueunten.

136. Yamada discusses water more extensively in Ibid., 113–22.

137. Ito, *Issei*, 39.

138. Turner, *Pacific Empresses*, 40.

139. Ito, *Issei*, 13.

140. "Big Games of Fan-Tan on the Chinas Steamers," *San Francisco Call*, November 6, 1898.

141. Kooiman, "James Hill's Great 'White Elephants,'" 12.

142. Michio Yamada, "The Anti-Japanese Problem and Passenger Ships on the North American Routes," *Sekai no Kansen*, May 1994.

143. Yamada, "The Anyō Maru."

144. Turner, *Pacific Empresses*.

145. Ito, *Issei*, 39.

146. Michio Yamada, "Voyage of Sōbō: Part 3: Daily Life on the Ships," *Sekai no Kansen*, January 1995.

147. Ibid.

148. Ibid.

149. "Sōbō" by Tatsuzō Ishikawa. Quoted in Yamada, *Fune ni Miru Nihonjin Iminshi*, 191, trans. Ann Sokolsky and Wesley Ueunten.

150. Ibid.

151. Yamada, *Fune ni Miru Nihonjin Iminshi*, 185.

152. D.A. Carmichael, N.V. Perry, and A.L. Parsons, Report on the Physical and Administrative Equipment at the United States Quarantine Station at San Francisco, California, ed. Public Health Service (National Archives, Record Group 90, 1918).

153. Anna Coxe Toogood, *A Civil History of Golden Gate National Recreation Area and Point Reyes National Seashore, California* (Denver: Historic Preservation Branch, Pacific Northwest Team, Denver Service Center, National Park Service, United States Dept. of the Interior, 1980).

154. *San Francisco Call*, July 27, 1912.

155. See Walter Willcox, *International Migrations* (New York: National Bureau of Economic Research, 1929), especially 160–66.

156. Maedakō Hiroichirō, *Santō senkyaku, Gendai Nihon bungaku taikei* 59 (Tokyo: Chikuma shobo, 1973), 12. Cited in Zelideth Maria Rivas, "Sea of Faces: Landscape and Boredom in Maedakō Hiroichirō's *Santō senkyaku*," unpublished paper (University of California, Berkeley, 2005).

157. Yong Chen, *Chinese San Francisco, 1850–1943* (Stanford: Stanford University Press, 2000), 105.

158. *San Francisco Call*, "Chinese Profit by a Rate War," December 3, 1903.

159. For "buying up" from steerage to cabin class, see Barde and Bobonis, "Detention at Angel Island."

160. See Keeling, "Transportation Revolution," 39. See also Drew Keeling, "The Economics of Migrant Transport between Europe and the United States, 1900–1914," May 11, 2005.

161. *New York Times*, June 18, 1993.

— 7 —

The Life and Death of the China Mail

Look Tin Eli was dressed for the occasion. Resplendent in his most formal banker's attire, he stood on the crowded ship's deck, surrounded by his many friends and business associates. He surely knew that this was his moment.

On October 28, 1915, in the thirty-third year of the Chinese Exclusion Act, after a third of a century during which Chinese in America had been ostracized, marginalized, and threatened with expulsion, *le tout San Francisco* was there to pay homage to him. Mayor Rolph, leading steamship officials, members of the Chamber of Commerce, hundreds of fellow Chinese, reporters from the *Examiner* and the *Chronicle*—all had come to Pier 42 to celebrate this enterprise, one that owed its existence to *him*, the President of the brand new CMSS.

He and the China Mail had just bought their first ship. The SS *China* was the *grande dame* of passenger service across the Pacific, and the old ship was dressed all in bunting for the occasion. In the dining saloon, a lavish luncheon awaited the hundreds of invited visitors. From the main mast flew the house flag of the CMSS, waiting to be hauled down and christened. When Captain Ryland Drennan and Purser Kent Clark brought down the ensign—a red field with a large blue ball inscribed with the monogram "C.M."—it was folded, then christened with a bottle of California champagne wielded by Rosa Lew Hing, daughter of the China Mail's vice president. The mayor's speech congratulated the Chinese community on its "entrance into the transpacific trade," and Look spoke of how much the new company would benefit San Francisco. It all felt like the start of something grand.[1]

And, for a while, it was.

Figure 7.1
At the christening of the SS *China* under the flag of the CMSS, October 28, 1915,
company officials were joined by the political elite of San Francisco.

Source: CMSS company report for 1915–19. Courtesy of Bruce Quan and Phil Choy.

For Ryland Drennan, too, it was a momentous day. His dream of becoming
master of a vessel was about to be realized, thanks to Look Tin Eli and the China
Mail. But close by, the big liner *Mongolia* was tied up, still under the guard of
Customs agents and Immigration Service watchmen. Drennan had been First
Officer on her last trip, and when eighty-six Chinese stowaways were discovered
during a search by Immigration inspectors, suspicion had fallen on him and his
crew. But today was not a day for being arrested.

That would come on the morrow. The *China* would leave port, but not under
the command of "Captain" Drennan. Deputy United States marshals would take

him from the bridge of the *China* and detain him pending results of the investigations. Captain F. E. Frazier, formerly of the Pacific Mail's lower coast service, was
hurriedly substituted as master of the *China*, and she made her one o'clock sailing.

The *Mongolia*'s last, inglorious voyage to San Francisco was, somewhat seren-
dipitously, immediately followed by a much more honorable endeavor. Where
the *Mongolia*, the property of a large, white-owned corporation, had been used
to smuggle Chinese into the United States, a new enterprise was being designed
by Chinese and Chinese Americans which from 1915 to 1923 would transport
their countrymen across the Pacific and land them legally on America's front
doorstep. That October rechristening of the *China* was a harbinger of things to
come during the brief existence of the CMSS. What follows is an account of
how the China Mail came to be, of its short life, and of its demise.

*****

Chinese had been in California for over sixty-five years before the China Mail
was formed, and this was not their first attempt to enter the immigrant transportation business. Like most of those from around the world who joined the Gold Rush,
thousands of Chinese often were more concerned with a vessel's availability than
with its amenities. Hong Kong merchants either bought or chartered Western sailing ships to transport their countrymen to the goldfields. The "first vessel owned by
a Chinaman which has ever entered this port under their flag" was the *Hamilton*,
arriving in San Francisco from Hong Kong in 1853, owned by Ton Kee and under
the command of Captain Keller. Another was owned by Mou Kee, who in 1853
bought the whaling ship *Potomac* and refitted her with an extra deck, and "on a
single voyage the Chinese owners transported more than five hundred emigrants
to San Francisco who represented the equivalent of thirty-seven thousand dollars
in passage fees." Later that same year, A. Choo chartered the clipper ship *Gazelle*,
plus its captain and American crew, to transport 350 Chinese *back* to Hong Kong.
And in 1855, the French *St. Germain* was chartered by Chinese companies in San
Francisco to take Chinese laborers back to Hong Kong.[2]

A generation later, the Chinese government organized the China Merchants
Steam Navigation Company in hopes of breaking the monopoly of British and
American shipping companies. In 1880 the 2,200-ton *Ho Chung* made two trips
from Canton to San Francisco, and a year later the 1,200-ton *Mei Fu* made
another two trips. But the four trips of these small ships were money losers and
the company soon gave up the service.[3]

Passage of the Chinese Exclusion Act in 1882 may have been sufficient to
discourage other would-be Chinese ship operators. During the Gold Rush
era, as Gunther Barth noted, "only Western shipowners profited immediately
from the transportation of emigrants through the money which Chinese charters
paid for the vessels. To Chinese merchants, as shipowners or charters, the
passage represented a considerable investment since they speculated not on
the shipping venture but on the labor potential of their countrymen in
California."[4]

Clearly, however, Chinese entrepreneurs had not been shy about entering such a risky, highly competitive field. Such entrepreneurial daring might yet surface again.

These early endeavors aside, most Chinese came to San Francisco (the major port of entry into North America for Chinese) in ships that were American, British, Canadian or, beginning in 1898, Japanese. By 1915, what seemed to be a fairly stable pattern had emerged: the major carriers of migrants from China to San Francisco were the PMSS (American) and the TKK (a Japanese company), with about 80 percent and 15 percent, respectively, of the passenger traffic between Hong Kong and San Francisco.[5]

An auspicious confluence of events would be needed for a newcomer to break into this cozy cartel. Politics on both sides of the Pacific could create an opportunity. A rising sense of being part of a Chinese *American* community might make it desirable to seize that opportunity. Economic and social institutions would have to emerge within the various communities of the Chinese diaspora to make it *possible* for the Chinese in California to seize the day. Key individuals would have to step forward to provide the final, indispensable ingredient—leadership. In 1915 all of these stars came into alignment.

WAR AND OPPORTUNITY

Ever since the Sino-Japanese War in 1896, Japan had clamored to join the ranks of nations gnawing on the carcass of an enfeebled China. Japan used its declaration of war on Germany in 1914 as justification for invading the German concession in Kiaochow (now Jiaoxian, Shandong province), then in 1915 secretly presenting China's President Yuan Shih-kai with an ultimatum—the infamous Twenty-One Demands, which would give Japan control of China's military, commercial, and financial affairs.

Such special rights and privileges had been exercised by European powers ever since the Opium Wars of the 1830s and were deeply resented by all Chinese. Japan's attempts to grab even greater power angered patriotic Chinese wherever they lived. The result was a widespread boycott, more or less spontaneously organized, of Japan and Japanese goods. Despite the Chinese government's own opposition, the boycott spread from San Francisco's Chinatown to other American cities. There was a long-standing feeling among Chinese that their unfavorable treatment in the United States was a reflection of China's weakness and powerlessness in international affairs. The Twenty-One Demands were a reminder of that impotence; standing up to the Japanese was not only the patriotic thing to do, but an assertion of Chinese immigrants' right to consideration in the United States.

While the Twenty-One Demands and the ensuing boycott fanned the desire of Chinese in America to do *something*, political developments in the United States—and the law of unintended consequences—were making "something" possible.

For twenty years, the president of the International Seamen's Union, Andrew Furuseth, had been lobbying for a bill that would improve the conditions under which American seamen worked. In 1915, Senator Robert La Follette finally shepherded the Seamen's Act through the Democrat-controlled Congress. He then, at the eleventh hour, brought Furuseth to see President Woodrow Wilson, who was reluctant to sign the bill. According to legend, Furuseth threw himself on his knees, begging Wilson to liberate the seamen. On March 4, one hour before Congress adjourned, Wilson signed the Seamen's Act into law.

One envisioned improvement lay in making it impossible for employers to have deserting crew members imprisoned—something that companies had long used to maintain discipline. Another lay in having specific requirements for adequate lifesaving equipment and procedures. Other aspects of the bill would protect sailors from a number of unfavorable conditions aboard ship—one of which was competition from low-wage "Oriental" sailors. The proviso that 75 percent of the crew must be able to understand the officers' orders (effectively, demanding fluency in English) may have meant little on the Atlantic, but it created turmoil among American shipping companies on the Pacific.

For over fifty years, the Pacific Mail had used crews that were almost exclusively Chinese—with, of course, a white officer cadre.[6] Chinese sailors were paid substantially less than white crew members: the *Mongolia,* for instance, carried "2 white oilers at Gold $45 per month each [and] 18 Chinese oilers at Mex. $18 each per month."[7] The same was true above decks, where "[t]he Chinese crews provided superb attention to the passengers and were excellent seamen as well, and Pacific Mail did not want to risk its reputation for quality service at the hands of new and untried crews of other nationalities."[8] The Pacific Mail's General Manager, Rennie Schwerin, and other shipowners waged a vitriolic after-the-fact campaign against Furuseth and the Seamen's Act. In a July 1915 letter to La Follette published as "La Follette's Ignorance Exposed," Schwerin threatened that "[t]here is nothing else for this company to do, when the La Follette Seamen's bill becomes effective on November 4, 1915, except one of three things: first, operate in some other sphere, where wages do not have such a serious effect in competitive oversea trade; second, lay up the ships; third, sell the ships and liquidate the company."[9]

The Pacific Mail took option number three. On August 14, the PMSS announced that it was selling its ships, including its entire fleet of transpacific passenger liners.[10]

The announcement stunned San Francisco. Not only was the Pacific Mail a long-established part of the commercial scenery, but the city's merchants *needed* the Pacific Mail. By August 1915 the effects of World War I were keenly felt on the Pacific. All British-flag ships had been requisitioned for England's war effort, and Germany's merchant ships similarly disappeared from their customary routes in Asia. A worldwide shortage of ships ensued—those that German submarines had not sent to the bottom of the North Atlantic were busy hauling men and supplies to the combatants. Those companies with ships on the Pacific had all made enormous profits during the first years of the war—even the Pacific Mail, which for years had paid no dividends.[11] Even with the high price that Pacific Mail received for its ships, the decision (especially in hindsight) seems ill-considered: the war would last for three more years, with profits aplenty for those with ships. Nonetheless, as Secretary of Commerce Redfield explained in an open letter to Secretary of the Treasury William Gibbs McAdoo, "the company after doing business for sixteen years without a dividend found that existing conditions gave them an opportunity of selling out a portion of their property at a price which would return them the full valuation of that property upon the company's books, plus at least a million dollars more."[12] Two months later, PMSS would cash out, reducing its capital stock from $20 million to $1 million and returning the difference to the shareholders.[13]

Merchants on the West Coast had good reason to be concerned. There be four fewer ships transporting passengers and goods across the Pacific, and virtually none of those remaining would be American. Transpacific shipping would be controlled by Japanese lines—the mighty NYK and the OSK operating out of Seattle, and the TKK out of San Francisco.

San Francisco newspapers had for some years periodically raised the alarm of Japan as an expanding military and commercial menace, and they were quick to seize on how American commercial interests in Asia would now be at the mercy of Japan's ships and shipping policy. On September 4, the U.S. Consul General in Hong Kong wrote to the *Chronicle* that the Japanese lines had just increased freight rates to "twice the rates obtaining on the same commodities before the opening of the war in Europe." Not only would freight rates increase on American goods (and not on Japanese goods, as that government was subsidizing the Japanese shipping lines), but it would be difficult simply to get American goods transported. In an ominous summing up, he warned that

> It is becoming quite evident, therefore, that all other trade in and with the Far East is to be under Japanese control. With the full pinch of the shortage of tonnage experienced it is becoming more and more evident that no Chinese cargo or through cargo transshipped at Hongkong for the United States by way of the Pacific can be expected...until all cargo has been carried from Japanese ports. Naturally, *the rate of freight to be charged on all such cargo will be all that the traffic will bear.*[14]

Caught in this vise was anyone in the United States trading with China—businesses large and small, white and Chinese. Of all those affected, only the Chinese community would respond quickly and effectively.

ECONOMIC AND SOCIAL INSTITUTIONS

On August 14, the very day that the Pacific Mail announced the sale of its ships, the Chinese business community in San Francisco began formulating its response. The CCC (Chinese Chamber of Commerce) proposed establishing a

Chinese shipping company and tried to get the Consolidated Chinese Benevolent Association—the famous "Chinese Six Companies"—to take up the idea.[15] After nearly a month of inactivity, the CCC held another meeting on September 8. The minutes brimmed with enthusiasm and resolve:

> As the Pacific Mail Steamship Company is going out of business, we are facing obstacles for transportation across the Pacific. However, to use the thief's (i.e., Japanese) ships would be a national disgrace. Therefore, there is a pressing need for us to own our own ships. Now, the founders and the Chinese Chamber of Commerce agreed to establish the China Mail Steamship Company through this meeting. This project depends on all of the overseas Chinese buying its stock; hence, we hereby urge (our members) to do so.[16]

And so the China Mail was born.

The men behind this initiative (and all were men) constituted the leading lights of the Chinese business community in the San Francisco Bay Area. Their businesses

Figure 7.2
Look Tin Eli, president of the Canton Bank, led the group of modernizing Chinese Americans who founded the CMSS.

LOOK TIN ELI,
President Canton Bank and president China Mail
Steamship Company, San Francisco.

Source: Coast Banker, August 1918, 175.

were not the laundries and restaurants with which most Californians associated Chinese. Rather, they were substantial enterprises run by visionaries who had grasped how to make money *in* America and *with* Americans. Three of the most prominent were Lew Hing, Ng Poon Chew, and Look Tin Eli.

Lew Hing had founded one of the larger Chinese businesses in California, the Pacific Coast Cannery, which canned fruit and vegetables under the "Buckskin" label. Based in Oakland after 1903, it was the city's largest cannery and one of its biggest employers. Lew Hing was a major stockholder in the Canton Bank and had served several terms as its president.[17] Other important businessmen who joined Lew Hing in investing in the CMSS were "Yu Ling, chief investigator of the National Salvation Association,"[18] and Woo Wai, "a prominent merchant."[19]

Ng Poon Chew of Oakland was the manager, editor, and one of the largest shareholders (along with seven other Ng family members) of *Chung Sai Yat Po* (*China West Daily*, or CSYP), the major Chinese-language local daily newspaper.[20] The major intellectual force behind CSYP, he had come from Guangdong Province in 1881, working near San Jose as a houseboy before learning English and entering the San Francisco Theological Seminary. After seven years, Chew (now using this as his surname, rather than Ng) left the ministry, and in 1899 founded a newspaper that was sympathetic to republican forces in China and opposed to mistreatment of Chinese in the United States. CSYP would run for over fifty years, and Chew would become "one of the most active and influential Chinese Americans of his time." He reportedly saved Sun Yatsen from deportation in 1904 and supported his early organizing activities—just the sort of man who would be attracted to a modernizer like Look Tin Eli and the China Mail.[21]

Under Chew's direction, the CSYP became a vigorous advocate for the China Mail. His newspaper regularly ran what today would be called "infomercials": pieces that were neither strictly advertisements nor strictly news, endorsing the China Mail and exhorting readers not only to patronize its ship but to purchase stock in the company. Here is but one example:

> It must be made clear that this company is not an enterprise serving the purpose of a small group. Its aim is to get a share for China in international maritime trade. There is absolutely no investment from non-Chinese sources....It will be unlike joint ventures between Chinese and foreigners, wherein non-Chinese often hold sway. Everyone who regards himself as Chinese should feel it his duty to invest in this. Let us hope that one day our company's banner will fly over every port in every continent.[22]

While support from Lew Hing, Ng Poon Chew, and other Chinese businessmen was important, in all likelihood, the CMSS would not have been born were it not for the vision and leadership of Look Tin Eli. No newspaper story of the China Mail fails to mention his name, as founder, president, and guiding spirit. It would not stretch things to say that the story of the China Mail is his story, too.

Look Tin Eli was born and educated in Mendocino on the northern coast of California. After high school, he took over the management of his father's store, and later went to San Francisco, where he worked for a large Chinese import-export business as assistant manager. He went on to apprentice in the banking business in San Francisco at the International Banking Corporation and at the Russo-Asiatic Bank.[23] Many banks of this era had a "Chinese department" through which they vied for Chinese customers. The Bank of Italy's bank booklet printed in Chinese was featured in *Coast Banker*, August 1917. Most managers of these departments were Chinese, and such positions represented one of the few avenues of advancement for Chinese—and especially for Chinese women—within the white-owned banking industry. A striking example was the profile and photograph of Miss Dorothy Gee Chang, "who at nineteen years of age is the highest paid woman employee in financial pursuits in the City of San Francisco, and, so far as we know, on the Pacific Coast."[24]

What brought Look Tin Eli to prominence, however, was his role as President of the Canton Bank. The Bank had actually been founded by his younger brother, Look Poong-shan, who had been Chinese manager of the Russo-Asiatic Bank. The latter was destroyed in the great 1906 earthquake and fire, as were many Chinese businesses. The banker Isaac Allen pointed out the need for a bank to supply credit to Chinatown merchants needing to rebuild, and Look Poong-shan seized the opportunity to call a meeting of the CCC. The Chamber's members quickly subscribed the capital necessary to launch the Canton Bank of San Francisco. Chartered by the State of California, with offices at the corner of Clay and Kearny streets in San Francisco, the Bank's first president and general manager was Look Poong-shan, with Allen its assistant manager; many of the staff were Chinese who had worked at banks that had closed following the earthquake.[25] It was not until Look Poong-shan left for Hong Kong in 1909 that his elder brother, Look Tin Eli, succeeded him as head of the Canton Bank.

By all accounts Look Tin Eli was an extraordinary person, recognized in both the Chinese community and in the broader white business world. His 1894 Immigration document for a trip to China has a photograph of him in traditional Chinese dress, but every subsequent publicity photo shows him in Western dress—usually formal attire. Similarly, his Canton Bank was run as an *American* institution by and for Chinese: its records always kept in English,[26] its new headquarters given a Greek revival (what for the day was a characteristically "American") architecture outside and Western conveniences within, and its Cashier was always, always a Caucasian. Most importantly, it would have the full confidence of the American banking community. As *Coast Banker* put it several years later, the Canton Bank "enjoys high respect with business men and financiers of the city (and) Look Tin Eli is personally one of the city's most popular bankers."[27]

By 1915, the Canton Bank had become a recognized, respected part of the San Francisco financial landscape, "for many years the principal banking house for about 100,000 Chinese scattered throughout the United States and Mexico."[28] Depositors had entrusted $660,000 to the Bank, and its capital stock and retained earnings represented another $150,000. Although only 1/20 the size of the Fleishackers' Anglo-California Trust Company, it was a solid bank showing a steady, if unspectacular, growth in deposits that paralleled that of other California banks.[29] The Bank's financial might (such as it was) was not its biggest contribution to the China Mail's success. Look Tin Eli actually put very little of the Bank's capital into the new steamship company. That the Bank was *seen* to be behind it gave the China Mail instant credibility and access to the San Francisco capital market to secure the needed loan for purchasing its first ship.

What the Canton Bank also provided to the new steamship line was a model for succeeding in an industry dominated by white-owned businesses. To assure credibility within banking circles, both the Manager (I.P. Allen, later E.F. Sager) and the Cashier (E.V. Spiganovicz) were Caucasians. The Bank's building *looked* "American," with none of the pseudo-traditional Chinese facades found in Chinatown. Pragmatism was the order of the day at the Canton Bank, and it carried over to the CMSS.

A PRECARIOUS OPPORTUNITY

The creation of the CMSS was a precarious thing. On several occasions the opportunity nearly slipped away. Without a ship, the CMSS would have been out of luck. With major competitors sponsored by both the American and the Chinese governments, the China Mail would have been out of business. Both such eventualities nearly came to pass, and at nearly the same moment.

The China Mail might have been stillborn had another, perhaps larger, company stepped in to provide service between San Francisco and China. There was no shortage of rumors of potential entrants. None of these—not even the Pacific & Eastern Steamship Company, with backing from the central governments of the United States and China—ever materialized.[30]

Still, it was not a sure thing that the CMSS would get its first vessel. Ships were scarce in 1915. Shipowners of other countries were making enormous profits on the ships they had and were not moved to sell them at reasonable prices. Those who had ships generally kept them; those who bought ships paid dearly. Only extremely well-capitalized companies could expect to purchase any ships that might come on the market.

Thus, the Pacific Mail's announcement that it would be selling its ships attracted intense interest from established shipping concerns. Its "Panama fleet" of ships plying the west coast of North America was sold to W.R. Grace. All five ships of its Pacific fleet of passenger liners were also put up for sale. They were

- The *China* (or *China II*), the oldest (1889) and smallest (5,600 tons) of the five ships.

- The *Korea* and the *Siberia*, both completed in 1902, the first ships that Pacific Mail had ordered since commissioning the *China* in 1889. At the time of their launching, they were the largest (11,000 tons) and fastest (18 knots) vessels on the Pacific, establishing records for the San Francisco–Yokohama crossing that would last until 1937.

• Buoyed by the success of these two vessels, PMSS had built the sister ships *Mongolia* and *Manchuria* in 1904. Larger than the *Korea* and *Siberia,* they were also somewhat slower. Nonetheless, these were substantial ships, prized all the more because of the worldwide scarcity.

In rather short order, all five were bought by the ATC (Atlantic Transport Company), a subsidiary of J.P. Morgan's International Mercantile Martine. The price was reportedly $8 million, and even at that price, ATC was convinced it could make handsome profits on the North Atlantic. However, ATC thought the *China* too old and too small for the transatlantic run and tried to find a buyer. The Japanese TKK line was interested, but offered too low a price. ATC was prepared to wait. The *China* was tied up and her funnels painted ATC's house color, red.[31] On October 11 she was still for sale when an offer came from the CMSS—not yet officially incorporated, but with the backing of the Canton Bank and an American banker. (W.C. Brunner suggests that of the purchase price, $75,000 came from local Chinese businessmen and that the remaining $225,000 was supplied by an American banker through a mortgage on the *China.*)[32] The offer was accepted: $300,000, cash on delivery. The China Mail had a ship.

For a further ten cents, the China Mail was given legal life. At least, that is what San Francisco County Clerk H.L. Mulcrevy required: a ten-cent IRS "documentary" stamp. There was, of course, a corporation license tax of $200 to pay (later, and under protest), and the true legal costs for the lawyer's services would have been considerably more. But on October 14, one-tenth of a dollar was what it took for the County Clerk to certify that fifteen people (all but two from San Francisco) had personally appeared before Notary James Mason and signed the articles of incorporation: Look Tin Eli (Oakland), Ting Mint, Mark Thus, Chin Lain, Jang Joe Sum, See Sing Hing, Chu Neu Chun, Fong Wing, Hom Yuey On, Wong Tong, M.Q. Fong (Oakland), Loo Kum Shu, Woo Wai, Lee Fay, and Yee Ling.

Capital stock was to be $2,100,000, consisting of 100,000 shares each with a par value of $21. The day of filing, the capital stock which had actually been subscribed was $315: one share by each of the fifteen directors.[33] The next step was to get the Chinese community to buy into the new venture.

According to the *Examiner,* "It was decided to assess every Chinese in the United States $10 if necessary to see this plan through."[34] This was clearly an exaggeration, typical of how the San Francisco newspapers credited the Chinese Six Companies with much more control of the Chinese community than they actually had. But while some of the China Mail's stock was purchased by wealthy Chinese, to a large extent financing the China Mail was an effort by the broader Chinese community—on the U.S. mainland, in Hawaii, and in China itself. *Chung Sai Yat Po,* the Chinese newspaper controlled by Ng Poon Chew, was one of the principal vehicles used to sell the China Mail's stock. Every issue carried an appeal to purchase shares in the new company. These public appeals did not use anti-Japanese rhetoric, but were instead couched in the language of "strengthening China" and creating something *for* the Chinese.

The China Mail also found investors among the Chinese living in Hawaii, a group of whom sent the new owners a congratulatory telegram: "We are very happy to learn that you have purchased the *China* and that you have set a date for its sailing to Hong Kong, with a stop in Honolulu. We are all so pleased to read this news. Please verify the date of arrival so that the passengers that we have gathered can be ready."[35]

Alas, the *China* was so fully booked with San Francisco passengers bound for Hong Kong that it was decided to skip Honolulu on the first voyage out.

Another large group of investors were Chinese merchants in Hong Kong. Like their counterparts in San Francisco, they found themselves at the mercy of the extortionate practices of Japanese shipping lines and were desperate for an alternative. While we do not know the precise amount of their investment in the China Mail, it must have been substantial. Other investors in Hong Kong included the Tung Wah Hospital ($20,000) and the Hong Kong Chamber of Commerce.[36] This infusion of capital was helpful at the beginning, but would later come back to haunt the China Mail, as we shall see.

Look and the other directors of the China Mail knew little about the steamship business, so they astutely retained many of the Pacific Mail's assets. These included not only the ship that they had purchased, but as much of the Pacific Mail's experience and expertise as they could hire. The officers (white) and crew (Chinese) of the *China* were retained, with the exception of Captain Hans Thompson, who was transferred to the *Manchuria*. The Pacific Mail allowed the new company to have its operational headquarters in the Pacific Mail's offices and for the *China* to use the Pacific Mail's docking facilities in San Francisco. More importantly, the Pacific Mail agreed to act as agents for the new line, providing a valuable store of managerial know-how and entrees into the worldwide shipping business. Having been in business in Asia for half a century, the Pacific Mail had a network of agents in Japan, China, the Philippines, and Singapore; many of them opted to switch over to the China Mail. A.M. Garland, the freight traffic manager for Pacific Mail, signed on as general manager of the China Mail, while H.N. Thomas continued as general passenger agent.[37]

There was, of course, the matter of the ship that would carry the fortunes of the CMSS. The *China* (or *China II*) was an old, familiar face on the San Francisco waterfront. She had been built in Glasgow by the Fairfield yard in 1889, the Pacific Mail's only British-built ship. Because only American-built ships qualified for American registry, until 1897 she flew the British flag. In that year, the Pacific Mail astutely had her registry transferred to the Kingdom of Hawaii; a year later, the U.S. annexation of Hawaii allowed all Hawaiian-registered ships to become eligible for American registry. This devious history of *China*'s registry would become important during her days in service to the China Mail.

Depictions of the *China* in her early days show her with four masts capable of carrying sail—a reflection of the period as a general transition from sail to steam.

Figure 7.3
The SS *China* (II), painted in 1889 by Alfred Finlayson, is shown as the ship departed Scottish yards to enter service between San Francisco and Asia for the PMSS.

Source: Original oil painting from the collection of Stephen J. and Jeremy W. Potash.

In her twenty-six years on the Pacific, she had taken part in her share of historic moments. When the Quarantine Station on Angel Island opened in 1891, the first ship to have its passengers held in quarantine was the *China*, which had come into San Francisco with 257 passengers and crew—and two cases of small-pox.[38] During the Spanish-American War, she did four months of duty as a char-tered Army transport, carrying over 2,000 troops to the Philippines. In her 246 (civilian) crossings of the Pacific, she had carried her share of celebrities. Having been refitted once in 1901 to carry 139 passengers in first class, 41 in second, and 347 in steerage, the *China* was given a quick makeover by her new owners. The total passenger capacity was increased, undoubtedly at the expense of cargo-carrying capacity, growing from 527 to 882.[39]

By the end of October the pieces were falling into place, and the *China* was ready for its first sailing under the flag of the China Mail.

And what a first sailing it was. On October 30 the *China* was filled to the brim with both cargo and passengers. There simply was not enough capacity to handle all the freight consigned to it. Passenger accommodations had been sold out for two weeks: 272 passengers in first class, 41 in second class, and 569 in "Asiatic steerage"—the largest number of passengers it had *ever* carried. So large, in fact, that extra boats and life rafts had to be found to comply with safety regulations. The Cathay Boys' Band was there to serenade the ship and the large crowd that had gathered to see her off. From the upper deck, "a party of Chinese Harvard graduates...gave one college yell after another." At 2:00 p.m. the heavily laden China made her way into the stream, picked up some of the Chinese crew from the *Mongolia,* and steamed out through the Golden Gate.[40]

On its first voyage under the new flag the *China* would go directly to Nagasaki, then Manila (where most of her cargo was destined), and on to Hong Kong. Her return would take her to Nagasaki and then direct to San Francisco.[41] The anti-Japanese boycott did not seem to preclude the China Mail from calling at Japanese ports. Her return on December 24 was noted in the San Francisco papers as again with a full cargo but a rather small passenger load of 184.

A second voyage was equally successful. "A shoehorn would have been necessary to have crowded any more of cargo into the holds of the liner China, of the China Mail Steamship Company, which sailed for the Orient yesterday. Every berth was sold out in all classes, and even up to the hour of sailing it was necessary for Kent Clark, purser, and Captain F.E. Frazier to turn away passengers."[42] On her return in March she brought 216 passengers to San Francisco, and in May 683—133 first class, 28 in second cabin, and a full house in steerage. The *Examiner* noted that "the China is naturally in high favor with the Chinese, who are willing to wait some time rather than travel on a Japanese vessel."[43]

That first year was a good one. The China Mail's first full year—1916—was its best year in terms of the percentage of capacity utilized. It was also a most profitable year for the China Mail. The initial mortgage on the China had been paid off by the third trip and, according to press reports, a large dividend had been paid.[44]

It was also high tide for the Canton Bank. Business was growing, and the following spring the Bank announced that it would build a new bank and office edifice to accommodate its customers and the offices of the CMSS. Look Tin Eli stated that the new site would be at the corner of Montgomery and Sacramento streets—not in Chinatown, but in the heart of San Francisco's financial district.[45]

When the new building opened in 1918, *Coast Banker* judged that the "Chinese-American Institution has Beautiful and Commodious Quarters Excelled by None in Convenience and Artistic Arrangement." Offices of the Canton Bank took up the ground floor and basement, while the China Mail occupied the second floor. In the minds of San Francisco's financial elite, the two companies were "sister institutions...strong and representative San Francisco institutions of the foremost standing."[46] Creating such an imposing new home for the Canton Bank and the China Mail was meant as a public display of their solidity. The truth, however, was that both were navigating rough waters.

RETURN OF THE DEAD

The Pacific Mail, it turned out, had not really died. At least not definitively. It had experienced a capitalist reincarnation and was back to compete on the Pacific.

Even reports of its original demise had been greeted with some skepticism. On the day of the *China*'s christening, the *Examiner* reported that "there is a well-defined rumor in Japan that the Pacific Mail intends to return to the transpacific business....One of Pacific Mail's most valuable assets was the wharf at Yokohama. This was sold for a mere song. Now they say in Japan that the wharf was bought by a Pacific Mail agent and that the company will take it over again and resume business before very long."[47] Within four months, they were right.

In February 1916 the W.R. Grace line bought the Southern Pacific Railroad's stock in the Pacific Mail, with the intention of reviving the shipping line, and the new Board of Directors rescinded the offer to sell the rest of its ships. In March the revitalized Pacific Mail bought three new Dutch steamers—the *Ecuador*, the *Colombia*, and the *Venezuela*—which it intended to put into service on the Pacific.[48] The rise in freight rates had more than compensated for the higher labor costs which the old Pacific Mail had so loudly bemoaned as the reason for selling its Pacific fleet. The new Pacific Mail was attempting to rebuild its old transpacific business—an experiment which, if successful, would lead to the purchase of new, larger ships.

How the new Pacific Mail managed to acquire these ships is something of a puzzle. Though large, they were not bigger than the old *China*—5,870 tons each, capable of a mere 13 knots, with a crew of 120 and room for 270 passengers. Built in Holland in early 1915 for the Royal Dutch West India Mail Co., they were bought by Pacific Mail for $1,100,000 each, then refitted from coal to oil-burning in New York. These were very much "dual purpose" ships, fitted out with four derricks for handling freight. Though not elegant in profile, the passenger accommodations were well-appointed—and, in contrast to the *China*, all were *new*.[49]

The *Ecuador*'s first sailing, in early April 1916, indicated that the new ships could rely on a good deal of residual goodwill from the old Pacific Mail. Returning to San Francisco that June, Captain Nelson "reported that the receptions which the vessel received in every port (Honolulu, Yokohama, Manila, Hong Kong and Shanghai) were wonderful." All three ships were painted with colors other than the old Pacific Mail's traditional black, but the house flag was retained, so "Chinese bumboatmen did not recognize the new colors on the vessel when she made port, but as soon as their eyes took in the striped red, white and blue house flag snapping aloft, familiar to them for half a century, they came off to the *Ecuador* in swarms." Several of the cabin passengers were Chinese as were, presumably, all 127 in "Asiatic steerage."[50] Soon all three ships were sailing virtually the same route as the *China*—formidable competition indeed.

A FLOATING PHOENIX

From its very inception, the China Mail had been looking for ships. Getting the *China* had been something of a coup—a known vessel, ready to sail, with a trained and proven crew. Enlarging the "fleet" to three or four ships had proven much more difficult. There were "reports," of course—the *Mongolia* might be purchased, Look was inspecting Austrian and German ships seized by the British in Hong Kong, the China Mail had signed a contract with the Wallace Shipyard in Vancouver to build two new ships at $1,500,000 each. Newspapers regularly described the China Mail as well funded, and Look once boasted that "I have been offered more money than I can possibly use until the war is over and ships are released and put on the market."[51] But none of these rumors or reports led to a ship.

In 1916 the CMSS did manage to buy the *Nile*, a British-registry ship that had been owned by another subsidiary of the Southern Pacific Railroad. But the acquisition came in a roundabout, devious way, and with a significant catch.

Look Tin Eli's brother, Look Poong-shan, was, as noted earlier, based in China. In early 1916 he learned that the *Nile* was for sale. It appears that he presumed on his connections with his brother's Canton Bank to purchase the ship...for himself. He then sold it to the China Mail for a fat profit. The China Mail's directors were irate—especially when the British government subsequently requisitioned the *Nile* for wartime service.[52] Only in late 1919 would she begin her career with the China Mail. This was not the last time that the company would be divided over the purchase of a ship.

Finally, in April of 1917, Look was able to buy another ship. But this one was an absolute wreck.

The *Congress* had belonged to the Pacific Coast Steamship Company when she caught fire off the coast of Oregon on September 14, 1916. Despite the fire —which left her "a smoldering skeleton"[53]—she had made her own way to Seattle. And there she sat for nearly seven months. Pacific Steamship had meanwhile merged with two other lines, and none of them wanted to repair her—as a coastwise liner she had been neither as fast nor as large as the new ships *Great Northern* and *Northern Pacific* that railroad magnate James J. Hill had recently put into service; worse, she was unprofitable. Sensibly enough, the owners sold her engines and boiler, which had escaped the fire, "and then abandoned the gutted, burned-out hulk...for scrapping at a later date." The China Mail's offer of $600,000 was pure windfall.[54]

Look thought that the ship could be repaired. The Union Iron Works had sent a representative from San Francisco, who estimated that it would cost $800,000 to put her in shape. Look decided to have the work done instead by the Seattle Construction and Dry Dock Company. His plan was to have the steamer, renamed the *Nanking*, fitted out so as to carry 123 passengers in first class, 100 in second cabin, and 554 in "Asiatic steerage."

It was a disastrous decision. The "repairs" became "the largest reconditioning job ever performed in an American shipyard"[55] as the cost ballooned to $2.5 million. Having compromised its financial solidity in the *Nile* fiasco, the China Mail now stood on the brink of financial ruin.

To increase the company's capital, Look called meeting of the Board of Directors on March 19. But the directors put him off, calling another meeting for July 19. In the meantime, notices were published in the *Daily Journal of Commerce* and mailed to all stockholders. Opposition was such that at the July 19 meeting Look could not raise a quorum. Nor could he do so at subsequent meetings on August 2, or in meetings in March, April, August, and December of 1918. In fact, the increase in capital would only come years later, once Look was long out of the way.[56]

With repair bills for the *Nanking* mounting, Look developed an alternative "financial restructuring" plan, but it stirred up even more animosity among the stockholders. In May 1918, he filed articles of incorporation for the China Mail Steamship *Corporation*. The idea was to raise $10 million in capital and have this new company take over the assets of the China Mail Steamship *Company*, "finance the debt, then supposedly return the company to its original owners."[57] What angered not a few of the China Mail's stockholders was that three of the five directors of the new Corporation would be white: John Barneson, Charles Blyth, and Harry Brandenstein. The other two would be M.Q. Fong and Look.[58]

This was not the first time that Look had tried to bring in non-Chinese investors. Writing in the 1920s, Brunner told the following story:

> In 1917 one of San Francisco's most prominent bankers approached Look:
> "Tin, I have great confidence in two things: the future of San Francisco as a great seaport and the future prospects of your steamship line. I am ready to back you to the extent of $10 million to purchase ships, and take shares in your company by way of security."
> "And," was Tin's quick reply, "at the first stockholders' meeting vote us Chinese out of our boots and take the whole works—nothing doing."
> "Nothing of the sort" was the banker's rejoinder. "On the contrary, I wouldn't give a hoot for your line with you Chinese out of it. It's the four hundred million inhabitants of China and the transportation facilities they are going to need very shortly that I am figuring on."
> Tin thought it over and seriously discussed it with his Board. He advocated accepting, but "mossbacks" rejected it.[59]

In 1918 the idea of having white investors was no more palatable to most China Mail stockholders than it had been the year before. Few had confidence that Look and his white investors would not try to take over the company to the detriment of the many small stockholders within the Chinese community.

The first attack on Look came in June 1918. The target was not the China Mail but, rather, Look's principal business, the Canton Bank, a number of whose directors also served on the China Mail's Board of Directors. At the annual meeting earlier in the year, an internal power struggle had led two of the directors to resign, to be replaced by Fong Wing (a Chinatown merchant) and M.Q. Fong (secretary of the China Mail). Business was reported as "extremely good," with deposits up nearly 25 percent from the previous year.[60]

So it came as something of a surprise when, on the morning of Saturday, June 23, just as managers were preparing to move the Bank (and the China Mail) into the new building at Montgomery and Sacramento, rumors spread that the China

Mail was in financial trouble and the Canton Bank with it. A run on the Bank began. In one day, reported the *Chronicle*, $175,000 of the $1,250,000 on deposit was paid out.[61] The run continued when the Bank opened on Monday morning, although the Bank managed to pay all depositors. Not only was the Bank threatened, but Look "and his fellow directors were simultaneously threatened with death."[62]

Support for Look from the white-dominated banking industry helped the Canton Bank weather the run. A statement was issued immediately by W.R. Williams, the State's Bank Examiner, to the effect that the Canton Bank was sound: only small depositors had withdrawn funds, and none of the larger accounts—including the China Mail—had withdrawn their deposits. Look also had the support of his fellow bankers:

> Within the bank the telephones were busy receiving offers of assistance from other institutions, none of which it was at any time necessary to accept. Further, the depositors who withdrew their money were told by other banks that it was not wanted by them and were advised to take it back immediately to the Canton Bank, as no better place could be found. The run lasted but two days, when all that had been lost began to come back. The bank's deposits...are now gaining daily.[63]

Having survived the orchestrated run on his bank, Look pushed ahead with his plans for the *Nanking*, which in June had motored down from Seattle to its new home port. On June 26, "one hundred and twenty-five of San Francisco's shipping men were the guests of the CMSS yesterday on board its new liner which was recently reconstructed at one of the Pacific Coast ports. The guests inspected its palatial fittings and accommodations and then partook of refreshments in the dining saloon."[64] The following month she would set sail for Japan and China, the largest ship in the China Mail's "fleet."

But even her maiden sailing would be disrupted by internecine warfare. John Sawyer, on his way to take up his new post as Vice-Consul at Shanghai, was booked on that inaugural sailing. Everyone was on board, lunch had been served, the crew ready to cast off. Then all were informed that the sailing was delayed and that they had thirty minutes to leave the ship before it went in the stream. Sawyer found this puzzling and, as the sailing was put off for at least a day, decided to investigate.

> I called at the "Six Companies" and met their attorney John L. McNab who told me there is still a chance of sailing tomorrow. He said the "Six Companies" has laid down certain terms to the China Mail SS Co. which the latter will have to yield; that the China Mail is calling a meeting for tonight to consider those terms. There is much mystery about the reason for postponing sailing, the usual explanation being that the action of the China Mail in admitting certain white men to important offices in the company has given offense to certain stockholders including the "Six Companies" and that the difficulty can not be straightened out without the raising of a large sum of money.[65]

A second attack on Look came in December. On the evening of the 22nd, Director Fong Wing was gunned down in front of his store. Fong Wing was owner of the Ye On Company, "one of the most prominent members of the Chinese Merchants Association...a close friend of Judge William W. Morrow of the Circuit Court of Appeals." In a personal communication from Lew Hing's granddaughter, the author was told that assassins got the wrong Fong—that the real Fong Wing had come to her family's home for breakfast *after* the reported killing.

"It was the first time in six months that [he] had disregarded a price that had been placed on his head and ventured into the streets of Chinatown unguarded. ...He had stepped but a few feet from his place of business, 16 Waverly Place, when he...received two bullet wounds in the abdomen...and sank into the arms of his wife."[66] The police and directors of the China Mail immediately put out the word that the killing was the result of a "financial war among the stockholders of the China Mail."[67]

Other China Mail directors began receiving anonymous death threats: "We got Fong Wing! We will get you!" The directors personally put up a $10,000 reward (rather than have the company offer it), but feared for their lives. "Closed automobiles, with drawn curtains, convey the hunted men from place to place, always escorted by their white guards." Their hiding places included an entire floor of the Cartwright Hotel, guarded day and night by six private

Figure 7.4
A lithograph depicts the China Mail's SS *Nanking*, ca. 1920, three years after the ruinously expensive refitting that led to violent dissension within the Company.

Source: Courtesy of Daniel Krummes.

detectives.[68] Several went into virtual seclusion, especially after both the *Chronicle* and the *Examiner* helpfully published the names *and addresses* of every director of the China Mail.

Look, too, went into hiding, then tried to enlist help from an unlikely quarter —the Immigration Service. His telegram to Washington urged federal action as "the murder was undoubtedly committed by hired assassins of Tong men.... These Tong are composed largely of undesirable citizens of China, and it is a matter of Federal interest that they be broken up and the undesirables deported." A week later he had the Commissioner of Immigration for San Francisco on the case: Commissioner Edward White and Assistant Commissioner Boyce met with M.Q. Fong of the China Mail and Walter Lum, President of the Chinese Parlor of Native Sons, who together "undertook to furnish us with the name of the offi-cers of these (tongs), and such data as could be secured which would assist this office in locating the records of these men...with the hope of securing facts which would make deportation possible."[69]

Five days later, the president of the China Mail surreptitiously left town. The *China* was sailing, but Look feared being shot if he attempted to board her at the pier. Instead, he was taken by ambulance to a dock where a red stack tugboat was waiting. The tug took him several miles out to sea where he could board the *China* in safety. Look left San Francisco, friends said, not because he feared for his life but "because he was ill and in need of a long rest."[70] He would remain in exile until his death in November 1919.

Look and his successors used the Chinese Six Companies (Chinese Consoli-dated Benevolent Association) as a forum for explaining and defending the operations of his two companies, both of which depended on widespread support from the Chinese community. Newspaper accounts ascribed varying causes to the dispute—small stockholders feeling edged out, large stockholders wanting a seat on the board, a desire for $50,000 in profits to be distributed to shareholders, as well as the criticisms about taking on debt and white investors. San Francis-co's 800 policemen never did find Fong Wing's killer, although several Chinese hit men were arrested in connection with other killings in Chinatown.

Once Look left the scene, however, things calmed down. There was a rather smooth transition to new leadership: in December 1919, following Look's death, Chin Lain, vice president of the China Mail and publisher of the *Chung Sai Yat Po* (China West Daily), was elected President. Ng Poon Chew, the editor of CSYP, was elected to the Board of Directors.[71] It helped that both the China Mail and the Canton Bank seemed to be making money. *Coast Banker* reported a $174,000 net profit for the Canton Bank for 1918, and the Bank had seen its deposits, despite the run of June 1918, more than double from the previous year.[72] The *Pacific Marine Review* similarly announced that "The report of the China Mail Steamship Company for 1919 shows that concern to be in a very prosperous condition. The net profits of the company, after deduc[t]ing a reserve for Federal income taxes and proper allowances for depreciation, amount to 12½ percent on the book value of the stock."[73]

Two things contributed to this cheery outlook, and both of them were ships. In July 1918 the *Nanking* made her first sailing under the China Mail's colors, and on her return brought 724 passengers—to that time the largest load ever on a China Mail ship. And in November 1919 the *Nile* was returned to the China Mail by the British government. She was undoubtedly a little the worse for wear, having served five years as a troop transport between Hong Kong, Singapore, India, and the Mediterranean. Nonetheless, a speedy twelve-day overhaul in Hong Kong led to her being pronounced "just as trim, neat and clean as when formerly employed in service out of this port."[74] If three ships constituted a fleet, the China Mail now had one on the transpacific run.

THE YEARS AFTER LOOK TIN ELI

Given Look's pivotal role in establishing the CMSS, his departure might have been fatal for the company. That it did not *immediately* come undone is, perhaps, testimony to the genuine esteem in which it was held by Chinese communities across the United States and to the basic soundness of its day-to-day (as opposed to long-term strategic) management. That it *eventually* failed may have been due in equal parts to Look's decisions continuing to burden the China Mail, a lack of leadership in his successors, an economic downturn, and legislation which, while perhaps not aimed specifically at the China Mail, had severe negative effects on it.

In 1920, peacetime caught up with the China Mail.

World War I had been a boon to shipping companies. Not only had they made money, but in many areas they were allowed to do business where, before the war, they might have been excluded. For over a hundred years the United States, for example, had prohibited foreign ships from picking up passengers or freight at one American port for delivery at another. These "cabotage" laws were relaxed during World War I, as the American government's first concern was that there be service between its various ports, regardless of the nationality of the ships providing that service. After the war, American policy put a premium on maintaining trade routes as an element of national security. "It created ground-breaking 'essential trade routes' plan and directed the United States Shipping Board to maintain those designated sea lanes through private management. If private enterprise was unable to provide services, the Board was authorized to operate ships on those routes until it was."[75]

Created in 1916 as the United States prepared for war, the Shipping Board was the 900-pound gorilla of the American shipping industry. In its right hand it held the legal authority to enforce every facet of the Shipping Act of 1916 and its successor, the Merchant Marine Act (or Jones Act) of 1920. In its other it held ownership to over one thousand ships that Uncle Sam had commissioned to transport men, arms, and supplies to the European battlefields and back. When peace finally came, the Board had to decide what to do with all those ships.

One thing the Board could do was to put some of its ships into the hands of private "managing operators." Another thing it could do was to keep out foreign competition. Section 28 of the Merchant Marine Act empowered it to fine "foreign" ships $200 per passenger if they engaged in the "coastwise" trade. And this, beginning in early 1921, it began to do.

Ships of the Japanese TKK line were clearly "foreign" ships, and they were prevented from allowing a stopover in Honolulu to passengers picked up in Asia or San Francisco. And though it had long been regarded as an "American" line, the China Mail suddenly became a "foreign" carrier.

First, the *Nile* was barred from the coastwise trade because of its British registry. Then in March 1921 the Shipping Board "also...denied to the China Mail the right to engage in coastwise trade with its two American flag vessels, the *China* and the *Nanking*, because 75 percent of the company's stock is not owned by American citizens, as required by the Merchant Marine Act....The wide distribution of China Mail stock, which is held in San Francisco, Honolulu and China, would make compliance with the law...exceedingly difficult."[76] As a final indignity, the Shipping Board questioned the *China*'s right to American registry, given that she had been built in Britain.

The China Mail chose to fight. It dispatched twenty-five cabin passengers to Honolulu by the American-built, American-registered steamship *Nanking* (formerly the *Congress*). At Honolulu a fine of $5,000 was imposed, at the fixed rate of $200 per passenger. From Washington, China Mail Attorney Walter Penfield advised his client not to pay the fine and, for good measure, instructed the line's Honolulu agency to accept one passenger for transportation by the *China* on its way to San Francisco. Penfield argued that "section 28 [of the Jones Act] grew out of the insistence of a single American company, which must compete with *Canadians*."[77] The China Mail was thus an innocent victim, caught in crossfire intended for another. However, despite support from San Francisco business circles and the editorials of the *Pacific Marine Review* (the industry's leading journal), the Shipping Board prevailed and the China Mail lost a valuable market.

In 1921, the China Mail began to founder. Looking at the passenger loads that its ships brought into port, a decline clearly began in the middle of that year. General market conditions, the worldwide surplus of ships, and the arbitrary enforcement of the Jones Act certainly contributed to the China Mail's woes. To them was joined another factor, one that some historians believe was aimed squarely and solely at the China Mail. And that factor was opium.

OPIUM TROUBLES

The Narcotic Drugs Importing and Exporting Act [Jones-Miller Act] of May 1922, signed into law by President Harding, made the "master of a vessel liable for all narcotics seized on his vessel, at a rate of $25 per ounce for smoking opium....It was estimated that the fine against the steamer *Nanking* on her last voyage from the Orient would have amounted to $1,400,000, for which a bond of $2,800,000 would have been required. Thus, the confiscation of one large lot of opium secreted on a steamer would financially wreck any Pacific Coast shipping company."[78]

It has been argued that the law penalizing the owners of ships carrying smuggled opium was aimed at putting the China Mail out of business, that there was "a ferocious campaign to destroy CMSS focused on the narcotics traffic that supposedly flourished on its ships."[79] However, there is little evidence for this. Reports and editorials in shipping journals denounced the new law as adversely affecting *all* shipowners. It is more likely that, again, the China Mail was simply caught in a law whose intent was much broader.

In 1922 it was illegal to import opium into the United States, but it had not always been that way. Until 1909 the importation of opium—for both immediate consumption and as the raw ingredient for morphine—had been a large and legal industry. In the period 1900–9 alone, over *six million pounds* of opium were *legally* imported into the United States. The structure of the industry was largely determined by the fact that an 1880 treaty with China had reserved to *American citizens* the right to import opium into the United States.[80]

After 1909, when the importation of smoking opium was made illegal, smuggling became the only way to satisfy the demand for opium. If the experience of "Chinese Merchant King" Joe Shoong was at all typical, Chinese merchant-investors teamed up with "white men who undoubtedly furnished the capital with which the contraband opium was purchased, and who hoped to reap immense profits."[81] In California, Chinese merchants played a large role as distributors and consumers, as well as often being the actual smugglers. Chinese seemed to get the headlines whenever there was an opium bust, or when Customs agent uncovered an attempt to smuggle opium into the United States, creating a widespread impression that opium and opium smuggling were "Chinese problems." This was so even where there was strong evidence that whites were involved—as when two San Francisco police officers tried to board the *Nanking* to purchase drugs.[82]

A decade later, all sorts of prohibitions were in the air. On October 28, 1919, Congress passed the Volstead Act to enforce the Eighteenth Amendment, ratified nine months earlier. Known as the Prohibition Amendment, it outlawed the "manufacture, sale, or transportation of intoxicating liquors" in the United States. Laws outlawing other vices simply followed the lead of the Prohibition on alcohol. Customs agents in San Francisco became busier than ever, owing to the growing list of items that were not only dutiable but illegal. The National Archives' "smuggling file" contains clippings not only on alcohol and opium, but cocaine, morphine, weapons (smuggled *out* of San Francisco), and Chinese stowaways.

Opium smuggling was not limited to the China Mail; it was a problem for all shipping lines. In the several years preceding the Jones-Miller law, Customs agents had seized drugs on the *America Maru, Korea Maru, Shinyo Maru, Siberia*

Maru, and *Tenyo Maru* (of the Japanese TKK line), *Batoe* (Java Line), *Lyman Stewart, Colombia, Ecuador, Venezuela*, and *Ventura* (Pacific Mail), plus the *Depere* and the *Birmingham City*. The China Mail was neither the cause of the smuggling nor the only target of the new legislation. Even after the China Mail went out of business, the business of opium smuggling persisted.

The first San Francisco arrest under the new law came on June 19, 1922: Louis Henriquez, chief electrician of the *Empire State*, was caught with three tins of opium. A subsequent search of the ship turned up $42,800 worth of opium, which *should have* led to a fine of $17,525 for Captain Henry Nelson and the Pacific Mail. However, they were exempted as the ship, although under charter to the Pacific Mail, was owned by the federal government, which presumably could not fine itself! Even after the new law went into effect, and it became known that Customs officers had been given additional resources for even more thorough searches, seizures were made on the *Siberia Maru* and *Taiyo Maru* (TKK), and *President Cleveland, President Wilson*, and *Sonoma* (Pacific Mail).[83]

Although other lines were involved, ships of the CMSS were heavily represented in opium smuggling cases. Just a few days before the Jones-Miller Act went into effect, the *China* was busted: not only did inspectors find 12,000 bottles of "Chinese gin," but underneath fifty tons of coal in the ship's bunkers they found 500 tins (4,000 ounces) of opium worth about $100,000, and a further 500 ounces of cocaine and morphine. The China Mail dodged this bullet, as the *China* had arrived in port before the law took effect, but a month later the company was not as lucky. On June 24, over $20,000 worth of opium and cocaine were found on the *Nanking*, the line was "libeled" (i.e., required to post a bond) for $60,000 and Captain Thomas B. Dobson personally fined $30,000—even though he had sent a wireless message to the San Francisco Collector of Customs conveying "his suspicion that large quantities of opium and cocaine had been smuggled on board despite his vigilance."[84]

The China Mail undertook all sorts of strategies to prevent smuggling. Captain Frank Wise "searched the China six times between Yokohama and Honolulu. . . . At Hong Kong, the regular squad of Hongkong police was doubled to prevent smugglers from bringing the contraband aboard the China. At every Oriental port visited the guards were increased."[85] To discourage small craft from approaching the *China* in American waters (presumably to pick up opium tossed overboard by accomplices), the *China* sported a machine gun.[86] There were even reports "that the China Mail was considering the employment of white crews [as] about the only way in which smuggling of narcotics aboard the company's liners can be successfully combatted."[87]

Despite these efforts, the *Nanking* continued to earn its reputation among Customs officials as the "prize dope ship operating in the Pacific."[88] In November 1922, drugs were found—9,600 ounces of opium—resulting in a fine of $240,000; a bond of twice that was required for her to leave port. In April 1923 the *Nanking* was again busted when a crew member with forty pounds of opium was caught by Customs agents. By then the accumulated fines totaled nearly $500,000, even though some had been reduced on appeal to Treasury Secretary Andrew Mellon. Where other lines had "deeper pockets" for paying and appealing fines, the China Mail found them an enormous burden.

SUPPLY AND DEMAND

In addition to the fines and to being excluded from the coastwise trade, the China Mail had another problem: business was terrible.

After the boom years of World War I, there came the inevitable retreat. The decision of the United States Shipping Board to put its many ships into private hands may have been an expedient alternative to simply scrapping them, but the effect was to so flood the market that most ships became unprofitable. "Beginning in midsummer 1920, cargoes for the world's merchant marines became extremely scarce. By early 1921, 35 percent of the USSB's vessels were idle; eventually this figure would read 70 percent....There were simply too many ships for the business."[89]

The China Mail tried various tactics to combat the winds of an adverse economy. In 1921 it announced that it would no longer abide by the rates set by the Pacific Westbound Conference.[90] Although a small player in these conferences (in effect, cartels organized to prevent rate wars), the China Mail's presence or absence was always noted by trade journals such as the *Pacific Marine Review* and the *Shipping Register*. But supply so greatly exceeded demand that international attempts at rate-setting (price-fixing) were unsuccessful.

If prices could not be raised and the traffic on existing routes was low, perhaps having a larger network would improve things. The China Mail duly tried to expand its reach, chartering ships that would feed passengers and cargo from Singapore and India to Hong Kong for transfer to the transpacific run. The British steamer *Gujurat* was chartered for six months[91] and the *Victoria,* reportedly sold to the China Mail, was in all probability chartered, too. In 1920 it opened a sumptuous office in Singapore, and the following January the *China* began including that port in its itinerary, while the *Nile* was consigned to feeder service between Singapore, Manila, and Hong Kong.[92] This arrangement lasted little over a year. In 1922 the China Mail agreed to operate the *Nile* on behalf of the new California-Tahiti Steamship Company for service between San Francisco and Tahiti. In between, the *Nile* was forced into such ignominious duties as ferrying a thirsty Shriners convention (to circumvent Prohibition) to Honolulu via Vancouver, where it took on "liquid goods from the mainland bonded warehouses."[93]

THE END

An attempt was made in 1922 to bring in additional funds. The directors arranged to have the authorized capital stock increased from $2,100,000 up to $10,500,000. This would have been a prelude to selling additional stock to new investors. What is impressive about this effort was that the documentation revealed the breadth of ownership—and thus community support—of the China Mail. The Certificate of Increase of Capital Stock filed with the California Secretary of State lists over 2,700 names and the number of shares owned by each. While several were in the range of the 1,100 owned by Look Tin Eli's estate, most were in the range of two to ten shares.[94] The larger infusion of new funds, though widely reported as imminent, never came to pass, perhaps a triumph of investor caution over investor patriotism.

By early 1923, the China Mail was clearly in desperate straits. As the previous year was drawing to a close, three of the *China*'s top officers had resigned while the vessel was en route from Yokohama to Honolulu.[95] In January the *Nile* was ordered tied up at Hong Kong: though still serviceable, as a coal-burner she was expensive to operate. In March the *China* was withdrawn from service and sent—empty of passengers—to Hong Kong: she had "failed to pass a boiler test and the company does not deem it advisable that repairs be made."[96] In early April, following the *Nanking*'s arrival, it was announced that she would be laid up pending a reorganization of the company. News that the *Nile* would make one last trip, arriving in May, only prolonged the China Mail's death throes.

All during March and April of 1923, stories appeared in the San Francisco press alluding to a pending reorganization or refinancing of the China Mail. Even with the April 6 announcement that the company would cease to operate, "the prevailing opinion in local shipping circles is that the suspension of operations...is only temporary, and it is known that strong financial interests are endeavoring to keep the company going."[97] Rumor had it that only disagreements over who would manage a revamped company were stalling the arrival of new capital, and that shipping interests (i.e., non-Chinese) in San Francisco wanted to maintain a competitor to the Pacific Mail.

A more plausible explanation was that "the Pacific Mail vessels have so completely cornered the trans-Pacific trade that all foreigners are practically excluded....(E)very Pacific Mail steamer arriving from the Orient is filled to capacity, both with passengers and cargo, while on other lines the cargoes and the passenger lists are light."[98] Shippers wanted the China Mail to continue, as "the Chinese back of the company...have long attempted to shift all possible trade in their control to the port of San Francisco."[99]

The *coup de grace* was delivered in May: on the 3rd, U.S. Marshals seized the *Nanking* to pay debts owed to the federal government and to private suppliers. Not only did the China Mail owe half a million dollars in unpaid fines, but it owed an equal amount to companies that included Shell Oil, Union Trust, Moore Drydock, and the Schirmir Stevedoring Company.[100] Two days later yet another indignity befell the *Nanking*: Federal agents, having already sent the crew back to China on the *President Cleveland*, discovered fifty-two Chinese stowaways in the hold.[101]

The next month, the *Nile* was sold at auction for a mere $47,800. The *Nanking* was sold in November to the Admiral Line, was rechristened the *Emma*

Alexander, and served until that line went bankrupt in 1936; the British bought her in 1942 for war duty, then sunk her at sea in 1946. The *China*, now thirty-four years old, was sent to Hong Kong to be broken up for scrap. In keeping with the anthropomorphic way that ships are often referred to, the *Marine Journal* offered an elegy to the *China*: "The China still retained her popularity with passengers—the 'little China,' as she was affectionately known. No more beautiful ship ever floated on Pacific waters. She had a well-bred, aristocratic look. Wherever fate may carry her, she will remain a ship of distinction and fame."[102]

The death of the China Mail, as summed up in the *Daily Commercial News*, "was received in shipping and business circles with expressions of regret. In the face of untold obstacles the company has made a brave battle for existence... and assisted to maintain the dignity and prestige of the American flag on the Pacific since it organized and began operations."[103] Three years later, the *Daily Commercial News* would announce the death of the Canton Bank, closed by the State Superintendent of Banks after its dealings with the failed Oriental Commercial Bank of Hong Kong led to a run on the Canton Bank's deposits. Most depositors would eventually be paid after the Bank's assets were distributed.

REFLECTIONS AND QUESTIONS

The identity of the China Mail as an American company fluctuated over time. For most of its career, it was seen by the public and by the U.S. government as an American business, with all the attendant rights and responsibilities.

Scarcely had the China Mail begun operations than her American character was asserted—and tested. Two days out of Shanghai on her second sailing back to San Francisco, the *China* was ordered to halt by the British auxiliary cruiser *Laurentic* (herself a former White Star liner), which fired a blank shot. The *China* continued on, coming to a stop only when a second shot—this time a live round—came across her bow. British marines came aboard and took off thirty-eight of the *China*'s passengers—twenty-eight Germans, eight Austrians, and two Turks.[104]

A diplomatic brouhaha ensued. With only a little encouragement from Look Tin Eli, Secretary of State Robert Lansing launched a loud and very public protest to the British government. A neutral ship—an *American* ship—heading to a neutral (American) port could be stopped and searched for contraband (arms) only; she and her passengers had every right to proceed unhindered. This was the same sort of protest that the U.S. government had made in 1914 when the *China* and the *Manchuria*, both then owned by the Pacific Mail, had similarly been boarded and German passengers taken off.[105]

In mid-1919, the U.S. government requisitioned the *Nanking* for patriotic service. The ship's assignment: bring back a contingent of Czechoslovakian troops from Vladisvostok who had been part of the Allied (mainly American) invasion of Russia aimed at toppling the new Soviet government. Returning via San Diego, she landed 772 Czech soldiers at San Francisco on the 4th of July.[106]

Later in 1919, treatment of the *Nanking* by Japanese quarantine officials was the subject of official protests by the American consul at Yokohama. The *Nanking* had been detained "for four days under circumstances that [were] declared by the ship's officers as more liable to spread disease than to check it." The *Examiner* noted that the ship was "owned by Chinese and Americans and is under American registry."[107]

It was, of course, not always to the company's advantage to be treated as an American business. Numerous regulations—such as certain aspects of the Jones/Merchant Marine Act—applied to American lines but not to foreign ones. One such was a ruling by the Shipping Board that ships under its control (which included the China Mail) could not load or unload at night "because it was found that stevedores, attracted by the night overtime, would not work so well by day."[108] Such rulings resulted in increased turnaround time that put the China Mail at a mild competitive disadvantage vis-à-vis its Japanese competitors.

The CMSS is often referred to as a "Chinese business." But one might well ask, how Chinese was the China Mail?

It was never the intention of the China Mail's directors to rely solely on Chinese clients to fill its passenger accommodations or its cargo holds. It was expected that the steerage quarters, commonly referred to as "Asiatic steerage," would be almost exclusively filled by Chinese passengers. To fill the profitable cabin quarters, however, would require a more broad-based clientele. Even in the midst of the anti-Japanese boycott, the China Mail courted and accepted Japanese passengers, just as it appealed to whites to "get the cream of the tourist trade."[109] Such a pragmatic policy resulted in a passenger distribution typified by the *China*'s July 20, 1917 arrival: "Europeans" comprised 78 of 141 first cabin passengers and 5 of the 39 passengers in second cabin; Japanese were 14 and 7, respectively; the other 399 were Chinese, including all 323 in steerage.[110]

Surviving China Mail brochures indicate that the CMSS sought that broader audience amongst white travelers. The brochures themselves are of the sort that appeal to white travelers seeking the "exotic Orient" and not too different, in fact, from those produced by cruise companies today. Never did an advertisement mention that the overwhelming majority of one's fellow passengers would be in steerage, and that they would be Chinese—kept totally separate, of course, from the cabin-class passengers. Newspaper accounts of the arrival in San Francisco of CMSS ships tell of the success of this policy—every sailing to San Francisco had numerous white cabin passengers that included businessmen, missionaries (an extremely loyal clientele), the occasional diplomat, and an assortment of travelers and tourists.

Not that the CMSS ignored its Chinese base. From the outset, advertisements were run in Chinese newspapers and in various Chinese publications, hoping to attract both cabin and steerage passengers. The CMSS regularly advertised in the *Chinese Students Monthly*, a publication of the federation of associations of Chinese students at universities across the United States: "Chinese Student Patronage to This First Big Chinese Enterprise 'Across the Pacific' is Earnestly Solicited." In this the CMSS was only one step behind the railroads: The Santa Fe courted Chinese passengers with being met by a Chinese representative and "no unnecessary details as to immigration inspection."[111]

Figure 7.5
A brochure for the CMSS, ca. 1916, courted non-Chinese clients for its cabin-class accommodations.

Source: The Huntington Library, San Marino, California.

There was at least one occasion when the entire passenger list was Chinese. In 1921

> for the first time in history an American vessel will arrive here with every passenger on board a Chinese. Traveling first cabin are 165 Chinese, both men and women. They are coming to attend American universities all over the United States at the expense of the Boxer indemnity. In her steerage are 400 Chinese, all en route to Havana.[112]

A similar pragmatism was evident in the filling of cargo holds, dictated by the pattern of trade between the United States and China that prevailed at the time. Even though *preference* was given to Chinese merchants, much of the outbound cargo came from white businessmen who sent manufactured goods (machinery, hardware, and food products) to China. On the return, a typical cargo would have been consigned to Chinese businessmen and might have included "2341 bales of gunnies, 500 bales of hemp, 1000 sacks of peanuts, 1032 cases of rubber, 235 packages of raw silk, 4629 sacks of rice, 300 packages of antimony, 1389 chests of tea and 6412 slabs of tin."[113]

With an ownership now composed entirely of Chinese, one might expect the composition of the crew to change. It did not. Crew lists show that the crews were largely the same combination of Europeans and Asians as before. A representative list from a year after the christening shows there are "Europeans"—i.e., whites—in each of the three major "departments" comprising the ship's company. Many of these "Europeans" are actually Americans (including the Captain), with the balance including a Greek carpenter, a Spanish quarter-master, an English watchman, an Australian steward, and a Russian butcher.[114]

Maintaining so many Chinese crew members was remarkable in itself, given that the China Mail had come into existence as the unintended by-product of a law (the La Follette Seamen's Act) enacted to *prevent* Chinese seamen from serving on American ships. The Act was not exactly a dead letter (at least not at the outset), nor were the examinations of a perfunctory nature. Newspaper stories noted that in advance of the November 4 (1915) deadline for registering and obtaining certificates of physical and professional competence, "Many Seamen Fail to Pass Test Required by New Law."[115]

Nevertheless, on January 6, 1916 the *China* made its second sailing under the China Mail flag, and the *Examiner* headline read that "Crew on China is All Chinese." This was not the result of sleight of hand. "Port Surveyor Justus Wardell...spent most of the preceding night examining the Chinese sailors, and found that all departments except the engineering measured up to the legal requirements." Twelve Filipino firemen were signed on for the "black gang" at the last minute, enabling the *China*'s crew to comply with the requirement that 75 percent of each department's crew be able to understand English. (On subsequent sailings, the requisite number of English-speaking Chinese firemen would be found.) President Look Tin Eli thought this proved that the China Mail could operate under American registry and still challenge the Japanese. He was quoted as saying that "about half of the crew of the China learned the business on Pacific Mail ships. We are paying our men more than the Pacific Mail ever did, and we feel that we can afford to do it. Of course, we could not pay what white sailors would demand."[116]

There does not appear to have been any concerted effort to train Chinese to become officers or to assume any of the more responsible crew positions. The lone exception is that Look's son was promoted to purser on the *Nanking*, a position held by white men on other American ships.

One thing, however, was clear and explicit from the outset: the China Mail would accommodate Chinese merchants first. On her initial sailing under the China Mail, *all* of the *China*'s cargo space was allocated to Chinese exporters. This was, according to the *Examiner*, in line with the company policy: "The officials of the company state that no outside cargo will be bid for until the Chinese merchants and shippers are accommodated. Then as space allows the cargoes of white shippers will be considered."[117]

The ownership was, indeed, initially all Chinese—"a majority of whom are citizens and residents of the State of California"[118]—although this was an informal understanding not written into the Articles of Incorporation. Several years later the Merchant Marine Act would make this a source of contention.

The management of the company's day-to-day affairs was clearly not Chinese. While Look Tin Eli was an activist President, his General Manager and Passenger Agent were white; in 1921, the Assistant General Manager was A.M. Garland and the Accountant W.G. Anderson (although by that date the General Manager was Lo Lok Chai). Overseas, its agents' offices were all headed by non-Chinese: Castle & Cooke (Honolulu), O.D. Martinez (Yokohama), Holme, Ringer & Company (Nagasaki), F.R. Barrett (Shanghai), C.T. Surridge (Hong Kong), Thomas Cook (Manila), and Francis Peek (Singapore).[119] This followed the model that Look had successfully established with the Canton Bank: have a complement of white officials to provide expertise and credibility beyond the Chinese community; court business from Chinese *and* white customers; and operate as an avowedly *American* company. Only when Lo Lok Chai arrived on December 15, 1919 from China as the new General Manager did daily management have a Chinese in charge.[120]

It is something of a puzzle that the China Mail never bought more than three ships—the *China*, the *Nanking*, and the *Nile*. There were certainly many rumors or reports that it had done so or was about to do so. But an examination of *Lloyd's Register of Shipping* shows only the three vessels. Undoubtedly there were vessels chartered or leased out of Hong Kong as part of the CMSS feeder network, but details on them are scant.

The most obvious source of ships in the immediate postwar period was the United States Shipping Board. It had hundreds of ships, and released them to "operating managers" on very favorable terms. The Pacific Mail put nearly a dozen of these "535s" into service on the Pacific, and other American steamship companies did the same. That the CMSS, which had a significantly better track record than many of the newly formed "operating managers," was unable to secure a single vessel is surely attributable to some form of racism: the owners of the China Mail were simply not viewed as "real" Americans and were thus ineligible to secure USSB vessels.

Still, there were many other vessels that the CMSS examined or negotiated for but never purchased. If the company had been as well funded as its leaders boasted, it should have been possible to purchase existing vessels or order new ones at *some* point. That the CMSS never did so hints that the company's access to funds was considerably less than many assumed. The white world seemed quite prepared to believe that "the Chinese" had an unlimited willingness to invest in this enterprise, even if there was little evidence for it.

Although the CMSS had a life of less than eight years, it should not be seen as a failure. It was, in fact, a rather remarkable achievement by any comparison. To start the CMSS and to keep it operating for that long were not trivial endeavors. Comparing it with two other efforts to start immigrant-ethnic steamship companies only heightens our admiration for Look's accomplishments.

In 1922, the American Line's aged *Philadelphia* (ex-*City of Paris*) was sold to the newly formed New York-Naples Steamship Company, her intended service being Gibraltar–Naples–Palermo–Piraeus–Constantinople. The *Philadelphia* left New York with Constantinople as destination, but by the time she approached her first port of call—Naples—the ship had become a floating problem. The company was facing heavy financial difficulties, and the crew had become mutinous. After an unsuccessful attempt by the crew to scuttle the ship, the officers were forced to patrol the decks with revolvers drawn. Upon the ship's arrival in Naples, the authorities came on board and arrested the crew. The ship was abandoned and it eventually drifted ashore. Shortly thereafter she was sold for scrap and towed to Genoa, where she was broken up, thus ending the ever-so-brief career of the New York-Naples Steamship Company.[121]

A second, more meaningful comparison is with the Black Star Line of Marcus Garvey. A Jamaican-born black nationalist who based his United Negro Improvement Association in New York, Garvey was an astute propagandist. Appealing to blacks with notions of racial purity and separatism, Garvey used his newspaper, the *Negro World*, as the vehicle for touting "a plan to unite Negrodom by a line of steamships."[122] In June 1919 Garvey incorporated the Black Star Line in Delaware, capitalized at $500,000, with the goal of transporting goods and raw materials between black-owned businesses in Africa, the Caribbean, and North America. He surprised the white world by quickly raising enough money to purchase his first vessel: the *Yarmouth*, an old World War I coal ship, which was to be renamed the *Frederick Douglass* and would sail under black captain Joshua Cockburn and an all-black crew.

Alas, the *Yarmouth* and the several other ships purchased by the Black Star Line came to sorry, soggy ends. Garvey knew nothing of ships or shipping, and what incompetence did not ruin, peculation did. Powerful though the line may have been as a symbol to American blacks, no Black Star ship ever made it to Africa.[123] "The established companies watched with amusement as shady white ship brokers and agents joined with no less unscrupulous blacks to fleece the Black Star Line for all it was worth."[124]

If one finds these comparisons unfair, a good case can be made that even comparisons to white American shipping companies are favorable to the CMSS. The shipping business was a difficult one, especially for American companies, and the passenger business was the riskiest of all. Many established American shipping lines perished around this time or survived only as wards of the U.S. government or of larger corporate parents. The mighty IMM never made money, and the Pacific Mail, reconstituted under the W.R. Grace ownership and with a long tradition of transpacific passenger service, was sufficiently enfeebled that the Dollar Line took it over in 1922.[125] The many "managing operators" that blossomed in the wake of World War I wilted within a year or two, with few approaching the life span of the China Mail.

CONCLUDING REMARKS

Many claims have been made on behalf of the CMSS. One is that the China Mail was "the direct outcome of Chinese nationalism, brought to a height by Japanese imperialism, and of racial discrimination against Asians in the United States."[126] Another view is that the China Mail was a heroic effort to protest Japanese imperialism or the U.S. racism, "the beginning of the struggle against accelerating Japanese aggression in China."[127]

The company itself made a more modest claim in 1919.[128] While anti-Japanese China patriotism and the fight against racism undeniably existed and conditioned the environment in which the CMSS was born, they were contributory in a distant way. More important, in my view, were the more immediate *opportunities* presented by the economic environment, the vision of Look Tin Eli and his colleagues, and the local Chinese American institutions that made it possible for them to exercise leadership and seize the day.

NOTES

1. *San Francisco Chronicle*, October 29, 1915.

2. Quotations are from early California newspapers, cited in Gunther Barth, *Bitter Strength: A History of the Chinese in the United States, 1850–1870* (Cambridge, MA: Harvard University Press, 1974), 60–62. See also L. Eve Armentrout Ma, "The Big Business Ventures of Chinese in North America, 1850–1930," in *The Chinese American Experience: Papers from the Second National Conference on Chinese American Studies (1980)*, ed. Genny Lim (San Francisco: The Chinese Historical Society of America and the Chinese Culture Foundation, 1984).

3. Schwendinger, *Ocean of Bitter Dreams*, 197.

4. Barth, *Bitter Strength*, 61.

5. Note that figures are based on the U.S. Department of Labor, *Annual Reports of the Commissioner-General of Immigration* (Washington: Government Printing Office, 1912–32), table "Passengers Departed from the United States," and assume that the inbound were roughly proportional to the outbound shares.

6. See Schwendinger, *Ocean of Bitter Dreams*.

7. Rennie Schwerin, "La Follette's Ignorance Exposed," *Pacific Marine Review*, 1915.

8. De la Pedraja, *Rise and Decline*, 16.

9. *Pacific Marine Review*, September 1915, 20.

10. "Pacific Mail Sells Five Ships," *Daily Journal of Commerce*, August 14, 1915.

11. J.H. Kemble wrote that Pacific Mail had paid no dividends during the entire period 1899–1915. See John Haskell Kemble, *One Hundred Years of the Pacific Mail* (Newport, VA: Mariners Museum, 1950), 21.

12. *Daily Journal of Commerce*, October 18, 1915.

13. *San Francisco Chronicle*, October 14, 1915.

14. Ibid., October 30, 1915; emphasis added.

15. *Chung Sai Yat Po*, August 14, 1915. The Chinese Six Companies were actually an amalgam of region- or clan-based associations, each headed by an influential power broker, rather than a strictly commercial entity.

16. Quoted in Po-Chi Liu, *Mei-Kuo Hua Chi'ia Shi* (Taipei: Hsing cheng yuan chi'iao wu wei yuan hui: Tsung fa hsing so Li ming we hua shih yeh kung ssu, 1981), 279–81, trans. Sophia Kam.

17. Ma, "Big Business Ventures," 105.

18. Ibid.

19. *San Francisco Examiner*, October 12, 1915.

20. Partnership list of CSYP, 809 Sacramento St, San Francisco, filed May 15, 1915.

21. See Corinne K. Hoexter, *From Canton to California: The Epic of Chinese Immigration* (New York: Four Winds Press, 1976).

22. *Chung Sai Yat Po*, November 24, 1915, trans. Danian Lu.

23. Ira B. Cross, *Financing an Empire: History of Banking in California*, vol. 2 (Chicago: The S.J. Clarke Publishing Company, 1927), 699.

24. *Coast Banker*, December 1918, 583.

25. William Luke, "The First Chinese Bank in the United States," *Chinatown News*, July 3, 1974.

26. In Japanese community banks, records were kept in Japanese until 1911. Supervision by state bank inspectors was thus more difficult, leading to numerous abuses and the banks being "simply looted." Cross, *Financing an Empire*, 728.

27. *Coast Banker*, August 1918, 175.

28. Cross, *Financing an Empire*, 699.

29. See annual *Report of Superintendent of Banks*. A table on page xxvi of the 1927 report shows "The Growth of Savings in California State Banks 1911–1927."

30. Noel H. Pugach, "American Shipping Promoters and the Shipping Crisis of 1914–1916: The Pacific & Eastern Steamship Company," *American Neptune* 35 (1975): 166–82.

31. Tate, *Transpacific Steam*, 71.

32. See W.C. Brunner, "Sixty Years of Steam Shipping, Part III," *Japan: Magazine of Overseas Travel*, June 1927.

33. Articles of Incorporation of China Mail Steamship Company, October 15, 1915. California Department of State.

34. *San Francisco Examiner*, October 12, 1915.

35. *Chung Sai Yat Po*, October 14, 1915, trans. Danien Lu.

36. See Liu, *Mei-Kuo Hua Chi'ia Shi*, 279–81.

37. *Pacific Marine Review*, December 1915.

38. Soennichsen, *Miwoks to Missiles*, 85.

39. René De la Pedraja, *A Historical Dictionary of the U.S. Merchant Marine and Shipping Industry, since the Introduction of Steam* (Westport, CT: Greenwood Press, 1994), 119.

40. *San Francisco Chronicle*, October 31, 1915.

41. Ibid.

42. *San Francisco Examiner*, January 7, 1916.

43. *San Francisco Examiner*, May 16, 1916.

44. *San Francisco Examiner*, October 2, 1916.

45. *Coast Banker*, June 1917, 439.

46. *Coast Banker*, August 1918, 175.

47. *San Francisco Examiner*, October 29, 1915.

48. Kemble, *One Hundred Years of the Pacific Mail*, 21.

49. *Pacific Marine Review* 13, no. 10 (1916): 27–28.

50. *San Francisco Chronicle*, June 20, 1917.

51. *San Francisco Examiner*, March 14, 1917.

52. Ma, "Big Business Ventures," 108.

53. Giles Brown, *Ships That Sail No More: Marine Transportation from San Diego to Puget Sound, 1910–1940* (Lexington: University of Kentucky Press, 1966), quoted in De la Pedraja, *Historical Dictionary*, 146.

54. De la Pedraja, *Historical Dictionary*, 145. Tate, *Transpacific Steam*, 71, gives $600,000 as the purchase price, while the *San Francisco Examiner* of April 12, 1917 states it as being $1,000,000.

55. Tate, *Transpacific Steam*, 72.

56. See "Certificate of Increase of Capital Stock of China Mail Steamship Company, Ltd.," California Secretary of State, February 2, 1922.

57. Ma, "Big Business Ventures," 108.

58. China Mail Steamship Company, "Articles of Incorporation," 1918.

59. Brunner, "Sixty Years of Steam Shipping, Part III," 35.

60. *Coast Banker*, January 1918, 68.

61. *San Francisco Chronicle*, June 23, 1918.

62. *San Francisco Examiner*, December 23, 1918.

63. *Coast Banker*, August 1918, 175.

64. *San Francisco Chronicle*, June 27, 1918.

65. John Birge Sawyer, "Diaries of John Birge Sawyer," 3:57–58.

66. *San Francisco Chronicle*, December 22, 1918.

67. *San Francisco Examiner*, December 23, 1915.

68. *San Francisco Chronicle*, January 24, 1919.

69. Alan Kraut and Randolph Boehm, eds., *Records of the Immigration and Naturalization Service*, vol. Reel 9 (Bethesda, MD: University Publications of America, 1992), Reel 9.

70. *San Francisco Chronicle*, December 29, 1918.

71. *Daily Journal of Commerce*, December 1, 1919.

72. *Coast Banker*, April 1919, 358, and Report of Superintendent of Banks, Canton Bank statement as of June 30, 1919.

73. *Pacific Marine Review* 17 (March 1920): 129.

74. *San Francisco Chronicle*, November 12, 1919.

75. J.J. Safford, "The United States Merchant Marine in Foreign Trade, 1800–1939," in *Business History of Shipping: Strategy and Structure*, ed. Tsunehiko Yui and Keiichiro

Nakagawa (Tokyo: University of Tokyo Press, 1985), 108ff. See also De la Pedraja, *Historical Dictionary*, 286.

76. *Pacific Marine Review*, April 1921, 251.

77. *Pacific Marine Review*, September 1921, 546, and October 1921, 607; emphasis added.

78. *Shipping Register*, June 3, 1922, 1.

79. De la Pedraja, *Historical Dictionary*, 121.

80. See Gregory Yee Mark, "Opium in America and the Chinese," *Chinese America: History and Perspectives* 11 (1997): 61–72.

81. Unidentified newspaper of January 1910, cited in Mark, "Opium in America and the Chinese," 71.

82. *San Francisco Examiner*, January 12, 1922, 1.

83. All stories seem to be from San Francisco newspapers, covering a period up to 1924.

84. *San Francisco Examiner*, June 25, 1922.

85. *San Francisco Journal and Daily Journal of Commerce*, December 23, 1922.

86. *San Francisco Chronicle*, March 3, 1923, 21.

87. *San Francisco Examiner*, March 15, 1923.

88. *San Francisco Examiner*, April 11, 1923. Dobson's reminiscences are among the oral histories in the collection of the J. Porter Shaw Library at the San Francisco Maritime National Historical Park. Cassette D13 contains an interview with Captain Dobson, recorded May 20, 1960, who mentions his stints as master of the *Olympia*, the *Victoria* (ex-*Parthia*), the *Colombia*, the *China* (when she was a Pacific Mail ship), the *Nile*, and the *Nanking* (among others).

89. Safford, "United States Merchant Marine," 110.

90. *Pacific Marine Review*, May 1921, 316.

91. *San Francisco Chronicle*, March 14, 1921.

92. *San Francisco Chronicle*, December 11, 1920.

93. *Shipping Register*, June 3, 1922, 2.

94. "Certificate of Increase of Capital Stock of China Mail Steamship Company, Ltd.," filed with the California Secretary of State, February 9, 1922.

95. *San Francisco Journal and Daily Journal of Commerce*, December 23, 1922.

96. *San Francisco Journal and Daily Journal of Commerce*, March 10, 1923.

97. *San Francisco Examiner*, April 7, 1923.

98. *San Francisco Examiner*, April 11, 1923.

99. *Daily Commercial News*, April 7, 1923.

100. *San Francisco Chronicle*, May 4, 1923.

101. *San Francisco Examiner*, May 5, 1923.

102. *Marine Journal*, April 14, 1923, 26.

103. *Daily Commercial News*, April 7, 1923.

104. *San Francisco Chronicle*, March 12, 1916, 3.

105. *San Francisco Examiner*, February 20, 1916, 1.

106. *Daily Journal of Commerce*, July 5, 1919.

107. *San Francisco Examiner*, September 22, 1919, 5.

108. *San Francisco Examiner*, December 21, 1919.

109. *San Francisco Examiner*, October 12, 1915, 1.

110. U.S. Bureau of Customs, "Customs Passenger Lists of Vessels Arriving in San Francisco, California, 1903–1918."

111. Both advertisements appeared in *Chinese Students Monthly*, November 1917.

112. *San Francisco Chronicle*, September 3, 1921, 19. Thousands of Chinese students came to the United States to study the so-called "Boxer indemnities."

113. *San Francisco Chronicle*, June 20, 1917, referring to the 4,078 tons of cargo brought in by the *China*.

114. Crew data taken from Alien Crew Lists, the "Recapitulation Passengers and Crew" portion of the Customs Passenger Lists, and the "Descriptive List of Chinese Seamen Arriving at the Port of San Francisco" for the respective voyages.

115. *San Francisco Chronicle*, October 31, 1915, 33.

116. *San Francisco Examiner*, January 7, 1916.

117. *San Francisco Examiner*, October 15, 1915, 10.

118. CMSS, "Articles of Incorporation," 1.

119. *Pacific Marine Review*, January 1921, ix.

120. *San Francisco Examiner*, December 16, 1919.

121. Found at http://www.greatoceanliners.net/cityofparis.html.

122. W.E.B. Du Bois, "The Black Star Line," *Crisis*, September 1922, 210–14.

123. See Ibid. The American Experience Web site on Marcus Garvey (http://www.pbs.org/wgbh/amex/garvey/filmmore/fr.html) has excellent summaries of Garvey's career, plus references and links to other sources on Garvey.

124. De la Pedraja, *Historical Dictionary*, 83.

125. See De la Pedraja, *Rise and Decline*, especially 4–8 and 63–69, for a brief history of the IMM. See also De la Pedraja, *Historical Dictionary*, for concise histories of IMM, Dollar, Pacific Mail, and China Mail.

126. Shehong Chen, *Being Chinese, Becoming Chinese American* (Urbana: University of Illinois Press, 2002), chap. 3.

127. Yong Chen, *Chinese San Francisco, 1850–1943* (Stanford: Stanford University Press, 2000).

128. China Mail Steamship Company, *Report 1915–1919* (San Francisco, 1919). The Report is in Chinese, and I thank Peng Lou for translating portions of it for me and Phil Choy and Bruce Quong for sharing the report itself.

— 8 —

The *Nippon Maru:*
A Career in the
Immigration Trade

M ost historical accounts of immigration to the United States focus, not unreasonably, on the lives of the immigrants. This chapter looks at another leading actor, the Japanese ship that brought Quok Shee, Chew Hoy Quong, and thousands of other Asian migrants into San Francisco: the *Nippon Maru*. If we think of the *Nippon Maru* in the anthropomorphic way dear to maritime historians, "she" had her own story, her own birth and life separate from those of the immigrants but for that one journey.

Even from afar, it was obvious that the *Nippon Maru* was destined mainly for transporting passengers. Any ability to transport cargo was carefully disguised by her graceful, elegant lines. Resting comfortably at the dock, she affected the air of a grand yacht, perhaps about to set off on a high society cruise, or carry statesmen on an important diplomatic mission. Nothing about her exterior hinted at so low a calling as the carrying of freight. And nothing gave away her being in the business of mass migration.

But graceful as she was, the *Nippon Maru* was a vessel of awkward fate, a ship with a history—and a past. She was also a carrier of controversy and death. Recounting that past conveys something of the transpacific immigration business and the role played by certain ships in that business.

The *Nippon Maru*'s maiden voyage in 1898 brought her to San Francisco, where she was received with much fanfare as a harbinger of a golden age of trade across the Pacific. Her journey across the Pacific in 1899, her third, brought her notoriety. Seventeen years later, the *Nippon Maru*'s seventy-fourth voyage brought Quok Shee and her "alleged husband." The ninetieth trip would be her last to

Figure 8.1

The *Nippon Maru,* photographed at the docks in San Francisco, ca. 1900, was the first Japanese passenger liner to call at San Francisco, and later brought Quok Shee and Chew Hoy Quong to California.

Source: Roy D. Graves Pictorial Collection, Bancroft Library, University of California, Berkeley.

San Francisco, one made as she neared the end of her career in the immigration trade. What follows is a retelling of several events in that career.[1]

MAIDEN VOYAGE

Long before the *Nippon Maru* first graced the Pacific—long, even, before her keel was laid—one man may have dreamed of such a ship: Asano Soichiro was a relative newcomer to the shipping business who had organized independent shipowners to challenge the mighty NYK (dominated by Mitsubishi) and the OSK. His strategy had been to operate in areas not served by the two larger lines, which had a stranglehold on Japan's shipping industry. Asano was so successful that by 1896 he was ready to try his hand at the high-stakes transpacific shipping business. His vehicle would be the TKK (Oriental Steamship Company).[2]

That year also saw the conclusion of the Sino-Japanese War. Many—mostly younger—Japanese, their worldview broadened by victory, wanted to go overseas. Organizations were created to serve people wanting to travel, a "law for the protection of emigrants" was enacted, and private emigration companies were established and began operating—but not to North America, which prohibited the entry of contract workers.[3] Japanese emigration to Hawaii increased sharply, and in 1899 the first Japanese emigrants went to Peru.

In the late 1890s, TKK was a rank newcomer to the transpacific shipping business. NYK was already in the business, having partnered in 1896 with James J. Hill, president of the Great Northern Railroad. Hill's idea was to connect Seattle—the end point of his railroad that crossed the northern part of the country—and the Far East so that he could transport cargo between New York and the Orient. NYK carried cargo (silks and teas, especially) and some emigrants outbound from Japan, and transported cargo such as cotton and flour on the return. In those days, at least two-thirds of the revenue came from shipping cargo, with revenue from carrying passengers accounting for only part of the rest. The cargo-first, passengers-second business model was extraordinarily successful: NYK's passenger service via Seattle lasted continuously for sixty-five years (allowing for a break during World War II), ending when NYK's last passenger ship on that run, the *Hikawa Maru*, was decommissioned in 1960.

NYK had chosen Seattle, not San Francisco, partly to avoid competition with the PMSS and the O&O line. In the same year that NYK started its service to Seattle, Asano looked to San Francisco, an area not served by the NYK. Asano decided that his TKK should try to break into the San Francisco route, then controlled by established *American* shipping companies.

In July 1896 Asano struck a deal with Collis P. Huntington, head of the Southern Pacific Railroad and owner of the Pacific Mail. They agreed that the Pacific Mail, the O&O, and TKK would divide the Far East–San Francisco market among nine ships: six ships from the American shipping companies and three ships from TKK. What made TKK an attractive partner was that Asano proposed to concentrate on passenger traffic, thus minimizing the amount of competition with the other two lines for the more lucrative cargo business. The cooperative arrangement disappointed San Francisco merchants, who had hoped that TKK's entry into that market would ignite a rate war.[4]

Asano had three markets in mind, three groups of emigrants who might welcome traveling in a ship that was not American, or to put it more positively, that was Japanese: Chinese, Japanese in Japan, and Japanese in Hawaii.

Before the Chinese exclusion laws, the bulk of the travelers across the Pacific were Chinese. After 1882 their numbers plummeted, but by the late 1890s had risen to several thousand each year traveling between San Francisco and China. Not all were official "immigrants." Many of the travelers were among the "exempt" categories—bona fide merchants, their wives, ministers and teachers, students—and the China-born children of Chinese residing permanently in the United States. Others were Chinese resident in the United States (including Chinese born in the United States) going to China on business, to visit, or to make their permanent return. Perhaps Asano saw in this modest upward trend the portent of a larger Chinese market.

Japanese migration was just taking off. Asano would certainly have been intimately familiar with this development. One thread followed the Japanese who came directly to the United States. From an abortive start in 1869 to a steadily increasing flow in the late 1890s, Japanese came to settle on the West Coast of the United States, particularly in California and Washington.

Japanese moving to Hawaii were potentially an even bigger source of passengers for TKK. Beginning in 1885, significant numbers of contract laborers came to Hawaii, recruited by Japanese immigration companies.[5] There were two sailings by Japanese ships that year which, along with a few individuals traveling on other vessels, brought 1,946 Japanese immigrants to Hawaii.[6] In each of the next dozen years, several thousand Japanese came to Hawaii. In 1898, the year of annexation, the number rose to nearly 10,000; the following year, to nearly 20,000. There was, indeed, a market.

A third thread in the fabric of Japanese migration consisted of Japanese already in Hawaii who were opting to move to the mainland of the United States. A song popular at the time among Japanese in Hawaii was "Horehorebushi," a phrase of which was "to go to the mainland, or return to Japan, we have to decide here and now." After the Sino-Japanese War, the number of Japanese emigrants moving to Seattle and San Francisco grew considerably, with over 50,000 Japanese coming to North America between 1901 and 1907.

Before launching TKK's transpacific services, Asano visited Hawaii and ran advertisements for his company in newspapers all over the islands. He made speeches to Japanese emigrants, saying, "We expect to transport 100,000 emigrants in ten years. Toyo Kisen Kaisha was founded with government subsidies and we promise to make your life comfortable in a foreign land."[7]

The following February, 1897, TKK ordered three vessels from major British shipyards on the River Tyne. Construction of the first ship, the *Nippon Maru*, began the next month in the shipyard of Sir James Laing in Sunderland. She was launched on April 23, 1898, completed four months later, then sailed in September to Yokohama by way of Port Said and the Suez Canal, Colombo, and Singapore. A second ship, the *America Maru*, came from Swan & Hunter in Newcastle, a large shipyard that would later build the famous *Mauretania*. The third ship, the *Hong Kong Maru*, came from James Laing. Each vessel cost ¥980,000 (about $500,000). The three ships would provide service from Hong Kong to Shanghai, Nagasaki, Kobe, Yokohama, Honolulu, and San Francisco regularly once every four weeks. But it was the first ship, the namesake of the "Nippon Maru Class," that captured the imagination of the Pacific shipping world.

In appearance she resembled the three *Empress* sister ships of the CPR, carrying an aura of style and comfort. The white hull, black topbands on the two buff funnels, a fancy carved wooden bowsprit, and the name written in Roman letters—an innovation that astonished people in Meiji Japan as somehow "too Western"—were all a product of TKK's relationships with American shipping companies.[8]

Graceful as she was, the Nippon Maru was a very large ship by the standards of the day. Bow to stern she measured 440 ft., 50 ft. across, with a hold 32 ft., 6 inches deep. Five boilers, two triple expansion engines, and twin screws enabled her to make a top speed of over seventeen knots (nautical miles per hour). In praise worthy of the Titanic, the Chronicle reported that "she has sixteen collision bulkheads and would be in no danger of sinking with any one of them smashed in." At 6,047 tons, when she arrived in San Francisco on January 24, 1899, the Nippon Maru was the largest passenger ship ever to have entered that port.

At that moment she was surely the most splendid ship on the Pacific. There was room for ninety-eight passengers in first class, forty in second class. As for steerage passengers—those carried below decks in open, dormitory-style accommodations—the Nippon Maru had "fixed accommodations for 335 steerage passengers in double-tiered bunk beds, each 2 ft. by 6 ft., with a further 735 passengers accommodated in open deck space for (converting to) steerage."[9] The San Francisco Examiner recorded her debut:

> The steamship Nippon of the Toyo Kisen Kaisha, the first of the long-talked-about Japanese liners, arrived in port yesterday morning and was berthed at the Pacific Mail dock. She looked large on the bay, the misty morning light lending a dimness to her lines and intensifying her massive appearance, but alongside the dock she resembled some huge monster of the deep.... (T)he gangway (which) even to the big China's main deck forms only a moderately steep incline...is converted into a regular ladder in the case of the Nippon Maru....The Nippon is splendidly equipped for the carrying of passengers, her second-class accommodations being as comfortable, if not quite as luxurious as her first.[10]

Asano and the TKK were not relying on just 138 cabin-class passengers to pay all the bills. Nor did TKK depend entirely on subsidies that the Japanese government paid its overseas shipping companies. The Nippon Maru and her sisters were built to haul emigrants: Japanese emigrating from Japan, Japanese quitting Hawaii for the mainland United States, Chinese leaving the turbulent Middle Kingdom, and members of all groups returning home for visits. Comparing the Nippon Maru and her sisters with the ships of the NYK that made the run to Seattle, the difference in strategies is obvious. The sizes (tonnage) of the various ships are comparable, but the TKK vessels had a much higher passenger capacity in both cabin class and steerage, with the NYK ships presumably having more room for cargo.[11]

Perhaps, then, it was not unreasonable for Asano and the TKK to envision a successful shipping business based on the emigration industry, and to build large, beautiful ships to carry those emigrants. But the number of Chinese emigrants to North America was small and, more seriously, a movement to exclude Japanese emigrants was building in California. Later, the TKK, and especially the *Nippon Maru*, would be greatly affected by restrictions on Japanese emigrants.

But in 1898, on her maiden voyage, the *Nippon Maru* seemed set to prove the wisdom of Asano's strategy. She carried a heavy complement of emigrants from Japan, and a few from China. Four hundred and eighty-six Japanese—all in steerage—were landed in Honolulu. Also aboard were forty Chinese, twenty-three of whom were destined for Honolulu. By the time the *Nippon Maru* arrived in San Francisco, the complexion of her passenger list had changed considerably. She carried sixty-nine cabin passengers, "including three Filipinos bound for Washington in Aguinaldo's interests." All fifty-seven Americans traveled in cabin class, including thirteen who were members of the American armed forces. A Russian engineer and his wife, plus seven Japanese, made up the rest of the cabin-class passengers.

Also on the ship were the remaining seventeen Chinese who had not disembarked in Honolulu. For seven, the United States was their final destination: five merchants with affidavits or Section 6 certificates; one "Return Laborer"; and one "Native" (i.e., born in the United States) who was refused landing and released only when he obtained a writ of habeas corpus in the U.S. District Court. The rest were "in transit": one was taking the Southern Pacific Railroad to Torreon, Mexico, while the others were transferring to another ship to travel to Panama.[12] Of the twenty-three Japanese on board, nineteen were bound for San Francisco (fifteen students, two merchants, and two farmers), while a merchant and three students were bound for New York.

For a ship hoping to haul large number of emigrants, the run Honolulu to San Francisco journey found the steerage quarters strangely empty. A mere thirty-five passengers in steerage! And not a particularly large contingent of Japanese passengers, either. Perhaps the business model of carrying emigrants would apply only as far as Honolulu, with the rest of the journey underwritten by cabin-class passengers and freight.

On her first voyage to North America, the *Nippon Maru* was severely tested. A heavy northeaster washed away much of her gingerbread work, twisted rails, and broke companion ladders. Seas were so rough that some of the cargo shifted, causing the ship to list slightly. Nevertheless, her passengers spoke highly of the performance of the ship and the captain in riding out the tempest. Passengers seemed to derive a certain comfort from knowing that the ship's lifeboats could be released from their lashings by the removal of a single wooden pin. Apparently all were impressed that even during the storm her eight iron lifeboats were "swung out instead of being brought inboard and lashed on chocks to the deck, as is the case with every other steamer coming into this port."[13]

Not everything about the *Nippon Maru* met with the approval of her cabin passengers. The third and fourth officers, Y. Yamamoto and N. Fujita, were Japanese, and the *Chronicle* recounted that "the passengers do not seem to care about having any but European officers on the bridge.... [They] all expressed a determination never again to take passage on a steamer officered, even in part, by Japanese."[14] The ship's surgeon, S. Kubo, was on loan from the Japanese navy; even he would be replaced by a European (i.e., white) surgeon based in San Francisco.

The reporter went on to say that "the Japanese deckhands did not prove exactly a success either, and it is not unlikely that their places will be taken by Chinese, who are said to make far better sailors." The crew was not a harmonious unit. "The Anglo-Saxon element refuses to associate with the Oriental and neither race will take an order from the other." Several engineers and junior officers resigned, rather than suffer a repeat voyage with a nearly mutinous crew.[15]

It was *de rigueur* for an Englishman to be the master of Japan's finest, newest passenger ship. When NYK inaugurated its service between Hong Kong and Seattle (August 1, 1896), the *Miike Maru* sailed under an English captain. It was not until the *Ryojun Maru* left Kobe for Seattle in June 1901 that a Japanese captain, Oono Kajitaro, commanded a Japanese passenger ship on the North American run. Only in 1920 did the last of the non-Japanese captains leave the Japanese transpacific passenger fleets. For the *Nippon Maru*, it would be seventeen years before she had a Japanese master.

The *San Francisco Chronicle* foresaw that the *Nippon Maru* would "be the pioneer of improved passenger travel across the North Pacific." The business class of San Francisco certainly hoped so. San Francisco would be the hub of American commerce on the Pacific, and the ships of many nations would tie it all together. The city fancied itself the Rome of the new American imperium stretching across the Pacific. The most recent tokens of expanding American influence were the annexation of Hawaii and the conquest of the Philippines, recently acquired in the tidy little war with Spain. Ownership was not to be merely part of a *mission civiliatrice*, but a key to increased trade with Japan and China. More passengers and freight moving through San Francisco meant wealth for the city's merchant and financial elites. Let nothing stand in the way of trade! Let there be ships!

After such a successful debut, the *Nippon Maru* seemed destined to have a part in that glorious expansion of America's ties with Japan and the Orient, and in the movement of Asians and Americans back and forth across the Pacific. It would play that role, along with another, less benign one that few would have foreseen when, on June 27, 1899, the *Nippon Maru* came to San Francisco for the third time. No winds or heavy seas had challenged her that time; the storm was of a different nature. The *Nippon Maru*, the loveliest ship ever to steam through the Golden Gate, was to become a carrier of death and, perhaps, of bubonic plague itself.[16]

THE PLAGUE SHIP?

The *Nippon Maru*'s maiden voyage had come just as the United States was increasing its presence in Asia. Troops moved back and forth to the Philippines and Hawaii, American businessmen and missionaries went prospecting for wider contacts with China and Japan. Asian passengers, too, were crossing the ocean in ships of all descriptions. Among the new dangers that might accompany such intercourse was the heightened possibility of diseases reaching the American mainland from Asia.

In an age aware of the process of "globalization" (if not the word itself), the spread of bubonic plague in other parts of the world was ominous. Up to 1899 the mainland United States had been spared, no cases of bubonic plague having been documented with absolute certainty.[17] But for a city such as San Francisco, open as it was to international intercourse, the threat was very, very real.

Such was the setting for the *Nippon Maru*'s fateful third trip to San Francisco. Having started out from Hong Kong on May 20, trouble surfaced six days later when a teenage Chinese passenger died less than an hour after the ship's surgeon had seen him in apparent good health. According to friends, the victim had a history of heart problems, and according to the ship's surgeon all the glands appeared normal. But Japanese medical officers in Nagasaki performed their own examination of the glands under a microscope. Their conclusion: bubonic plague.

The *Nippon Maru*'s passengers were taken to the Nagasaki quarantine station, there to have their bodies bathed, their clothing, bedding, and baggage disinfected by steam, and the ship itself given a thorough washing with strong carbolic acid. "The Japanese sent us up for fumigation," reported passenger J.A. Welch, a veterinary surgeon. "The women put on old kimonos and the men attired themselves in their oldest clothes. After fumigation, we threw the old things away."[18] A week later the ship was allowed to continue on to Hawaii.

Three days from Honolulu, death again visited the *Nippon Maru* when one of the Chinese steerage passengers died in twenty-two hours, accompanied by "convulsions, suppression of urine, and symptoms of pulmonic congestion." The ship's surgeon decided not to have the body buried at sea, but kept for examination in port. Microscopic examination by Dr. Alvarez, the bacteriologist of the Hawaiian government, showed "considerable numbers of a short bacillus, rounded at both ends, and like the bacillus of bubonic plague." That was enough for Dr. D.A. Carmichael, Sanitary Inspector and Surgeon at Honolulu's Marine Hospital Service. He dashed off a letter to his colleague at the Quarantine Station on Angel Island and to the Surgeon General, alerting them to the strong possibility of plague aboard the *Nippon Maru*. Absent any telegraphic connection to the mainland, his warning had to be carried by the *Rio de Janeiro*, leaving for the coast that very afternoon.[19]

In Honolulu, none of the passengers bound for the mainland were permitted to disembark. Only after four days of strict quarantine did the *Nippon Maru*, still with all of her 2,500 tons of freight, continue her sad journey to San Francisco. Still aboard in "Asiatic steerage" was a 29-year-old Japanese woman, originally bound for Honolulu. She had been ill—suspiciously so—and the Honolulu port physician had refused to let her land. During the onward voyage to San Francisco, her condition worsened, "and the signs of the plague became more manifest day by day. She died on June 25th and her body was at once thrown over the side."[20]

It was later reported that conditions on board the *Nippon Maru* were deteriorating, to the point "that almost all the cabin passengers were in a state of panic." The captain did manage to enlist three physicians among the cabin passengers to aid the ship's surgeon in disinfecting the steerage compartments. It is unclear whether the steerage passengers themselves assisted in this, or whether anyone questioned why the first and second-class cabins were not also disinfected.[21]

When the *Nippon Maru* finally entered San Francisco early on the morning of Tuesday, June 27, she carried 61 cabin-class passengers, plus 32 Japanese and 106 Chinese passengers in steerage.[22] Another, most unwelcome, passenger was indicated by the bright yellow flag flying ominously from her mast, one recognized everywhere as "the dread symbol of violent disease."[23]

Chauncey St. John, the Deputy Surveyor of the Port, took no chances. His Customs men would normally have been among the first to board a ship, usually as soon as she reached Meiggs' Wharf (now Pier 39). With the yellow flag flying over the *Nippon Maru*, however, he decided against putting his inspectors aboard her, opting to have a launch keep a tight patrol of the suspect ship day and night.[24]

Joseph Kinyoun, head of the Federal Quarantine Station, did visit the ship. He questioned Ship's Surgeon Deas and Captain Allen to verify the recent medical events on board. Kinyoun quickly decided the fate of the *Nippon Maru* and her cargo, directing the ship to Angel Island, where all passengers and crew were to be transferred to the Quarantine Station and held "in antiseptic imprisonment" (as the *Chronicle* put it) for the required fourteen days. The ship and her cargo would be taken "to the fumigating hulk [the *Omaha*] off San Quentin, where disinfectants will be forced into every nook and cranny."[25] After the ship had been cleansed of possible contaminants, Kinyoun would allow a temporary crew to take her to berth at the Pacific Mail's docks for unloading.

In accordance with Kinyoun's orders, the *Nippon Maru* continued to a spot about a mile and a half to the leeward side of the Quarantine Station on Angel Island. That evening, all cabin-class passengers were transferred to the Quarantine Station. The following morning, the steerage passengers and most of the crew were landed at the Station. Kinyoun then ordered a thorough search of the ship, one that turned up nine stowaways. All were Japanese who had boarded at Yokohama and "had been hidden and provided with food by the Japanese firemen of the steamer. They had found sleeping quarters in the coal bunkers, and until the ship was searched by Dr. Kinyoun's order their presence was unknown to the Maru's officers."[26]

There ensued a very fierce, very public debate between Kinyoun and the local health authorities. At issue was who had the final say about preventing disease from entering through the port of San Francisco. In dispute were the most basic of facts: whether there was evidence that the plague had actually arrived (as the local and state quarantine officers had come to believe) or not (as was Kinyoun's opinion).

Giuseppe Casarino changed the debate on Wednesday afternoon. He and his partner were lying off Fort Point (what would today be the south end of the Golden Gate Bridge), on their way to fish for crabs, when they caught something rather unexpected: two lifeless bodies, held upright in their life preservers, floating on a strong tide and headed out the Golden Gate. Giuseppe got close enough to see that they were Asian and to read the words on the life preservers: *Nippon Maru*.

The bodies were those of Japanese stowaways. They had attempted to swim to the Marin mainland several miles away, drowning in the rough waters of Raccoon Strait. Their bodies were eventually hooked by the astonished Giuseppe, who towed them to the landing at the foot of Baker Street, where they could be examined by W.F. Barbat, the bacteriologist of the Board of Health. He reported that the drowned men had swollen glands and that his microscopic examination showed the presence of bacilli that *looked* like those of bubonic plague. This led to an escalating war of words with Kinyoun that was amplified by headlines in the *Examiner*. At the top of its front page on Friday, June 30, the *Examiner* shrieked that "San Francisco Is Endangered by the Federal Quarantine Officer."[27]

Barbat's report convinced the public—or, at least, the *Examiner*—that the plague had arrived in the person of the two drowned Japanese, and that more of it could come ashore from the *Nippon Maru*. By now the *Examiner* was fully on the side of the local health authorities, and its front-page headlines on July 1 were unequivocal: "Dr. Barbat Positive That Bacilli Are Those of the Bubonic Plague."

The Board of Health ordered that *no one* land, even though the *Nippon Maru* was almost at the docks. State Quarantine Officer Cohn ordered it taken into the stream for a second fumigation, even though Kinyoun, the Federal quarantine officer, deemed this unnecessary. Agent W.B. Curtis, acting for TKK, was in a quandary as to which quarantine authorities his company should obey. He had never had any dealings with quarantine authorities. Which orders should his company comply with? He might win a judicial reprieve, but any further delay would be risky—perhaps another week of losses of $400 per day plus dock charges, not to mention all the negative publicity focused on the fledgling passenger line.

On July 1, the TKK agreed to having the ship towed to the south quarantine grounds near Mission Rock and re-fumigated. The new State Quarantine Officer, Dr. Cohn—on his first official day of duty—oversaw the preparation of

chemical solutions which destroy every form of infectious bacilli, and the sprays and gases were soon forced into every crevice where a germ might be lodged. The disinfectants used are formaldehyde, formaline, corrosive sublimate, black oxide of manganese, and sulphuric acid. The cabins were sealed up and the gas was injected through the keyholes until the rooms were filled. To disinfect the cargo covers of the hatches were raised sufficiently to permit the insertion of the nozzles through which the gas is pumped....Other men were engaged in washing every inch of

Figure 8.2
The caption to this newspaper drawing dramatized the possibility of a ship bringing plague to San Francisco: "Under a magnifying power of 1,200 diameters, the bacilli found in the glands taken from the dead bodies of the Japanese who escaped from the *Nippon Maru* closely resembled the bacilli of bubonic plague, but the final tests were not completed yesterday."

SAN FRANCISCO IS ENDANGERED BY THE FEDERAL
QUARANTINE OFFICER.
INFECTED NIPPON MARU SENT TO THE MAIL DOCK

Police Captain Spillane, Under Orders From the Board of Health, Will Station a Guard This Morning to Prevent the Landing of Freight or Passengers.

BUBONIC PLAGUE GERMS

DR. WILLIAM F. BARBAT'S MICROSCOPIC EXAMINATION OF THE GLANDS

Source: San Francisco Examiner, June 30, 1899.

exposed surface with a strong solution of corrosive sublimate. Forty chlorine lamps were lighted and the fumes soon permeated the whole ship.[28]

Over on Angel Island, Kinyoun reigned supreme and would not let Cohn come ashore. He reported merely that everyone was in good health, that there had been no signs of plague, and that he would continue to share the passengers' confinement for the full fourteen days.

The following day, July 2, the *Nippon Maru* was released from her quarantine by the State. The TKK had been incurring heavy losses each day, sustaining a blow to its corporate bottom line. First, there was the condition of the ship itself:

> At present the steamer is not a fit place in which to live, for the stench of the disin-fectant is so intense that in some of the cabins it is stifling. What of the bedding and blankets was left aboard [were] soaked with the liquid and cannot be used before passing through the laundry. The upholstering is impregnated with the stuff, and on the return trip will furnish a constant reminder of the bubonic plague scare, which not only startled San Francisco, but caused a fight between the State and Federal authorities that has not ended yet.[29]

Then there was the matter of the *Nippon Maru*'s cargo. Seventy tons of cargo destined for Honolulu was still in the hold and would have to be delivered on the return journey. Chinese merchants in San Francisco had a big consignment of fireworks on board, and it was unlikely that they would be delivered in time for the Fourth of July. And all the overland freight would be more than two weeks late. With the ship's return sailing to Asia also delayed, much of what would have been her return cargo was diverted to other lines. The current passengers were being handsomely fed while on Angel Island—at TKK's expense—but the *Nippon Maru* would have few passengers on her return journey. Many people who had intended taking passage had cancelled their trips, or changed to another vessel. And no wonder—who would travel on the "plague ship?" Each of these items clanked into the TKK's loss column.

More consequential was the disruption of the port of San Francisco. It became a chaotic place indeed, as the *Nippon Maru* had monopolized the Pacific Mail's docking facilities, leaving other ships waiting in the stream until the affair was settled.

Most seriously inconvenienced, of course, were the passengers themselves. As they were held more or less incommunicado during their confinement, little of their predicament or condition was reported in the press. What we do know is limited largely to the cabin-class passengers. Of the Chinese and Japanese steer-age passengers, nothing was thought important enough for the major dailies to report.

Of all the fifty-six persons in cabin-class quarantine, the most celebrated had not even been on the original list. May Jackson of Sausalito was returning from Hong Kong where, as a Salvation Army missionary, she met and married Lieu-tenant Hill of the Royal Artillery. She was about to give birth to her first child, only to be delayed by *force majeure*. Her baby came into the world on Friday, July 7, to great fanfare among the cabin passengers, several of whom suggested that she be baptized "Angelina Quarantina." The more prosaic Marguerite Frances Hill was chosen, and the "Child of the Quarantine" was announced in all the dailies—although true to their rivalry, the *Chronicle* and the *Examiner* could agree on neither the day of her birth nor the spelling of her given names.

On July 11 Kinyoun at last lowered the yellow flag, ending the quarantine. Two hours and $200 in duties later, the cabin passengers were cleared by Customs, then cleared by Immigration and told that they would leave the following day. The steerage passengers were informed that their effects would take another two days to go through. The stern-wheeler *Caroline* left the Jackson Street wharf at 6 o'clock the next morning, July 12, to bring the cabin passengers back from Angel Island. All were in a festive mood. Even Kinyoun, who handed each person a Certificate of Health, was praised for his handling of the situation and absolved of responsibility for the cramped conditions. They cheered as the *Caroline*'s whistle blew for departure, and some sang as the little steamer made for the city.

The *Nippon Maru* incident would give credence to future business claims that admitting the presence of plague would result in great losses to those who depended on the movement of people and goods. Exhibit A, of course, was the TKK, which certainly had sustained serious financial losses.

It is curious that local attention subsequently centered exclusively on the Chinese community. After all, it was a *Japanese* ship that (possibly) brought the plague, and *Japanese* stowaways who were widely presumed to have been infected. Yet a subsequent cleanup campaign focused on San Francisco's Chinese.

The following year, plague irrefutably made its way across the Pacific. In March 1900, deaths in San Francisco's Chinatown were attributed to the plague. Chinatown and the Chinese would be the locus of death and of blame, and the focus of competing, contradictory interpretations and courses of remedial action. Again there would be arguments over how the plague was transmitted, and even whether or not those dying actually had the plague. And again, blame for transmitting the plague from Asia to America would fall on a ship in the immigration trade.[30]

A VETERAN OF THE IMMIGRATION TRADE

When the *Nippon Maru* brought Quok Shee and Chew Hoy Quong to San Francisco that September morning in 1916, the ship was no longer young. The vessel that had mesmerized San Franciscans when she first arrived in 1899 had long been eclipsed by the larger ships of the Pacific Mail and by the *Tenyo Maru* class of ships of her own TKK line, which were twice her size (in tonnage) and powered by three screws (propellers) to the *Nippon*'s two. The speed records foreseen for her for crossing the Pacific were now held by other, newer vessels. She had settled into comfortable middle age as a regular on the passenger routes between eastern Asia and the west coast of North America. When she had arrived back in January, her seventy-second round-trip across the Pacific, the *San Francisco Chronicle* had courteously bowed to "the faithful old *Nippon*, one of the best money-makers on the Pacific."[31]

This particular voyage had been relatively uneventful, despite facing more than the usual risks. Japan was a belligerent in the Great War on the side of England, France, and Russia, and German threats to Japanese shipping were mounting. Japanese civilian ships—at least those on routes to Europe—were being armed,[32] an uncomfortable reminder of when Japan's first war with a European power had interrupted the *Nippon Maru*'s early career in the immigration trade.

That had been from January 1904 to February 1906, when the *Nippon Maru* completely disappeared from the arrival records of the United States Customs Service in San Francisco,[33] she had been drafted. During the Russo-Japanese War the *Nippon Maru*, like many Japanese civilian ships, was conscripted into the Japanese Navy and she shows up in some sources as a "battle cruiser" in Japan's "volunteer navy." It is unclear how the ship was modified—whether guns were mounted on her decks, or armor added, or its interior and passenger accommodations reconfigured to carry troops or supplies—but the *Nippon Maru* of 1906 was surely far less elegant than the one that had entered wartime service two years earlier. When she first returned to San Francisco after the Russo-Japanese War ended, the *Chronicle* noted that "The Nippon Maru Shows Signs of Battle":

> Scarred by black marks that were inflicted during the great naval fighting in the sea of Japan, the Japanese liner Nippon Maru came to port yesterday under the command of Captain W. W. Greene, who was in command of another of the auxiliary cruisers during the war with Russia. This is the first arrival here of the Nippon Maru since the war. She was formerly a well-known and popular liner on the Oriental route, but was impressed into service by Japan for the conflict with Russia. It was at one time reported that the Nippon Maru was sunk, or run ashore, after having been punctured by the enemy. But she is still afloat....
>
> After having been converted into an auxiliary cruiser at the outbreak of the war, the Nippon Maru...was in the fight between Admiral Togo and the Russian fleet under Admiral Rjoestvensky [where] the Nippon Maru received her honorable wounds. She was on the outskirts of this famous conflict [the battle of Tsushima Straits—Ed.] and not prepared to give or receive any particularly severe blows, but, as it happened, the Nippon Maru received a rain of fragments from exploding shells fired by the Russians. All about the promenade deck pieces of redhot shell broke and fell, and these marks still remain, deeply marked in the white woodwork. But no fragment or shell caused serious damage.[34]

Over the years the *Nippon Maru*'s arrivals and departures were regularly noted in the San Francisco newspapers. Each daily normally devoted an entire page to news from the port—wireless messages received from vessels at sea, ships arrived, ships cleared, ships sailing or scheduled to sail. Occasionally the *Nippon Maru* was given special notice, as in 1911, when the *San Francisco Call* announced the "Nippon Maru Here From The Far East; Japanese Steamship Brings 85 Passengers and Large Cargo of Great Value....Mexican silver valued at $100,000 and 3,193 tons of cargo, which included a shipment of raw silk valued at more than $1,000,000." Not uncommon were notices connecting the *Nippon Maru* with some sort of smuggling—opium or purported prostitutes, as when the *Maru*'s interpreter, Long Moon, was caught attempting to smuggle four "Chinese slave girls" ashore for "immoral purposes."[35] More tragically, the ship made the headlines in late 1916 when a fumigation procedure went terribly wrong: entering the ship's hold before the cyanide gas had completely dispersed, one Chinese deckhand was killed, and a second barely escaped with his life.[36]

On some occasions the reportage combined flippant remarks with observations of technical advances. In June 1916, for instance, the *Examiner* noted that "in anticipation of the celebration of the Fourth of July in a noisy style, the liner also had a shipment of 36 tons of fireworks so that Young America will be supplied with fizzers, crackers, bombs, and rockets." Of real military significance was "a new attachment [to the Nippon Maru's wireless], a secret of the Japanese government, which kept the vessel in constant contact with the big government wireless stations in Japan right up to the vessel's arrival in port yesterday."[37]

Until 1916, the *Nippon Maru* was commanded by European captains. Four years later, all masters of Japanese vessels would be Japanese, but for the *Nippon Maru* the big change took place in March 1916. This important event in the life of "'the little white yatch' [sic], until her color was changed to black,"[38] was reported in rather low-key fashion by the *Chronicle*: "Captain H. Stanley Smith, her regular commander, was relieved in Honolulu and waited there to take command of the big turbiner Tenyo Maru, outward bound." The *Examiner*, lamenting that "the genial face of Captain Stanley Smith did not show above the bridge railing" when the ship arrived, noted without fanfare that "the Nippon was under the command of first officer, H. Nagano."[39]

First Officer—now Captain—Hyakuichi Nagano, age 39, thus became the *Nippon Maru*'s first Japanese master, and he would be on the bridge when the *Nippon Maru* brought Quok Shee and Chew Hoy Quong to San Francisco. Seventeen years earlier, when the *Nippon Maru* first appeared in San Francisco, the conventional wisdom was that white passengers were not comfortable with any Japanese officers—let alone a captain—on the bridge. The 1916 change of command to Captain Nagano, however, seemed to have no ill effects on the ship's competitive position: she continued to sail full of cabin passengers, many of whom "were missionaries from India and the Orient with their families, on the way home on furlough."[40]

The changes on the bridge, from an officer cadre composed largely of Europeans to one composed exclusively of Japanese, were mirrored in the changes to the crew itself. On the *Nippon Maru*'s maiden voyage the crew (officers aside) had been exclusively Japanese, and reporters had speculated that they might be replaced by Chinese sailors.

Such speculation was not born out by events. While ships of the Pacific Mail and the O&O lines did have largely Chinese crews,[41] the crews of the *Nippon Maru* and other ships of the TKK line were virtually all Japanese. Captain Nagano had but two non-Japanese amongst his crew when the *Nippon Maru* arrived on September 1, 1916: Purser H.J. Grasett (British) and Ship's Doctor F.B. Galbraith (American).

Those two aside, every officer (6, in addition to Nagano) and crew member (123) was a Japanese national: 25 sailors, an engine room complement of 16 firemen and 15 coal passers (the "black gang"), and a hotel staff of 67 with stewards (including 2 stewardesses), waiters, cooks, a butcher and a baker, and a printer (presumably for printing menus and communiqués to the passengers).[42] Curiously, where other lines had separate Chinese kitchen crews, the TKK line saw no need to cater to its many Chinese passengers in this way.

And Chinese passengers it did carry. Many of the destinations for Japanese emigrants also received sizeable numbers of migrants from China, a goodly proportion of whom sailed on Japanese ships. It is not clear what food the Chinese emigrants were served, if their passage was proportionately more (or less) expensive than that of (subsidized) Japanese passengers, and what mechanisms existed for signing up Chinese passengers and allotting them space. Still, we have some intriguing glimpses into the accommodations provided for Chinese migrants, showing the importance of the Chinese in the economics of Japanese migration and Japanese ships. The layout of the *Anyō Maru* (see "Asiatic Steerage"), for example, shows clearly that it had steerage space for nearly as many Chinese as Japanese.

Thus, it was not surprising that Quok Shee and Chew Hoy Quong would choose a Japanese ship. In the first few years of the new century, the TKK line had garnered nearly 50 percent of the passenger traffic between Honolulu and the Orient, and a fifth of the business out of San Francisco. When the Pacific Mail sold its transpacific fleet in 1915, the TKK came to have an even larger share: 75 percent out of Honolulu and fully half of San Francisco's outbound traffic. While most of the TKK's passengers were carried on its newer ships, the reliable old *Nippon Maru* remained an important part of the fleet.[43]

The sailing that ended in San Francisco on September 1, 1916 was, according to press reports, fairly typical of her passenger loads that year. Over half her passengers (146) were in steerage, 107 in first class, and 9 in second class. Cabin class was a very international group. In first cabin, Americans (74) predominated, but there were also Japanese (16), Russians (3), Chinese (3), and Europeans (10). Second cabin, like steerage, was more Asian: 3 Chinese, 1 U.S.-born Chinese American, and 5 "Siamese."

Steerage was not exclusively an Asian affair, as two Russians occupied berths below decks. The remaining passengers were evenly divided between Japanese (75) and Chinese (67). In this way, the *Nippon Maru* was quite different from the ships of the Pacific Mail: on the transpacific run to San Francisco, 73 percent of the steerage passengers were Chinese and 20 percent were Japanese.[44] About one-third of each group had been in the United States before.

The seventy-five Japanese traveling in steerage included thirty-eight women, a function of there being fifteen couples traveling together. Among the Chinese traveling steerage class—and generally among Chinese traveling to North America—there were very few women. This sailing was no exception. Quok Shee was one of only four women among the sixty-seven Chinese (including American-born citizens).

END OF THE LINE

After bringing Quok Shee and Chew Hoy Quong to America, the *Nippon Maru* would continue on that route for another three years, making sixteen more round-trips, one every ten weeks or so. Eventually, hard times and her advancing age forced TKK to put the *Nippon Maru* on the market for $750,000. On October 20, 1919, she was sold to the CSAV (Compania Sud Americana de Vapores), based in Santiago, Chile. The vessel was at San Francisco at the time, and CSAV's Engineering Superintendent, David Stuart, had reported her to be in satisfactory condition. On November 3 it was decided to name her *Renaico*, after a minor tributary of the Bio-Bio River. On January 4, 1920, her flag was changed from Japanese to Chilean, and she sailed for Valparaiso on the 14th.

Ahead lay a brief stint carrying passengers and freight between South America and Europe. CSAV records show her as having space for 180 in cabin class and 100 in steerage—a significant change from the TKK configuration. On April 26, the vessel was sent to New York via Havana. Despite minor difficulties vis-à-vis the European Cargo Conference, the *Renaico/Nippon Maru* made several trips to Europe with cargo and passengers for Le Havre, London, Antwerp, and Hamburg. At the end of 1922, CSAV decided to mothball the *Renaico*, which was losing money and had been relegated to the coastal trade to Arica, until better times. In April 1923, she was put up for sale, but not until the second half of 1929 was she sold—for 5,000 pounds sterling for scrap.[45]

The TKK line itself was bought out by NYK in 1926. Today, the NYK is a global corporation which, among many other things, operates the elegant Crystal Line of cruise ships.[46] The *Nippon Maru* name lives on, today gracing a "tall ship" in the Japanese navy. When that incarnation of the *Nippon Maru* called at San Francisco in 2003, no member of the crew seemed aware of the earlier *Nippon Maru* and its tempestuous, historical association with emigration to the United States.

Maritime historians and other people with an affection for ships refer to a seagoing ship anthropomorphically—as "she," as having a "life" or a "career." In an article that led to *Fune ni Miru Nihonjin Iminshi*, Michio Yamada traces the earliest migration of Japanese contract laborers to Brazil, beginning in 1908 with the eponymous *Kasato Maru*. That ship had been built in England (as the *Potosi*), sold to the Russian Volunteer Fleet (as the *Kazan*), then seized by the Japanese Navy. As the *Kasato Maru*, it was later leased to TKK, then to the OSK line for carrying emigrants to Brazil, then sold several more times.

Its last days were rather inglorious as a sardine fishery ship that was finally sunk by Soviet forces off the Kamchatka Peninsula in the closing days of World War II. Yamada's words might serve as an epitaph for the *Nippon Maru*. "I heard an old song playing on TV the other day. It told of the *Kasato Maru*'s last years as a fishing ship. I could not help but think back on that ship and on its long, poignant history."[47]

NOTES

1. This story is told in more detail in Robert Barde, "Prelude to the Plague: Public Health and Politics at America's Pacific Gateway, 1899," *Journal of the History of Medicine and Allied Sciences* 58, no. 2 (2003).

2. Michio Yamada, *Fune Ni Miru Nihonjin Iminshi*. The origins of the TKK line are from Michio Yamada, "Emigrants to North America in the Meiji Era," *Seki no Kansen*, January 1994, trans. Yuko Okubo, with Robert Barde.

3. Act of February 23, 1885: Prohibition of Contract Labor ("Foran Act"), 23 Stat. 332: 8 U.S.C.

4. W.C. Banner, "A History of Trans-Pacific Service," *Japan: Magazine of Overseas Travel* 16, no. 5 (1927); Yamada, *Fune Ni Miru Nihonjin Iminshi.*

5. This story is well told in Alan Takeo Moriyama, *Imingaisha: Japanese Emigration Companies and Hawaii, 1894–1908* (Honolulu: University of Hawaii Press, 1985).

6. Robert C. Schmidtt, *Historical Statistics of Hawaii* (Honolulu: University of Hawaii Press, 1977), table 3.6, p. 97.

7. Michio Yamada, "Emigrants to North America."

8. Ibid.

9. U.S. Customs Service, "Report of Examination of Passenger Vessel," June 14, 1918; Records of the U.S. Customs Service (Record Group 365), NARA—Pacific Region (San Bruno, CA).

10. *San Francisco Examiner*, January 15, 1899.

11. Comparative figures are given in Yamada, "Emigrants to North America."

12. Information on the Chinese passengers comes from the U.S. Department of Labor, "List of Chinese Passengers Arriving in San Francisco, California, 1882–1914," ed. Immigration Service (NARA), arrival #9666. All other passengers are listed in Series M1410, Passenger Lists of Vessels Arriving in San Francisco, California, 1893–1953.

13. *San Francisco Chronicle*, January 15, 1899.

14. Ibid.

15. "Color Line on Nippon Maru," *San Francisco Chronicle*, January 19, 1899.

16. See Barde, "Prelude to the Plague."

17. A possible case of plague in late 1898 so perplexed the bacteriologist of the San Francisco Board of Health that he rendered a verdict of "not proven." See Board of Health of the City and County of San Francisco, *Biennial Report of the Board of Health of the City and County of San Francisco for the Fiscal Years 1898–1899 and 1899–1900* (San Francisco: The Hinton Printing Company, 1901), 145–47.

18. *San Francisco Examiner*, July 11, 1899, 3.

19. Public Health Service (formerly Marine Medical Service), *Public Health Reports*, 14, no. 27 (July 7, 1899): 1066–67.

20. *San Francisco Chronicle*, June 28, 1899, 7.

21. See the report by Surgeon Kinyoun, Quarantine Officer at Angel Island, in the August 18, 1899, *Public Health Reports*.

22. Figures quoted in the press differ slightly from those of the Immigration Service and those given by Kinyoun in the August 18, 1899, *Public Health Reports*. I have used the latter.

23. *San Francisco Examiner*, June 26, 1899, 5.

24. *San Francisco Call*, June 28, 1899, 23.

25. Ibid., 7.

26. *San Francisco Chronicle*, July 1, 1899.

27. *San Francisco Examiner*, June 20, 1899.

28. Ibid.

29. *San Francisco Chronicle*, July 3, 1899, 10.

30. See Marilyn Chase, *The Barbary Plague: The Black Death in Victorian San Francisco* (New York: Random House, 2003); and Nayan Shah, *Contagious Divides: Epidemics and Race in San Francisco's Chinatown* (Berkeley: University of California Press, 2001).

31. *San Francisco Chronicle*, January 15, 1916, 15.

32. Personal communication from NYK Museum.

33. Immigration Service U.S. Department of Labor, *Alphabetical Index of Ship Arrivals in San Francisco* (NARA).

34. *San Francisco Chronicle*, February 10, 1906, 9. The names of all cabin-class passengers were given, Chinese and Japanese as well as "European."

35. *San Francisco Chronicle*, November 27, 1912.

36. "Cyanide Gas Imperils 2 on Nippon Maru," *San Francisco Examiner*, November 21, 1916.

37. *San Francisco Examiner*, June 16, 1916, 23.

38. *San Francisco Chronicle*, April 2, 1916, 57.

39. *San Francisco Examiner*, April 2, 1916, 9. The paper actually misspelled his name as "Hagano."

40. Ibid. Newspaper reports for sailing in April, June, and September all indicate a ship whose cabin accommodations were full and with well over 100 steerage passengers.

41. See Schwendinger, *Ocean of Bitter Dreams,* for a thorough discussion of the Chinese as "the major labor force that made possible the extraordinary history of transpacific voyages," especially 169–93.

42. "Alien Crew List" for the *Nippon Maru*, U.S. Department of Labor Immigration Service, ship arrival number 15530.

43. Immigration Service annual reports, 1909–1920: tables on "Passengers departed from the United States."

44. Barde and Bobonis, "Detention at Angel Island."

45. My thanks to Georg Fendt, Fumio Nagasawa, and most generously, Edmundo Adriasola of Compania Sud Americana de Vapores, for information on the last years of the *Nippon Maru*.

46. See NYK Web site, http://www.nykline.co.jp/english/seascope/200110/index.htm.

47. Michio Yamada, "First emigrants to Brazil by the *Kasato Maru*," *Sekai no Kansen*, 1994.

— 9 —

Keepers of the Golden Gate

The Detention Shed and Angel Island have come to symbolize enforcement of the Chinese exclusion laws, but the actual enforcers were the men (and a very few women) of the Immigration Service. We meet these people in several different ways in two chapters that follow: through a reconstruction of one of the more sensational immigrant smuggling cases of the early twentieth century, and through the diaries of an immigration inspector. The former shows the workings and weaknesses of immigration enforcement at the time, while the latter provides insights into the character of one thoughtful, if perhaps atypical, frontline guardian. The rest of this section is an extended introduction to the workforce at the Angel Island Immigration Station—those charged with enforcing the general immigration laws and, at San Francisco especially, the Chinese exclusion laws.

At the apex of the enforcement structure, of course, were the authorities in Washington, D.C. In 1916, the year of Quok Shee's arrival, the Democrats were in the White House and thus controlled Federal patronage appointments. The Labor Department oversaw immigration enforcement, and William B. Wilson was "labor's voice in the Cabinet" as Secretary of Labor.[1] He could be counted on to continue organized labor's long-standing opposition to Asian immigration and so-called "coolie labor." Anthony Caminetti, a career California politician, had been appointed Commissioner General of Immigration over the opposition of Wilson's deputy, Louis F. Post.[2] A longtime exclusionist, Caminetti's ability and performance came to be held in rather low esteem by both Secretary Wilson and Assistant Secretary Post. The commissioner of immigration at Ellis Island had an even lower opinion of Caminetti's abilities: "The Commissioner General... was as untrained in administrative work as I was in higher mathematics, and his consciousness of his inexperience led him to refuse to take any action at all.

His table was piled mountains high with undespatched business, with records of men and women held in immigration stations awaiting his decision."[3]

At the local level, enforcement was largely the responsibility of the Commissioner of Immigration for San Francisco. Even in the Progressive Era, this was still a patronage position, appointed by the ruling party in Washington, usually on the advice of the Senator from the state in question. When Quok Shee arrived at Angel Island in 1916, the Commissioner of less than a year was Edward H. White. While he differed from previous Commissioners in some important particulars— the most recent Commissioners had been appointed by Republicans—in many ways he typified the sort of person who got appointed to such positions.

White was Old California. When he died in 1931, he was reported to have been the oldest "Native Son" (i.e., white person born in the State of California). Newspapers described him as the "son of a typical pioneer family. His father and mother came around the Horn in 1849 and he married a girl who was born in a covered wagon."[4]

His father, William Francis White, a native of County Limerick, Ireland, died in 1890 at the age of 73 years and 11 months. The elder White "settled in the [Pajaro] Valley and was one of the founders of the town of Watsonville." He had been prominent in state Democratic politics, but broke in 1878 to join the virulently anti-Chinese Workingmen's Party as its first candidate for governor. Running under the slogan "The Chinese Must Go!" he came in second to George C. Perkins.[5]

William White's eldest son, Stephen Mallory White, was the family's most successful politician. As a lawyer and California State Senator from Los Angeles, he was selected in 1889 to represent the State before the U.S. Supreme Court in a case involving the constitutionality of the Scott Act (officially, the Act of September 13, 1887: "Immigration of Chinese Laborers Prohibited," 25 Stat. 476, 8 U.S.C.). Stephen White was a power in the state's Democratic Party and an ally of Anthony Caminetti, presiding over the Democratic state conventions in 1884 and 1886 and being elected Lieutenant Governor in 1888. He shared his father's opposition to Chinese immigration and to large corporations and railroads.[6] But he thought that California went overboard with its anti-Chinese prejudices, fearing they might become a distraction from more important issues or give Easterners cause to mobilize against California and its peculiar prejudices.[7]

In 1892 Stephen White was elected to the United States Senate and served a single term, dying in 1899. He continued his lifelong mission of securing "minority representation" in the political process—although in this context the expression meant protecting Catholics from discrimination. Any differences with his father's anti-Chinese sentiments were merely differences of degree, as evidenced by his speeches in the U.S. Senate.[8]

Younger brother Edward H. White was born in San Francisco in 1851 and educated at Santa Clara University. After leaving school he engaged in ranching and was the owner of a large tract near Watsonville.[9] His life seems to have been a pale shadow of his more famous and more talented sibling. After the Senator's death, Edward sought elected office, drawing on his late brother's name and connections, but proved ineffectual in the game of politics. In 1914, he ran in the Democratic primary for governor on a platform that included "efficiency [as] the sole qualification for public service; opposition to all Asiatic immigration and colonization...opposition to all freak and useless legislation."[10] He came in seventh in a crowded field.

But his connections were still of some worth. When Caminetti was named Commissioner General of Immigration, White's ties to the California politician became quite valuable. His nomination as Commissioner for San Francisco came as something of a surprise to many observers, his town already having harvested such political plums as District Judge and Port (of San Francisco) Surveyor. He was a political hack, but a safe one, having offended few and showing no signs of further political ambition.

On October 27, 1915, Edward H. White swore the Oath of Office as "Commissioner of Immigration at the Port of San Francisco, California." The official Oath that he was required to swear—an act repeated in every subsequent year—is most instructive. It clearly conveys the dominant prejudice against the Chinese, an "anti-coolie" mentality, and an undercurrent of suspicion of all aliens entering the United States:

> I will use my best endeavors to prevent and detect frauds against the laws of the United States regulating immigration, forbidding the importation of aliens under contract to labor, and relating to the exclusion of Chinese persons.

Like his predecessors, White kept an office in the administration building on Angel Island, and another in the City Office in the Appraisers Building. His annual salary of $4,000 was about double that of his inspectors (John Sawyer's was $2,100)—substantial, but not princely. Nonetheless, White clung to his job long after Woodrow Wilson's Democrats had been replaced by Warren Harding's Republicans. Unable to get White to resign gracefully, the new administration fired him by Executive Order in 1923.[11]

INSPECTORS

Commissioner White's forces were split between Angel Island and the City Office, located in the Appraisers Building at Sansome and Washington streets. Many of the records were kept at the latter location, as the inspectors who would go out to meet incoming ships were based there. The rest of White's staff was employed at Angel Island, and White's principal office was there. Each day they would all make the same pilgrimage from Pier 7 to the Island aboard the government ferry *Angel Island*—White and his forces, plus the friends and witnesses of the detainees, the very people whom the inspectors might be interrogating later in the day.

An early and astute observer of the Chinese exclusion laws and their enforcement was Stanford Professor Mary Roberts Coolidge. A chapter in her 1909 volume on *Chinese Immigration* contained a particularly trenchant assessment of the "Administration of the Exclusion Laws," in which she concluded that "the personnel of the immigration service and the traditions of the Chinese Bureau itself have been responsible for the larger part of the odium attached to the administration of the law." She found that up and down the West Coast, "the most casual mention of the immigration service brings out stories of the treatment of the Chinese illustrating the ignorance, prejudice, untrustworthiness and incompetence of some immigration officer."[12] A few of her observations will give the gist of her low opinion of those guarding the gates.

> The bulk of the work has been done by inspectors and interpreters at salaries ranging from twelve to eighteen hundred a year and the higher officials have based their decisions on the investigations and testimony of men of this grade....The employes [sic] of the immigration bureau have generally been appointed by political influence solely, and from a class imbued with the tradition that the object of the exclusion law is not only to exclude laborers but all Chinese as well. To this class tradition has often been added the race prejudices of the European-born against the Oriental, for the service has been largely recruited from Irishmen and others of foreign extraction....Such men as these have been detailed to receive not only Chinese laborers but officials, scholars and cultivated travelers. It could scarcely be expected that their manners would be equal to the social requirements...but it appears that they have often omitted the ordinary American courtesies and hospitality.

John Birge Sawyer, whose career we explore in a chapter that follows, was an exemplar of the better sort of immigration inspector, one who saw the Immigration Service as a profession rather than an opportunity for self-enrichment. His appointment and subsequent promotions represent the increased professionalization of the Immigration Service, a trend that made corruption less common, though not extinct.

INTERPRETERS

Interpreters were indispensable intermediaries in the immigration process. Few, if any, immigration inspectors had any facility with Asian languages. John Sawyer, "Mr. Section 6," who spent a lifetime dealing with Chinese immigration, was fluent in German but never acquired more than a smattering of Chinese. He was probably one of the more diligent inspectors, at times taking classes and hiring tutors variously in Mandarin or Cantonese. But despite the "interpreter" rating in his early personnel record, his Chinese never rose to where he could carry on a conversation.[13]

The interpreters' influence extended beyond serving as translators at interrogations and Boards of Special Inquiry. They were employed by many businesses, including banks and steamship companies, and often served as important cultural intermediaries, gaining personal wealth and influence from their knowledge of American institutions (courts, administrative agencies, business practices) and the people who ran them. While a number of the early interpreters were white missionaries who had worked in China, most were either Chinese or Eurasian.

An early example was Moy Jin Mun (1848–1936), who learned English in a Chinatown mission school shortly after he arrived in San Francisco in 1861. He became wealthy as a miner, then railroad labor contractor, then as merchant in San Francisco. In the 1870s he became "the Chinese interpreter in the United States District Court at a salary of $75 per month,"[14] and subsequently "he became good friends with several of the judges on the court, including Judges Fields, Sawyer, Hoffman, Cooks and Murasky.... [By] the turn of the century, Jin Mun's knowledge of English was invaluable among the Chinese of his age, and he became a minor political power in Chinatown, gaining many friends among the city officials. Court and treasury officials were numbered among his acquaintances, and he later became a close friend of Mayor James Rolph."[15] Like many interpreters, he was not above suspicion. The *Examiner* alleged that "he exacts a fee from every Chinese habeas corpus petitioner in addition to his salary, and he has been enabled to save enough money to lease a large building in Chinatown and furnish it in the comfortable and luxurious manner of Chinese hotels."[16]

Other well-known examples in this mold were Joseph Tape (or Chew Diep, 1852–1935) and his son Frank (1878–1950). Joseph was interpreter in the Chinese consulate in San Francisco and had two profitable businesses: a firm that had a monopoly on transporting Chinese who came to the United States in bond and handled large drayage contracts for wholesale merchants in Chinatown, and another as a bondsman for Chinese crewman seeking to spend some time ashore. His son, Frank, and his sons-in-law Herman Lowe and Robert Park also worked as interpreters—the first two for the Immigration Service, the latter for the San Francisco courts.[17] Frank Tape worked for the Immigration Service in both Portland and Seattle. In Portland, a review of all Immigration interpreters by Said Gain Back, Jr., found him lacking in "character, qualifications and antecedents" and recommended that Tape be dismissed—a recommendation ignored by the Service.[18] In Seattle, he appeared to live well beyond his means. He was suspected of corruption and was investigated and suspended from the service in 1914.[19]

Many came from within the missionary community or had been mission-educated. One of the more fascinating examples was Tye Leung: educated in Donaldina Cameron's Presbyterian Mission Home, hired by the Immigration Service on Angel Island as an assistant to the matron, she regularly acted as interpreter for Chinese immigrants. She also fell in love with Immigration Inspector Charles Schulze, a romance that led to a long and happy marriage, but which cost them both their jobs.[20]

Another example of interpreters from the missionary community was the longtime interpreter for the Immigration Service in San Francisco, John Endicott Gardner, a Eurasian whose career illustrates the possibilities and perils inherent in the position. Son of an English father and a Chinese mother,

Figure 9.1
John Endicott Gardner served as both interpreter and inspector for the Immigration
Service in San Francisco, 1910–15.

Source: Photograph courtesy of Susan S. Briggs.

Gardner grew up in Hong Kong and had an excellent command of both spoken
and written Chinese and English.[21] His eleven years of mission work for the
Methodist Church in Victoria, British Columbia, gave him not only the title
"Dr." that he went by, a seemingly solid claim of honesty, but also the experi-
ence of having been accused of *dis*honesty in work as an interpreter for Chinese
dealing with the Canadian immigration authorities.[22] Such credentials were
enough to offset the Immigration Service's early policy of not employing
Chinese as interpreters: for several years up to 1884 (when he was known as
Vrooman), and then again from 1896 to 1915, Gardner was employed by the
Immigration Service.

At times he also held the title of Inspector, an unusual set of responsibilities
fraught with conflict-of-interest possibilities. On several occasions he was investigated on suspicion of corruption. In 1899, Port Collector Jackson engaged in a

long and acrimonious exchange of charges and countercharges with Gardner through the office of the Secretary of the Treasury; both sides submitted lengthy documents detailing (or refuting in detail) charges that Gardner extorted bribes from immigrants and their attorneys. In 1915 he resigned his post as "Chinese inspector and interpreter" rather than accept a transfer to New Jersey ordered by Commissioner General Caminetti.[23] Suspicion continued to fall on Gardner: two years later, Federal agents and police raided his Berkeley home and that of his son-in-law, carting away "several hundred pounds of report and other documents...records belonging to the immigration station at Angel Island."[24] It was the lot of many interpreters to be accused of corruption; just as many accusations were undoubtedly well founded, others were surely acts of revenge against interpreters in highly visible, and vulnerable, positions. A 1915 newspaper article featuring Gardner as a "notable Californian" offered the curious praise that there had been "never a word of newspaper criticism of the man or his work" during thirty-two years of public service.[25]

These and other cases indicate how interpreters came to be held in rather low esteem, despite being indispensable to the immigration industry. Mary Roberts Coolidge's low opinions and prejudices of immigration inspectors extended to the interpreters as well.

> With the exception of a very few individuals of American parentage, the position of Chinese interpreter in the immigration service has been filled by half-breed Chinese-Anglo-Saxons. Their knowledge of both languages is imperfect and in the interpretation of Chinese documents and testimony this leads to technical mistakes which make it appear that the Chinese immigrant has been coached or that there are discrepancies in the testimony of himself and his witnesses....Interpreters of nondescript social class and superficial linguistic attainments have been despised and distrusted equally by Chinese and Americans. There is abundant evidence that in collusion with inspectors they have held up the exempt classes for bribes and that they have for the same reason been the chief instruments of all the Chinese schemes for securing the admission of laborers.[26]

In the report on his first investigation into immigrant smuggling, John Densmore was equally dismissive of interpreters, especially if they were Chinese. In keeping with the racialized notion of Chinese being inherently untrustworthy, he recommended that only whites be considered for such positions.

AT THE BOTTOM

The Angel Island Immigration Station required, in addition to immigration inspectors (around ten) and translators (a similar number), a small force of around thirty clerks, watchmen, and messengers. The Densmore investigations revealed that corruption at Angel Island spread from the inspectors down to those at the bottom—W.J. Armstrong, a file clerk who removed files, and Theo Kaphan, a watchman who delivered them to immigration lawyers for alteration—men who for $5 would steal a file.

LAWYERS

A final element in the enforcement equation was the immigration lawyers. If there were mixed motives behind the actions of the enforcement officers, this was doubly so among the lawyers. It is enormously difficult to differentiate between greed and altruism, between self-promotion and genuine hostility to arbitrary power. Mary Roberts Coolidge was of the opinion that immigration lawyers, though perhaps essential to the process of subverting the exclusion apparatus, were not necessarily getting rich from it:

> It is commonly said that lawyers have made a great deal of money out of landing cases but this is true only in an occasional case. Ordinarily a lawyer makes only his contingency fee which is not more than fifty or seventy-five dollars. The money spent does not go to the lawyers, for the Chinese have learned that a lawyer can do very little for them; the only man who can do anything for them is the examining inspector.... If the interpreter and the inspectors agree the Chinaman is landed, and if the money is spent it is probable that it goes to one or the other.[27]

Who were the San Francisco lawyers working on immigration? We have already met several of them: George McGowan and his partner, Alexander Worley, and Dion Holm and his patron, Samuel Shortridge. In the next chapter we will meet two more, the notorious firm of Oliver Perry Stidger and Henry C. Kennah. McGowan & Worley and Stidger & Kennah were the two largest firms, with perhaps 75 percent of the business, but there were others. One indication came out of the Densmore investigations, from a list of lawyers (and brokers) doing immigration work, "found in a barrel in the plumbers shop by [Clerk] Hendricks, who stated that Clerk McFarland used said barrel in which to hide records."

- Bellingall, R.W.: 510 Battery St.
- Catlin & Catlin: 628 Montgomery St.
- Chinese Consul General: 885 Clay St.
- Coo, Carroll: Chronicle Bldg.
- Dye, Clarkson: 649 Kearny St.
- Harper & Co.: 510 Battery St.
- Horn, H.L.: 604 Montgomery St.
- Jones, R.H.: 626 Montgomery St.
- Lee, H. Embert: 851 Clay St.
- Marcuse, S.C.: 508 Battery St.
- McCulloch, Ben: 776 Sacramento St.
- McGowan & Worley: Bank of Italy Bldg.
- Monroe, H.E.: 106 Montgomery St.
- Rickards, Carleton: 819 Grant Ave. (broker)
- Strauss, Gaston: 604 Montgomery St.

- Swayne, Hoyt: 450 Sansome St.
- Tape, Joseph: 755 Dupont St. (broker)
- Thornley, Wm. H.: 520 Battery St. (broker)
- Worley, F. B.: 502 Washington St.

It may have been true that lawyers did not keep all the money paid out as bribes, but that money largely went *through* them.[28] Employing Chinese-speaking assistants, immigration lawyers courted Chinese business. This could be done formally, as when both McGowan & Worley and Stidger & Kennah ran ads in the Chinese newspaper *Chung Sai Yat Po*. Informally, Chinese merchants often asked the lawyers who handled their commercial business to assist in immigration matters. This was probably more true in the nineteenth century; by the time Quok Shee and Chew Hoy Quong arrived at Angel Island, it is likely that most immigration cases were handled by lawyers who specialized exclusively in immigration law. Surely one of the "skills" they touted was their ability to avoid an unfavorable outcome by "influencing" those in a position to make a decision. While it is doubtful that lawyers were often able to bribe judges making *legal* decisions, there is incontrovertible proof that they were quite able to bribe immigration service employees making *administrative* decisions.

How this could happen is part of the chapter that follows, viewed through the Densmore Investigations of 1915–18.

NOTES

1. John Lombardi, *Labor's Voice in the Cabinet: A History of the Department of Labor from Its Origin to 1921* (New York: Columbia University Press, 1942).

2. Joseph Preston Giovinco, "The California Career of Anthony Caminetti, Italian-American Politician," University of California, Berkeley, 1973.

3. Frederick C. Howe, *The Confessions of a Reformer* (New York: C. Scribner's Sons, 1925), 255. Quoted in Lombardi, *Labor's Voice in the Cabinet*, 128.

4. Obituary in the *San Francisco Chronicle*, May 18, 1931.

5. Peter Thomas Conmy, *Stephen Mallory White, California Statesman* (San Francisco: Dolores Press, 1956).

6. Kenneth M. Johnson, *Stephen Mallory White* (Los Angeles, CA: Dawson's Book Shop, 1980), 26–27.

7. Edith Dobie, *The Political Career of Stephen Mallory White: A Study of Party Activities under the Convention System* (Stanford, CA: Stanford University Press, 1927).

8. Stephen M. White, *Stephen M. White: Californian, Citizen, Lawyer, Senator. His Life and His Work. A Character Sketch, by Leroy E. Mosher. Together with His Principal Public Addresses, Compiled by Robert Woodland Gates* (Los Angeles, CA: The Times-Mirror Company, 1903).

9. Obituary in *San Francisco Examiner*, May 18, 1931.

10. *San Francisco Examiner*, July 3, 1914, 9.

11. Edward H. White's Oaths of Office, along with letters of appointment and dismissal, are found in his Official Personnel Folder at the National Personnel Records Center, St. Louis, MO.

12. Coolidge, *Chinese Immigration*, 312.

13. Personal communication from Sawyer's daughter to the author. Sawyer's personnel file also indicates that he was not proficient in Chinese.

14. *San Francisco Examiner*, December 19, 1883.

15. Information on Moy Jin Mun comes from Thomas W. Chinn, *Bridging the Pacific: San Francisco Chinatown and Its People* (San Francisco, CA: Chinese Historical Society of America, 1989), 73–74.

16. *San Francisco Examiner*, December 19, 1883.

17. Daniella Thompson, *The Tapes of Russell Street: An Accomplished Family of School Desegregation Pioneers*, 2005, available at http://www.berkeleyheritage.com/essays/tape_family.html.

18. Marie Rose Wong, *Sweet Cakes, Long Journey: The Chinatowns of Portland, Oregon* (Seattle: University of Washington Press, 2004), 195.

19. Thompson, *The Tapes of Russell Street*, pt. 2.

20. For Tye Leung Schulze's "autobiography," see Judy Yung, *Unbound Voices*, 281–88.

21. For more on Gardner's early life, see Lee, *At America's Gates*, 62–63.

22. See Staley, "Gum Moon," 14. The charges of dishonesty are found in Stevens, "Brokers between Worlds."

23. "Dr. Gardner Resigns U.S. Post in S.F.," *San Francisco Examiner*, November 12, 1915.

24. "U.S. Agents Make Raid on Home of Dr. Gardner," *San Francisco Examiner*, January 24, 1918.

25. *San Francisco Chronicle*, January 16, 1916.

26. Coolidge, *Chinese Immigration*, 313–15.

27. Ibid., 317–18.

28. For a study of this process in the Pacific Northwest, see Stevens, "Brokers between Worlds."

— 10 —

The Great Immigrant Smuggling Scandal

THE *MONGOLIA* SCANDAL

The big steamer's last voyage across the Pacific could have been a graceful farewell. After fifty-three round-trips, ferrying passengers and cargo between Asia and California, the *Mongolia* was being transferred to New York. She was not a particularly old ship, but her owner, the PMSS, was getting out of the transpacific market and selling her. The *Mongolia*'s Pacific career was set to end when she arrived in San Francisco on Wednesday morning, October 27, 1915.

"Arrival" meant more than steaming right up to Pier 42 and having the ship's passengers walk down the gangway. The process of clearing a ship—especially one capable of carrying over 1,000 passengers, plus cargo—began well before the ship tied up. After navigating the "Golden Gate" and passing the grounds of the Panama Pacific Exhibition, the *Mongolia* stopped opposite Meiggs Wharf (present-day Pier 39, at the foot of Powell St.) and received a small flotilla of government boats and agents. The cutter *Argonaut* of the U.S. Public Health Service's Quarantine Station arrived. A Coast Guard cutter also came alongside, carrying the U.S. Customs Service boarding officer as well as several newspaper reporters and a representative of the Pacific Mail. They were soon joined by the Immigration Service's cutter *Inspector*, carrying Acting Commissioner Mehan, Inspector Clendennin, and other Immigration inspectors. The *Mongolia*'s Captain, Emery Rice, provided the inspectors with a list of all aliens aboard, and the Immigration men immediately began their examinations of the passengers.

As the *Mongolia* resumed her progress toward Pier 42, cabin-class passengers were inspected in their cabins. "Steerage" passengers, three quarters of whom were Chinese, were inspected in the *Mongolia*'s steerage eating areas. Some

Chinese were cleared for landing right away—"natives" (i.e., Chinese born in the United States), first cabin Chinese holding Section 6 certificates stating that they were bona fide merchants, and Chinese officials. Most Caucasians, and all Caucasian Americans, were immediately admitted. Everyone else—Chinese, Japanese, and Russians—was destined for Angel Island.

Captain Rice and Chief Officer Ryland Drennan were on the bridge as she eased into the Pacific Mail's docks. By the time she was firmly berthed, fifteen Immigration officers were aboard the *Mongolia,* and perhaps thirty or forty customs officers were on hand. Plainclothes agents of the Treasury Department were on the dock. This was all standard operating procedure, nothing out of the ordinary. The *Mongolia*'s last Pacific crossing had come to an end. She had given good service, service that deserved a stately salute at its conclusion, but her actual reward would be two acts of the inelegant—first farce, then scandalous high drama.

On October 27, the farce was acted out on that most American of stages, the movie set. What cinematic story line could have been more tailored to San Francisco than a raid on Chinese opium smugglers? As the *San Francisco Chronicle* told it on the next day's front-page, the "Movie 'Opium Raid' Is Cause of Customs Squabble":

> Surveyor of the Port Justus S. Wardell and Collector of Customs John O. Davis are far from agreed as to the propriety of permitting a motion-picture concern to have free run of the dock upon the arrival of the Japanese liner *Nippon Maru* and the Pacific Mail liner *Mongolia* in a "correct imitation" of "A Terrible Opium Raid."
>
> "I have been informed that the motion-picture actors were actually permitted to wear regulation uniforms and badges," said Surveyor Wardell yesterday. "This can serve no good public purpose and tends to belittle the United States Customs Service."
>
> The matter has been put up to Special Agent W. H. Tidwell [who] said he would investigate.[1]

As the following day's headlines made clear, the Special Agent had another investigation to attend to, and it was about nothing so frivolous as a motion picture.

Tidwell had been worrying about smuggling, and he had been worrying about it for some time. As Special Agent in Charge of the United States Customs Service at the Port of San Francisco, that was his job. Import duties were the federal government's biggest source of revenue (this was two years before the first federal income tax laws), and his office, as in every port, was charged with making sure that duties were collected. His many responsibilities included two that differentiated San Francisco from most other ports: he was charged with (among many other things) preventing the entry of smuggled opium and, increasingly, smuggled Chinese and Japanese trying to enter the United States.

A year earlier he had received a most disturbing letter from "a native born Chinaman at this port."[2] It was a tip, accompanied by numerous examples.

One of the most graftiest bunch in the U.S. Services of the Pacific Coast, is the immigration band with its organization in San Francisco.... The business of making money in the immigration services is to employed Chinese secret agents so as to landed Chinese labours unofficially. And the bunch of Chinese inspectors is those that reaped the golden harvest.[3]

On the day the *Mongolia* steamed into San Francisco, another letter was delivered to the Customs office, addressed to Tidwell. It arrived shortly before noon, about three hours after the *Mongolia* had tied up, and was all in Chinese—all except the word "Graham," which was written clearly in English.

The steamer *Mongolia* has stowaways on board. The No. 1 boatswain has eight of them. Fireman Cheung has 25. The No. 1 Saloon waiter has 20. The Chief Engineer gets $100.00 (gold) for each one. The trip before, the No. 1 boatswain had 4, No. 1 Fireman had one, the Interpreter and the No. 1 Saloon waiter had 10. All were safely landed. It was done through collusion with the "fat boy" in the Department of Labor, who whenever passengers were landed, would stand at the head of the gangway to take up the passenger tickets. The name of the "fat boy" is Mr. Graham.... Do not let any of the crewmen go ashore. Do not let the fat boy be at the steamer.... Don't let one person land until you have searched the vessel and you will then know what is what.[4]

Just two weeks before, someone had tipped off Immigration that the *Manchuria* had a load of stowaways to be smuggled in, and Tidwell had heard the news. He was ready to have his men join a search of the ship the night of its arrival, but for some reason the Immigration men wanted to wait. Not until the next morning did a force of forty Immigration and Customs agents search the ship, and by then it was clean. Not a stowaway to be found.[5] Something was amiss, but nothing that Tidwell could act upon.

But on that Wednesday, October 27, it was Tidwell who had the tip, and this time he would not let such information go to waste. The *Mongolia* was to be closely guarded by Immigration and Customs officers until the morning, when they would make a thorough search. This was to be a Customs operation, even though the smuggling of people came under the jurisdiction of Immigration. That Customs did not trust Immigration was well known, having been reported a year and a half earlier under the headline "Nobody Wants to Catch Smugglers."[6] Certain customs officials suspected that whatever smuggling of Chinese there might be was carried out with the connivance of corrupt Immigration officers. Everyone had heard such gossip, and the suspicion had wide circulation in San Francisco. The newspapers printed such rumors as a matter of course.

Immigration sent Inspectors Strand and Hays from Angel Island. By the time they reached the Pacific Mail's docks at 6:30 p.m., they found that most of the Immigration officers had gone home, and most of the ship's passengers were *already* off the ship. During the day the *Mongolia*'s passengers had all been examined: some had been landed, and most of the others—the Chinese who were to be detained—had been transferred to Angel Island on the Pacific Mail's own tugboat, the *Arabs*. Only ninety-three remained on board, waiting to be transferred to Angel Island the following morning. Perhaps Strand and Hays were too late.

A nighttime search of such a large ship had not seemed like a good idea, but Customs Captain Sackett arrived at 7:15 p.m. and led all three, unannounced, below decks to the steerage quarters. They found what seemed like a very large number of Chinese, all dressed and walking about—certainly more than the ninety-three passengers supposedly remaining on the ship, and quite clearly not people readying themselves to spend the night in their quarters aboard ship. Hays motioned for one of the Chinese men to show him his steamship ticket. No ticket. Hays asked the next man—no ticket either. Stowaways, without a doubt. The tipster had been right.

By midnight Sackett had nearly thirty Customs men on the *Mongolia*, and he set them to searching every possible hiding place. They found eighty-six Chinese stowaways.

There were stowaways everywhere imaginable. There were ticketless Chinese under benches in the dining room, others in the fireroom. Some had mingled with the Chinese crew and wore uniforms.

> Ten were found hidden under an enormous steel bucket which had been buried under the coal in the bunkers, where there were blankets and remnants of food. The stowaways had spent the long days and nights in darkness, but were supplied with rice and dried fish. Two tubs of *shoyu* and teapots were also found in the lair. Others had apparently had a little the better of it, evidently having lived sumptuously in the crew's quarters, only concealing themselves when Captain Rice and his officers made daily inspections.[7]

None of the searchers could remember ever having seen so many stowaways discovered all at once—small parties of four or five, perhaps, but never eighty-six. And those were just the ones they caught; others, surely, had gone undetected or had already made it to the mainland.

On Thursday, the *Call* and the *Examiner* had small stories on page one: "86 Hidden Chinese Captured on Liner" was the *Call*'s headline. By Friday, all of the major San Francisco dailies had pushed the story to the top of the page, in big, bold type. The headlines had been dominated by news from the European front in World War I, but on Friday the "Wholesale Smuggling of Chinese" (the *Call*) and "Big Smuggling Plot Found" (the *Chronicle*) had superseded news that the "Kaiser Masses Army to Invade" (*Call*). Over the next few days, the newspapers offered San Franciscans a smorgasbord of graft, corruption, incompetence, and bureaucratic infighting and ineptitude. What kept these stories alive were charges that the *Mongolia* affair was not an isolated incident, but part of an organized, ongoing conspiracy that enabled Chinese to enter the United States illegally.

These disclosures were so amazing, said the *Call*, that "officials of the United States Immigration Service find them almost unbelievable." Anthony

Caminetti, Commissioner General of Immigration, found them believable enough. He took the Friday night train from Washington, announcing to the *Examiner* that he would take personal charge of an investigation into whether "United States Immigration inspectors connived with members of the crew of the steamer *Mongolia* and with agents ashore to permit the landing of the contraband Chinese who were found aboard the vessel fourteen hours after it tied up." It probably irritated him that while he was rushing out to California, his new San Francisco Commissioner of Immigration, Edward White, thought the appropriate response was to head down to Watsonville to pass the Sunday at home.

Caminetti's would not be the only investigation. The Pacific Mail immediately launched one of its own, as it was responsible for the stowaways' transportation back to China and for their care and feeding at the Angel Island Immigration Station. Surveyor of Customs Wardell announced that he, too, had launched one. The United States District Attorney for San Francisco, John W. Preston, ever responsive to local whites' demands to keep the Chinese out, said he would investigate and bring criminal charges. "I intend to shake every branch of the immigration tree at Angel Island."

For the first few days after the *Mongolia* story broke, the District Attorney was busy organizing the Grand Jury, having the forty grand jurors empaneled by Judge Maurice Dooling. D.A. Preston said that he would merely be *assisting* Commissioner General of Immigration Caminetti by centralizing all the information being gathered by Customs Surveyor Wardell, Immigration Commissioner White, and by his own staff, but it quickly became clear that Preston was in fact the driving force behind the investigation. The newspapers gave a running account of those being quizzed by the District Attorney. On November 4 Preston and White examined Sackett, six of his inspectors, Watchman David Graham, and eight Night Officers. Several days later he summoned M.H. Hunt, purser of the *Mongolia*; Stewards Wolf and Richardson; Ryland Drennan; James Campbell, checker for the Pacific Mail; and J.C. Hamilton, the company's ticket agent in Hong Kong who had arrived aboard the *Mongolia*. By the time the *Mongolia* case was actually presented to the Grand Jury on November 11, Preston had already questioned dozens of people, including employees of the Immigration Service.

At the same time, Preston set about making sure that no potential witnesses left town. Customs officers had already taken fifteen Chinese crew members into custody on Saturday, October 30. Much of the rest of the crew had been preparing to return to Hong Kong on the steamer *China*, a former Pacific Mail ship now under the ensign of the new, Chinese American–owned CMSS.

None of the other officers of the *Mongolia* were Chinese, but all seem to have come under suspicion. Captain Rice was supposed to take the *Mongolia* to New York and on to Europe, scheduled to leave on November 9. With the prospect of a lengthy investigation, it looked as though Rice might have to remain in San Francisco. Over the next few days, more Pacific Mail employees were identified as objects of the DA's investigation. Captain Rice, Chief Engineer Robert Paul, and Assistant Engineer Walter Scott were detained, then released on $1,000 witness bonds. The Pacific Mail's assistant general manager, H.A. Frey, added the company's assurances that the three would appear before the Grand Jury even if they were permitted to leave the city temporarily.

Caminetti initially let it be known that he would stay in California for some time to supervise the investigation. Then on Friday, November 5, he announced that the Justice Department was sending investigators of its own and it would not be necessary for him to remain in San Francisco. The press, however, unanimously and relentlessly insisted that all those who were making it easy for the Chinese to enter the United States should be exposed. That many such persons were in the Immigration Service, and that they were either dupes or connivers, was part of the daily fare in the San Francisco papers. On Friday, November 12, the *Examiner* summed up the general perception that something was very rotten at Angel Island:

> The publication in "The Examiner" of the details of the secret indictment in Los Angeles several months ago of Immigration Inspector W. H. Chadney for alleged complicity in a Chinese smuggling conspiracy, and Chadney's charge that he was indicted in order that "a club might be held over his head"...the *Mongolia* matter, the disclosures that Anthony Caminetti, Jr., has handled immigration cases at Angel Island, the contested appointment of Edward White as Immigration Commissioner at San Francisco, the resignation of Dr. John E. Gardner as interpreter at Angel Island, following an order transferring him to an obscure Eastern town, and other recent developments in the immigration service upheaval are declared to have contributed to the interest manifested by the Department of Labor.[8]

Caminetti's response was to name an investigating team of James L. Hughes, Assistant Commissioner of Immigration at Philadelphia, H.R. Sisson, head of the Chinese Section at New York, and some third member.

The third member, it turned out, would be John B. Densmore (1877–1939). As the *Examiner* had announced in a front-page story headlined "U.S. Agent Is Here to Sift Alien Scandal," Densmore had "arrived secretly in San Francisco" on November 11. The following day he boasted to the dailies, "You can count on me to clear up the entire immigration situation in San Francisco."[9]

Densmore was introduced to the public as "the most expert investigator in the Labor Department...having conducted the most vital part of the McNamara investigation, the settlement of the bloody teamsters' strike at Indianapolis, Indiana, and many of the most sensational governmental scandals of the past decade."[10] The photo that stares out from the *Examiner* is that of the steely-eyed inquisitor come to rescue the honor of the Immigration Service.

Densmore was more than just another gumshoe from Washington: he was a family friend of Labor Secretary William B. Wilson: In the 1880s Densmore *père* had been superintendent of the water supply system for the Illinois Central Railroad and had given the young Wilson, then an organizer for the United Mine

Figure 10.1
John B. Densmore, solicitor and investigator for the Labor Department and its Bureau
of Immigration, led a series of high-profile investigations into immigrant smuggling at
San Francisco. He later became the first Director General of the U.S. Employment
Service.

Source: The only known photograph of Densmore is from the *San Francisco Examiner*, December 3,
1918.

Workers, a job and a home when Wilson was on the coal operators' blacklist.[11]
Wilson promoted Densmore *fils*, an editor of the UMW journal and a
Democratic party apparatchik, over the objections of his own Assistant Secre-
tary more than once—first to Department solicitor, then in 1918 to the position
of Director General of the newly created United States Employment Service.
Densmore was no stranger to California, for he frequently visited on Democratic
Party business and had had another, more pleasurable, association with the
Chinese, when he escorted a high-profile delegation of Chinese industrialists
on a tour around the United States in early 1915; his name appears on the list
of dignitaries attending the farewell party in San Francisco.

Much was made of the team of investigators summoned to assist Densmore.
H.D. Ebey was assistant commissioner of Immigration at Chicago and, according

to the San Francisco newspapers, a much-feared investigator sent to interrogate the Chinese interpreters at Angel Island and to assist Preston.[12] Unquestionably, the Wilson administration wanted it known that Washington was pursuing this scandal vigorously. The dailies were only too happy to assist the Administration in telling the public how hard it was trying to find those who were smuggling Chinese into the country—such sensational headlines did, after all, help to sell newspapers.

The furor aroused by the *Mongolia* incident was not limited to newspaper headlines. San Francisco's Chinese community was distressed, fearful that it would unleash California's widespread anti-Chinese sentiment. The first signs of that happening came on November 17: "Immigration Officials Raid Chinatown for Stowaways; Imposing Squad of Inspectors, Headed by Special Agent from Chicago, Batter Down Doors on Waverly Place but Find No Smuggled Orientals."

Under instructions from United States Commissioner of Immigration Anthony Caminetti a search of Chinatown was made last night for contraband Chinese who escaped from Pacific Mail liners.

A corps of special agents of the Immigration Service, headed by H.D. Ebey of Chicago, and a squad of twenty-five inspectors, went into the Chinese quarter at 9 o'clock last night. They hoped to find at least a few of the stowaways who have been smuggled ashore.

The squad first raided Waverley Place. Doors of suspicious buildings were battered down, but no stowaway was found. The squad then turned its attention to other sections of Chinatown where it was suspected the fugitives might be hidden.

Immigration officials admitted yesterday that while eighty-six Chinese were captured on the liner *Mongolia,* from thirty to fifty escaped from the vessel between the time it docked early in the afternoon of October 25th and the time the first stowaways were discovered toward midnight of that date.

The raid in Chinatown last night is said to have been advised by United States District Attorney Preston who had admitted that his investigation, without corroborative testimony, was weak.[13]

In hindsight, such raids could be seen as precursors of the anti-immigrant, anti-labor "Palmer Raids" a few years later. The revived fear of officially sanctioned raids in the night was unsettling, but even more disturbing for Chinese was the prospect of organized efforts to be rid of the entire Chinese community. The *Examiner* reported these fears on November 23: "Chinese Fear Wholesale Deportation."

Wholesale deportation of Chinese smuggled into California may be the outcome of the investigation into the immigration service scandal which is to be conducted by John B. Densmore, Assistant Secretary of Labor.

Chinese colonies throughout the State are worrying over the coming probe of the *Mongolia* Chinese-smuggling conspiracy and the accompanying charges against the immigration department. That, at the very lowest estimate, one-quarter of the Chinese now in California have gained unlawful entry was the declaration made yesterday by a high authority on Chinese immigration affairs.

Speculation in local Federal circles as to how far Densmore will be allowed to go with his inquiry gave rise yesterday to various speculations. It was reported that powerful influences in Washington will be brought to bear to prevent a complete expose, for the reason that a deep and energetic probe would involve big men in the immigration service.

It was also rumored that attention might be diverted from the charges against the immigration service by a sweeping deportation of Chinese. In this connection it was said that Densmore may require Chinamen throughout California to produce certificates entitling them to admission to the country. During an investigation of an immigration service scandal in Philadelphia several years ago such a method was resorted to and scores of contraband Chinese were discovered, many of whom were compelled to divulge information as to how they were smuggled into the United States.

Rumors that Densmore might take a similar action has caused the Chinese Six Companies no little anxiety. The Six Companies, through their attorney, John L. McNab, have taken steps to protect responsible Chinese in California....

It was reported that [U.S. Attorney] Preston had expressed the opinion that the immigration situation gave promise of being one of the greatest scandals in official life in this city, but that he feared he would never be able to prove it to its depths. There is a well-defined conviction in Federal quarters that what Preston is reported as saying means that determined efforts may be made to cover up rather than expose the immigration department scandal.[14]

Some Chinese were, indeed, deported. Eighty of the *Mongolia*'s stowaways were sent back to China on January 8, sailing on the *Tenyo Maru* (of the TKK line). The government paid the $50 passage per man, then filed suit against Pacific Mail to recoup that cost and the twenty-four cents per person per day the government had spent to board the men at Angel Island. Six of the stowaways were forced to remain on Angel Island: Assistant District Attorney Ornbaum had demanded their continued presence as potential witnesses, and none of them were able to post the $500 bail required by Judge Maurice Dooling.[15]

Densmore sought out both the smugglers (unsurprisingly, he would find none of them amongst the men of the Immigration Service) and the weaknesses in the system that might allow the smugglers to succeed. For the latter, he focused on three theories of how the smuggling operation might have been carried out:

1. The stowaways were to be landed with the passengers on the day of arrival.
2. The stowaways might be landed by the members of the crew at some point between the pier and Angel Island.
3. The stowaways were to be landed as bonded members of the crew.

Densmore and his investigators gathered information that could test each of these theories. In the Roshomon-like text of his report, Densmore pointed to the differing stories and perspectives of those involved in the inspecting and clearing of incoming ships. He pieced together a picture of the complex, and at times cumbersome, way a ship, its passengers, and crew were treated from the time they entered the harbor to the time the ship sailed again.

Theory Number One: Stowaways Landed with the Passengers on the Day of Arrival

The most obvious theory came from the anonymous letter to Tidwell. In support of this theory was the fact that over the past two years, Immigration
Watchmen Robert J. Smith and David F. Graham had been the only watchmen
assigned to helping land passengers and crew. If Watchman Graham played a
key role in landing stowaways, then presumably he would have been in a
position to allow undocumented Chinese who presented passage tickets to pass
down the gangway and out into the great city. But in the course of his interviews, Densmore found that almost all customs guards were ignorant of how
Immigration officials actually landed passengers. The actual procedure, in his
opinion, made it virtually impossible for one official, acting alone or even in
concert with another, to allow illegals to land.

> On the arrival of the *Mongolia* at quarantine the Immigration boarding crew went
> aboard, and in the usual manner proceeded with the examination of the Chinese
> passengers, continuing until the ship docked and thereafter until all the passengers
> were landed. Acting Commissioner Mehan was aboard to approve the findings of
> the primary inspectors; Inspector Clendennin was the landing inspector and
> Watchman Robert J. Smith assisted him in landing the passengers....
>
> [The practice of] landing Chinese passengers by ticket or card at San Francisco
> [existed] prior to 1913, when it was abolished by the Commissioner at that port for
> the reason that it afforded a possible means for illegal landing of Chinese. As a matter
> of fact, the Chinese who are landed at the pier have been...passed upon by the exam-
> ining inspector and approved by the Acting Commissioner [and] are given to the
> landing inspector who proceeds to the head of the gangway. The Immigration
> watchman is stationed opposite him across the gangway. The landing inspector then
> calls out the name of a Chinese passenger whose papers he has, and the passenger
> approaches and produces his steamship ticket which he hands to the watchman. The
> watchman verifies the passenger's name by manifest number from his steamship ticket
> and returns the ticket to him. The landing inspector then compares the passenger with
> the photograph and description on his papers, and he is passed down off the boat.
>
> ...All other Chinese passengers are examined at Angel Island. The passports
> given Japanese are examined, and passengers other than Chinese holding tickets
> with their examination O.K'd on the back thereof by the examining inspector, are
> permitted to land.
>
> The Chinese passengers are permitted their steamship tickets which contain
> their name and manifest number, for the express purpose of facilitating the securing
> of certificates of identity to which they are entitled and for which they later apply at
> the Immigration office....
>
> There were approximately fifteen Immigration officers on board and about the
> vessel performing various duties in connection with the landing of the passengers;
> there were thirty or forty customs officers on board and about the vessel constantly
> on duty; there were several plain-clothes agents of the Treasury Department about
> the dock; the gangway down which the stowaways would have to come led immedi-
> ately into the baggage corral guarded by the customs inspectors, and it would have

been impossible for any stowaways to have escaped to the dock from the gangway, as the foot of the gangway was inside the customs corral; the customs inspectors are furnished with the number of passengers of all classes and could readily discover if there were any Chinese in the corral who were not entitled to be there. In view of the fact that no Chinese passenger can leave the vessel unless passed by the landing inspector at the head of the gangway, and in the circumstances above recited, it seems absurd that one man, a watchman, with no authority whatever to land passengers, would undertake to land these eighty-six stowaways in the manger charged, or at all.[16]

Theory Number Two: Stowaways Could Escape During Transfer to Angel Island

[T]he steamship officials are notified of the number of and manifest reference to those detained who are to be sent to Angel Island. The vessel is then left in charge of the customs officers. The steamship officials, in keeping with the practice, transfer the detained passengers to Angel Island in the tugboat "Arabs." On the steamship *MONGOLIA* ninety-three detained passengers were held aboard during the night, it having been found impracticable for the steamship company to transfer all the passengers in the daytime.

. . . It is true that the transfer of detained passengers to Angel Island is left solely to the steamship officials, there being no Immigration officials present when the detained passengers are transferred to the tug boat, nor during the trip across the bay from the pier to Angel Island. The practice imposes upon the steamship officials the duty of delivering to the Immigration station certain detained Chinese passengers indicated in the notice delivered by the landing inspector to the ship's officer. While this method of transfer to Angel Island, involving more than an hour's travel, no doubt affords an opportunity for the landing of contraband Chinese, still it would necessarily involve members of the ship's crew and practically the entire crew of the "Arabs" or other transfer boat and would be apparent to the detained passengers aboard such transfer boat. As these transfers are always made in the daytime and the transfer boat would have to land at some point where detection would be likely, it would appear that this method of illegal landing of Chinese would scarcely be undertaken.[17]

Theory Number Three: Stowaways Landed as Members of the Crew

With the exception of a small cadre of white officers, the crew was overwhelmingly Chinese, manning (for they were all males) the engine rooms, the dining and cooking facilities, the passenger cabins and steerage quarters, and the deck operations. This was true in 1915 and it had been true on American ships crossing the Pacific for over a generation: those ships had employed over 100,000 Chinese sailors in facilitating the great maritime migration of Chinese to the United States.[18] A ship like the *Mongolia*, which could carry 1,500 passengers, would also carry a very large crew: on average, about 270 men. For this voyage, over 220 Chinese crewmen from the *Mongolia* were ready to ship back to Hong Kong on the SS *China*; perhaps a few others had chosen to remain in San Francisco. A new crew was ready to take her to New York. Perhaps smugglers had a plan to use the commotion of switching two rather large crews—one of which was nearly all Chinese—to land the eighty-six stowaways.

As it was Watchman Graham who usually attended to landing the members of the crew under bond, suspicion naturally fell on him. But the process of bonding crew members so that they could go ashore was sufficiently complex that suspicion could also fall on any number of persons. One such was Joe Tape, a resident Chinese who worked as an agent for the Southern Pacific Railroad and for a number of the steamship companies. His specialty was the bonding process by which a crewman who was normally not entitled to enter the United States—in practice, a Chinese crew member—could enter for thirty days. The bond—somewhat like a bail bond, but issued by a customs broker—was redeemable when the crewman sailed on an outbound ship. This bond was what guaranteed that he did not remain in the United States.

Joe Tape would board a ship the day she entered San Francisco. He would be given the names and photographs of all the crewmen whom the officers would allow to go ashore. The normal procedure was for Tape to take the photographs to Wm. H. Thornley, a customs house broker, who would attach an individual's photograph to that individual's bond. Tape would then take the bonds to Angel Island for approval by the Commissioner. The approval came in the form of a letter, signed by the Commissioner, to the master of the ship, advising him which crewmen would be permitted to go ashore and at what time an Immigration officer would be at the ship to land the men. Tape would then take the bonds to the Immigration office in the City and give them to the Immigration officer on duty—in this case, Watchman Graham. At 5:00 p.m., Graham and Tape would walk over to the ship and give the vessel's officer a list of all those who had been bonded. The officer gave passes to the crew going ashore, who then passed down the gangway. The Immigration watchman would identify each one by his name and photograph on the bond; each pass was collected.

The weakness in the system was that no one checked the crewmen back *on* to the ship. To redeem the bond, a crewman had only to appear at muster the morning the ship was to sail. An immigration officer would compare his face and description with that on the bond and, if they matched, presumed that the crewman had returned to the ship.

On October 27, Joe Tape did some unusual things. Normally, he would wait until the next day to arrange for the crew's bonds. But on October 27 he immediately boarded the *Mongolia*, got a list of names, then showed up at Angel Island with forty-two bonds for members of the crew. This surprised Inspector Hays, for the day before he had been informed by Pacific Mail that *no* crewmen from the *Mongolia* would be allowed ashore. Hays thought to call the Pacific Mail office for verification, and was told that, indeed, no crewmen from the *Mongolia* would be allowed ashore. Hays informed Joe Tape that the bonds would not be approved. Tape then destroyed the bonds, after first cutting out the photographs and returning them to their owners.

The DA suspected Tape of trying to land at least forty-two of the stowaways as crewmen. But Tape countered that haste was necessary if the crew—scheduled to leave for Hong Kong in three days—were to have any shore leave at all. Tape also suggested that investigators check the photographs that had been returned to the crew. Those photographs were found to be not those of stowaways, but of the crew members, as claimed.

Densmore found that suspicions of Tape did not hold up and, further, that Tape's complicity would have been unnecessary. A corrupt Immigration man could simply pass the stowaways off the boat as crewmen,

> as he is the only officer who sees the photographs, compares them with the crewmen as they leave the boat, and passes them off if satisfied that they are the ones represented in the bond; and no check being made of the return of the crewmen to the vessel...the landing of the stowaways would not be detected, as the entire crew would be accounted for on muster by the watchman on sailing day.[19]

Densmore's report completely exonerated the local Immigration Service aside from

> several matters of administration...that could and should have been improved....
> The fact that 86 stowaways were brought right to the door of the United State and there prevented from landing by the Immigration officers in the ordinary performance of their duty, far from bringing condemnation or accusation upon them, should and does reflect credit upon their integrity.[20]

His report to the Secretary did, of course, make a number of recommendations. Most were sensible and quite practicable, and nearly all were aimed at making it more difficult to avoid the gantlet of Immigration control. One set of recommendations focused on the inspection of arriving ships: changing procedures to make sure that a ship always be under guard, with a landing inspector at the head of each gangway continuously from the time the vessel docked until all passengers were landed; that no one be allowed to board a ship prior to the Immigration and Customs officers and, preferably, not until all passengers had been examined; that individual, rather than group passes, be issued to visitors to a ship and that people on the pier not be allowed to communicate with Chinese and other passengers; "that all passenger and cargo vessels *from the Orient* should be thoroughly searched as soon after arrival as practicable";[21] and that an inspector accompany detainees being transferred to Angel Island.

Densmore also recommended an end to the pandemonium that occurred on sailing day. The custom was for the Commissioner of Immigration to issue passes for people to visit a ship the day it was to sail. Lawyers and the steamship company could request passes for relatives and friends of Chinese passengers, who would naturally prolong their visit as long as possible. Shortly before sailing, when the "last call" was given, they would "rush pell mell for the gang planks.

There are hundreds of visitors, Chinese, and others, and they practically swamp the officers at the gang planks."[22]

There were the inevitable recommendations/pleas for more—more watchmen, more Immigration inspectors, more Chinese interpreters, more matrons (there was only one at the time) at Angel Island, more stenographers on the Island and in the City office. Finally, there was the matter of the Angel Island Immigration Station itself:

> The Immigration Station should be established on the mainland in the city of San Francisco. It is now most inconveniently located, and the cost of operating and maintenance is far in excess of what it should be for a station at that port. The likelihood of fire and loss of life at the present station...is worthy of immediate and serious consideration. The costs of a suitable fire-proof station on the mainland would be covered in a very few years by the saving from the amount now necessary to expend with the station located on Angel Island.[23]

The Immigration Service offered the Densmore report as evidence that something was being done to close loopholes in the bulwarks against Chinese immigration, even though the report found no wrongdoing by employees of the Service nor recommended that any Immigration Service personnel be punished. "We have," Densmore said publicly, "no grounds for changes in the Angel Island immigration service."[24]

Few San Franciscans were so thoroughly satisfied. The *Examiner* charged that "Densmore was more interested in preventing a scandal than in exposing one."[25] Whispers of a Densmore "whitewash" could be heard, whispers that grew louder on February 8 when the Federal Grand Jury released the results of *its* investigation, headlined in the *Examiner*'s front page: "27 Indicted as Chinese Smugglers." The Federal Grand Jury had voted "true bills" against five members of the Immigration Service, six officers of the *Mongolia*, Tape and Thornley (they who bonded crewmen), and Chinese members of the crew (although District Attorney Preston later asserted that the Grand Jury had issued the indictments against his advice, and while he was out sick for a protracted period). As the *Examiner* headline on February 10 asserted, the "True Bills Contradict Densmore."

Those indicted included Assistant Immigration Commissioner Boyce, Inspectors Strand, Hayes, Clendenin, and Smith, and Watchman Graham. From the *Mongolia*'s officers: M.H. Hunt (purser), Robert S. Paul (chief engineer), Walter Scott (first assistant engineer), J.J. Richards (chief steward), Joseph Wolf (steerage steward), R.E. Gerathy (watchman). Also indicted were thirteen Chinese crew members: Wong Joe, Yip Foo, Kwon Yook, Hoong Sun, Hue John, Chun Bing Tong, Han Sung, Yip Mo, Chun Sing, Tam Yim, Sue Hoong, Chen Tan, and Chen Foo.[26] The indictments of the Immigration Service officers were curious indeed, in that most of those implicated were the very men who had uncovered the *Mongolia*'s stowaways and had been subsequently exonerated by Densmore.

Densmore did not speak directly to the press; he issued no denial of a white-wash. But he, too, must have been upset at the DA having issued indictments where he, Densmore, had seen no sign of criminal activity. The following week he wrote to his patron and family friend, the Secretary of Labor, taking the unusual step of asking that "*the report as pertains to the investigation of the Mongolia smuggling matter be withdrawn* for further investigation and that only such matters as touch the general administration of the Immigration Service at San Francisco now receive your consideration and action."[27]

Over the next few months, the *Mongolia* investigations slowly ran out of steam. With little in the way of sensational new developments to report, the scandal faded from view as the newspapers turned to other things—the war in Europe, the forthcoming election, the trial of Germany's consul in San Francisco for conspiring to violate American neutrality, and armed forays and incursions along the Mexican border. There was not a single conviction from the investiga-tion of the Great Scandal that was to have shaken the Immigration Service to its very roots. No one was even put on trial.

As far as Commissioner White in San Francisco was concerned, the scandal and the investigations all came to an end on September 1, 1916. He wrote to Commissioner General Caminetti in Washington that his men were at last to be absolved:

> In *Mongolia* smuggling case before Judge Dooling, yesterday, district attorney Preston...announced that he was seeking authority from Washington to dismiss the indictment, as the men should not have been indicted, the evidence being insuf-ficient to justify the charges and that he had advised the Grand Jury against bringing an indictment.[28]

On the same day, the *Nippon Maru* arrived in San Francisco, carrying Quok Shee and her "alleged husband," Chew Hoy Quong. The political and bureau-cratic waters they sailed into were anything but calm. They would be there for yet another immigration scandal and investigation. Densmore would be back. And this time, heads would roll.

DENSMORE'S RETURN

On October 10, 1916, the slumbering *Mongolia* investigation was momen-tarily roused when Commissioner White received a tip from an anonymous source:

> Mr. Commissioner:
>   There is a short man from your office. He says he name Aleck but we find out his name is McFarlin. He say he go record room now and can change any picture or do any thing. His good friend Hilky you discharge two or three months ago for stealing China boys paper....If you do not watch McFarlin or take him out record room he and Hilky and two bad men from Chinatown will make heap lot trouble for Chinamen with good paper.[29]

Put on the alert, it still took Commissioner White's office another two months to stumble on the plot described by the tipster.

> On Friday morning, December 8, 1916, Clerk Richard Rankin reported to the Commissioner's office that he had detected Under Clerk Presley A. McFarland removing record No. 15669/8-15 from the filing cabinets in the vault. There was apparently no reason for Mr. McFarland having the record in his possession.... Upon being confronted with Mr. Rankin, who stated that he personally saw Mr. McFarland remove this record, Mr. McFarland confessed.[30]

This serendipitous discovery would revive the investigations into immigrant smuggling. Within days of McFarland's confession, practically every clerk and watchman at the Immigration Station had been interviewed by the team of Assistant Commissioner Boyce, Law officer Wilkinson, Immigrant Inspector Lorenzen, and Clerk Rankin. Although Clerk McFarland's confession had not been taken down by a stenographer and was later repudiated, he had already implicated other low-ranking employees of the Immigration Station on Angel Island: Junior Clerk (Stenographer and Typist) Robert Fergusson, Under Clerk William Armstrong, Junior Watchman Theodore Kaphan, and former Under Clerk Agathon Hilkemeyer. McFarland's confession led Commissioner White's men to other conspirators, including attorney Henry Kennah and ultimately to interpreters and inspectors in the Immigration Service itself. The more searching the inquiry became, the more it appeared that there had been extensive theft and manipulation of records. San Francisco's newspapers maintained a drumbeat favoring further, "honest" investigations, as did State Assemblyman Leo Friedman of San Francisco and the city's Chamber of Commerce.[31] By February, Commissioner White wrote to the Secretary, asking that "an experienced investigator be assigned to the duty of ferreting out those who are guilty of this nefarious business."[32] That investigator would again be John B. Densmore.

In March 1917, Secretary of Labor Wilson directed Densmore to proceed to San Francisco and perform a "complete administrative clean-up of the service at this station which...ha[s] been a source of considerable annoyance and embarrassment to the Department for a number of years."[33] Densmore concluded that the usual holding of semipublic hearings, as he did in his earlier investigation, would be ineffective in the face of such widespread corruption. He devised "a probe conducted in the most secret way possible, without the knowledge of even the officials of the service at this port."[34] While he and F.C. Howe, head of the Ellis Island Immigration Station, maintained a public appearance of interviewing employees and speaking to the press, the other members of his team went about their business more clandestinely. One approach involved the surveillance of the principal white suspects, whether in the Immigration Service or not, while another was to establish contact with various Chinese "smugglers and manipulators." This team was as multicultural as the confederation of smugglers, and although their identities were never publicly revealed, it included Inspectors George Parson and Thomas Fisher, Special Agent McCarty, and

Chinese Interpreter Ah Jon. The latter is probably the person referred to in Densmore's report as "an intelligent young Chinese of demonstrated probity and courage, whose place of residence must not be disclosed."[35]

At first, "surveillance" meant simply watching the meetings of the inspectors under suspicion. The conspirators were seen meeting at the office of Stidger and Kennah in the Montgomery Block, at the Bank Exchange Saloon in the same block, on the ferry from Berkeley to San Francisco, and—favorite meeting place of all—on Sundays at the baseball park at 41st and San Pablo in Oakland. Tips came in, some meant to mislead, others genuine like the one from typist Jennie Garcia at the Immigration Station:

> At the risk of being laughed at as a "female detective"...Interpreter McClymont...
> for the last two or three weeks has taken up the habit of going in the Chinese toilet
> ...where as you know no white men but the janitor ever goes....I have also
> observed that the Chinese witnesses sometimes almost run from the boat up to the
> building and dash in there before they can be called on the cases.[36]

Generally, however, visual surveillance revealed little, and Densmore felt it would be an "interminable job...as they were extremely cautious in their movements." Displaying a ruthless disregard for the law, he decided to tap the telephones of key subjects. It was illegal in California to do this, as it had been since 1905, but Densmore was not deterred by such niceties. "Inasmuch as wire tapping is a statutory offense in this state, I need only...point out the necessity of the utmost secrecy."[37] He would resort to illegal eavesdropping in an even more famous case that we shall come to later.

In May 1917, Densmore began to tap the telephones at the Oakland residences of Henry Kennah, four immigration inspectors, and "Chinese steerer" Lee U Ong. It was a simple thing to tap the suspects' telephones. The Labor Department talked to the head office of the Pacific States Telephone Company, which instructed a Mr. McFarland (no relation to the suspect Clerk) in San Francisco to cooperate. He "directed his general manager to place at my disposal whatever equipment I requested....The switchboard was so set up that incoming and outgoing calls on these lines would be announced in our office without the knowledge of the regular operators. Our equipment also consisted of multiple head receivers permitting four people to hear one conversation at the same time." Inspectors Parson and Fisher, Special Agent McCarty, and Clerk Armstrong did the listening, transcribing everything they overheard—unless it was spoken in Chinese by a "Chink."

Those being overheard were slow to catch on. Even if one party might hear a clicking sound, the other would attribute it to someone else in the house being on the line. Even as the noose tightened around them, as Densmore continued to investigate and as more and more inspectors and interpreters were removed from office, the conspirators continued to "fix" things. Only after a month had elapsed did they start worrying about being seen together, and in early July they ceased communicating by phone.

The transcripts reveal both the excitement and the tedium of illicit surveillance. The listeners heard the amusing or mundane (Inspector Ebey trying to convince women to go for a ride in his new car), the ridiculous (Mrs. Kennah calling home to remind her son to go to the bathroom before going to bed), and of course, the crooked:

Chink: This Yee Jim. How about Louie Ming?

[Inspector J.T.] McCall: The testimony is all wrong. I am afraid he will be rejected.

Chink: How is that?

McCall: Lots of things wrong; the witness was all wrong.

Chink: I send the witness over again.

McCall: No; don't send him over again.

Chink: You want a different witness? I will wait two days and then I send a different witness. I send a good one this time. You think then I have chance?

McCall: I am afraid I can't.

Chink: I will give you double price you do.

McCall: I will see what I can do.[38]

Never does an actual immigrant call—all the conversations are between lawyers, immigration inspectors, and "steerers"—Chinese brokers or fixers. A Chinese "steerer," not knowing which inspectors would be assigned to any particular cases, would call *all* of the inspectors in the ring, giving each the same list of the cases to be fixed. The evidence gained is unequivocal in its depiction of certain inspectors as corrupt—and in its absolute inadmissibility in court. Densmore had to make sure that any charges were so written as to avoid indicating the extralegal source of some of the evidence behind them.

Densmore's first investigation had focused solely on the possibility that the smuggling was somehow carried out by a ship's crew as the arrivals were transferred from ship to shore. This time, he learned that the smuggling was carried out by the employees of the Immigration Service itself—its inspectors, interpreters, clerks, and messengers—and the smuggling involved two types of activities: manipulation of records and fraud in the examination of applicants for admission.

Manipulating records involved stealing records and then doctoring them in some way, most commonly by changing the photograph on a valid document. Fong Get, a photographer at 914 Stockton Street, was quizzed by Densmore in September 1917 about a photograph he had taken about a year previously. His subject had come dressed in American clothes, then changed into Chinese clothes, cap and wig appropriate for an earlier generation—in this case, 1899, when Fong's subject had supposedly first entered the United States.[39]

The examination of immigrants could be manipulated in a variety of ways. Densmore uncovered quite a list:

Fraud in connection with examinations manifests itself in the employment of fake witnesses and affidavits; the surreptitious coaching of applicants, by means of letters secretly delivered to them in the detention quarters of the Immigration Station; purposely easy examinations on the part of the inspectors; underhanded assistance rendered applicants, during the course of examinations, by the official Chinese interpreters; changing of notes on the part of stenographers who report the hearings; reconciling discrepancies in testimony by the inspectors who conduct the examinations.[40]

The lower employees were the first to be dismissed. In April, Clerk McFarland and Watchman-Messenger Kaphan were fired, followed by Watchman-Messenger Harry Akers. In June, it was the turn of the inspectors: William Heitman, then William Gassaway ("one of the best known Immigration men on the Pacific coast," according to the *Examiner*), then McCall. By early July the trickle of resignations and suspensions had become a torrent that included Chinese interpreters Edward Park, Joseph Gubbins, C. Alves, J. Olivera, Julius McClymont, Robert Lym, and W. T. Thatcher. Inspectors Clarence Ebey, William Thiess, W. H. Clendenin, and Albert Long; Clerk Arthur Hyman; and Laborer Rolub Hendricks were removed. And those were just the current employees at Angel Island.

Densmore also produced evidence against a number of outside parties: attorney Embert Lee (one of the few Chinese lawyers in San Francisco), former employees Agathon Hilkemeyer, Robert Fergusson, and Robert Riley, photographer Fong Get, forger E. L. Mills; and fifteen Chinese, headed by Lee U Ong, variously labeled as steerers, manipulators, or fixers. But Densmore's special wrath was reserved for the law firm of Stidger and Kennah, who told the Inspectors "what to do, received their reports, and paid them for their work. [Stidger and Kennah] stand guilty, individually and as a firm of attorneys, of the most fraudulent practices...through bribery and perjury, they are directly responsible for the corrupt methods so long prevalent at the Station."[41] He made sure that the firm of Stidger and Kennah was disbarred from practicing before the Immigration Service.

Stidger and Kennah was no ordinary law firm. Their share of the "business before the Immigration Station is by far the largest of any of the attorneys similarly engaged, amounting to one-half of all the business done at this Station."[42] This translated into an enormous opportunity for graft. Densmore charged that the five inspectors controlled by Stidger and Kennah "handled 50 per cent of all the cases that came up for action in the three years ended December 31, 1916,—*or 1947 cases out of 3847* [emphasis in the original]."[43] Two other inspectors that he suspected of being controlled by Stidger and Kennah handled another 787 cases.

These figures reveal something of the dynamics of the business of immigration law, especially how controlling a majority of the immigration inspectors could give a firm a decided competitive advantage over other firms. Stidger and Kennah, of course, got a reputation for being able to deliver favorable decisions on behalf of their clients. But they could also affect the entry of another firm by securing *adverse* decisions against that firm's clients. Densmore quoted attorney Joseph P. Fallon (later a partner of George McGowan) that "this is sometimes done, especially in the case of new attorneys who are seeking to break into the Chinese field. The new man probably secures his first case with difficulty, and when it is reported on unfavorably by the examining inspector, it will be a long time before he gets another."[44]

The two men, Stidger and Kennah, were an interesting contrast in personalities and styles, and point up how the exclusion laws could engender varying motives that were not necessarily incompatible with each other. Henry Kennah was thought by Densmore to be the key corrupter. Kennah's intimate knowledge of the Immigration Service came from serving as Chinese Inspector for some twenty-one years. He resigned from his $2,000 annual salary in 1912 following an into corruption in the handling of Chinese immigration cases. Densmore thought him a "man determined years ago to be a crook and to profit from conditions which make it a comparatively easy matter for an unscrupulous man of brains to grow rich in the Immigration Service at this port." Kennah's pleasing, outgoing, grand personality resulted in a genuinely "generous fellow who is devoid of any feeling of moral accountability... generous and lovable, and at the same time unscrupulous. This strange combination makes him a dangerous man."[45]

Stidger was another matter, "a small man in every way," in Densmore's estimation. But Stidger's motivations included more complex notions than greed alone. He and his family had a long association with the Chinese in California, and it is not unreasonable to think that some sense of fighting for an aggrieved community came into play.

Oliver Perry Stidger (1873–1959) was the son of James Allen Stidger and grandson of O.P. Stidger. The latter had been a "famous pioneer lawyer and editor." He had been Editor of the *Marysville Herald* and was "a staunch friend and unyielding enemy, he espoused the cause of the Chinese and did much to aid them." His highly principled defense of the Chinese is typified by an address delivered July 4, 1855 in North San Juan (Nevada County):

> As true Americans we must defend and protect the stranger within our gates. If we be true to American liberty and freedom and the flag, we must in this state defend the Chinese strangers far from their native land however meek and down trodden they may be. These Chinese people we have found to be hard working and friendly and faithful and we must defend them against the grievous wrongs they have suffered at the hands of lawless elements in our state especially those in our mining communities.[46]

Something of that spirit was surely passed along to his son and grandson. James Allen Stidger began practicing law in San Francisco in 1869, and in 1893 took on his son as partner. Oliver Perry Stidger carved out a career working with Chinese clients in business and immigration law. He was known to fellow lawyers as "attorney for the Chinese Six Companies; for Chinese Chamber of Commerce, Chinese Merchants' Association and Chinese Republic Association. Mason, Republican."[47] His obituary noted that the "Constitution of the

Republic of China was drawn up in Montgomery Block in 1911. Pictured is Sun Yat-Sen, Republic founder, and lawyer Stidger, in whose office the doctrine was drafted."[48]

Stidger was not above trying to bribe inspectors himself. Densmore showed that the relationship between the two lawyers went back at least a decade, to cases where (then) "Inspector Kennah has placed the details of the record within the grasp of the attorney (Stidger), who, for the sake of the dollars in the fee took advantage of the betrayal of the confidential records." Densmore's report also included Inspector Joseph Strand's report of an incident where "Stidger attempted to give Strand $150 to influence his recommendation in a certain Chinese case, following up this offer with a proposition to pay him a flat rate of $25 for each case handled."[49]

It is difficult to know how much of Stidger and Kennah's business involved corrupt practices, and how much was straightforward immigration work. In applying in 1919 for reinstatement to practice before the Immigration Service, Stidger had his former accountant produce the firm's cash book for the period September 1914 to June 1917. The cash book recorded monies paid to the firm and offers an insight into the role played by Stidger and Kennah (and, presumably, other lawyers) in the immigration process. Each month the firm received around one hundred payments of various sorts, totaling approximately $2,500. Most are for what one would expect of lawyers involved with immigration cases: preparing papers so that arriving Chinese could be landed immediately and preparing appeals for those who could not, and helping with passports for American-born Chinese. Accountant Sadie Curtis summarized the fees charged by Stidger and Kennah:

> All cases were handled on a contingent basis and only in appeal cases was a retainer obtained. A merchant's or native's son who was landed outright, a fee of $25 was charged; in cases of a small family applying, $35 or thereabouts was charged for the family's case. Merchants, Natives, and laborers returning a fee from $5 to $10 was charged, the fees being charged according to the amount of work done in their case. A fee of $2.50 was charged for all affidavits made.[50]

But a number of other, interesting transactions show up. Until September 1915, when the "last check" was received, Stidger and Kennah received a monthly payment of $250 from the PMSS. A very few non-Chinese clients ("three Mexican girls") are taken on. Appeals cost anywhere from $40 to $100. It appears that Stidger and Kennah also acted as a source of credit for newly arriving Chinese or for people assisting them. There are numerous receipts of $500 or $1,000 for payment on "loans" or "credit account" or, simply, "cash." In addition, the lawyers clearly paid many of the up-front costs of being detained at Angel Island. Nearly every journal page, representing approximately one week, records "payment from Island" or "hospital treatment" or, in one case "deposit trachoma, $300."[51] Accountant Curtis noted that the ledger also contained "moneys deposited for hospital treatment out of which possibly

$7.50, or $15 was used and the balance returned to the client." Such financial intermediation clearly facilitated the flow of Chinese through the inspection-detention process.

Densmore, however, was not interested in facilitating the immigration of Chinese immigrants. His mission was to "eradicate graft and place the whole immigration establishment at the port of San Francisco on a firm basis of honesty and efficiency." Initially, he had seen his charge as being "to correct an intolerable condition in [the Labor Department's] service solely; it conceivably [having] neither the time, inclination, nor authority in law to clean up the entire community." But as the extent of the scandal became larger and larger, and as public opinion expressed through the newspapers insisted on punishment for the "higher ups," Densmore came to the conclusion that "something more than an administrative house-cleaning would be in order."[52] Having discovered the "grafter and corrupters" and fired or transferred those who worked for the Immigration Service, he then launched criminal proceedings against them and their civilian accomplices.

Despite the preponderance of evidence, this was not a simple matter. The indictments were drawn up by Assistant United States Attorney Caspar Ornbaum, whom Densmore found to be "a crony of Stidger's and an unscrupulous up-country lawyer who places the personal interests of his grafter friend above any considerations of duty, honor, or public good."[53] Densmore discovered Ornbaum's "despicable double-dealing and rank treachery" only when a member of the Grand Jury resigned to protest Ornbaum's blatant leaking of information to Stidger. Ornbaum was denounced to the U.S. Attorney Preston, who removed Ornbaum from all Immigration cases and took them over himself.

Fifteen people were indicted and tried, only one of them an Inspector (Ebey). Eight of the Immigration men, all clerks or watchmen, were found guilty. The juries disagreed on Ebey and mechanic Mills, Wong A. Wong was acquitted, and the indictments against translator McClymont, notary public Riley, and lawyers Lee and Stidger were dismissed—the latter a particularly bitter blow to Densmore, largely owing to the fact that he eavesdropped on his own star witness, Hilke-meyer, and discovered him trying to sell out for $4,500. Kennah died in 1918, before the cases went to trial, and several of the other Chinese fled the country or went into hiding. A number of other cases against the inspectors did not result in indictments, presumably through the machinations of Ornbaum and Stidger. Nonetheless, Densmore felt the results "as gratifying as they were salutary... considering the unusual difficulties under which the prosecution labored."[54]

Despite the taint to his reputation, Stidger continued his practice. In advertisements in all the local Chinese newspapers, Stidger and Kennah published a letter to the CCC, saying that they were no longer able to practice immigration law but could still practice other types of law. They attributed their being barred from representing clients before the Immigration Service to the Service persecuting them for having earlier organized a petition-signing to protest harsh treatment of Chinese trying to enter the United States. When a Republican administration came to power in Washington in 1921 and brought in a new Commissioner for San Francisco, Stidger was again allowed to represent clients in immigration matters. He continued to work for the Chinese and to call attention to the discriminatory and counterproductive nature of legislation aimed at the Chinese, including the 1924 National Origins Law.[55]

Densmore would be on the front page one more time. His second bout of notoriety stemmed from a bomb that went off at the July 22, 1916 Preparedness Parade in San Francisco. Ten people died from the explosion, and suspicion fell most heavily on two trade union leaders, Tom Mooney and Warren Billings. The two were found guilty; Billings received a life sentence, and Mooney was sentenced to death. As Densmore was in San Francisco anyway, conducting his investigation into the immigration scandal, Secretary of Labor Wilson assigned him to look into the Mooney Case. Densmore did so, using two of his investigators (inspectors McCarty and Parson) to plant a Dictaphone in the Hall of Justice office of District Attorney Charles Fickert. Over the next two months, all of Fickert's office conversations and telephone calls were recorded and transcribed. Released to the *San Francisco Call* at about the same time they were given to Secretary Wilson, "the Densmore Report" was a bombshell of its own: it revealed that Fickert had tried to frame Mooney and engaged in a number of other practices that were questionable and perhaps corrupt.

Densmore's report was more than just a compilation of his illicit recordings. He added his own highly partisan commentary that incited those wanting to see Mooney's conviction upheld. "Densmore's comments and the impropriety of a federal bureau chief's wiretapping the office of a city official—particularly when the results were scurrilous rather than conclusive...may have harmed the Mooney case considerably."[56] Mooney's conviction was not overturned, but his death sentence was commuted to life in prison, where he remained for another twenty years.

Densmore may have thought that he had stamped out the smuggling of immigrants at Angel Island, but it merely died down for a while. The demand for entry into the United States, and the rewards for gaining such entry, was motivation enough to insure that smuggling did not end with Densmore's investigation. Nor was immigrant smuggling restricted to Angel Island. Corruption continued to flourish to varying degrees, but especially in those ports where the Chinese exclusion laws affected large number of people passing through. One operation was uncovered in 1924 in Honolulu and reported in the *New York Times,* which pegged the bribes of $1,200 a head, alleging that 5,000 Chinese had been smuggled into Hawaii in recent years. The chief smuggler was Richard Halsey, the head of the Immigration Service in Honolulu. Halsey had apparently been taking bribes for years. On the day the Commissioner General of Immigration was to visit Halsey and confront him with these charges personally, Halsey went to his office, sat in his big Director's chair, and killed himself.[57]

This was the same Halsey who in 1917 gave John B. Sawyer a guided tour of the Honolulu immigration station. Sawyer was on his way back from Hong Kong to take up a position as Chinese Inspector at Angel Island. Halsey's corrupt activities had begun well before 1917, and it seems strange that they were unobservable to the uncorruptable straight arrow, "Mr. Section 6," whom we meet in the next chapter.

NOTES

1. *San Francisco Chronicle*, October 28, 1915, 1.

2. Tidwell to Secretary of the Treasury, November 11, 1914. *Records of the Immigration and Naturalization Service*, editorial advisor, Alan Kraut. Series A, Subject Correspondence Files.

3. Tidwell to Secretary of the Treasury, November 11, 1914. Alan Kraut and Randolph Boehm, eds., *Records of the Immigration and Naturalization Service*, vol. Reel 9 (Bethesda, MD: University Publications of America, 1992). Series A, Subject correspondence files, Supplement Reel 4. Referred to hereafter as "INS Microfilms." All errors of grammar, spelling, etc., are in the original document.

4. Report of John B. Densmore to Secretary of Labor, January 11, 1916. INS microfilms, Supplement Reel 4.

5. This incident came to light after the *Mongolia* story broke. See the *Call*'s front-page headline and story on "Wholesale Smuggling of Chinese" on Friday, October 29, 1915.

6. *San Francisco Call*, July 21, 1914.

7. Information on the various hiding places comes from contemporary newspaper accounts, especially the *Chronicle*. Densmore's report minimized the role of the Customs officials and omitted the colorful detail so dear to the dailies.

8. *San Francisco Examiner*, November 12, 1915.

9. *San Francisco Examiner*, November 21, 1915.

10. *San Francisco Examiner*, November 20, 1915.

11. See Lombardi, *Labor's Voice in the Cabinet*, 78 and 194.

12. *San Francisco Chronicle*, Tuesday, November 16, 1915.

13. *San Francisco Chronicle*, Thursday, November 18, 1915.

14. *San Francisco Examiner*, November 23, 1915.

15. *San Francisco Examiner*, January 9, 1916.

16. Densmore Report.

17. Ibid.

18. See Schwendinger, *Ocean of Bitter Dreams*, especially the chapter on "America's Invisible Merchant Marine," 169–79.

19. Densmore, Report to Secretary of Labor Wilson, January 11, 1916, 16; INS microfilms, Supplement Reel 4.

20. Densmore Report, 19.

21. Densmore Report, 22; emphasis added.

22. Densmore Report, 23

23. Densmore Report, 31.

24. *San Francisco Examiner*, February 10, 1916.

25. Ibid. The quotation comes from the edition photocopied for the INS microfilms series; it is not found in the edition in the UC Berkeley Library's newspaper microfilm collection.

26. *San Francisco Chronicle*, February 11, 1916.

27. Densmore, letter to Secretary of Labor Wilson, February 21, 1916; INS microfilms, Supplement Reel 4; emphasis added.

28. INS microfilms, Supplement Reel 4.

29. October 10, 1916. Exhibit "B," accompanying White's letter to Caminetti.

30. Memorandum of Assistant Commissioner William Boyce, December 14, 1916. Document 12016/1076.

31. *San Francisco Examiner,* January 30 and February 7, 1917.

32. White to Commissioner General of Immigration, February 6, 1917; file 12016/1076.

33. Densmore to Secretary of Labor, May 1, 1919, document 54184/138-A. Hereafter referred to as "Densmore Final Report."

34. Densmore Final Report, 2.

35. Ibid., 3.

36. Undated memo from Jennie Garcia to Inspector Strand, Densmore Investigation File, NARA.

37. Densmore to Commissioner General of Immigration, July 16, 1917. NARA document 54184-138-C. This cover letter accompanied transcriptions of the telephone taps.

38. Transcripts of Densmore wiretaps, May 27, 1917. In Ibid.

39. Densmore investigation, Box 4, file 1.

40. Densmore Final Report, 4.

41. Densmore report to W.B. Wilson, Secretary of Labor, July 24, 1917; quoted in Densmore's letter to Wilson, March 19, 1919. Referred to as "Densmore Report to Wilson. 1917."

42. Ibid.

43. Ibid.

44. Ibid.

45. Ibid.

46. In the collection of the Society of California Pioneers, file B001747, donated to the society by Oliver Perry Stidger, November 11, 1944.

47. Bates, *History of the Bench and Bar of California,* 519.

48. *San Francisco News,* March 14, 1959.

49. Densmore Report to Wilson. 1917.

50. Sadie Curtis to J.H. Ralston, April 24, 1919. Densmore Investigation File, NARA, Washington.

51. Cash book of Stidger & Kennah, Densmore Investigation File, National Archives and Record Administration, Record Group 85, Washington, D.C.

52. Densmore Final Report, 7.

53. Densmore Final Report, 8.

54. Densmore Final Report, 11.

55. Oliver Perry Stidger, *Highlights on Chinese Exclusion and Expulsion. The Immigration Law of 1924 as It Affects Persons of Chinese Descent in the United States, Their Business Interests, Their Rights and Their Privileges* (San Francisco: Chinese Chamber of Commerce, 1924).

56. Richard H. Frost, *The Mooney Case* (Stanford, CA: Stanford University Press, 1968).

57. "Immigrant Director in Hawaii a Suicide," *New York Times,* March 15, 1924.

— 11 —

Mr. Section 6: John Birge Sawyer and the Enforcement of Chinese Exclusion

John Birge Sawyer (1881–1970) quite literally "wrote the book" on procedures for issuing visas to Chinese coming to the United States. He also wrote another sort of book: six volumes of diaries, now housed in the Bancroft Library at the University of California, Berkeley, along with a collection of his professional papers.[1] For nearly eighteen months, from January 1916 to June 1918, Sawyer was stationed at Angel Island as an inspector in the Chinese Division of the Immigration Service. His diaries[2] are the only first-person accounts by an Inspector at the Immigration Station, accounts that give us an insight into the character and motivations of at least one of the key people charged with enforcing the Chinese exclusion laws.

Sawyer devoted nearly half of his eighty-nine years to work that enforced the immigration laws of the United States. His life, from birth to retirement in 1943, neatly coincided with the Chinese exclusion laws. He worked for two agencies charged with implementing those acts—the Labor Department's Immigration Service and the State Department's Consular Service. Sawyer's specialty was Chinese immigration. He spent nearly thirty years in China as a consular officer, responsible for vetting Chinese who wanted to go to the United States, and another ten years in the United States as an immigration inspector and along the Mexican border as Vice-Consul.

John Sawyer interests us as an exemplar of the modern, professional administrator that emerged in the early Progressive period, someone who "represented a new type of bureaucrat that the Bureau of Immigration was now attracting.... He exemplified a new kind of government bureaucrat who viewed his work not as a stepping stone to an elected political office, but as a career."[3] The diaries trace in painful, sometimes maddening, detail Sawyer's aspirations and (generally unsuccessful) attempts to further that career.

YOUTH/BACKGROUND

John Birge Sawyer was born in Appleton, Wisconsin, into a comfortably middle-class family where scholarly ambitions abounded. His father was a scholar of German and a devotee of opera, tastes shared by Sawyer's mother. They frequently spoke German at home and spent several years in Germany when their children were in elementary school. Sawyer *père* then brought his young family to San Jose, California, holding teaching and, later, administrative positions at the University of the Pacific. The family put down roots in the San Jose–Berkeley area and remained there.

The family arrived in San Jose when John was but six years old and the anti-Chinese feeling not far from its fever pitch of the early 1880s. Yet despite prevalent anti-Chinese attitudes, the Sawyer family developed relatively positive feelings toward the Chinese. His grandfather employed Chinese workmen on his farm near San Jose, keeping a bunkhouse for their use.

> I remember how they pasted bright red papers around the door of the shack and shot firecrackers to usher in their new year; how, at that time of year, they brought us children colorful toys and ornaments and things to eat, especially dried lichee nuts and sugared cocoanut. I recall too that sometime they assembled with sticks and tin pans and made a terrific din as they drove the devils into a pond which was caused by the overflow of an artesian well. Perhaps we did not correctly interpret this performance but that was the explanation which we believed.... We children thought the Chinese were a strange people but we had every reason to like them. It was a case of friendly coexistence.[4]

Sawyer notes that "the Chinese in California were having a rough time then and for years after." He personally saw several instances where violence was inflicted on the Chinese. In a separate document, Sawyer recalls an incident from the late 1880s:

> On my way to school on Julian Street in San Jose I saw the body of a "Chinaman" hanging from the limb of a pepper tree. "Chinaman" was the term invariably used in those days. I never learned the circumstances of the lynching, but such things were happening from time to time as a result of violent racial hatred against the Chinese.[5]

When he was nineteen years old, he witnessed the lynching of a Chinese man. In his diary he gives a rather detached, almost callous, account of the event:

I was at the Mt. Breckenridge mill and worked for $1.25 a day and board and, at different times, filled every position in the yard and mill, except head-sawyer and carriage tender. After the lynching of a Chinaman by the mill hands, an inquest was held at which I had to be a witness. Doherty, the manager of the company, was present and when he learned that I was a Berkeley student he gave me the position of tally-man and superintendent of the lumber yard at $50 per month and board.[6]

Sawyer gives two other accounts of this incident, and they show how his own feelings changed over time. In 1957, writing on "My Undergraduate Days," he looked at the incident differently, providing more detail and more of a sense of moral outrage:

Junior Year: During the summer vacation, I worked in a lumber mill at Mt. Breckenridge, near Bakersfield. I ended up as superintendent of the lumber yard at $60 per month. The mill hands lynched the Chinese cook, dragging him up the canyon and hanging him to a tree. All on the story of the woman in charge of the cook house, who said that he threatened her with his butcher knife. I was sick with malaria in the bunkhouse but saw a good deal of what went on. This was a disgusting and painful episode.[7]

In his 1958 account, he recalls that "this was to me a sickening experience. I could not do a thing; at least I thought I couldn't."[8]

John Birge had three siblings: older brother Wilbur, younger sister Edna, and younger brother George. Wilbur was two years his senior, but they attended the same elementary and high schools, then entered the University of California at Berkeley together in 1898. Their paths diverged when Wilbur subsequently transferred to Harvard. Wilbur Sawyer eventually became a medical doctor and had an illustrious career in the field of tropical medicine, best known for his role in developing a vaccine for yellow fever and as an internationally renowned public health official. He worked for the Rockefeller Foundation from 1919 to 1944, primarily within its IHD (International Health Division). He became the IHD's director in 1935 and also founded and directed the Rockefeller Foundation's Yellow Fever Laboratory.[9]

In the middle of his sophomore year, John Sawyer transferred from the College of Social Sciences to the College of Commerce. "My object in entering the College of Commerce was to prepare for the government service, preferably the diplomatic or consular service."[10] He graduated in the class of 1902 with solid but unspectacular grades. As Sawyer later recalled, "It doesn't seem to me that I had very high ambitions at that time. Probably if I had been told that I would for many years hold the position of chief of the Passport Office in the Consulate General at Shanghai, I should have been satisfied."[11]

EARLY CAREER IN IMMIGRATION ENFORCEMENT

After graduation, Sawyer had short stints as a freight clerk for the American Hawaiian Steamship Company and as a clerk for the Sperry Flour Co. He did well in the "Custom House examination" and on January 27, 1903 was "sworn in by Collector F.S. Stratton as an Inspector of Customs at $3 per diem. Sperry Flour Co. offered me $75.00 per month if I would continue in my position, but I had high hopes of my opportunity in government work, and took the new position."[12]

At the time, the Customs Service, an arm of the Treasury Department, was charged with enforcing the Chinese exclusion laws. This was Sawyer's introduction to a lifetime in that line of work. But for the moment, he viewed government work as unglamorous in the extreme.

> My work was now very monotonous and irksome, as I had to stand guard for eight hours each day at a foreign steamer. The three watches of the day rotated so that my hours of eating and sleeping changed each month, and often the arrangements were very unsatisfactory.... However, I won the confidence of my superior officers and was never reported for any violation of rules.[13]

Disagreeable though his work may have been, it was not without its moments of excitement.

> For three months, beginning July 1st, I was detailed for duty searching baggage and ships. The work was now all in the daytime, and was much more interesting. I made a few seizures of smuggled goods, and discovered three "Imperial Jade Tablets", on Aug. 12th in the baggage of Capt A. Van T. Anderson, returning from the Orient on Transport "Logan." They were a present to him from a Russian officer who had looted them in the "Forbidden City" of Peking and were greatly valued by the Chinese government.[14]

Sawyer's promotions from Customs Inspector to Messenger to Clerk No. 1 were all duly noted in the San Francisco newspapers. Nursing aspirations to the State Department's Consular Service, he took the civil service examination three times but became discouraged about his possibilities in that regard. "I wrote to the Secretary of State about examinations for the Consular Service. The reply showed the futility of any ambition along that line without very powerful friends at Washington."[15]

Finally, his perseverance in the civil service examinations paid off. "On Sep 3 [1904] I received a telegram from Acting Commissioner [of Immigration] Larned asking me if I would accept the position of Chinese Inspector at Portland, Oregon. I replied that I would."

PORTLAND IMMIGRATION STATION

Sawyer's long career enforcing immigration laws, particularly as they concerned Chinese seeking entry into the United States, had already begun in San Francisco when he was in the employ of the Treasury Department and its Customs Service. Only in 1903 were Treasury's responsibilities for enforcing the Chinese exclusion laws transferred to the new Immigration Service within the Department of

Commerce and Labor. Sawyer's transfer to Portland neatly coincided with the shift in bureaucratic responsibilities from Treasury to Immigration.

On becoming Inspector in the Chinese Division at the Portland immigration station, Sawyer came into frequent contact with the Chinese coming to (and occasionally leaving) the United States. As he would throughout his life, Sawyer saw his first duty as upholding the law, following the rules, almost without regard to the effect of those rules. Charged with upholding and enforcing the Chinese Exclusion Act, he did not stint in his efforts to detect those trying to evade the barriers erected against their entry:

> Portland presented many of the contradictions and tensions that inevitably accom-
> panied enforcement of the Chinese exclusion laws, but with a local twist that
> distinguished it from San Francisco. Oregon in general, and Portland in particular,
> was quite different from California or Washington in their relationships with the
> Chinese. Where Tacoma or San Francisco had seen riots that drove many Chinese
> away, Portland remained relatively calm. Other cities tolerated or abetted white
> worker-based anti-Chinese vigilante committees, but Portland made them
> unwelcome.[16]

Not that Portland's leaders had a high opinion of the Chinese. When the Oregon Territory was drawing up its constitution for statehood in the late 1850s, convention delegate Matthew Deady opined that even "the Negro was superior to the Chinaman, and would be more useful" to the new state.[17] Deady, however, eventually became a federal judge and adopted a more pragmatic attitude toward the Chinese. As a judge, he recognized that the Chinese had rights under the law, rights that he upheld despite his profound distaste for the Chinese. His overriding goal, like that of many of Portland's leaders, was to help the new state grow, something which demanded a source of cheap labor. Harvey Scott, editor of the *Oregonian* from 1869 to 1910, was a tireless and forceful advocate of allowing the Chinese to remain and of using them to further the business community's goals of economic growth. Both Scott and Deady (and, indeed, other members of Portland's elite) were firm opponents of the anti-Chinese vigilantes, whom they saw as threats to order and the rule of law.

For these reasons, Portland was much more hospitable to, or at least tolerant of, the Chinese than were other major ports of entry. Such attitudes surfaced in the way that the exclusion laws were enforced, and especially in the interplay between the courts and the officers of the Portland station of the Bureau of Immi-gration. The Bureau's officers were charged with enforcing the Chinese exclusion laws, the courts with hearing appeals of the Bureau's administrative rulings such as deportation orders or writs of habeas corpus. Major figures on the U.S. District Court for the District of Oregon were Presiding Judges Matthew Deady (1859–93) and Charles Bellinger (1893–1905). In general, it seems the District Court seated in Portland was unsympathetic, even antagonistic, to the local Bureau's efforts to enforce the exclusion laws. Sawyer mentions the judges by name in a rant against what he perceived to be the court's pro-Chinese attitudes:

During my six months probationary period, ending March 24, 1905...arrests were made occasionally in this district in the case of Chinese unlawfully in the country but they were futile for the most part owing to the attitude of Judge Bellinger of the District Court and Commissioners Sladen and McKie who were all outspokenly for the Chinese.

The attacks against the Exclusion Laws and the Chinese Inspectors were numerous and bitter at this time. The Chinese boycott of American goods was a daily news topic. The rules and regulations were changed frequently and on June 26, Pres. Roosevelt and Secretary Metcalf issued orders requiring courteous treatment of all Chinese under penalty of dismissal, and ordering thorough investigation by U.S. officials in China before granting Section 6 Certificates.[18]

His first observations of his new post were of a station in turmoil. Chief Inspector J.H. Barbour had been there less than a year and had just divested himself of two troublesome officers; one was "Major Ryan whose place I took had been incapable and was a man of such immoral character and unpleasant habits that he had been transferred to Ellis Island."[19]

Not only was the Portland station in a political milieu quite different from San Francisco's, the station's staff were also unusual. One of the most exceptional staff members was Seid Gain Back Jr., shown in Figure 11.1 with the other officers of the Portland Immigration Station.

Back's father was a merchant and labor contractor, one of the wealthiest and most influential members of Portland's Chinese community. The younger Back, born in the United States, had been educated in China and in Portland's private Bishop Scott Grammar School. From 1900 to 1903 he was a contract interpreter for the U.S. district court, and in 1903 he secured a career appointment as the Portland immigration station's Chinese interpreter; his $1,000 annual salary was the equal of an immigration inspector's. In addition to becoming the Bureau of Immigration's top Chinese interpreter, evaluating all the interpreters in the Bureau's employ, Back also became the first Chinese to be admitted to the bar when he passed the examinations of the University of Oregon and the Oregon bar. His distinguished career with the Bureau of Immigration was somewhat at odds with his contentious nature and with a later indictment in a tong-related murder (the charge was dropped). Nonetheless, he had a long record of achievement and of leadership within the Chinese community.[20]

Sawyer somehow qualified as both an Inspector and an Interpreter—even though he never became fluent in either Cantonese or Mandarin.[21] Sawyer loved everything about his job—his boss, his colleagues, his office, the city itself. He was enthusiastic about his work as Chinese inspector. Only later did he come to have misgivings about it.

My new duties were fascinating from the start. As the steamer lines had ceased to bring passengers to Portland our office had none of the duties of landing Chinese. The Chinese business consisted principally: 1st of investigation of applicants for admission at other ports alleging that they were returning merchants of firms in Oregon or native born in Oregon; 2d, Examination of laborers arrested on

Figure 11.1

In a photograph of officers of the Portland Immigration Station, ca. 1904–10, Inspector John Birge Sawyer is on second step right. Translator Seid Gain Back is on the fourth step left.

Source: John Birge Sawyer photo collection, courtesy of the Bancroft Library, University of California, Berkeley, and Jo Sawyer and Craig Steele.

suspicion of being unlawfully in the country; 3d Pre-investigation of departing Chinese (laborers or members of the exempt classes) and 4th applications for duplicate certificates.[22]

"Section Six C" of the Chinese Exclusion Act allowed certain categories of Chinese to enter the United States—merchants, students, teachers, ministers, and their families. Section 6 Certificates were issued to Chinese *before* they left China, indicating that the Chinese government had vouched for their qualifications for admission to the United States; American consular officials often felt compelled to verify those qualifications. All other Chinese were vetted for admission at the port of arrival. This vetting frequently involved detailed interrogations and long periods of detention at Immigration Stations such as the one on Angel Island in San Francisco Bay.[23]

The officers of Portland's Immigration Station were charged not only with "sifting the arrivals" (although much of the initial "sifting" was done at Astoria)

Figure 11.2
John Sawyer (with clipboard), another inspector, and an interpreter question Chinese aboard an arriving ship, ca. 1904–10.

Source: John Birge Sawyer photo collection, courtesy of the Bancroft Library, University of California, Berkeley, and Jo Sawyer and Craig Steele.

but with ferreting out those who might be in the country illegally or had been ordered for deportation. For most of 1909 Sawyer was "engaged in enforcing the provisions of the immigration law relating to the 'White Slave Traffic'.... I made a number of sensational arrests: Izawa Rui, Anna Fuhrer, Eugenia Legris, Maria Efenicio, and Louise Marie Targuet."[24] He recounts his exploits in the case of Ms. Legris, a French prostitute, in "On the Trail of the Immigrant (Apologies to Dr. Steiner)," an entertaining story included in his professional papers. It is amusing to follow this most modest and straightlaced of men as he goes undercover—"with my hat pulled down over my eyes and my coat collar turned up"—in his searches through the red light districts of Pendleton and Baker City, Oregon, in search of the elusive prostitute whom he must (and did) arrest for deportation.

He was not infrequently sent to arrest Chinese for deportation on grounds of "illegal residence." One such case was "The Arrest of Ng On" in January 1908. Sawyer did his duty in this instance, but not without misgivings as to the justice of the case—misgivings that never completely harmonized with his many years of diligent service in administering the exclusion laws. He recounts how he was sent to Pendleton, Oregon, to arrest Ng On for being in the country without a Certificate of Residence.

> With Interpreter Frank Tape, I arrived in Pendleton at noon on January 7, 1908. I showed photographs of Ng On to a deputy sheriff, who recognized our man and led us to his laundry. It was a sight to provoke Heaven to anger to see three officers of the law swoop down on that laundryman—53 years old, his face wrinkled beyond his years, of slight build and short stature, his expressionless gaze bespeaking an indifference to fate resulting from years of hardship, his bare feet protected from the Winter's cold only by a pair of slippers, his buttonless vest held together by safety-pins, the sleeves of the coat given to him by some charitable white man reaching to his finger tips.
>
> Through the interpreter, I told Ng On what I knew about his past and he simply answered "Yes". A little later he braced himself to make some defense and asserted that he had lost his Certificate in a cannery on Puget Sound. I told him to get ready to go to Portland. He complied. The operation was simple. First he removed his slippers and pulled over his bare feet a pair of heavy shoes, then he unlocked his bed-room door and got his worldly wealth in coin and then said "All right". (The money when counted in the jail amounted to $18.65.)
>
> At Ng On's request I took him to see his landlord, who was also the lawyer who had written the fatal letter [of appeal] to the Bureau of Immigration in Washington. Ng On said little. I told the story and then Ng On said in a barely audible voice, "You please can help me" and the interpreter explained that Ng On wanted someone to put up $250 bail so that he might be released and be free to dispose of his business interests before leaving the U.S. for ever....
>
> At Ng On's request we next visited the store of Yee Ngaw, the leading Chinese merchant of the city. The interpreter and I were given seats. Ng On preferred to stand. In a few minutes the room filled with Chinese who appeared almost at the same moment from all of Chinatown....In a desire to be helpful to Ng On I said

in English (most of those present understood some English), "Why don't you put up the bail. You will get it back. This man is too old to run away and make you lose your money. And if he should run away, he will leave his laundry, and that ought to be worth $250." At these words those who understood smiled and repeated my words in Chinese and then others smiled. Then I understood that this man's wash-house was worth nothing. Ng Goey spoke up....He said, "Mr. Sawyer, this man hires three men; he pays them 10 dollars one week each; this makes $30 a week; it takes lots of clothes to bring in $30; steam laundry does the work better and cheaper; he no got money to pay his men all their wages; nobody want to buy him out; his laundry worth nothing at all." The conference was ended and we proceeded to the county jail. On the way a fat, brown dog appeared (no one noticed just when he attached himself to us). I asked Ng On, "Whose dog?" and he answered "My". We arrived at the jail door and all of us entered—except the dog. We shut the door on him, and he and his master were parted doubtless forever.

There had been a tragedy in two lives that day.[25]

On other occasions, Sawyer's sense of fair play brought him to the defense of individual Chinese. The following incident took place the day before Sawyer went to Grace McConnell's home to ask her father for her hand in marriage:

On the night of June 9th 1906 I got involved in a street fight with a mob through my endeavor to protect a Chinaman from the attack of 3 hoodlums. The trouble began at 11:30 pm and it was just about 1 a.m. when I got [the hoodlums] in jail. The result was my swearing to a complaint against Johnson, Donovan and McDonald for assault. They plead guilty and were fined $25.00, $10.00 and $10.00 respectively. City attorney Fitzgerald filed a second charge of assault on the Chinaman but the 3 boys were allowed to go under suspension of sentence pending good behavior. The outcome of the fight would have been very different were it not that officer Wearmouth of the SS "Tottenham" came to my assistance at a critical moment and stuck to me all through. He was considerably cut and bled profusely. The mob that followed me and attacked me had fully 15 fellows in it, though only part of them attacked me.[26]

Writing in 1958, Sawyer indicated that he might have been doing more than simply protecting someone from bullies. "To my mind, what I had done that night made up in a small degree for my failure to do anything at the time of the Bakersfield lynching."[27]

The following day Sawyer arrived at McConnell's home still sporting the bruises and cuts from his fight. Rather than finding him a ruffian and an undesirable suitor, the McConnells must have found him a righteous, sympathetic man. Sawyer and Grace McConnell were engaged the next day.

Sawyer thus found Portland congenial personally as well as professionally. He became attached to the city, built a home, and made numerous requests to be transferred there from other posts—requests that were never honored. A daughter, Nancy Ellen, was born in 1911. That same year, his life took another major, and unexpected, turn when, "without the slightest warning," he was transferred to the Consular Service at Hong Kong.

AMERICAN CONSULATE, HONG KONG

In the early twentieth century, the American consular service in China had a poor reputation when it came to honesty or efficiency. In *Chinese Immigration*, Stanford sociologist Mary Roberts Coolidge had advanced the view that

> From 1880...until now, it has been no secret that the consular visé was of no value. Even when the Consul was honest it was impossible that he should investigate thoroughly the facts stated in the certificates so as to vouch for their truth. Yet no vigorous effort has been made to make the consular visé authoritative or, in default of that, to send, as Commissioner-General Sargent proposed, a trained officer of the immigration service to China whose business it shall be to ascertain the truth of the statements made by Chinese officials.

Sending Sawyer and people like him was a partial response to such criticisms. Sawyer was, indeed, a trained immigration officer and scrupulously honest. But despite his desire to investigate Chinese claims to exempt status—and thus eligibility for a Section 6 visa—he found it difficult to do so. This was due partly to the press of work and partly to the lack of funds for the required travel. Sawyer perceived the problem quite clearly, and many of the memoranda and letters in his professional papers are requests for the staff and funds to remedy it.

In Hong Kong, Sawyer still saw himself as an officer in the Immigration Service, but his position as a Consular officer made his status ambiguous. It was the beginning of a career in limbo between the Immigration Service and the State Department. Sawyer and his family began what would be a thirty-year exile, broken only by an eighteen-month hiatus while stationed at Angel Island.

His work in Hong Kong was almost entirely related to "Section 6" and other Chinese immigration matters. But the context was quite different, as he explained in a letter to Barbour, his former station chief in Portland:

> In Portland, I could make no very serious mistake because you were watching, and the officers at the port of arrival were watching, and the Chinaman's lawyer and the Commissioner-General and the Secretary at Washington all had their turn in looking over my work if the Chinaman felt aggrieved. Out here a Chinese applicant has no lawyer and no one to whom to appeal; so he will be practically helpless excepting by boycotting the United States.[28]

Shortly before Sawyer's arrival in Hong Kong, Consul General George Anderson had written to the Secretary of State to point out the contradiction between enforcement of the exclusion laws and promotion of American interests, especially those of businessmen and missionaries.

> Sir:
> I have the honor to present for the attention of the Department complaints of Chinese business men in Hongkong and Canton....The Chinese complain of the general enforcement of the law at San Francisco....On the one hand we are instructed, are expected...to advance American interests....On the other hand

we are made instruments in dealing with the same people of enforcing a law which strikes at the very foundation of their self respect, their national interests, and their commercial betterment.[29]

In Hong Kong, Sawyer seemed to feel that his office enabled him to aid, rather than hinder, Chinese going to the United States. He uncovered a scheme where doctors were providing fictitious "cures" for Chinese with hookworm or trachoma, "loathsome diseases" that would preclude their entry into the United States. He also used his power to grant or withhold "Section 6" certificates for students as a means of protecting Chinese from shady immigration entrepreneurs.

> The most difficult problem so far has been as to how to deal with such student-collecting undertakings. Previous to Miss Greenlee's undertaking [an American seeking visas for a large number of Chinese students] there had been a number of collections of students which had abandoned their studies and disappeared from sight almost immediately after landing. As a result the immigration service officers condemned all such efforts and seemed justified in their attitude. I have asked and obtained reports on some of those undertakings which show that the promoters did not apply to the education of the boys the money which they took with them for that purpose. I passed Miss Greenlee's boys with the idea that they were a better lot of boys than composed these other parties having been more carefully investigated, and that the promoter was actuated by purer motives. If government desires to provide any further safeguards against bad immigration of this sort, it should provide for investigation of these student cases at the homes of the boys in the interior and it should provide for bonding the boys on arrival in the U.S. for the length of time necessary for them to attain to high school standing.[30]

Hong Kong was a posting that Sawyer viewed with mixed emotions. He appreciated the many opportunities for sport—he became a dedicated golfer—and the great quantities of cheap domestic help that made it easy to entertain. But there was a shallow downside to it all, as he explained in a 1916 letter to old friend Rafe Bonham:

> The main part of the social life here is going to dinner and tiffin and bridge parties. There is an interminable series of those. When you have spent a year in the colony you have seen it all except what you intentionally leave out....If a comparison of the advantages of life in Hongkong and in Portland as regards health conditions and social enjoyments seems fairly evenly balanced, I now have to suggest a factor which is completely to the advantage of life at home. That is the sense of banishment felt in the Orient....You have a feeling that the real life is over there across the Pacific, that your stay here is a temporary detail like that of nearly everyone that you know here....It is that more than anything else that makes one sometimes determine to quit and go home.[31]

Not that Sawyer found the time in Hong Kong devoid of pleasure or reward. While on an investigative visit to Sun Ming City shortly before his departure for California, he allowed himself a rare moment of sentimentality:

[T]he city itself seems quiet for a city where all work is by hand and does not make such noises as our American cities. Almost directly below me I hear the occasional thump of wooden pole or basket against bucket as one of the women dips up water from a hollow and carries it to one of the vegetable patches on the hill slope slightly above the rice fields. I hear the shouts of a farmer to his awkward water buffalo which appears to be anxious to get home to its dinner and persists in leaving the furrow and dragging plow and master far out of the proper course.

As the coming darkness compels me to make my way back to the Railway building I hear the soldiers on guard there beating a tattoo and sounding a bugle call marking nightfall; the electric light plant by the railway building is humming busily and lights are coming out in many places in the city. The tall pagoda to the west of Sai Ming See rises seven stories above the crest of its hill against the sunset glow. I am loath to leave the scene for I know I shall never experience it again save in memory. In less than a month I shall be in the Pacific with Grace and Nancy, returning home.[32]

Still, after four years in Hong Kong, Sawyer was anxious to get back to the States. He was concerned about his family's health and the need "for a different social atmosphere with less of formality and caste and more of family ties and enduring friendships...[and] my need of development in my work if I am not to deteriorate."[33] His wish to leave Hong Kong was answered on June 10, when a cablegram arrived from Secretary of State Lansing: "Washington. Sawyer American Consulate Hongkong. Ninth. Department Labor says is impractical transfer Schnare from Shanghai offers you position Chinese and immigrant inspector San Francisco. Salary not quite as large as present one."[34] Sawyer accepted. He was going home.

ANGEL ISLAND

Returning to the United States was a desirable thing, but the same could not be said for being assigned to Angel Island as an inspector in the Chinese Division. On November 6, 1916, Sawyer expressed some uneasiness about returning to the United States to work on Chinese immigration matter:

Two days ago I was in a veritable panic at the prospect of going to work in the San Francisco office. I have been struggling with a voluminous record in a tangled Chinese case from San Francisco and as I worked I could think of nothing but the horror of being kept at that one thing month after month and perhaps year after year.[35]

Nonetheless, on January 15, 1917, Sawyer reported for duty as Chinese Inspector at Angel Island. He did not like what he found.

After two weeks of work at Angel Island what has impressed me most is the remarkable system that has been developed *to protect the Government against its own officials*. (1) No inspector can know in advance of a hearing what case he will have for investigation....The interpreter and stenographer on the case are similarly assigned so that it is absolutely impossible for any one of the three men of the "crew" on this case to direct the progress of the hearing along prearranged channels. (2)...No interpreter acts for more than one witness in any case, and each interpreter can have no knowledge of the testimony given by a previous witness.

This method...seems a most admirable protection against crookedness but also most obstructive to the efforts of conscientious officers....I feel that the government's inspectors should be trusted or fired.[36]

Although he probably did not know it, Sawyer had already come in contact with a most corrupt part of the immigration service. On his way back from Hong Kong, his ship had stopped at Honolulu. As was his wont, Sawyer took time ashore to visit members of the local immigration service. His host was Richard Halsey, the same station chief who would commit suicide in 1924 when his corrupt activities were uncovered:

Jan 5, 1917. We arrived at Honolulu at 11 in the morning. I took time before lunch to walk over to the Immigration Station and have a visit with the inspector in charge, Mr. Halsey....About 60 Japanese "picture brides" were detained in the building. They make up the bulk of the Japanese immigration which is 85% of the whole. Mr. Halsey pointed out that the Japanese government allows its citizens residing in the Hawaiian Island to bring in their children and their parents and in this way they get in all their brothers and sisters and nephews and nieces and consequently the Gentlemen's Agreement is proving very unsatisfactory.[37]

Sawyer would again become a player in the perpetual cat-and-mouse game between the Immigration Service and the Chinese who tried to enter the country in the guise of membership in one of these "exempt" classes. As an Inspector in the Chinese Division, Sawyer would perform many such interrogations, attempting to verify an arrival's bona fides, trying to understand whether that person was who or what he said he was.

An excellent example of this process is in the file of Yee Yit Jeung, who on August 13, 1917 arrived in San Francisco from Hong Kong aboard the *Korea Maru*. Yee was accompanied by his eighteen-year-old "alleged son" claimed to be a merchant, and to prove it had a certificate issued by the Chinese Commissioner of Foreign Affairs at Canton and a Section 6 visa, No. 23/1917, issued by the American Consulate General, Hong Kong. His visa indicated that he was a member of the firm Tai Hing Jan in Hong Kong and was coming "to establish a new general merchandise business in San Francisco with capital promised by members of his present firm." These claims had been verified in Hong Kong by the consular staff: "Examination has been made of the applicant and the manager. Store and books inspected. There are no material contradictions in the claims made and appearance of the applicant indicates genuine mercantile occupation."

Still, the procedure at U.S. ports of entry was to verify, as best the inspectors could, both that Yee was a bona fide merchant and that he really was the father of the "alleged son" traveling with him. To do this, Sawyer asked Yee seventy-one questions and, separately, his son a further fifty-five. The process being more art than science, Sawyer noted that "Having compared the applicant with his alleged father I am of the opinion that their noses are similarly straight, and that their ears are very different, and I am unable to say whether they bear to one another any family resemblance." He then recalled both, separately, to ask a further half dozen. This was on August 20, by which time the Yees had already been in the Angel Island detention barracks for a week, guilty of no crime but that of being Chinese.

Sawyer was not quite satisfied. The next day he asked Yee, "Do you have any objections to our searching your baggage?" He noted that a "search is made of applicant's baggage resulting in the discover of two wooden name chops bearing the names Yee Yit (Yick) Jeung and Yee Sing Lung, thus indicating that he is traveling under his rightful name." Later that day Sawyer concluded that "his examination developed nothing calling for special comment. Only the two applicants have been examined as to their alleged relationship to one another. Their testimony was given in a straight forward manner and is free from any material discrepancies. I have to recommend the landing of both applicants."[38]

Not all cases went so smoothly, if eight days in detention constitutes "smoothly" from the detainee's perspective. In July 1917 Sawyer dealt with thirteen "cases [that] must necessarily all be considered together because it is evident that they have all been prepared in a similarly irregular manner by the same person or persons." This was a particularly inept attempt to bring nonexempt Chinese into the United States, including clumsy forgeries of the signatures of several notaries—all by the same hand—and "alleged fathers" who did not exist or refused to appear. "In each case the applicant has now expressed his abandonment of further effort" to verify his claim to exempt status. By the time they were deported, the seven who had arrived on the SS *Colombia* (the only ones for which we have data) had been detained over three months.[39]

Among the unique aspects of Sawyer's diaries are his insights into how Immigration Inspectors actually carried out their work, and how the enforcement process appeared from *their* perspective.

Feb 15, 1917. I to-day had a fine object lesson of the way an inspector is sometimes driven in his work. I had the cases of two alleged brothers claiming to be citizen applicants for passports. This "double header" was handed to me about 9:30 with the information that the two applicants and two supporting witnesses were present awaiting a hearing. The cases proved long and involved and at 2:30 I went to Mr. Mehan to ask what was to be done if I could not get through. He said nothing could be done but let the applicants and witnesses go back to the City by the 4:30 boat as there was no later boat and they could not be detained. If I could not cover the ground in the usual way I must just hit the high places. I went back to work and by tremendous crowding I made my investigation exactly fit the time that was left. I think I have ample grounds for denial of the two applications but I hate to think of the risk of utter failure that I faced at 2:30 this afternoon. If I had been compelled to release one or more witnesses without examination they would have come the next day ready for examination and prepared to reconcile every serious discrepancy.[40]

While Sawyer learned to cope with the demands of his heavy workload inspecting Chinese arrivals, an investigation into immigrant smuggling swirled around the Angel Island Immigration Station. The scandal had exploded in October 1915, when the Feds uncovered the *Mongolia* immigrant smuggling operation. Sawyer's diaries give us an inside eyewitness to the investigation, complementing the extensive coverage given in the San Francisco daily newspapers and the interrogation transcripts and reports in the National Archives.

On August 15, 1917 Sawyer wrote how the investigation had touched his fellow Immigration inspectors:

> It begins to look as though the overhauling of the officers at our Station is about finished. There have been no removals for a month. Solicitor Densmore and his two Secret Service assistants still spend much time at the Station but my guess is that they are putting their evidence in shape for the grand jury. Out of the eleven inspectors engaged in hearing Chinese cases when the investigation started only four are left as shown below:
>
> Ebey: Fired
> Gassoway: Fired
> Theiss: Fired
> Warner: Fired
> Heitman: Fired
> McCall: Fired
> Long: Transferred
> Becktel, Jones, Scully, Butler: unscathed[41]

One of the curiosities is that Densmore talked to the Immigration Inspectors about his investigation of *them* and their colleagues as it drew to a close.

> October 22, 1917. To-day all the inspectors at the station were called together to listen to Mr. J.B. Densmore talk on his investigation of graft. He told us that when the newspapers asserted that he had uncovered an international smuggling ring grafting $100,000 per year, he thought it was a wild flight of fancy but he now knew that the figure is much larger. He pointed out the principal ways of grafting.[42]

Sawyer thought that the investigation and attendant suspicion tainted even good men, Inspectors who were not ogres despite having to enforce the unfair exclusion laws. As Sawyer wrote on November 17, 1917, "Three days ago Mr. Mehan who has been chief of the Chinese Division for fourteen years was transferred to the City Office....Practically everyone in our division seems to feel a sense of personal loss in Mr. Mehan's departure and a sense of resentment that such a fate should come to such a faithful and able officer."[43]

Despite being near his parents and siblings, Sawyer's tour of duty at Angel Island had been unhappy in several ways. Not only was he embroiled in the turmoil at the Immigration Station—"the expulsion of officers and disbarment of attorneys and indictment of many connected with Chinese immigration is having its results in demoralization of the immigration game"—but he had lost his only child in a streetcar accident. In mid-1918, Sawyer's ongoing maneuverings for a new post bore fruit when he was appointed as Vice-Consul in Shanghai. He had managed to escape from Angel Island.

> June 26, 1918 [S]pent two hours at the office saying good-bye. I felt a genuine regret at parting with such men as Jones and Trumbly, Root, Butler, Mehan, Tomkins, Franklin, Harry Tang, Louis Fong, Ben Yiu, Wilkinson and Walsh. But I feel much relieved to be done with the Station. It is not a safe place to be connected with and I feel that I will have to be pretty desperate to return to it....I see only stormy seas ahead for them and consequently for the Service.[44]

BACK TO SHANGHAI: A CAREER IN CHINA

Sawyer's second tour of duty in China, this time in Shanghai, lasted from 1918 to 1942. Despite his many efforts to get a more desirable posting—Europe was his preference—the best offer Sawyer received was to be posted to New York as a Chinese Inspector at Ellis Island. On visiting that Immigration Station in 1925, Sawyer was unimpressed with his prospective colleagues and dismayed at the cost of living in New York. "[A]n inspector...show[ed] me anybody and anything I would care to see....I found the atmosphere of the Island rather depressing and am sure I should never wish to serve there. The officers are unrefined and not well educated and their work is not of a sort to stir enthusiasm."[45]

Sawyer's Official Personnel File casts some light on why European positions were never offered to him. While he was recognized as "diligent and willing and has a great capacity for work...[h]is vision is limited. He has worked all the time at one thing and learned little outside of it in so far as the Service is concerned." He was considered "most valuable at Shanghai rather than at some other post."

His Berkeley classmates from the class of 1902 were an important part of his "support group" (a term not yet invented) and of the University of California's "China Connection" over the century's first four decades: Robert Roy Service and Grace Service, missionaries and leaders in the YMCA movement (and parents of John S. Service, one of the "old China hands" falsely accused by Joe McCarthy), and Julian Arnold, the U.S. commercial attaché to Shanghai and Beijing and a leader in the Rotary movement in China. They all figure in Sawyer's diaries.

Despite having in Consul General Cunningham a boss whom he loathed, Sawyer professed to enjoy his work at Shanghai. The accompanying 1929 photograph is in the spirit of paternalistic colonialism, with Sawyer seeing off his "native protégés" as they head to America for study. Perhaps he counseled them as he had a similar group a decade earlier:

> Your advisors have urged you to put forth your best efforts to get certain American things, American learning, American spirit, American this and that. My message to you would be to hold on to what you have that is good. You have inherited many valuable things from your thousands of years of history and from your leaders of

thought....They are too precious to be cast aside as a man would change his coat.[46]

Over time, more and more of his efforts were devoted to the Consulate's passport section and to registering Americans living in China. By the 1930s, "Section 6" work had become distinctly secondary.[47]

In a section of his professional papers, we find Sawyer's "Personal Note Book—Official Matters," in which he placed "everything dealing with official matters, which may be of personal interest in future." Here he related particularly interesting cases such as "the Mah Jong Fraud" and "Chinese woman with 84 American-born descendants," vented his exasperation at "Depleted Staff," and expressed his personal views on immigration policies. In particular, he looked unfavorably on the Quota Act of 1921.

The Quota Law (as Sawyer referred to it) was the first law to limit the overall number of immigrants allowed into the United States, which it did by establishing a quota for each country based on 3 percent of the foreign-born residents of that country who resided in the United States at the time of the 1910 census.[48] Sawyer characterized it as "The Quota Law—a dishonest law" and "The Quota Law—an inhuman law." He railed against it on behalf of the many non-Chinese (Russians, especially) living in China who wanted to go to the United States. It was often unclear to the American consulate in Shanghai whether that particular country had used up its quota for the year, which could lead to an immigrant from that country being sent back from the U.S. port or unnecessarily rejected by the steamship line (on the ground that they *might* be barred from entry).

Figure 11.3
As American Vice-Consul at Shanghai, John Birge Sawyer hosted farewell parties for students going to the United States. At this party on August 17, 1929, Sawyer is seated front row center, wearing glasses.

Source: John Birge Sawyer photo collection, courtesy of the Bancroft Library, University of California, Berkeley, and Jo Sawyer and Craig Steele.

Other anomalies in the law, and the confusion surrounding implementation during the first years of its existence, created numerous hardships for Chinese students and other immigrants, cases that Sawyer relates in detail both in his diaries and in his professional papers.

Still, "Chinese work" was Sawyer's entrée into Chinese society and formed the basis of his warm relations with individual Chinese. Among his proudest accomplishments was that he quite literally "wrote the book" (although he would never put it so immodestly) on Section 6 procedures for issuing visas for Chinese traveling to the United States. On a number of earlier occasions, he had developed new forms for the use of immigration offices or in other ways sought to systematize the daily practice of enforcing the Chinese exclusion laws.[49] In 1923, "the regulations and instructions governing American consular officers in the enforcement of the Chinese Exclusion laws were so extensive and so scattered that I took it upon myself to collect them and reduce them to writing."[50]

On July 26, 1924, he noted the arrival of a printed copy of "Outline of Section 6 and Other Chinese Immigration Matters" by J. B. Sawyer, American Vice-Consul at Shanghai.[51]

> This came as a great surprise to me. I thought it was worth printing but did not look for it yet if ever. . . . This year's law makes the most radical change in procedure in a quarter-century and more. It is the irony of fate that such a revolutionary law should be passed just as my Outline of the old procedure reaches circulation among consuls. In fact the new regulations reached us in the same pouch to-day.[52]

The "Section 6" manual embodies the text of the various acts that comprised the Chinese exclusion laws and also refers to the various practices and departmental instructions that gave them vigor. It is also, according to Sawyer—who was not given to boasting—quite clearly *his* work, compiled on his own initiative without much input from superiors. Here are some of the more salient issues raised in Sawyer's manual:

Who is Chinese? The concept of "blood" runs thick through this document in defining who is Chinese and who is not. All citizens of China "without regard to race" are defined as Chinese, as well as

> all persons who are wholly or chiefly of Chinese blood. (Dept. of Labor to Dept. January 28, 1914 and Dept. to Hongkong February 21, 1914). Persons should be regarded as of other than Chinese descent if the admixture of Chinese blood is less than one-half. In cases where there is an equal admixture of European and Chinese blood, the racial stock of the male parent controls in the enforcement of these laws. (Dept. to Shanghai, June 18, 1923).[53]

Who is exempt? One is struck by the constant references to the Chinese Exclusion process as flowing from *economic* considerations, rather than from any notion of racial bias. "The purely economic nature of the Chinese exclusion legislation must be constantly kept in the foreground (Dept. Circular March 25, 1907)."[54]

Likewise, the four "exempt" classes entitled to admission—merchants, students, teachers, and travelers for curiosity or pleasure—are defined not by their occupation in China but by the consular officer's estimation of their *likely* occupation in the United States.

How are exempt visas granted? A person's Section 6 certificate, while only prima facie evidence, "constitutes the only evidence permissible...to establish his right to enter the United States." Once the Section 6 certificate had been approved by the applicant's own government it went to the U.S. consul at Canton, Hong Kong, or Shanghai (assuming the applicant was a Chinese citizen in China) who was expected to "examine the truth of the statements set forth in said certificate...with great tact, kindness and consideration, and with full regard to Chinese sensibilities (Dept. Circ., March 25, 1907.)."

How to anticipate fraudulent cases? (vague criteria, etc.) Applicants are to be apprised of the laws and rules governing the process. Information is to be given out—but not too generously. Anticipating Chinese efforts to game the system, "care is exercised not to give out any unnecessary information regarding the nature of the consular investigation, which might be used to perpetrate a fraudulent case....The Department has instructed that it can not prescribe precisely the evidence which must be required."[55]

Sawyer thought he understood, to some extent, the Chinese resentment of foreigners. Writing in 1925 during serious antiforeign disturbances, he compared local xenophobia to the American nativist hysteria that had produced the Chinese Exclusion Act:

> It seems to me that the situation is analogous to the anti-Chinese disturbances in the US in the '70s and '80s. Hiatt contended that the foreigners are a benefit to China. Of course they are. So were the Chinese to America. Everybody recognizes the importance of their help to develop the West. In each case the country got frightened at the increase in numbers and influence of the alien invaders. China doesn't understand clearly where the danger lies but she does know that the danger would be removed if she could get rid of us.[56]

Chinese were not the only ones hoping to travel from Shanghai to the United States. Shanghai in the 1930s was something of a safe haven for those fleeing Hitler and Stalin and the gathering storm in Europe. With America seen as a refuge, many were desperate to go there. This included not only Jews and citizens of the Soviet Union, but people with all sorts of tenuous ties to the United States. The plight of such people, and American policy toward them, tested Sawyer's sense of fairness.

Sawyer's diaries record, somewhat erratically, many of the struggles between various warlords, between the Nationalists and the Communists, and between China and the various foreign powers, especially Japan. Other major events, such as the 1937 "Rape of Nanking," are conspicuously absent or only hinted at. What does come across is the unreality of life within the International Settlement as these events swirled around it. Even in December 1941, when the

Japanese invaded Shanghai and interned all enemy nationals, life serenely continued for the diplomats: golf (while on parole), visiting Chinese staff to say good-bye, attempting to have one's car protected from confiscation by the Japanese, endless days playing cards or learning Spanish, and all the while waiting to be exchanged and repatriated (as they were in 1942). The Japanese occupation seems more a major inconvenience than a disaster.

Once repatriated (the exchange took place in Laurenço Marques), Sawyer briefly resumed his career. He was posted to Ciudad Juarez and Nogales where, as even the State Department recognized, his "previous experience does not fit him for [the] Mexican border." In less than a year, he retired and returned to California, settling into a quiet retirement in Modesto.

JOHN BIRGE SAWYER AND THE CHINESE

If we are to believe his diaries, Sawyer's sense of propriety and seriousness earned him the respect of Chinese with whom he interacted professionally. Actual friendship would come much, much later.

Work at Angel Island surely must have heightened the tension he felt between upholding the law and providing justice. In 1917, as the Densmore investigation into immigrant smuggling swirled around the Immigration Station, Sawyer noted with sadness how a good man, the inspector in charge of the Chinese Division, had come unjustly under suspicion:

> [Inspector Charles Mehan] maintained a very sympathetic attitude toward every subordinate and every Chinese coming before the office. It was evident to me that he worked with higher motives than one generally finds among civil service officers. I have heard him tell of instances of injustice to Chinese and their patient submission to acts of injustice and indignities and then add that the Chinese needed a friend in the office he held and this made him contented in his work.

Note his approval of Mehan's acting as a "friend" to the Chinese. Sawyer, too, saw himself as promoting, rather than inhibiting, relations between Chinese and Americans. He repeatedly stated his belief that his immigration work, whether at Angel Island or in Hong Kong or Shanghai, "in controlling Chinese immigration is as important as any work I might do as a consul, more important in cultivating good relations between China and the U.S. than anything I could hope to do in a commercial way."[57]

Even in the late 1950s, long after the exclusion laws had been repealed, Sawyer was of two minds about the laws he had worked to uphold. On the one hand, he minimized the impact of those laws on Chinese in the United States and in China. "The Chinese exclusion laws had been an irritation and an insult to the Chinese for 61 years, but in the main they accepted the situation calmly and in a friendly spirit."[58] But he also recognized the basically unjust nature of the laws, in that "one can hardly blame the Chinese who sought by wiles and crooked schemes to defeat our exclusion laws. Those laws were not of their making. They owed them no duty of loyalty and submission. Those laws stood in the way of their natural and commendable ambition to gain a better way of life."[59]

In summing up his life's work, Sawyer hinted at the underlying tension between enforcement and fairness, yet continued to avoid acknowledging the racial animosity that underlay the Chinese Exclusion Act and its successors.

> You perhaps ask yourselves, as I have often asked myself, why an American citizen should devote the best years of his life to the enforcement of a law to keep Chinese people out of the United States. It must be remembered that when the law was passed it seemed to our legislators the only way to handle the tense racial conflict in California. Undoubtedly much bloodshed and property damage has been averted by passage of these laws. If I succeeded in my efforts at enforcing those laws fairly and in a way to gain the respect of the Chinese with whom I dealt, perhaps my time was not wasted.[60]

NOTES

1. All of the Sawyer materials were donated by his daughter, Jo Sawyer, and grandson, Craig Steele. I am extremely grateful to Ms. Sawyer and Mr. Steele for their generosity in sharing these items. The diaries are in six volumes and were given to the University in 1980 at the suggestion of John Service, son of one of Sawyer's dearest friends and himself a former Foreign Service officer. The Sawyer collection also includes a separate set of professional papers, miscellaneous writings, and photographs that were donated in 2005.

2. John Birge Sawyer, "Diaries of John Birge Sawyer: Holograph and Typescript, 1910–1962," Bancroft Library, University of California, Berkeley.

3. Lee, *At America's Gates*, 71.

4. John Birge Sawyer, "Some Personal Observations of Chinese American Relations," Unpublished manuscript, March 1, 1958, 2. Courtesy of Josephine Sawyer.

5. Ibid.

6. Sawyer Diaries, vol. 1, p. 31.

7. John Birge Sawyer, "My Undergraduate Days," one-page typescript dated 1-12-57. Document courtesy of Josephine Sawyer.

8. Sawyer, "Some Personal Observations."

9. The papers of Wilbur A. Sawyer are in the National Library of Medicine. A finding aid is at http://www.nlm.nih.gov/hmd/manuscripts/ead/sawyer69.html.

10. Sawyer Diaries, vol. 1, p. 37.

11. Ibid., vol. 6, p. 2.

12. Ibid., vol. 1, p. 41.

13. Ibid., 41 and 47.

14. Ibid., 43. Confirmed in "Historic Tablets of Forbidden City: Three of the Twelve Stolen Jade Plates Turn Up Here and Are Returned to the Chinese Consul-General," *San Francisco Examiner*, August 13, 1903.

15. Sawyer Diaries, vol. 1, p. 48.

16. For comparisons of Portland, Seattle, and San Francisco on several levels, see Stevens, "Brokers between Worlds."

17. Quoted in Wong, *Sweet Cakes, Long Journey*, 32. Her monograph is the source for the descriptions of the political and social context of immigration enforcement in Portland.

18. Sawyer Diaries, vol. 1, pp. 57–58.

19. Ibid., 55.

20. For more on the Backs, father and son, see Wong, *Sweet Cakes, Long Journey*, 187 ff. Stevens questions Back's credentials as a bona fide lawyer.

21. This inability to speak Chinese is confirmed in Sawyer's "Official Personnel Folder."

22. Sawyer Diaries, vol. 1, p. 56.

23. See Barde and Bobonis, "Detention at Angel Island," and Gee, "Sifting the Arrivals."

24. Sawyer Diaries, vol. 1, p. 85.

25. John Birge Sawyer, "The Arrest of Ng On," in "Professional Papers of John Birge Sawyer" (Collection of the Bancroft Library, University of California, Berkeley, 1908).

26. Sawyer Diaries, vol. 1, p. 65. The visit to McConnell's home is from a personal communication with Josephine Sawyer.

27. Sawyer, "Some Personal Observations."

28. Letter to J.H. Barbour, January 27, 1912, in "Professional Papers of John Birge Sawyer."

29. Letter from Consul General George E. Anderson to the Secretary of State, ca. July 1911, "Professional Papers of John Birge Sawyer."

30. Sawyer Diaries, vol. 2, pp. 14–15.

31. Letter from J.B. Sawyer to Rafe Bonham, April 4, 1916, in "Professional Papers of John Birge Sawyer."

32. Sawyer Diaries, vol. 2, pp. 93–94.

33. Ibid., 66–67.

34. Ibid., 64.

35. Ibid., 89–90.

36. Ibid., 117–20.

37. Ibid., 106–7. The "Gentlemen's Agreement" of 1907 between the United States and Japan had the effect of the Japanese "voluntarily" limiting immigration to the United States.

38. All material on the Yees comes from Chinese Arrival Files, 16432/8-1. Not that the younger Yee's trials were not over: he was found to have hookworm, for which he was treated at the Immigration Station Hospital after his father's lawyers paid a deposit of $50.

39. Chinese Arrival Files, 16243/7-13.

40. Sawyer Diaries, vol. 2, pp. 124–25.

41. Ibid., 152.

42. Ibid., 158–59.

43. Ibid., 124.

44. Ibid., vol. 3, p. 53.

45. Ibid., vol. 4, pp. 178–79.

46. From speech to Chinese students departing Shanghai for America, August 9, 1919. Document courtesy of Josephine Sawyer.

47. In 1919 he listed his duties as "Section 6 Chinese Certificates, Alien Passport Control, American Passports, American Registration, Swiss Registrations & Passports." Sawyer Diaries, vol. 3, p. 135.

48. For the full text, see LeMay and Barkan, *U.S. Immigration and Naturalization Laws and Issues*. This Act was superseded by the Immigration Act of 1924 (the "Johnson-Reed Act") that established the system of "National Origins" quotas that remained in place until 1965.

49. For example, Sawyer Diaries, vol. 1, p. 58.

50. Sawyer, "Some Personal Observations," 12.

51. The actual title is John Birge Sawyer, Procedure in "Section 6" and Other Chinese Immigration Matters (Washington, D.C.: Government Printing Office, 1923). Available from the Library of Congress Web site at http://lcweb2.loc.gov/service/gdc/scd0001/2005/20051119001pr/20051119001pr.pdf.

52. Sawyer Diaries, vol. 4, pp. 74–75. Sawyer's revised "Procedure in 'Section 6'" was printed in 1926.

53. "Procedures in 'Section 6,'" 1–2.

54. Ibid., 4.

55. "Procedure in 'Section 6,'" 6–8.

56. Sawyer Diaries, vol. 4, pp. 122–23.

57. Ibid., vol. 3, p. 137.

58. Sawyer, "Some Personal Observations," 5.

59. Ibid., 12.

60. Ibid.

— 12 —

Epilogue

I have told the tantalizingly ambiguous story of Quok Shee many times. Those who hear her tale always ask what became of her. Was she really what she said she was? Did she have children? What of the rest of her life?

We know only that in 1927, when returning from another trip to China, her "alleged husband" Chew Hoy Quong told immigration authorities that he was single. The Immigration inspector, ever vigilant, caught him in an apparent lie: What of this woman, Quok Shee? Ten years ago, you said she was your wife? Chew replied—convincingly, it seems—that his wife had complained of not receiving enough money and had run off with another man. And there we lose track of her. There is nothing more, nothing beyond what was in her own file. Does she have descendants, and could they answer our questions about Chew Hoy Quong and his "alleged wife"? I simply do not know.

What became of the other actors from the preceding chapters—the immigrants, lawyers, and government officials, the ships and ship captains? Some of the people from "Angel Island" continued their relatively modest careers. John Sawyer, for instance, remained in government service until 1943 (fittingly, the year the Chinese Exclusion Act was repealed), kept in touch with his classmates from Berkeley who had worked in China, and continued to write in his diary. Oliver Perry Stidger carried on with his law practice on behalf of Chinese clients for another quarter century.

Others acquired a modicum of fame. Dion Holm, who secured the writ of *habeas corpus* that ensured Quok Shee's release, resumed his legal career after World War I, defended the Hetch Hetchy dam on behalf of the Public Utilities Commission, and served as Attorney for the City and County of San Francisco for thirteen years. John Densmore's illegal wiretaps in both the immigration scandal and the Mooney case were overlooked—or, perhaps, rewarded—when he was appointed the first Director General of the U.S. Employment Office in 1918.

Perhaps the greatest renown accrued to the *Mongolia,* whose last voyage across the Pacific launched the first Densmore investigation. On November 9, 1915, the *Mongolia* left the San Francisco scandal behind her as Captain Rice, out on bond, took her to New York to begin a new life dodging U-boats and hauling war materiel to England. When American neutrality ended in March 1917 with the United States' declaration of war on Germany, Rice and the *Mongolia* were put even more directly in harm's way. And more surely on the path to glory. On April 25, 1917, her gun crew, with but a single shot, sank a German U-boat off the coast of England. Rice was hailed as a hero, captain of "the ship which boasts of being the first of Uncle Sam's maritime traders to sink a U-boat...the steamship *Mongolia.*"[1]

The Immigration Station on Angel Island continued its rather unhappy existence until 1940. When the administration building burned—and its records with it—the Immigration Service decided to move its operations back to the mainland. The Angel Island facilities, symbol of immigration on the West Coast, then fell into disuse after World War II. Only with the discovery of numerous Chinese poems inscribed on the walls was the Immigration Station saved from slow decay. Today it is recognized as a National Historic Landmark and is being restored to something of its former glory. Exhibits and docent tours will enable visitors to learn about the Immigration Station, the people who were "processed" there, and the laws that were the Station's *raison d'être*.

In writing about Angel Island, it occasionally seemed that I was writing about a remote past: nearly a hundred years since the Immigration Station opened, seventy since it closed. At other times, it seems that while Angel Island may have been of another age, it is one that speaks to us still. Many of the same questions about immigration policy are still with us. How many outsiders should we let in? Which ones? Why these ones and not those? And new questions have been added: What effects will our policies have on other countries? Who will hold us to account for the justness of our immigration laws? What can we learn from our experience with restricting the entry of newcomers?

We might well remember that until 1882, there was no such thing as "illegal immigration." The Chinese Exclusion Act changed that. What San Franciscans initially referred to as "the Restriction Law" created an artificial shortage, much as Prohibition would, that led to a booming smuggling business: Chinese wanted to come here to work—in the mines of Gold Rush California, in building the transcontinental railroad, then in the agricultural, commercial, and industrial sectors. Americans, too, wanted Chinese to come here—not just big industrialists needing laborers, but businessmen wanting partners for trading with China and well-off families enjoying services that the Chinese provided. Even the most ardent proponents of exclusion were routinely exposed as hypocrites for employing Chinese in their homes or on their farms. Demand (for legal immigration) exceeded supply.

Exclusion had unanticipated effects. Exclusion heightened the need for documents attesting to one's nationality. The normal back-and-forth of immigrant travel was disrupted by the possibility of not being allowed back in if one returned to China for a visit. Courts became clogged with appeals of rejections and deportation orders. An expanded bureaucracy was needed to enforce it all. Corruption flourished. Appalling injustices of all sorts flowed from overzealous or callous enforcement and from the widespread notion that Chinese were people without "the right to have rights."

Much of "Angel Island" does have a familiar, contemporary ring. This is particularly true when we recall that the Immigration Station was a detention center. When I was first writing about Quok Shee's travails, a story in the *New York Times* grabbed my attention. "No Refuge" recounted the story of a young Congolese man, Mubenga Kanyinda, who had tried to enter the United States as a refugee fearing persecution. He was detained in the Wackenhut facility near New York's John F. Kennedy airport, a "200-bed detention facility...equipped with cameras and metal detectors...with a windowless dorm room crammed with 40 detainees who eat, sleep, shower and go to the bathroom under the surveillance of armed guards."[2] Kanyinda was kept there for nine months, gaining his freedom only because a law firm took his case *pro bono*.

His experience was evocative of Quok Shee's in many ways—not nearly as long, but equally terrifying in its loneliness and in the indeterminacy of his sentence. A psychiatrist asked if he had been tortured at Wackenhut, and Kanyinda replied, "Being in detention is a kind of torture. There is physical torture and then there is the torture of one's morale."[3] Quok Shee would have understood him, for this is what differentiates detention facilities from mere prisons. Their ordeals serve as reminders of the need for continuing judicial oversight of the administrators enforcing immigration laws, and of the need for considering the unintended consequences of laws severely restricting the admission of newcomers to this nation of immigrants.

NOTES

1. *San Francisco Examiner*, April 26, 1917, 1.
2. Eyal Press, "No Refuge," *New York Times Magazine*, September 17, 2000.
3. Ibid.

Bibliography

Abbott, Edith, ed. *Immigration: Select Documents and Case Records.* Chicago: University of Chicago Press, 1924. Reprint, New York: Arno Press and the *New York Times,* 1969.

Architectural Resources Group. "Poetry and Inscriptions: Translation and Analysis." San Francisco, 2004.

Ball, J. Dyer. *Things Chinese: Being Notes on Various Subjects Connected with China.* London: S. Low, Marston, 1892.

Bamford, Mary. *Angel Island: The Ellis Island of the West.* Chicago: The Women's American Baptist Home Mission Society, 1917.

Banner, W.C. "A History of Trans-Pacific Service." *Japan: Magazine of Overseas Travel* 16, no. 5 (1927).

Barde, Robert. "Prelude to the Plague: Public Health and Politics at America's Pacific Gateway, 1899." *Journal of the History of Medicine and Allied Sciences* 58, no. 2 (2003): 153–86.

Barde, Robert, and Gustavo Bobonis. "Detention at Angel Island: First Empirical Evidence." *Social Science History* 30, no. 1 (2006): 103–36.

Barde, Robert, and Wesley Ueunten. "Pacific Steerage: Japanese Ships and Asian Mass Migration." *Pacific Historical Review* 73 (2004): 653–60.

Barde, Robert, Susan B. Carter, and Richard Sutch. "International Migration." In *Historical Statistics of the United States, from the Earliest Times to the Present: Millennial Edition,* edited by Susan B. Carter, Scott Sigmund Gartner, Michael R. Haines, Alan L. Olmstead, Richard Sutch, and Gavin Wright, 523–657. New York: Cambridge University Press, 2006.

Barde, Robert, William Greene, and Daniel Nealand. "The EARS Have It: A Web Search Tool for Investigation Case Files from the Chinese Exclusion Era." *Prologue* 35, no. 3 (2003): 24–45.

Barth, Gunther. *Bitter Strength: A History of the Chinese in the United States, 1850–1870.* Cambridge, MA: Harvard University Press, 1974.

Bates, J.C. Bates, ed. *History of the Bench and Bar of California.* San Francisco: Bench and Bar Publishing Co., 1912.

Becker, Jules. *The Course of Exclusion, 1882–1924: San Francisco Newspaper Coverage of the Chinese and Japanese in the United States*. San Francisco: Mellen Research University Press, 1991.

Birn, Anne-Emanuelle. "Six Seconds Per Eyelid: The Medical Inspection of Immigrants at Ellis Island, 1892–1914." *Dynamis* 17 (1997).

Board of Health of the City and County of San Francisco. *Biennial Report of the Board of Health of the City and County of San Francisco for the Fiscal Years 1898–1899 and 1899–1900*. San Francisco: The Hinton Printing Company, 1901.

Brinnin, John Malcolm. *The Sway of the Grand Saloon*. New York: Delacorte, 1971.

Brown, Giles. *Ships That Sail No More: Marine Transportation from San Diego to Puget Sound, 1910–1940*. Lexington: University of Kentucky Press, 1966.

Brownstone, David, Irene Franck, and Douglass Brownstone. *Island of Hope, Island of Tears*. New York: Wade Publishers, 1979.

Brunner, W.C. "Sixty Years of Steam Shipping, Part III." *Japan: Magazine of Overseas Travel*, June 1927.

Camp, Constance Willis. *Kuan Yin, Goddess of Mercy of Angel Island*. Cincinnati: The Woman's Home Missionary Society, Methodist Episcopal Church, n.d.

Carmichael, D.A., N.V. Perry, and A.L. Parsons. Report on the Physical and Administrative Equipment at the United States Quarantine Station at San Francisco, California, edited by Public Health Service, 11. National Archives, Record Group 90, 1918.

Castro de Mendoza, Mario. *El transporte marâitimo en la inmigraciâon China, 1849–1874*. Lima: Consejo Nacional de Ciencia y Tecnologâia, 1989.

———. *La Marina Mercante en la Republica, 1821–1968*. 2 vols. Vol. 1, Miraflores [Peru] Talleres de Artes Gráficas Martínez, 1980.

Chan, Sucheng. *Entry Denied: Exclusion and the Chinese Community in America, 1882–1943*. Philadelphia: Temple University Press, 1991.

Chang, Iris. *The Chinese in America: A Narrative History*. New York: Viking, 2003.

Chase, Marilyn. *The Barbary Plague: The Black Death in Victorian San Francisco*. New York: Random House, 2003.

Chen, Shehong. *Being Chinese, Becoming Chinese American*. Urbana: University of Illinois Press, 2002.

Chen, Yong. *Chinese San Francisco, 1850–1943*. Stanford: Stanford University Press, 2000.

Chew, Kenneth S.Y., and John M. Liu. "Hidden in Plain Sight: Global Labor Force Exchange in the Chinese American Population, 1880–1940." *Population and Development Review* 30, no. 1 (2004): 57–58.

China Mail Steamship Company. "Articles of Incorporation," 1918.

———. "Report 1915–1919." San Francisco, 1919.

Chinn, Thomas W. *Bridging the Pacific: San Francisco Chinatown and Its People*. San Francisco, CA: Chinese Historical Society of America, 1989.

Chung Sai Yat Po, "American Newspaper Describes Prison as Inferno," December 18, 1903 (original in Chinese).

Cohn, Raymond L. "The Transition from Sail to Steam in Immigration to the United States." In *Maritime Aspects of Migration*, edited by Klaus Friedland. Koln: Bohlau Verlag, 1989.

Compton, Samuel Willard Crompton. "Chew, Ng Poon." Review of Reviewed Item. *American National Biography Online*, 2000. http://www.anb.org/articles/15/15-00510.html.

Conmy, Peter Thomas. *Stephen Mallory White, California Statesman.* San Francisco: Dolores Press, 1956.

Coolidge, Mary Roberts. *Chinese Immigration.* New York: Henry Holt and Company, 1909.

Corbitt, Duvon Clough. *A Study of the Chinese in Cuba, 1847–1947.* Wilmore, KY: Asbury College, 1971.

Cross, Ira B. *Financing an Empire: History of Banking in California.* 4 vols. Chicago: The S.J. Clarke Publishing Company, 1927.

Daniels, Roger. "No Lamps Were Lit for Them: Angel Island and the Historiography of Asian American Immigration." *Journal of American Ethnic History* 17, no. 1 (1997): 3–18.

De la Pedraja, René. *A Historical Dictionary of the U.S. Merchant Marine and Shipping Industry, since the Introduction of Steam.* Westport, CT: Greenwood Press, 1994.

———. *The Rise and Decline of U.S. Merchant Shipping in the Twentieth Century.* New York: Twayne Publishers, 1992.

Dobie, Edith. *The Political Career of Stephen Mallory White: A Study of Party Activities Under the Convention System.* Stanford, CA: Stanford University Press, 1927.

Dougherty, Mary Agnes. *My Calling to Fulfill: Deaconesses in the United Methodist Tradition.* New York: General Board of Global Ministries Women's Division, United Methodist Church, 1997.

Du Bois, W.E.B. "The Black Star Line." *Crisis* September (1922): 210–14.

Ebrey, Patricia Buckley, ed. *The Cambridge Illustrated History of China.* New York: Cambridge University Press, 1996.

Emmer, Piet C. "Immigration into the Caribbean: The Introduction of Chinese and East Indian Indentured Labourers between 1839 and 1917." *Itinerario* 14, no. 1 (1990): 61–89.

Emmer, Piet C., and A.J. Kuipers. "The Coolie Ships: The Transportation of Indentured Labourers between Calcutta and Paramaribo, 1873–1921." In *Maritime Aspects of Migration,* edited by Klaus Friedland, 403–26. Koln: Bohlau Verlag, 1989.

Fairchild, Amy L. *Science at the Borders: Immigrant Medical Inspection and the Shaping of the Modern Industrial Labor Force.* Baltimore: The Johns Hopkins University Press, 2003.

Frost, Richard H. *The Mooney Case.* Stanford, CA: Stanford University Press, 1968.

Gee, Jennifer. "Sifting the Arrivals: Asian Immigrants and the Angel Island Immigration Station, San Francisco, 1910–1940." PhD diss., Stanford University, 1999.

Gillis, John. *Islands of the Mind: How the Human Imagination Created the Atlantic World.* New York: Palgrave MacMillan, 2004.

Giovinco, Joseph Preston. "The California Career of Anthony Caminetti, Italian–American politician," University of California, Berkeley, 1973.

Gontard, Jean. "Second Class on Angel Island: Immigrant Hell." *The Californians: The Magazine of California History* 12, no. 4 (1995).

Gyory, Andrew. *Closing the Gate: Race, Politics, and the Chinese Exclusion Act.* Chapel Hill: University of North Carolina Press, 1998.

Hao, Fu Chi. "My Reception in America." *Chinese America: History and Perspective* 1991 (1991): 153–56.

Healy, Patrick J., and Ng Poon Chew. *A Statement for Non-Exclusion.* San Francisco, 1905.

Hoexter, Corinne K. *From Canton to California: The Epic of Chinese Immigration.* New York: Four Winds Press, 1976.

Hsu, Madeline Y. *Dreaming of Gold, Dreaming of Home: Transnationalism and Migration between the United States and South China, 1882–1943*. Stanford: Stanford University Press, 2000.

Igler, David. "Diseased Goods: Global Exchanges in the Eastern Pacific Basin, 1770–1850." *American Historical Review* 109, no. 3 (2004): 693–719.

Immigration Commission. *Steerage Regulation, 1819–1908*. Vol. 39, *Reports of the Immigration Commission*. Washington, DC, 1911.

Irie, Toraji, and William Himmel. "History of Japanese Migration to Peru." *Hispanic American Historical Review* 31, no. 3 (1951).

Ito, Kazuo. *Issei: A History of Japanese Immigrants in North America*. Translated by Shinichiro Nakamura and Jean S. Gerard. Seattle: Japanese Community Service, 1973.

Jensen, Joan M. *Passage from India: Asian Indian Immigrants in North America*. New Haven: Yale University Press, 1988.

Johnson, Hugh. *The Voyage of the Komagata Maru: The Sikh Challenge to Canada's Colour Bar*. Delhi: Oxford University Press, 1979.

Johnson, Kenneth M. *Stephen Mallory White*. Los Angeles, CA: Dawson's Book Shop, 1980.

Jones, Maldwyn A. "Aspects of North Atlantic Migration: Steerage Conditions and American Law, 1819–1909." In *Maritime Aspects of Migration*, edited by Klaus Friedland. Koln: Bohlau Verlag, 1989.

Keeling, Drew. "The Economics of Migrant Transport between Europe and the United States, 1900–1914," May 11, 2005.

———. "The Transportation Revolution and Transatlantic Migration, 1850–1914." *Research in Economic History* 19 (1999): 39–74.

Kemble, John Haskell. "Notes: Cabin Plan of the Pacific Mail Steamer *Japan*." *American Neptune*, 1942, 243.

———. *One Hundred Years of the Pacific Mail*. Newport, VA: Mariners Museum, 1950.

———. "Side-Wheelers Across the Pacific." *American Neptune* 2, no. 1 (1942).

Kikumura-Yano, Akemi, ed. *Encyclopedia of Japanese Descendants in the Americas*. Walnut Creek, CA: Altamira Press, 2002.

Kooiman, William. "James Hill's Great 'White Elephants.'" *Sea Classics*, 1991, 10–13.

Kraut, Alan. *Silent Travelers: Germs, Genes, and the "Immigrant Menace."* New York: Basic Books, 1994.

Kraut, Alan, and Randolph Boehm, eds. *Records of the Immigration and Naturalization Service*. Vol. Reel 9. Bethesda, MD: University Publications of America, 1992.

Lai, Him Mark, Genny Lim, and Judy Yung. *Island: Poetry and History of Chinese Immigrants on Angel Island, 1910–1940*. San Francisco: Hoc Doi (History of Chinese Detained on Island), San Francisco Study Center, 1980.

Lee, Erika. *At America's Gates: Chinese Immigration during the Exclusion Era, 1882–1943*. Chapel Hill: University of North Carolina Press, 2003.

———. "The Chinese Exclusion Example: Race, Immigration, and American Gatekeeping, 1882–1924." *Journal of American Ethnic History* 21, no. 3 (2002): 36–62.

LeMay, Michael, and Elliott Robert Barkan. *U.S. Immigration and Naturalization Laws and Issues: A Documentary History*. Westport, CT: Greenwood Press, 1999.

Liu, Po-Chi. *Mei-kuo Hua chi'ia shi*. Taipei: Hsing cheng yuan chi'iao wu wei yuan hui: Tsung fa hsing so Li ming we hua shih yeh kung ssu, 1981.

Lombardi, John. *Labor's Voice in the Cabinet: A History of the Department of Labor from its Origin to 1921*. New York: Columbia University Press, 1942.

Lubbock, Basil. *The Coolie Ships and Oil Sealers*. Glasgow: Brown, Son and Ferguson, 1981.

Luke, William. "The First Chinese Bank in the United States." *Chinatown News*, July 3, 1974.

Ma, L. Eve Armentrout. "The Big Business Ventures of Chinese in North America, 1850–1930." In *The Chinese American Experience: Papers from the Second National Conference on Chinese American Studies (1980)*, edited by Genny Lim. San Francisco: The Chinese Historical Society of American and the Chinese Culture Foundation, 1984.

Mark, Gregory Yee. "Opium in America and the Chinese." *Chinese America: History and Perspectives* 11 (1997): 61–72.

Markel, Howard. *Quarantine! East European Jewish Immigrants and the New York City Epidemics of 1892*. Baltimore: Johns Hopkins University Press, 1997.

———. "Which Face? Whose Nation? Immigration, Public Health, and the Construction of Disease at America's Borders, 1891 to 1928." In *Immigration Research for a New Century: Multidisciplinary Perspectives*, edited by Ruben G. Rumbaut, Nancy Foner, and Steven J. Gold. New York: Russell Sage Foundation, 2000.

Martin, Mildred Crowl. *Chinatown's Angry Angel: The Story of Donaldina Cameron*. Palo Alto, CA: Pacific Books, 1977.

McConaghy, Sharon Boswell, and Lorraine. "Arrival of the Miike Maru." *Seattle Times*, 1996.

McKeown, Adam. *Chinese Migrant Networks and Cultural Change: Peru, Chicago, Hawaii, 1900–1936*. Chicago: University of Chicago Press, 2001.

———. "Global Migration, 1846–1940." *Journal of World History* 15, no. 2 (2004): 155–89.

Moltman, Gunter. "Steamship Transport of Emigrants from Europe to the United States, 1850–1914: Social, Commercial, and Legislative Aspects." In *Maritime Aspects of Migration*, edited by Klaus Friedland. Koln: Bohlau Verlag, 1989.

Moriyama, Alan Takeo. *Imingaisha: Japanese Emigration Companies and Hawaii, 1894–1908*. Honolulu: University of Hawaii Press, 1985.

Moriyama, Iwao M. "Epidemic Cerebrospinal Fever Among Transpacific Steerage Passengers." *University of California Publications in Public Health* 2, no. 2 (1936): 183–234.

Ngai, Mae M. "The Architecture of Race in American Immigration Law: A Reexamination of the Immigration Act of 1924." *Journal of American Ethnic History* 86, no. 1 (1999): 67–92.

———. *Impossible Subjects: Illegal Aliens and the Making of Modern America*. Princeton: Princeton University Press, 2004.

Pan, Lynn, ed. *The Encyclopedia of the Chinese Overseas*. Cambridge, MA: Harvard University Press, 1999.

Pascoe, Peggy. *Relations of Rescue: The Search for Female Moral Authority in the American West, 1874–1939*. New York: Oxford University Press, 1990.

Perkins, Dorothy. "Coming to San Francisco by Steamship, 1906–1908." In *The Chinese American Experience: Papers from the Second National Conference on Chinese American Studies*, edited by Genny Lim. San Francisco: Chinese Historical Society of America, 1980.

Pierson, Carrie Isabelle. "The Immigrant on the Pacific Coast." *Woman's Home Mission*, 1912.

Pitkin, Thomas M. *Keepers of the Gate: A History of Ellis Island*. New York: New York University Press, 1975.

Pugach, Noel H. "American Shipping Promoters and the Shipping Crisis of 1914–1916: The Pacific and Eastern Steamship Company." *American Neptune* 35 (1975): 166–82.

Rivas, Zelideth Maria. "Sea of Faces: Landscape and Boredom in Maedakō Hiroichirō's Santō senkyaku." Unpublished paper, Berkeley: University of California, 2005.

Safford, J.J. "The United States Merchant Marine in Foreign Trade, 1800–1939." In *Business History of Shipping: Strategy and Structure*, edited by Tsunehiko Yui and Keiichiro Nakagawa. Tokyo: University of Tokyo Press, 1985.

Sakovich, Maria. "Angel Island Immigration Station Reconsidered: Non-Asian Encounters with the Immigration Laws, 1910–1940." Sonoma State University, 2002.

Salyer, Lucy. *Laws Harsh as Tigers: Chinese Immigrants and the Shaping of Modern Immigration Law*. Chapel Hill: University of North Carolina Press, 1995.

Sawyer, John Birge. "Professional Papers of John Birge Sawyer," Bancroft Library, University of California, Berkeley, 1908.

———. "The Arrest of Ng On." In "Professional Papers of John Birge Sawyer," Bancroft Library, University of California, Berkeley, 1908.

———. "Diaries of John Birge Sawyer: Holograph and Typescript, 1910–1962," Bancroft Library, University of California, Berkeley, 1908.

———. "Official Personnel Folder." St. Louis, MO: National Personnel Records Center.

———. *Procedure in "Section 6" and Other Chinese Immigration Matters*. Washington, DC: Government Printing Office, 1923.

Schmidtt, Robert C. *Historical Statistics of Hawaii*. Honolulu: University of Hawaii Press, 1977.

Schwendinger, Robert J. "Investigating Chinese Immigrant Ships and Sailors." In *The Chinese American Experience: Papers from the Second National Conference on Chinese American Studies*, edited by Genny Lim. San Francisco: Chinese Historical Society of America, 1980.

———. *Ocean of Bitter Dreams: Maritime Relations between China and the United States, 1850–1915*. Tucson, AZ: Westernlore Press, 1988.

Schwerin, Rennie. "La Follette's Ignorance Exposed." *Pacific Marine Review*, 1915.

Service, John S., Rosemary Levenson, John King Fairbank, and Bancroft Library. Regional Oral History Office. *State Department Duty in China, the McCarthy Era, and after, 1933–1977: Oral History Transcript and Related Material, 1977–1981*.

Shah, Nayan. *Contagious Divides: Epidemics and Race in San Francisco's Chinatown*. Berkeley: University of California Press, 2001.

Sharrock, John. "Three Seas and Two Oceans." *Japan: Magazine of Overseas Travel*, 1924.

Shuck, Oscar T., ed. *History of the Bench and Bar of California*. San Francisco: The Commercial Printing House, 1901.

Smith, John H. Letter from Jno [John] H. Smith to Henry Rose Carter, May 10, 1923 in *Philip S. Hench Walter Reed Yellow Fever Collection*. http://etext.lib.virginia.edu/etcbin/fever-browse?id=01102019 (accessed July 27, 2007).

Soennichsen, John. *Miwoks to Missiles: A History of Angel Island*. Tiburon, CA: Angel Island Association, 2001.

Sprague, E.K. "Medical Inspection of Immigrants." *Survey* 30 (1913): 420–22.

Staley, Jeffrey L. "'Gum Moon': The First Fifty Years of Methodist Women's Work in San Francisco Chinatown, 1870–1920." *Argonaut (Journal of the San Francisco Museum and Historical Society)* 16, no. 1 (2005): 4–25.

Stevens, Todd. "Brokers between Worlds: Chinese Merchants and Legal Culture in the Pacific Northwest, 1852–1925." PhD diss., Princeton University, 2004.

Stickland, Eunice Jones. "More Than an Angel." *World Outlook*, 1944, 15.

Stidger, Oliver Perry. *Highlights on Chinese Exclusion and Expulsion. The Immigration Law of 1924 as it Affects Persons of Chinese Descent in the United States, Their Business Interests, Their Rights and Their Privileges.* San Francisco: Chinese Chamber of Commerce, 1924.

Stolarik, M. Mark, ed. *Forgotten Doors: The Other Ports of Entry to the United States.* Philadelphia: Balch Institute Press, 1988.

Tang, Vincent, ed. *Chinese Women Immigrants and the Two-Edged Sword of Habeas Corpus, the Chinese American Experience: Papers from the Second National Conference on Chinese American Studies.* San Francisco: Chinese Historical Society of America, 1980.

Tate, E. Mowbray. *Transpacific Steam: The Story of Steam Navigation from the Pacific Coast of North America to the Far East and the Antipodes, 1867–1941.* New York: Cornwall Books, 1986.

Thomas, Brinley. *Migration and Economic Growth: A Study of Great Britain and the Atlantic Economy.* Cambridge: Cambridge University Press, 1954.

Thomas, Gordon, and Max Norgan Witts. *The San Francisco Earthquake.* New York: Stein and Day, 1971.

Thompson, Daniella. 2005. The Tapes of Russell Street: An Accomplished Family of School Desegregation Pioneers. http://www.berkeleyheritage.com/essays/tape_family.html (accessed June 15, 2006).

Thomsen, Neil L. "No Such Sun Yat-Sen: An Archival Success Story." *Chinese America: History and Perspective,* 1997, 16–25.

Tinker, Hugh. *A New System of Slavery: The Export of Indian Labour Overseas, 1830–1920.* London: Oxford University Press, 1974.

Toogood, Anna Coxe. "A Civil History of Golden Gate National Recreation Area and Point Reyes National Seashore, California." Denver: Historic Preservation Branch, Pacific Northwest Team, Denver Service Center, National Park Service, United States Dept. of the Interior, 1980.

Torpey, John. *The Invention of the Passport: Surveillance, Citizenship and the State.* New York: Cambridge University Press, 2000.

Trauner, Joan B. "The Chinese as Medical Scapegoats in San Francisco, 1870–1905." *California History* 57, no. 1 (1978): 70–87.

Tsurutani, Hisashi. *America-Bound: The Japanese and the Opening of the American West.* Translated by Betsey Scheiner with Yamamura Mariko. Tokyo: The Japan Times, 1989.

Turner, Robert D. *The Pacific Empresses: An Illustrated History of Canadian Pacific Railway's Empress Liners on the Pacific Ocean.* Victoria: Sono Nis Press, 1981.

U.S. Bureau of Customs. "Customs Passenger Lists of Vessels Arriving in San Francisco, California, 1903–1918." San Bruno, CA: National Archives and Records Administration.

———. "Press Copies of Letters from the Collector of Customs, San Francisco, to the Secretary of the Treasury, 1870–1912." Collector Sears to Secretary McCulloch, December 30, 1884.

U.S. Department of Labor. "Annual Reports of the Commissioner-General of Immigration," 1903–1932.

———. "Annual Reports of the Commissioner-General of Immigration." Washington: Government Printing Office, 1912–32.

———. "List of Chinese Passengers Arriving in San Francisco, California, 1882–1914," edited by Immigration Service: National Archives and Records Administration.

U.S. Department of Labor, Immigration Service. "Alphabetical Index of Ship Arrivals in San Francisco." National Archives and Records Administration.

U.S. Public Health Service. "Annual Report of the Supervising Surgeon-General, Fiscal Year 1899," 1899.

Van Sant, John E. *Pacific Pioneers: Japanese Journeys to American and Hawaii, 1850–80.* Urbana and Chicago: University of Illinois Press, 2000.

White, Stephen M. *Stephen M. White: Californian, Citizen, Lawyer, Senator. His Life and His Work; A Character Sketch, by Leroy E. Mosher. Together with his Principal Public Addresses, Compiled by Robert Woodland Gates.* Los Angeles, CA: The Times-Mirror Company, 1903.

Willcox, Walter. *International Migrations.* 2 vols. Vol. 1, Statistics. New York: National Bureau of Economic Research, 1929.

Wilson, Andrew, ed. *The Chinese in the Caribbean.* Princeton: Markus Wiener Publishers, 2004.

Wong, Marie Rose. *Sweet Cakes, Long Journey: The Chinatowns of Portland, Oregon.* Seattle: University of Washington Press, 2004.

Wray, William. *Mitsubishi and the N.Y.K, 1870–1914: Business Strategy in the Japanese Shipping Industry.* Cambridge, MA: Harvard University Press, 1984.

Yamada, Michio. "The Anti-Japanese Problem and Passenger Ships on the North American Routes." *Sekai no Kansen,* May 1994.

———. "Emigrants to Hawaii in the Meiji Era, Part 1." *Sekai no Kansen,* November 1993.

———. "Emigrants to Hawaii in the Meiji Era, Part 2." *Sekai no Kansen,* December 1993.

———. "Emigration to Mexico and Peru in the Meiji Era." *Sekai no Kansen,* March 1994.

———. "First Emigrants to Brazil by the *Kasato Maru.*" *Sekai no Kansen,* April 1994.

———. "The First *Santos Maru,* Part 1." *Sekai no Kansen,* September 1994.

———. "The First Ship Specially Built for Emigrants, the *Anyō Maru.*" *Sekai no Kansen,* June 1994.

———. *Fune ni Miru Nihonjin Iminshi: Kasato Maru kara Kuruzu Kyakusen e.* Tokyo: Chūō Kōronsha, 1998.

———. "Voyage of Sōbō: Part 1: National Emigration Center." *Sekai no Kansen,* November 1994.

———. "Voyage of Sōbō: Part 2: Meals on Japanese Emigrant Ships." *Sekai no Kansen,* December 1994.

———. "Voyage of Sōbō: Part 3: Daily Life on the Ships" *Sekai no Kansen,* January 1995.

———. "Voyage of Sōbō: Part 4: Epidemics Aboard Emigrant Ships." *Sekai no Kansen,* February 1995.

Yun, Lisa. "Under the Hatches: American Coolie Ships and Nineteenth-Century Narratives of the Pacific Passage." *Amerasia Journal* 28, no. 2 (2002).

Yung, Judy. *Unbound Feet: A Social History of Chinese Women in San Francisco.* Berkeley: University of California Press, 1995.

———. *Unbound Voices: A Documentary History of Chinese Women in San Francisco.* Berkeley: University of California Press, 1999.

Index

About the Author

Robert Eric Barde is Deputy Director and Academic Coordinator of the Institute of Business and Economic Research, University of California, Berkeley. He is the author of nearly three dozen articles on immigration history and the social sciences and has written for numerous award-winning programs on TVOntario.